Western Frontiersmen Series
XXXVII

Robert Newton Baskin, from
mayoral portrait by John Willard Clawson,
grandson of Brigham Young. The portrait hangs in the
magnificent Salt Lake City-County Building, erected
under Baskin's leadership. *Photo by Michael Roberts
of Michael Roberts Photography of Salt Lake City.*

ROBERT NEWTON BASKIN
and the
MAKING OF MODERN UTAH

by
JOHN GARY MAXWELL

THE ARTHUR H. CLARK COMPANY
An imprint of the University of Oklahoma Press
Norman, Oklahoma
2013

Also by John Gary Maxwell
Gettysburg to Great Salt Lake: George R. Maxwell,
Civil War Hero and Federal Marshal among the Mormons (Norman, Okla., 2010)

Library of Congress Cataloging-in-Publication Data
Maxwell, John Gary, 1933–
 Robert Newton Baskin and the making of modern Utah / by John Gary Maxwell.
  p. cm. — (Western frontiersmen series ; 37)
 Includes bibliographical references and index.
 ISBN 978-0-87062-420-9 (hardcover : alk. paper) 1. Baskin, R. N. (Robert Newton), 1835–1918. 2. Utah—History—19th century. 3. Mormons—Utah—History—19th century. 4. Utah—Politics and government. 5. Frontier and pioneer life—Utah. 6. Legislators—Utah—Biography. 7. Utah—Biography. I. Title.
 F826.B32M39 2013
 979.2′02092—dc23
 [B]
                    2012031222

Robert Newton Baskin and the Making of Modern Utah
is Volume 37 in the Western Frontiersmen Series.

The paper in this book meets the guidelines for permanence and durability
of the Committee on Production Guidelines for Book Longevity
of the Council on Library Resources, Inc. ∞

1 2 3 4 5 6 7 8 9 10

Contents

Preface 11

Acknowledgments 17

Abbreviations and Conventions 21

Introduction 23
  1. Ohio Origins 31
  2. Forewarned and Prepared? 43
  3. Arriving in Utah 53
  4. A Theocratic Society 67
  5. A Climate of Violence 85
  6. The Combative Years 107
  7. "The Canker Worm of Their Souls Ever Since" . . 125
  8. The Year of the Prophet's Death . . . 141
  9. Elections, Challenges, and Ill Winds . . . 153
  10. Lying for the Lord 169
  11. The Tide against the Mormons Strengthens . . 179
  12. Baskin and Public Education in Utah . . . 201
  13. Challenge and Controversy 213
  14. Mayor of Salt Lake City 227
  15. Epiphany or Transformation: Reelection . . 249
  16. Mayors, Industrial Armies, and City Crises . . 261
  17. Unrelenting Problems but Statehood Arrives . . 271

18. Into the Judicial Arena 281
19. Evanescence of Financial Success . . . 301
20. Obey the Law 315
21. Gently They Go 323
22. The Father of Modern Utah 339

Chronology 353
Bibliography 357
Index 375

Illustrations

Mayor Robert Newton Baskin . . . *frontispiece*

William S. Godbe 101

Charles C. Goodwin 180

Parley Lycurgus Williams, friend 203

Cornerstone laying of City and County Building, Salt Lake City

. . . . 240

Completed City and County Building . . . 243

Clock tower of City and County Building . . . 244

Portrait of Mayor Baskin 246

Patrick H. Lannan 251

Orlando W. Powers, politician 255

Celebration of Brigham Young's one hundredth birthday . 287

Brigham Young, man of energy and purpose . . 288

Enos Dougherty Hoge, law partner . . . 303

Robert Baskin, Alta Club member 304

Mary Edna Brown Hall, younger 330

Mary Edna Brown Hall, older 333

Preface

Freedom of thought must include protection against
"the tyranny of prevailing opinion."
PAUL M. EDWARDS

CONTRADICTIONS AND PERPLEXITY APPLY TO THE LIFE of Robert Newton Baskin. Educated in private schools and at Harvard Law School, he killed a farmhand bully in a street brawl. First living with the enlightened elements of society in Highland County, Ohio, he spent most of his life within an isolated minority in a distant territory that was ruled by a theocratic monarch. Rationality usually prevailed for him, but a left jab to an opponent's nose or an application of his Irish shillalah to the head could quickly circumvent reason. Hated in his early years in Utah, he became respected and admired despite being the author of the most severe federal laws ever enacted against the theocratic society of the Mormon people.

Baskin was a Utah contemporary of George R. Maxwell, the U.S. marshal of whom I authored an earlier biography. Until Maxwell's death in 1889, the two shared a span of years and the disdain of theocratic rule.[1] They worked, both together and separately, to establish a republican government in Utah and to bring Mormons into compliance with federal law. Baskin, unlike most non-Mormons of this period, left a record rich in civic contributions and a modest written history filled with his observations of Utah events. His two books,

---

[1]Maxwell, *Gettysburg to Great Salt Lake*.

Reminiscences of Early Utah and *Reply to Certain Statements by O. F. Whitney*, were published to revise what he considered an intentionally incorrect history. Baskin's insightful works yield scores of nuggets of detail rarely found in other records. *Reminiscences* and *Reply* are the best-known substantive renderings from the pen of a non-Mormon whose life spanned more than fifty years of conflict between non-Mormons and Mormons in Utah. They are the record of a well-educated, analytical lawyer who lived through the time of Utah's Sisyphean struggle for statehood, while the Mormon priesthood hierarchy held a vise grip on government and plural marriage.[2] Baskin became a major contributor to the changes that finally brought statehood to Utah's ardent, intransigent Mormons.

After learning that this biography of Baskin would follow mine of Maxwell, historian Ronald O. Barney provided the following reminder from distinguished British historian George Macaulay Trevelyan: "While it is true that 'a single biography is more likely to mislead than a history of the period,' it is equally true that 'several biographies are often more deeply instructive than a single history.'"[3] However, a caveat to Trevelyan's assessment is needed. If several biographies have the same author, the reader may also be misled, constricted by one point of view. Therefore history can be more assuredly correct if biographies by different authors, describing the life and conditions in Utah, are juxtaposed with this account of Baskin.

Consider, for example, Edward Leo Lyman's massive oeuvre of Mormon apostle and articulate theologian Amasa Mason Lyman. Reflective and introspective, Amasa Mason Lyman was an intellectual giant who found Mormon theology too restrictive for his expansive mind. Originally attracted to Mormonism by Joseph Smith's teaching, Lyman found his views changed under the second prophet. He observed that "a 'most vile apostasy, so apparent in the wonton and reckless departure from the principles, spirit, and genius of the Gospel,' . . . had taken place during the time when Brigham Young led the church."[4] John D. Lee, in his autobiography, also held Young guilty of violating fundamental principles espoused by Smith.[5] Compare

---

[2]Baskin's books are not faultless, as Brigham D. Madsen noted in his 2006 foreword to *Reminiscences*. Save for legal citations, documentation is scant; several errors of fact are evident.

[3]George Macaulay Trevelyan, "Clio, a Muse," in Vaughn, *Vital Past*, cited in Barney, *One Side by Himself*, xviii.

[4]Lyman, *Amasa Mason Lyman*, xiii.

[5]Lee, *Mormonism Unveiled*.

also Barney's biography of his ancestor Lewis Barney, a man living near poverty in the periphery of society, that tells of a worker in the Kingdom's vineyard. Not a prince among Mormon leadership, he was one of the "last wagon" men whose life was "rich and quiet . . . outside the boiling currents of their times."[6] Historian Ronald G. Watt sensitively describes the impoverished beginnings of his ancestor George D. Watt, whose decline from grace resulted from his defiance after Brigham Young refused to pay him a fair rate after sixteen years of service as Young's scribe and shorthand recorder.[7] Biographies of Gen. Patrick Edward Connor, the U.S. Army officer who dealt with the Mormons through the Civil War years, provide a military officer's perspective.[8] While the autobiographical letters of Jotham Goodell are limited to a single winter in Zion, they document the clench-fisted control over non-Mormons by Utah's theocracy.[9] Polly Aird's biography of her relative Peter McAuslan describes the abusive treatment of Mormon apostle Orson Pratt by Brigham Young, and the violence of central Utah that moved McAuslan and other formerly faithful Saints to seek the protection of federal troops when traveling to California, out of the Kingdom of God.[10]

Historian Thomas Alexander posits that recording history is "always perspectival."[11] His observation applies to this biography, for its purpose, like that of *Gettysburg to Great Salt Lake*, is to present one man's life story as he sought to effect profound change among the Saints in Utah. Alexander further emphasizes that "honesty is the most important ideal of the historian."[12] Honesty is intended here, in my telling about a good but not perfect man. However, honesty is not to be defined as a "balanced" presentation of non-Mormon and Mormon accounts. Historians never granted Baskin a "balanced" evaluation, and this work aims to place ballast on the unused side of the scale. Quickly perceived as anti-Mormon, Baskin was dismissed, and found unworthy of serious mention by most authors. Until now, no historian has volunteered the possibility that Baskin did more to bring Mormons closer to mainstream acceptance, to statehood, to access

---

[6]Historian Dale L. Morgan, cited in Barney, *One Side by Himself*, xviii.
[7]Watt, *Mormon Passage*.
[8]Madsen, *Glory Hunter*; Varley, *Brigham and the Brigadier*; Rogers, *Soldiers of the Overland*; Wagner, *Patrick Conner's War*.
[9]Bigler, *Winter with the Mormons*.
[10]Aird, *Mormon Convert, Mormon Defector*.
[11]Alexander, "Faithful Historian Responds," v, 37.
[12]Ibid., vi.

to the rights and privileges offered by a modern America, than did revered figures like Wilford Woodruff or George Q. Cannon.

Baskin's years in Utah—1865 to 1918—were a time of embedded divisiveness, with little nonpartisan, thoughtful dialogue between Mormons and non-Mormons. Baskin saw Utah as many of his non-Mormon contemporaries saw it. He would never have judged Brigham Young a divinely inspired, spiritual prophet who employed persuasion, democratic voice, and introspection, as some have painted him with the soft, endearing title of "Brother Brigham." The context of Utah for much of Baskin's life was one of a tightly controlled state of obedience and conformity, enforced by violence or its threat. Historians of any background would prefer evidence—beyond context—for proof that the many Utah murders committed before and during Baskin's lifetime either were or were not at the instigation of, or at the hands of, those who controlled the territory.[13] Evidence is rare, for the men who controlled it were likely the perpetrators.

The Mormon narratives of conquering a hostile wilderness, of making the high desert productive, of organization, colonization, and conquest by sheer energy and will over legions of obstacles, bring well-deserved praise to Mormon pioneers. Among those so honored are my own ancestors, who risked all in leaving Scotland. My first Maxwell emigrant drove an oxcart from Westport, Missouri, arriving in Utah in September 1854. More Maxwell family arrived pushing their handcarts 1,400 miles in the second handcart company, in 1856. Into the twentieth century, they were the groundlings, the commoners, and repeatedly obeyed calls to conquer the wilderness. Narratives of faith and labor have justifiably fueled their testimonies of belief and dedication and those of many other Mormons. However, by their very origin and purpose these testimonies tell less than the full and honest history of Utah.

There is in this biography neither desire nor intent to disparage any interpretation of Utah history. Rather, I hope readers will appreciate the "other" reality experienced by the non-Mormons. Their perceptions have not been included in the barbicans, the often-told, faith-promoting depictions that have dominated Utah history. It may be overreach to suggest Baskin's desire that the "imputation of improper

---

[13]"Context is a reconstruction of the social patterns, climate, and characteristics of a given time and place, but . . . historical evidence is the product of the mind . . . such as . . . journals, letters, buildings, furniture, art." Alexander, "Historiography," 36.

motives to those who opposed the hierarchy of Utah" will be recognized and corrected.[14] Perhaps balance will result if the long-ignored contributions by or about non-Mormons gain a respected place on history's shelf.

In his prizewinning epic, Will Bagley acknowledges that the saga of western migration is not a legend with heroes or villains, culprits or victims, but a story of people who struggled to do the best they could for themselves and their families in a time and place marked by hardship, peril, and rapid change."[15] This should be equally true of the conflicting Mormon and non-Mormon renditions that weave the rich tapestry of Utah history.

This biography of Robert Newton Baskin does deserved honor to its man, naming him to the Valhalla of Utah's early Gentiles. I hope that when it is added to the biographies of such Mormon figures as Amasa Mason Lyman, George Darling Watt, Lewis Barney, John Doyle Lee, and Peter McAuslan and to those of non-Mormons like Jotham Goodell, Patrick Edward Connor, and George R. Maxwell, together they will become, as Trevelyan suggests, "more deeply instructive" than "the narrative generalizations we call history."[16]

---

[14]Baskin, *REM*, 236.

[15]Bagley, *So Rugged and Mountainous*, xx.

[16]"Instructive": Trevelyan, *The Recreations of an Historian* (New York: Thomas Nelson and Sons, 1919), 50n; "narrative generalizations": Barney, *One Side by Himself*, xviii.

Acknowledgments

For history is a pontoon bridge.
Every man walks and works at its building end,
and has come as far as he has over the pontoons laid by others.
WALLACE STEGNER

GRATEFULLY ACKNOWLEDGED IS THE ASSISTANCE OF Nancy Boskoff, director of the Salt Lake City Arts Council, in securing permission for photographing the portrait of Robert N. Baskin that hangs in the City and County Building in Salt Lake City. Baskin's portrait was skillfully photographed by Michael Roberts of Michael Roberts Photography of Salt Lake City. Michael is also a graduate student in the Department of Geography, College of Social and Behavioral Science, University of Utah, Salt Lake City. Thanks to Kristin M. Giacoletto, assistant photograph archivist, for the images from the Alta Club Photographic Collection in the Special Collections at the Marriott Library, University of Utah. Credit and thanks are due Steven Leathem Malia, who graciously provided photographs of his great-great-grandmother Mary Edna Brown Hall, who was for many years a friend of Robert Baskin.

Historical details of Utah's Masonic Lodges, Baskin's Masonic activities, and the correct designation of Masonic titles were generously provided by Aaron E. Saathoff, Past Worshipful Master, Wasatch Lodge No. 1, 33rd Degree Scottish Rite Mason, and Past Potentate of El Kalah Shrine, of Salt Lake City. Suggestions and corrections were given by Michael Homer of Salt Lake City, the acknowledged expert of Mormon-Mason history.

Legal advice and opinion regarding court jurisdiction matters in Utah Territory were generously given by Kenneth L. Cannon II, of Durham Jones & Pinegar, P.C., Salt Lake City. Thanks are also due Lonnie P. Merritt, attorney at law, Wilmington, North Carolina, and Scott K. Wilson, attorney at law of the Utah Federal Defender Office in Salt Lake City, for their review of the 1863 records of the Highland County, Ohio, Court of Common Pleas.

Thanks to Patrick Ragains, business and government information librarian at the University of Nevada, Reno, for searching for federal resolutions concerning Utah's theocracy that originated from Nevada.

The patient assistance of Justine Roach, law librarian at the New Hanover County Law Library in Wilmington, North Carolina, who skillfully aided my online search while teaching me the rudiments of searching the unfamiliar files of long-forgotten Utah Supreme Court records and U.S. Supreme Court records, is gratefully acknowledged. Julia Huddleson, archivist at the Salt Lake County Archives, West Valley City, Utah, was very helpful in locating Baskin property records.

Special thanks are reserved for Ronald O. Barney, former senior archivist in the Church of Jesus Christ of Latter-day Saints' Department of Family and Church History and now executive director of the Mormon History Association. In several instances his kind words encouraged my responsible pursuit of a different perspective on Utah history.

My debt to Wallace Stegner follows a trail with many turns, some easily identified, some subconscious, but I shamelessly acknowledge that I have borrowed from his tribute to his wife, Mary, in the dedication of this work to my wife, Cheryl Gunn Maxwell. She has been an ever-willing, vigilant critic and an unacknowledged copy editor.[1] This work has also benefitted immensely from the patience, meticulous copy editing, and persistence of Rosemary Wetherold, who deserves recognition and my thanks.

William P. MacKinnon, a model for those who would build bridges among Utah historians, while deftly managing to keep one foot in the river of Mormon history and the other in the stream with the non-

[1]Mary Stegner obituary, *SLT*, May 23, 2010. The author certifies that beyond the publisher's contract, he has no commissions, contracts, financial interests, or obligations to any organized body in the publication of this work; he also has no allegiance to Robert Newton Baskin's descendants.

Mormon writers, deserves my gratitude for his thoughtful evaluations that have given encouragement when it was sorely needed.

Independent historians David L. Bigler and Will Bagley very graciously relinquished their own opportunity of setting Robert Newton Baskin into his proper place in Utah history to me, a newcomer. Selfless in their sharing source materials and adept at suggesting improvements, they have provided the proper balance of encouragement and criticism that is the trait of the true teacher and friend. With their works, both men have laid uncountable pontoons for others of us to cross over.

Abbreviations and Conventions

BOP	*Blood of the Prophets*
BYLC	Brigham Young Letterpress Copybooks, 1844–79
CDBY	*The Complete Discourses of Brigham Young*
DavCC	*Davis County (Utah) Clipper*
DN	*Deseret Weekly News* (Salt Lake City)
DEN	*Deseret Evening News* (Great Salt Lake City)
DJMT	*Dialogue: A Journal of Mormon Thought*
GGSL	*Gettysburg to Great Salt Lake*
GQC	*George Q. Cannon: A Biography*
GQCJ	*George Q. Cannon Journal*
HIGH	*Highland Weekly News* (Hillsborough [Hillsboro], Ohio)
HILL	*Hillsboro (Ohio) Weekly News*
HOU	*History of Utah*
IMR	*Inter-Mountain Republican* (Salt Lake City)
JOD	*Journal of Discourses*
JMH	*Journal of Mormon History*
NYH	*New York Herald*
NYT	*New York Times*
NYTrb	*New York Tribune*
OS	*Ogden (Utah) Standard*
REM	*Reminiscences of Early Utah*
RCSW	*Reply to Certain Statements by O. F. Whitney*
SLH	*Salt Lake Herald*
SLMinR	*Salt Lake Mining Review*
SLT	*Salt Lake Tribune*
SLTel	*Salt Lake Telegram*

UHQ	*Utah Historical Quarterly*
USHS	Utah State Historical Society, Utah State Archives, Salt Lake City
UV	*Union Vedette* (Camp Douglas, Utah Territory)
WOR	*The War of the Rebellion: A Compilation of the Official Records of the Union and Confederate Armies*

WHEN CITING THE ONLINE, DIGITALIZED VERSIONS OF NEWS-papers, particularly the *Salt Lake Tribune* and the *Deseret News*, the citation is listed as follows: "Article Title," *Newspaper Name*, date of publication, and, when available, page number and column in the digitalized record, rather than the original imprinted page number. Example: "That Hero and Martyr," *SLT*, September 19, 1888, 2/1.

Introduction

The one duty we owe to history is to rewrite it.
OSCAR WILDE

ROBERT NEWTON BASKIN, A TWENTY-EIGHT-YEAR-OLD lawyer from Hillsboro, Highland County, Ohio, arrived in Utah Territory on a dog-day of summer, in August 1865. He was not a Mormon. A tall, lean body topped with sorrel-red hair, and his cool, blue eyes were gifts from his Irish father and Pennsylvania-born mother. A sound mind, an articulate tongue, and a flash temper were also included. To these had been added excellent private school education, followed by time at Harvard law school, and social status that shortly permitted a meeting with a wealthy, well-known Philadelphian by the name of Hirst, agent for James P. Bruner's North Star mine.[1] Allegedly bound for opportunity in California, Baskin stopped to travel with Hirst to see the mining ventures of Little Cottonwood Canyon, a U-shaped glacial cleft in the Wasatch Mountain range, not far from Great Salt Lake City. At an altitude of 9,100 feet, in the small mining settlement of Alta, they inspected the North Star and Emma silver mines. Baskin saw in the argentiferous galena ore the possibility of its silver and gold expanding his own purse, or at least

---

[1]Baskin, *REM*, 5. Baskin's naming of "Thomas Hearst" is an error. His host was either William L. Hirst, Jr., or Anthony A. Hirst, both sons of William Lucas Hirst, Sr., a wealthy Philadelphia lawyer. With Bruner, wealthy from cotton and woolen mills, Hirst invested in mines in Utah and elsewhere. Prior to his son's meeting with Baskin, the senior Hirst purchased a gold mine in North Carolina; Bruner assumed its operation. "America's First Gold Rush," www.rocksandminerals.com/reedmine.htm, accessed March 2012.

some promise that a new, expanding economy would bring demands for legal expertise beyond those arising from the Mormons' predominantly agrarian works. Rather than continue to California—and perhaps never intending to go there—Baskin set himself to an uncertain future in Utah. The remainder of his long and productive life was spent there.[2]

Robert Baskin entered a Utah society that was unique among the settlements of the West. Conflict arising from social, political, and religious differences defined the interface between the Mormons and the non-Mormon minority. The origins of the conflict were found in the polarity of American mores, religious beliefs, and societal institutions outside Utah, against the parochial assertions and the peculiar theological beliefs of the Mormons.

The early years of the Church of Jesus Christ of Latter-day Saints (LDS Church) are memorialized by their difficult migrations. Soon after the LDS Church's emergence in 1830, near the Erie Canal city of Palmyra, New York, the Mormons relocated to Kirtland, Ohio, then to Jackson County, Missouri, designated as the site for their "New Jerusalem" by the church's founder and first prophet, Joseph Smith. Severe conflicts with the established residents of Jackson, Clay, Caldwell, and Daviess counties in Missouri necessitated retreat north to Illinois, where on the east bank of a sharp bend of the Mississippi River they rebuilt an existing city, renaming it Nauvoo. The seeds of the practice of polygamy, sown in the Illinois soil by Smith, came to full bloom in Utah under the second church leader, Brigham Young. The marriage practices of the Mormons, together with the inseparable fusion of their religion and their government—which defined their unique Kingdom of God on earth—were primary causes of conflict.[3]

The reasons for the Mormons' move west were far different from most of those underlying manifest destiny's westward continental expansion. Under immense pressure from hostile non-Mormon neighbors and the State of Illinois following the murder of Joseph Smith in 1844, Mormons were forced to abandon their homes and property. Faced with great hardships from weather, primitive travel, and hunger, the Saints, under Brigham Young's iron hand, migrated into the Great

---

[2]Baskin, *REM*, 5.

[3]For thorough treatment of the exodus, see John E. Hallwas and Roger Launius, eds., *Cultures in Conflict: A Documentary History of the Mormon War in Illinois* (Logan: Utah State University Press, 1995).

Basin's vastness and isolation, stopping alongside the briny Great Salt Lake, in what was then part of Mexico. Rooted in the revelations of Joseph Smith and the scripture he recorded, faithful Mormons saw themselves as innocent victims, continually persecuted in their peregrinations. However, America's Protestant majority held mistrust and hostility for a people seen as peculiar, unyielding, and fanatic.

To reform their Kingdom of God, Mormons considered founding a new nation or a new state in 1847 on the land now possessed by the United States following its war with Mexico, but a territory named Utah was imposed on them in 1850. By 1857 President James Buchanan declared the Mormons to be in rebellion, instigators of the nation's first civil war. Buchanan sent 30 percent of the U.S. Army toward Utah in the summer of 1857 to restore order and install a replacement for Acting Governor Brigham Young. To this federal action the Mormons mounted armed resistance, destroyed immense amounts of government property, and responded treasonously against the United States and its military forces.[4] Mormons ominously feared another religious pogrom, with repetition of the violence, suffering, and expulsion they had experienced at the hands of government in Missouri and Illinois. Brigham Young also saw in the armed conflict an even more serious specter, the initiation of the end of times, the final war of good against evil that would end with the dominance of God's Kingdom ruled by the men of the Mormon priesthood.

Young's edict, declaring martial law in the early fall of 1857, closed the borders of Utah Territory, virtually bringing travel to a halt across the Great Basin, isolating California, and cutting the nation in half.[5] On the eleventh of September, at a lush green valley in the southwestern corner of Utah Territory, the lives 120 to 140 men, women, and children would send the tragic and undeniable message that Brigham's word was law. Bound for southern California, almost the entire immigrant train was massacred by several score of worshipping, God-fearing men of the Mormon Militia, together with a handful of Utah Indians. The search for the motives and responsibility among the Mormon leaders for the Mountain Meadows atrocity would engage Baskin for a lifetime. Despite his efforts and those of many others, the answers remain controversial and under intense study, with the

---

[4]Bigler and Bagley, *Mormon Rebellion*.
[5]Brigham Young's closure of transcontinental travel was considered by many to be a treasonous act that, by itself, justified a military response.

irretrievable harm incurred, the responsibility not placed, and justice not served remaining as deep and unhealed wounds.[6]

For the four years of 1861 to 1865, America's second civil war, later named the War of the Rebellion raged across the mid-Atlantic and southeastern segments of the nation, along the course of the Mississippi River, and even into the western territories. To Utah's Mormons it was nothing more than God's punishment, deserved by the American people and their iniquitous government for the murders of Joseph Smith and his brother Hyrum, and for their failure to recognize the re-establishment of God's true church. Other than a company of ninety-six soldiers and thirteen teamsters of the Mormon Militia guarding mail and telegraph routes at Fort Bridger, Utah provided no volunteer units to the Union.[7] When the Utah War of 1857–58 did not escalate into complete destruction of federal rule, the Civil War's onset rekindled this apocalyptic vision, that North and South would destroy each other and that Mormons, under God's revelation and through his restored priesthood, would reign. War widows would be welcomed into Mormon plural marriages, along with thousands of fatherless children gathered into the bosom of Mormon society.[8] The Kingdom of God would be hastened by this war's outcome.

Like the Mormons, Baskin sat on the sidelines of this war, observing the crimson tsunami of blood and death that inundated the nation. It was neither apathy nor anesthesia that resulted in Baskin's not serving. In fact he exhibited strong patriotism, Copperhead sympathies, Democrat allegiance, and support of Southern states' secession and continued slavery.[9] But circumstances in Ohio demanded his presence for most of the war's duration.

The eight years prior to Baskin's arrival in Utah saw a series of trials and traumatic events, including a jeremiad call from the Mormon

---

[6]Bagley, *bop*; MacKinnon, *At Sword's Point*; R. W. Walker, Turley, and Leonard, *Massacre at Mountain Meadows*; Bagley and Bigler, *Innocent Blood*.

[7]Ninety-six men served, ostensibly under the command of Brig. Gen. James Craig, but in the de facto command of Mormon Militia lieutenant general Daniel H. Wells, who had commanded their ranks in the 1857 Utah War. Serving from April 28 to August 14, 1862, they guarded the telegraph, mail, and coach transport along the two hundred miles from Green River to Salt Lake City. Hewett, "Utah Territory," 43; MacKinnon, *At Sword's Point*, 472–74.

[8]Maxwell, *GGSL*, 96–102.

[9]"Copperheads," a pejorative term coined by Republicans, referred to those who advocated negotiations with the South, associating them with the poisonous snakes indigenous to the south.

leadership for drastic repentance by its church members. Known as "the Reformation," the voices of Brigham Young and Apostle Jedediah M. Grant thundered from the pulpit. Rebaptism was needed to cleanse the sins that were allegedly running rampant, leading God to forsake his chosen people. The reformation period still hung heavy in Utah when Baskin arrived.

Of his first twenty years in Utah, Mormon leaders said Baskin was in collusion with a tight band of non-Mormons, mostly Civil War veterans and federal civil service appointees, dubbed by the Mormon leaders as the conspiring "Utah Ring." Baskin and the other émigrés were not simply conspiring. They battled—not subversively but openly—against Mormon polygamy and the entrenched government that fused church and state. Non-Mormons saw both the taking of multiple wives and the impenetrable theocratic rule as immoral, illegal, and un-American.

Because his efforts for change were forceful and sustained, Baskin earned this description from one of the Mormons' highest leaders, Apostle George Q. Cannon: "We probably never had a more cruel and unrelenting enemy than he."[10] Another Mormon apostle, Joseph F. Smith, prayed that Baskin "should be made blind, deaf and dumb unless he would repent of his wickedness."[11] Baskin was pleased with the credit given him by his contemporary adversary Orson Ferguson Whitney, a historian who said Baskin was a "Bourbon of the dead past who 'learns nothing' and 'forgets nothing'" and was the "human mainspring of nearly every anti-Mormon movement that Utah has known."[12] Recently, historian David L. Bigler described Baskin as "brash, outspoken, combative, and absolutely fearless" when he shocked the Saints in 1871 by indicting Brigham Young, first for lewd and lascivious conduct under a "territorial law never meant to apply to polygamy" and shortly thereafter for murder.[13]

Baskin drafted the federal legislation that was introduced as the fiercely anti-polygamy Cullom Bill, and later the even more feared Cullom-Struble Bill. He lobbied for the passage of many congressional acts against theocracy and its abuses, which came to be called the "Mormon problem." He challenged Mormon dominance in Utah

[10]Bitton, *GQC*, 198.

[11]Quoted in Baskin, *REM*, xi, cited from *JMH* 14, April 18, 1877.

[12]Baskin, *RCSW*, 3, 29.

[13]Bigler, review of *Reminiscences*, 191.

by aiding the formation of the first non-Mormon political party, the Liberal Party, and urging non-Mormon William McGroarty to run against Mormon congressional incumbent William H. Hooper. Following a very lopsided loss, Baskin then convinced McGroarty to officially contest Hooper's seat.[14] Baskin assisted Gen. George R. Maxwell in his run against the influential Utah pooh-bah and territorial representative George Q. Cannon and later vied unsuccessfully with monogamous Mormon John T. Caine for Utah's seat. Baskin served as *the* dominant force in Washington that placed the LDS Church upon the procrustean bed of the Edmunds Act and the Edmunds-Tucker Act, with dissolution of the incorporation of the church and seizure of its assets and property.

Despite the enmity his opposition generated within the overwhelmingly Mormon population of Salt Lake City, he was twice elected the city's mayor, only the second non-Mormon to be elected to that post. He led the way for improvements in the city's waterworks and sewer system and had many streets paved and sidewalks constructed. He brought Salt Lake City, as he said, from the third-highest mortality rate in the nation "to the standard of a city of the first class."[15] Elected to serve in the Utah legislature, he became a prime mover in establishing free public education. As he and Mormon factions mellowed, Baskin ascended to be elected chief justice in Utah's Supreme Court, serving with distinction.

For at least nineteen of his widowed, senior years, Baskin lived unmarried under the same roof with widow Mary Edna Brown Hall, twenty-three years his junior. Curiously, it was Baskin who had pushed for legislation to make cohabitation a crime punished by imprisonment when practiced by Mormon men under the aegis of plural marriage.

Baskin came to Utah from Ohio as a nonveteran, a loner; he remained distanced from the easy camaraderie among the Civil War veterans of the so-called Utah Ring. An investor and speculator in mining and real estate, a thoroughbred race horse owner, and a highly capable lawyer, he was also a visionary city planner who was the force behind the construction of the classically beautiful Salt Lake City and County Building. Baskin was also an active Master Mason, serving as Grand Orator and Grand Chaplain of Utah's Mount Moriah Lodge,

---

[14]Baskin, *REM*, 23.
[15]Ibid., 27.

and was a founding member of the Alta Club, a prestigious, exclusive group of Utah's business and professional men.[16] Already a longevity outlier at age sixty when he became a Utah State Historical Society founding member, he was even more so at ages seventy-seven and seventy-nine when he published his corrections of what he decried as the "dishonest and despicable" history of Utah.[17] When he died at age eighty-one, the average age of death was forty to fifty; he outlived many Grand Army of the Republic men and Confederate veterans, his contemporaries in Utah following the Civil War.

Forever with an eye to a better Utah, Baskin deserves placement as the cynosure among the handful of little remembered, non-Mormon men like George R. Maxwell, Jacob Smith Boreman, and Frederic Lockley. They were among the earliest non-Mormons in Utah who worked to qualify the territory for statehood. For a half century Baskin fought for the basic freedoms enjoyed by American citizens to be granted to the people of Utah. The distinguished statesman of Utah history David L. Bigler fittingly nominates Robert Newton Baskin, ahead of any other man, as the unsung father of modern Utah.[18]

---

[16]Malmquist, *Alta Club*, 130.
[17]Baskin, *REM*, 236.
[18]Bigler, review of *Reminiscences*, 192.

I

Ohio Origins

Lawyers, I suppose, were children once.
CHARLES LAMB

ORN ON DECEMBER 20, 1837, IN JACKSON, HIGHLAND
County, Ohio, Robert Newton Baskin was the fourth son,
and the seventh of nine children, of Irish immigrant Andrew
Baskin and Nancy Fulton, formerly of Pennsylvania.[1] The men of the
Baskin family were accomplished and highly regarded. Andrew, an
affluent man with substantial property, was well-known in Hillsboro;
he was, for four years, Highland County's sheriff, and, for twenty
years, the Highland County representative in Ohio's state legislature.
John Baskin, Robert's uncle, served in 1856 and 1863 as the Highland
County recorder. Two of Robert's older brothers, John and James,
were steady farmers; the third brother, Thomas H., was elected county
sheriff in 1858, opened a law practice after the Civil War, and, as his
father had done, served in the Ohio House of Representatives.

Robert Baskin was twelve when his father died, in 1849. The eldest
son of the family, John, was the only sibling then married; three of
Robert's sisters were younger than sixteen. Details of Robert's early
childhood education are uncertain, but he first attended the log
schoolhouse built in 1842 three miles east of Belfast township. The
school consisted of a single large room, heated by a giant stove in winter, with glass panes as its small windows.[2] Despite whatever financial

---

[1]U.S. Federal Census, 1850. The 1900 census lists Robert Baskin's birth date as December 1837.
[2]Elderly John R. Emrie was the school's first teacher. Johnson, *Highland Pioneer Sketches*, 509.

strains this fatherless family may have experienced, Robert began private school in 1853 at South Salem Academy at age sixteen.

Founded by Presbyterian minister Hugh Stewart Fullerton, Salem Academy, as it was known, was built just over the state line in Ross County, Ohio. Its primary purpose when it opened was the preparation of ministers and teachers bound for the West.[3] Professor J. A. Lowes served as its principal during the "golden age" from 1848 to 1858 that encompassed Baskin's tenure there. While at Salem, Robert also worked for, and studied law under, the tutelage of practicing attorney James H. Thompson of Hillsboro.[4]

Encouraged by his education at Salem Academy, and perhaps at the suggestion of Thompson, Baskin chose to attend Harvard Law School in Boston. The school's 1856–57 catalog defined its purpose as "to afford a complete course of legal education for gentlemen intended for the Bar in any of the United States, except in matters of mere local law and prudence."[5] Harvard's requirements were simple and plain: "No examination, and no particular course of previous study are necessary for admission; but the Student, if not a graduate of some college, must be at least nineteen years of age, and produce testimonials of good moral character." A $200 bond was required, and the tuition was $50 each term. Two years were required to complete the course of study.

Baskin entered Harvard Law School on April 7, 1856, and boarded at the home of a Mr. Torry.[6] Upon completing two terms, he qualified as a member of the "Middle Class" and was listed a "Class of 1857" member. However, he did not enter the second year of study and did not receive a law degree. This aspect of his education at Harvard was apparently not discussed in Utah.[7]

In the summer of 1857 Baskin returned to Hillsboro, where he joined the law practice of highly respected William Oliver Collins. Collins, a graduate of Amherst College, had studied law from 1833 to

---

[3] Such schools were called normal schools, and the word "normal" was often part of the school's official name.

[4] Chillicothe's Presbytery ministry took over Salem Academy in 1859; thereafter it functioned as a junior college. Betty and Dwight Crum, Crum Sinking Spring, Highland County, Ohio, pers. comm., July 2009; Ohio Historical Society, "Marker #4-71 Salem Academy," *Remarkable Ohio*, www.remarkableohio.org/HistoricalMarker.aspx?historicalMarkerId=456, accessed March 2012.

[5] Harvard Law School, *Catalogue*, 10.

[6] Ibid. Baskin's costs at Harvard would have totaled approximately $11,400 in 2007 dollars.

[7] Harvard Law School, *Quinquennial Catalogue*.

1835 under the tutelage of judges John C. Wright, Timothy Walker, and Edward King at Cincinnati Law School and was admitted to the Ohio bar in 1835.[8]

While Baskin was attending law school in Boston, his mentors James H. Thompson and William Oliver Collins, along with his childhood teacher John R. Emrie and one of his uncles, John Baskin, joined with other men to found the Hillsboro Female College.[9] This progressive move for educational equality for women would contrast sharply with the climate in Utah, where Baskin would find neither free public schools nor special schools for women. Women in the male-dominated society of the Mormons were generally less educated, their primary roles restricted to domesticity, procreation, and child care.[10]

RAISED IN COPPERHEADISM

During the pre–Civil War period, a substantial percentage of people in the southern counties of Ohio, where Baskin was raised and first practiced law, were in sympathy with the South. Loyalties "vacillated between Union and Confederate," and because the region had "the poorest soil in the Midwest," it was severely affected by "the agricultural depression precipitated by Lincoln's closing of southern markets in 1861" and became "a hotbed of Copperheadism, Negrophobia, and the political machinations of northerners with southern sympathies."[11] In the 1860 election in Morgan Township, near Highland County, only 36 percent of voters cast their ballots in support of Abraham Lincoln, and "in southern Ohio counties, especially Highland and Ross, support for the Union cause was lukewarm."[12] When fighting erupted in 1861, an Ohio Democratic State Convention adopted

---

[8]*Amherst College Biographical Record.*

[9]Klise, *County of Highland*, 212. The college was incorporated in 1855, and the building was completed in 1857, with J. M. Matthews as its president.

[10]Outside Utah, the woman was seen as the stabilizing force in the home, a bastion against corrupting influences. With Mormons, the husband, the church, and priesthood authority stood as the moral ramparts, a fact seen by many non-Mormons as "an inherent degradation of womanhood." Marquis, "Diamond Cut Diamond," 169, 173. Nonetheless a number of early Mormon women achieved professional status, with claims that "no concentration of women in medicine ever occurred proportionately to equal the number of women doctors among the pioneers of Utah." Noall, "Utah's Pioneer Women Doctors," 16–17. Lawrence Foster notes, "Polygamy itself may have helped to free some women for a broader range of activity in society." Foster, *Religion and Sexuality*, 233.

[11]Unrau, *Tending the Talking Wire*, 8.

[12]Mowery, "Copperheadism."

resolutions declaring that two hundred thousand Democrats of Ohio sent greetings to their southern brethren.[13]

Given that he was nurtured in this environment heavy with sympathy for the southern causes, Baskin's allegiance with the South was not surprising. His politics were at odds with his colleagues Thompson and Collins, who shared programs as featured speakers in Republican gatherings in 1858. Both were outspokenly critical of President James Buchanan's "doughface" Democratic administrative policies.[14] Throughout his tenure in Utah, Baskin made the necessary compromises, affiliating with the Liberal and Citizen parties, but he proudly maintained that he was a lifelong, unwavering, to-the-core Democrat.

At age twenty-four, in good health and well-educated, Baskin was prime material for leadership in volunteer service in the Civil War, yet, unlike his colleagues and family members, he served neither side. His first law associate, Thompson, served in the Union cavalry.[15] His second, Collins, compiled a commendable record. From 1837 to 1840, Collins had been prosecuting attorney for Highland County; from 1848 to 1851, the Cincinnati and Hillsboro Railroad's president; and from 1860 to 1862, a member of Ohio's state senate. In the summer of 1862 it was Collins, a volunteer lieutenant colonel, who organized Ohio men into the Eleventh Ohio Cavalry. It became the only Ohio unit active in the territories. The Eleventh did not fight Confederate units but ranged widely over Nebraska, Dakota, Colorado, Utah, Oregon, Idaho, and Montana, engaging in battles with the Snakes, the Sioux, and the Cheyennes, while enduring severe privations in the winters. General Collins's military record was distinguished, but at a high price. His only son, Lt. Caspar W. Collins was killed on July 26, 1865, by Indians near Platt Bridge at the Battle of Red Buttes, near present-day Mills, Natrona County, Wyoming.[16]

Nurtured in Temperance

The temperance movement in Hillsboro, Ohio, had smoldered among wives and mothers for a substantial period long before "Mother Thomp-

---

[13]*NYT*, November 23, 1876.

[14]*HIGH*, September 23, 1858.

[15]Thompson was a sergeant in Company C, Ohio Fifth Cavalry.

[16]Fort Collins, Colorado, was named for General Collins, and the city of Casper, Wyoming, for his son. The Postal Service's misspelling as "Casper" has persisted. Collins and Family Papers; Unrau, *Tending the Talking Wire*, 8.

son," commanding a phalanx of women protestors, marched to the doors of drinking establishments. As early as 1857 the Hillsboro Town Council passed an unusual ordinance against selling liquor: whenever a written complaint was made by a wife that her spouse was given to intoxication, the mayor was required to notify "each dealer in Intoxicating drinks, . . . directing such person or persons to refrain from selling or giving him liquor for six months, under a penalty of fifty dollars," with jail time of "not less than three nor more than twenty days for each offense." Another article of the ordinance made similar complaints by children against their father or mother also legal.[17]

As the Civil War neared its end, temperance became increasingly important to southern Ohio residents. Baskin's home city sported as many as twenty saloons, and "Mother Thompson" was none other than Eliza Jane Trimble Thompson, the wife of Baskin's former tutor and law associate Judge James H. Thompson, and the daughter of former Ohio governor Allen Trimble. By 1873 she and a number of like-minded women were determined to stop alcohol consumption in their town: seventy-five of the city's women marched on the saloons, demanding that owners pledge to no longer serve alcohol.

The Women's Christian Temperance Union grew from these origins in Highland County into a national effort. Baskin had been years in Utah by the time the temperance movement gathered full strength in Hillsboro, but he was apparently influenced by its conservative ethic. Utah's Mormons were always eager to publicize any tendency to overindulge in strong drink by their non-Mormon agitators, but Baskin was never the object of such criticism, and no comment on his alcohol use is found in Utah's historical records.

A HEATED WINTER

Copperheadism kept southern Ohio politically hot in the cold fall and winter of 1862–63. Editor of the weekly *Dayton Empire* and Democratic politician Clement Laird Vallandigham had become the acknowledged leader of this faction. Elected from Ohio to the U.S. House of Representatives in 1858 and 1860, his ardent antiwar stance led to defeat in his reelection bid in October 1862. A states' rights and secession supporter, he believed that the federal government had no legal power to regulate slavery. Vallandigham's voice,

---

[17]*HIGH*, May 28, 1857.

with others, rang out through the winter of 1862 and the spring of 1863, with a tone of defeatism that skirted disloyalty. So disturbing were his criticisms of the war and his support of the Confederacy that Gen. Ambrose E. Burnside, then Department of Ohio commander, issued General Order No. 38 from his headquarters in Cincinnati in April 1863, declaring: "Sympathy for the enemy will not be allowed in this department. Persons committing such offenses will be at once arrested . . . or sent beyond our lines into the lines of their friends. . . . [T]reason, expressed or implied, will not be tolerated."[18] Vallandigham's agitations were particularly irritating to Burnside, who was carrying the burden of Fredericksburg's stunning defeat of Union forces under his command. More than thirteen thousand men had been slaughtered there in mid-December of 1862. Of Fredericksburg the *Cincinnati Commercial* exclaimed: "It can hardly be in human nature for men to show more valor or generals to manifest less judgement, than were perceptible on our side that day."[19] Vallandigham was undeterred by Burnside's general order; a speech in May 1863 led to his arrest and conviction, with a sentence of two years in federal prison.[20]

Public unrest was further stirred when President Lincoln issued the Emancipation Proclamation in January 1863, declaring that all slaves in those states in rebellion were, by federal decree, free. Shortly thereafter came the Conscription Act, by which men of the states, ages twenty to forty-five, were liable for service under the Union banner.[21]

The men of Highland County who volunteered into Union service were well aware of the division of allegiance among those still at home. The substance of a letter from a Twenty-fourth Ohio volunteer was printed in the city paper, describing the "intense feeling of disgust and indignation which [we] feel for those men at home who were instrumental in causing many . . . brave fellows to go into the field, by promise of their sympathy and support, but who are now found

---

[18]"General Order No. 38," *Ohio History Central*, www.ohiohistorycentral.org/entry.php?rec=1481, accessed March 2012.

[19]When Lincoln was told of Fredericksburg that "it was not a battle, it was a butchery," he wrote in his diary, "If there is a worse place than hell, I am in it." Quoted in Goolrick, *Rebels Resurgent*, 92–93.

[20]Lincoln reduced Vallandigham's sentence, and Vallandigham was transported to nearby Confederate lines. Rather than fight, he fled to Canada.

[21]Service could be avoided by paying a fee or finding a substitute. This policy was seen as an unfair targeting of the poor, and protest riots in working-class sections of New York City resulted.

bitterly opposing the war and basely deserting the gallant men who relied upon their professions of patriotism."[22]

In this incendiary, divisive atmosphere, the ardent Democrat of short temper Robert Newton Baskin spoke at a political meeting sponsored by the Union faction: "The gallant Union men of Old Paint had a glorious meeting at Rainsboro . . . [and] the large School House was filled to its utmost capacity. Stirring speeches were made . . . and the spirit manifested . . . showed that the friends of the Union are fully aroused . . . and determined to do their duty. A Union League is organized . . . and has a large list of members."[23] Baskin spoke at this meeting, undoubtedly in vigorous opposition, and was brusquely challenged by Union-aligned men in the audience. Hot words were spoken, a disturbance ensued, and Baskin was "roughly handled" by several men, according to witnesses. Seeds of ill will planted in this Rainsboro meeting grew into a second encounter only seven days later. An account of the "Shocking Tragedy" was reported in the local newspaper:

> Our usually quiet town has been in a state of intense excitement . . . caused by the shooting of Andrew J. West, of Paint township by Rob't Newton Baskin . . . resulting in the death of the former about 24 hours after receiving the wound. The parties met in the street in front of Brown's Drug Store, about 11 o'clock . . . when some word passed between them, and a scuffle ensued, in which Baskin shot West twice, the first ball merely grazing his head, the second entering his left side[,] . . . causing his death. . . . Baskin was arrested immediately and held to bail . . . in the sum of $2,000 . . . but owing to the absence of an important witness, the examination was postponed. . . . About noon, West died, and Baskin was re-arrested on a charge of murder in the first degree.[24]

Andrew West, about age thirty, was generally well-liked and was engaged to be married in a few weeks. The newspaper report went on: "There are . . . contradictory reports in regard to the deplorable occurrence, but . . . we desire to say nothing which might add to the excitement already prevailing. Let the law take its course, should be the feeling of every prudent, law abiding citizen."[25]

---

[22]*HILL*, April 16, 1863.
[23]"A Rousing Union Meeting in 'Old Paint,'" *HILL*, March 26, 1863.
[24]"Shocking Tragedy," *HILL*, April 4, 1863.
[25]Ibid.

Witness testimony, given several days later, clearly indicates that West's death at Baskin's hand was more a matter of self-defense than a result of Baskin's hot temper:

> The first witness . . . testified that he was coming up Main Street with Baskin when they met West. Baskin said, "How are you, Andy?" West replied, "How are you, Bob?" . . . Baskin replied, "I don't think you fellows acted gentlemanly." . . . West responded, "I think you lied." Baskin replied, "I am not in the habit of being called a 'liar.'" West retorted, "Well, . . . you are . . . a G——d d——d liar." . . . Both then stepped back a pace, and West took hold of his coat as if to draw it. Baskin said, "Don't strike," and took hold of the lappel [*sic*] of his coat as if to draw something from the inside pocket. West immediately struck him in the face . . . five or six times, Baskin fending off the blows. . . . [The] witness heard the first report of a pistol and called for help. West then caught Baskin around the body and threw him . . . into the gutter. . . . Baskin was lying in the gutter on his back, West kneeling on his breast, holding him by the collar . . . and striking him about the face. . . . Before he could have struck more . . . blows [the] witness heard the second report of the pistol. West fell forward . . . exclaiming, "I am shot." He crawled up on the sidewalk, holding both hands to his left side. Some other persons came up and took him into Brown's drug store.[26]

A second witness corroborated the statements of the first, and a third witness added more details: "Baskin was standing on the pavement after the second shot, with a pistol in his hand. West staggered toward him . . . when Baskin raised his pistol and said, 'Don't come any further, or d——m, I'll shoot you the third time.'"[27] Following the testimony, and after "able arguments" by lawyers on both sides, the magistrate ruled that Baskin would be charged with second-degree murder. He was freed on $6,000 bail.[28]

West's funeral, conducted by Masonic order members, was followed shortly by the issuance of a resolution by Highland Lodge No. 38: "With the most profound sorrow we mourn the murder and untimely death of our beloved brother. . . . [I]n his death the Lodge has lost one of its true and best friends, the community a good citizen, and the

---

[26]"Charge of Killing A. J. West," *HILL*, April 9, 1863.

[27]Ibid.

[28]The sureties on the bail bond included Robert Baskin, Sr., uncle; Thomas H. Baskin, brother; James Baskin, brother; and Allen Trimble, former governor of Ohio. *HILL*, April 9, 1863.

Nation and State a loyal subject." West's Masonic brothers were urged to wear a badge of mourning for him for thirty days.[29]

In May 1863 a grand jury was convened, and after a protracted examination, an indictment for the lesser charge of manslaughter was brought against Baskin.[30] Judicial matters progressed slowly in the Court of Common Pleas of Highland County, for the case was not called for trial until November 1863. During this six-month span it appears that Baskin and his counsel may have honed an effective defensive legal skill—namely, packing a jury:

> Of public interest . . . is that of the State vs Baskin, indicted for manslaughter. In this case the Prosecutor . . . entered a *nolle*, and the defendant was released from bail. We learn that the reason [was that] . . . in spite of his [the prosecutor's] utmost efforts to prevent it, the special jury empaneled in the case *was composed entirely of men of the same political party as the defendant.* This . . . rendered it next to impossible to expect a fair . . . verdict. . . . He therefore decided to quash the indictment, rather than subject the county to the expense of a trial, which, with a jury so constituted, must be but a mockery of justice. The effect of the *nolle* is to discharge the defendant from all liability under the indictment to which it applies; but he may again be arrested and tried under a new indictment.[31]

The Civil War raged in 1864 while court proceedings in the case proceeded slowly with delays and continuances brought about by missing witnesses and other issues.[32]

In 1865 Baskin was rearrested on the charge of killing Andrew J. West and held on $1,000 bail should a new indictment be found against him at the next term of court.[33] The final action concerning Baskin in the Court of Common Pleas, in March 1865, was very disturbing to the Republican editor of the *Highland Weekly News*:

> The Grand Jury . . . refused to find any bill against Baskin for killing West. . . . [T]he Grand Jury last spring found a bill against him

---

[29]"Tribute of Respect to the Late Andrew J. West," HILL, April 16, 1863. West applied for membership in Highland Masonic Lodge No. 38 in 1858 and became a Master Mason on February 9, 1860. Les Brower, Past District Deputy Grand Master, 7th Masonic District of Ohio, e-mail message to author, November 28, 2009.

[30]"Indicted for Manslaughter," HILL, May 28, 1863.

[31]"Court Matters," HILL, November 5, 1863; italics in the original. Baskin's paternal uncle John was, at the time, the Highland County recorder and could have been responsible for a jury impaneled with only Democrats.

[32]"Matters about Home," HIGH, June 16, 1864.

[33]HIGH, March 9, 1865.

for Manslaughter, which was *nolle'd* by the Prosecuting Attorney . . . together with all the other indictments found at the Spring term, on account of legal informality in the manner of drafting the Jurors. The refusal of the Grand Jury for the present term to find any indictment against Baskin cannot fail to excite strong suspicions that a majority of the Jury were influenced by *party feeling* in disregard of their sworn duty as Jurors.

The editor then expressed his perspective on what happened after the court instructed the grand jury members on the various degrees of homicide: "It then became their sworn duty . . . to inquire into the facts and present an indictment in accordance therewith. By their refusal to do so, they have virtually declared that the killing of West was *not* a violation of law—*not a crime at all!*" The article then restated the editor's concern about political connections: "A majority of the Jurors are known to be of the *same political party* as Baskin. Putting all these circumstances together, we leave the public to decide whether the Jury did or did not discharge its duty, in accordance with its sworn obligations."[34]

Even though the Republican-aligned *Highland Weekly News* suggested that the grand jury's impaneling had been subverted by packing it with Democrats, its editor did not name John Baskin or any other as having done so. Baskin was freed.[35]

Two independent reviews of original Ohio court records by experienced lawyers have recently concluded that the evidence was insufficient to establish either that the jury was packed or that any questionable legal practice took place. Information is not available regarding the regulations governing jury impaneling and selection or the proportion of Democrats and Republicans among the population eligible for jury call. Both legal reviewers interpret Baskin's release without an indictment as a practical consideration, the prosecutors and judge considering it not worth the court's investment to press for an indictment, since Baskin's plea at trial would certainly have been one of self-defense, with which the jury, in all probability, would have agreed.[36]

[34]*HIGH*, March 23, 1865; italics in the original.

[35]Records of legal actions arising from the death of Andrew West: Court of Common Pleas, Hillsboro, Highland County, Ohio, General Index, Order Book 13, May term 1864, no. 54, 83, p. 568.

[36]Lonnie P. Merritt, attorney at law, Wilmington, North Carolina, and Scott K. Wilson, attorney with the Utah Federal Defender Office, separately reviewed the court records.

Baskin left no written record describing the traumatic events in Ohio that preceded and precipitated his leaving. It is speculation to ask if he planned to leave, never (as far as we know) to return to the family hearth. Did John West, the father of Andrew J. West, or either or both of Andrew's brothers, Allen P. and Joseph, openly seek retribution? Did they place a price on Baskin's death? Did Baskin's relatives banish him from the family constellation? Did his killing of Andrew West erase any prospect of a thriving legal practice in Highland County? All are reasonable scenarios, but his reasons for leaving Ohio remain unknown.

In the protracted period during Highland County's court action against Baskin in the killing of West, the Colorado territorial governor Dr. John Evans visited Hillsboro and spoke enticingly of riches to be found in the mountains, saying, "It is confidently asserted that the mineral wealth of Colorado exceeds that of California, and that her gold is sufficient to pay off the national debt."[37] It is speculation, but reasonable, that the potential for mining success led Baskin to formulate a western-bound exit plan, possibly with a detour to Colorado to evaluate prospects there before going to Utah, Nevada, or California. Hillsboro newspaper accounts confirm that many citizens of Highland County were leaving, attracted by the postwar opportunities in Missouri, Iowa, and Illinois. Whether his path to his decision was complex or simple, Baskin, like so many others, was attracted to the opportunities afforded in the western expansion.[38]

---

[37]*HIGH*, January 28, 1864.
[38]*HIGH*, October 5, 1865.

2

Forewarned and Prepared?

The first duty of a newspaper is to be accurate.
If it be accurate, it follows that it is fair.
HERBERT BAYARD SWOPE

A T THE TIME ROBERT BASKIN RETURNED FROM HARvard Law School, the news of happenings in Utah Territory appeared in the newspapers in Highland County, readily available to a young lawyer with an inquisitive mind. Certainly Baskin read the Democratic-leaning *Highland Gazette* and gave some attention to the Republican-aligned *Highland Weekly News*, whose articles frequently dealt with polygamy and anti-federalist unrest in Utah. Polygamy was treated humorously at times, as in one ditty that told of the duties of the Mormon man's first wife:

> Now sisters, list to what I say;
>   With trials this world is rife,
> You can't expect to miss them all,
>   Help husband get a wife!
> Now this advice I freely give,
>   If exalted you would be,
> Remember that your husband must
>   Be blest with more than thee.[1]

Far more serious were reports in both newspapers in the spring and summer of 1857 describing the events that would escalate into the Utah

---

[1]"Mormon Poetry," *HIGH*, May 21, 1857, 1/1. A slightly different version published elsewhere noted the ditty's source as the *Deseret News*. "Mormon Wives," *The National Magazine*, October 1857, 876.

War. A piece titled "Mormon Outrages" carried the message that President Buchanan's attention and "perhaps a touch of powder and ball" would be required after "a party of Mormon dignitaries, acting under the advice of Brigham Young, . . . entered the offices of the U.S. District Judge, and Clerk of the Supreme Court and carried away all the papers . . . together with nine hundred volumes of the laws." Mormon threats said that federal officials "must leave at once or be 'sent to h——l across lots.'"[2] Shortly thereafter another report claimed that the house of federal judge George P. Stiles had been burned and that death threats had been made against surveyor general David H. Burr and U.S. Indian agent Garland Hurt. These men were the "only United States officials remaining in the territory." The safety of these three was said to be "so precarious at last accounts, that in all probability they are now on their way to the States."[3] Land distribution and ownership in Utah were the subjects of a midsummer article, which stated: "Mormons have sequestered the public lands of the United States, ignored the surveys, and bought and sold the soil, precisely as if they held the same by original right of proprietorship. . . . [T]hough Utah has been organized for nine years . . . not an acre of land has been bought from the Government."[4]

July's articles described Gen. Winfield Scott's preparation for the dispatch of troops to Utah. "No attempt will be made to interfere with the religious or social institutions of the Mormons, but the United States laws will be rigidly enforced," said Scott.[5] The movement of the U.S. Army columns from Fort Leavenworth was described, as were details about the newly appointed territorial governor, Alfred Cumming of Georgia. Reports indicated that troops were sent to escort the new official, assert federal authority, and protect federal officers among those believed to be in rebellion and insubordinate to the laws of the United States.

What was not made clear by Ohio's publications was the Mormon perspective on Buchanan's military expedition. Young and his leaders saw renewed persecution in this military action, fearing that another heinous pogrom would develop as they anticipated the march of more

---

[2] "Mormon Outrages," *HIGH*, April 16, 1857, 1/7. Mormon officials countered that these reports were untrue or overblown, and that official records remained.

[3] "Further Outrages by the Mormons," *HIGH*, May 28, 1857, 2/5. Mormon versions insist that threats against Burr and Hurt were questionable; nonetheless both men left the territory in fear of death.

[4] "Mormon Titles in Utah," *HIGH*, July 9, 1857, 1/6. The divisive issues of Mormon claims of land ownership and non-Mormon denial of their claims are treated in Maxwell, *GGSL*, 117–42.

[5] "Troops for Utah," *HIGH*, July 9, 1857, 4/2.

than a thousand troops whose first assigned commander, Gen. William Selby Harney, carried a reputation for grisly cruelty. When Albert S. Johnston was moved to replace Harney, it brought small comfort. Experience gave Mormons no assurance they would be immune from harm at the hands of government. The possibility that Young envisioned a chiliastic conflagration initiating the end of time was a theological detail not found in the information then available to Baskin.

The Hillsboro newspapers continued throughout the remainder of 1857 to report the events unfolding in Utah. The Mormons' exploratory trek to Fort Limhi in Idaho was misinterpreted to be a Mormon effort to entrap a pursuing army and was not recognized for its true purpose: Young's personal evaluation of escape routes and sites for a possible mass migration.[6] This venture northward in November was erroneously described by the *New York Times* correspondent who wrote from Nebraska, saying, "Some seceders from the Mormon Church have arrived, bringing the news that a large force of Mormon militia . . . were preparing to leave Salt Lake City with provisions for a six weeks campaign in the mountains."[7] In addition to the reports in Ohio newspapers, extensive press coverage of Mormons, Utah, and the Utah War was provided by big-city publications of wide circulation, as Kenneth Alford has recently documented. More than 1,200 related articles appeared in the *New York Times* during this period.[8] Baskin's mind was no tabula rasa regarding Mormons when he arrived in the mountains of Utah Territory.

September 1857 Tragedy

Baskin and his law colleagues in Ohio may not have heard, despite widespread reports, of the awesome calamity in Utah in the fall of 1857. From Los Angeles, Omaha, Chicago, and New York came stories of a nightmare of death that had befallen travelers that September in a little-known western valley.[9] Baskin would have read the accounts

---

[6]See Bigler, *Fort Limhi.*

[7]"Important from Utah," *HIGH*, November 5, 1857, 2.

[8]Alford, "Utah and the Civil War Press," 76.

[9]"Horrible Massacre of Emigrants!! Over 100 Persons Murdered!! Confirmation of the Report," *Los Angeles Star*, October 10, 1857; "The Emigrant Massacre," *San Francisco Herald*, October 15, 1857; "The Mormon Outrages," *Omaha Nebraskan*, December 2, 1857; "Murderous Outrages by the Mormons and Their Indian Allies Confirmed," *Chicago Daily Tribune*, December 4, 1857; "Complicity of the Mormons in the Late Emigrant Massacre—Indians Were Tools in the Hands of the Saints," *NYH*, December 4, 1857; "Horrible Massacre of Emigrants!! The Mountain Meadows Massacre in Public Discourse," http://mountainmeadows.unl.edu/archive/index.html.

with particular interest had he known the depth to which he would become involved in its aftermath, and the lifelong burden of working for justice that he would come to accept.

In Utah Territory a company of 120 to 140 individuals, mostly children and women, led by trail captains Alexander Fancher and John T. "Jack" Baker, were camped three hundred miles southwest of Great Salt Lake City. Coming from prosperous farms in Arkansas, they carried gold coin and herded hundreds of fine animals as they traveled the Old Spanish Trail to a destination in southern California. On September 7 they were attacked at daybreak in the beautiful grassy valley called Mountain Meadows, in what is now the far southwestern corner of Utah. By September 11, the fifth day of the siege, many of their men were dead. Without water, their ammunition nearly spent, the remaining company of exhausted, terrified travelers were lured from the scant protection of rifle pits beneath their wagons by a white-flag promise held in the hand of a white man. This man talked of safe transport to nearby Cedar City, Utah. Believing themselves safe at last from an attack by Utah Indians, they relinquished their arms. Shortly after their surrender, the adult men were walking single file when a Mormon militiaman called out, "Halt!" Each emigrant man was then killed, shot at arm's length by the Mormon guard walking immediately beside him. Hearing the gunfire from the back side of the low ridge they had just crossed, the women and teenage boys of the Fancher train rushed back toward their men, only to be systematically slaughtered as they attempted to flee or hide. Seventeen children under the age of eight years were not killed, as they were judged too young to report the event and Mormon doctrine considered them "innocent."[10]

Despite attempts by Utah Mormons to keep the killings secret, news of the massacre raced across the nation, and within a month a San Francisco newspaper called for military action: "If the government was incapable of handling the Mormon question, from this state alone, thousands of volunteers could be drawn, who would ask

---

[10]The interconnection of the U.S. Army advancing to Utah and the mass murder of the Arkansas travelers, have become the subject of intense research as the history of the Utah War and the LDS theocracy of the time is untangled. Juanita Brooks's *Mountain Meadows Massacre* (1950) remains a classic. More recently, Bagley's *Blood of the Prophets* and Walker, Turley, and Leonard's *Massacre at Mountain Meadows* have dealt, from different perspectives, with the causes and responsibility for the massacre.

no better employment than the extermination of the Mormons."[11] It was an amazing omission that Buchanan's 1857 annual message in December did not mention Mormon involvement in the killings but addressed other significant problems in Utah: "Whilst Governor Young has been both governor and superintendent of Indian affairs . . . , he has been at the same time the head of the church called the Latter Day Saints. . . . His power has been . . . absolute over both Church and State. The people of Utah . . . , believing with a fanatical spirit that he is governor . . . by divine appointment, . . . obey his commands as if they were direct revelations from Heaven." Buchanan charged that Young "has . . . declared his determination to maintain his power by force, and has already committed acts of hostility against the United States." The line had been crossed, Buchanan said, adding, "This is the first rebellion which has existed in our Territories, and humanity itself requires that we should put it down in such a manner that it shall be the last."[12]

As Colonel Johnston's troops were held in check by political negotiations and enduring the cold and severely reduced rations at Fort Bridger and Camp Scott in the 1857–58 winter, news came to Highland County, reprinted from a California paper, of Young's message to his Saints: "We will destroy our enemies by millions, if they send them here to destroy us, and not a man of us be hurt. As soon as they start to come into our settlements, let sleep depart . . . until they sleep in death."[13] In the spring and summer of 1858, newspapers told Ohioans of the entry of Johnston's forces into Utah's heartland as well as the evacuation of the Mormon people from Salt Lake City. They had been ordered by Young to go south, into the refuge of central Utah villages in anticipation of harm at the hands of federal troops.[14]

1862 MORRILL ACT IGNORED

When the Morrill Anti-bigamy Act was signed into law in July 1862, the nation's capital was whirling with Civil War preparations and military assignments. A frustrated Lincoln watched Gen. George B. McClellan perform his Kabuki dance of nonengagement with Rob-

---

[11]*San Francisco Daily Evening Bulletin*, October 12, 1857.
[12]"President's Message, Utah," HIGH, December 24, 1857, 1/2.
[13]"What Brigham Young Says," HIGH, January 28, 1858, 3/2.
[14]"Interesting Letter from Utah," HIGH, July 25, 1858, 1/4.

ert E. Lee's Confederate forces on the Richmond peninsula. Justin Smith Morrill, a senator from Vermont, pushed through two bills during this stressful time. The first was a land grant bill whose provisions set aside thirty thousand acres of federal land for each member of Congress, for endowment of a home-state college. The second focused on plural marriage in Utah, legislation that earned him the enmity of the Mormons. The intent of this anti-bigamy, anti-polygamy bill was "to punish and prevent the practice of polygamy in the Territories of the United States, and for other purposes, and to disapprove and annul certain acts of the Legislative Assembly of the Territory of Utah." The bill stipulated that anyone engaged in polygamy would be guilty of bigamy, with fines up to $500 and up to five years in prison. Additionally, it specified that no religious corporation could hold more than $50,000 in real estate. No funding was provided for the enforcement of the bill's provisions, and a preoccupied Lincoln administration allowed the bill to lie fallow. If this landmark legislation came to the attention of Robert Baskin in his law practice in Ohio, he likely gave it the same brief consideration that it received elsewhere. Again, Baskin could not have foreseen that the problems in Utah that led to this relatively obscure act would consume a major portion of his life.

Four Years of Anesthesia, 1861–1865

From Andrew West's death in March 1863 to May 1865, Baskin was confined—held by bail—to Highland County and engaged in legal proceedings stemming from the shooting. Learning that the Civil War was a matter from which the Mormon people were uniquely insulated by distance, culture, doctrine, and prophecy was probably inescapable. In one broad sense the Mormons' view of the Civil War was not different from that of the majority of Americans. They shared the belief in a "pervasive, providential interpretation" of human events:[15] "History was directed by providence, meaning that God was in charge and that all events reflected God's will."[16] Wins and losses, even each battle's death counts—all reflected God's favor or disfavor, reward or punishment. As historian George Rable's Civil War treatise notes, "Brigham

[15]Rable, *God's Almost Chosen Peoples*, 1.
[16]Richards, review of *God's Almost Chosen Peoples*, 283.

Young rejoiced that the Lincoln administration had become so desperate for soldiers that 'they have begun to empty the earth, cleanse the land, and prepare the way for the return of the Latter-day Saints to the centre Stake of Zion.'"[17] Mormons considered the war as an inevitable, deserved punishment by God for the persecution heaped on them by the heads of government in Ohio, Missouri, and Illinois and for the murder of their prophet in Carthage, Illinois. Young was gratified that "the nation 'that has slain the Prophet of God [Joseph Smith] . . . will be broken in pieces like a potter's vessel; yes, worse, they will be ground to powder.'"[18] Battles over secession and slavery would escalate into the destruction of an ungodly government and the reestablishment of Christ's true church on earth, said Mormon leaders. In 1861 Mormon apostle John Taylor denied that the war was a matter that concerned his people: "We have been banished . . . and forced to make a home in the desert wastes. . . . Shall we join the North to fight against the South? No! Shall we join the South against the North? As emphatically, No! Why? . . . [We] have had no hand in the matter. . . . We know no North, no South, no East, no West."[19]

Although Utah did nothing to benefit either combatant, the Civil War brought immense financial largesse to the territory's cash-starved economy. As they had in 1858–59 at Camp Floyd, Mormon suppliers turned a heady profit from the meat, hay, and other staples required by the troops and animals, benefitting the barter-based system with the substantial infusion of federal currency. When the U.S. Army liquidated the buildings, furnishings, wagons, and provisions of Camp Crittenden and Fort Bridger in preparation for the posts' abandonment, Mormon buyers were on hand, obtaining for a mere $100,000, goods whose worth was said to be $4 million.[20] During the war years, southern Utah's counties produced a marketable surplus of cotton. At least seventy thousand pounds of cotton was exported to markets along the Mississippi River, where southern buyers purchased it either for their own needs or for export "to British and European ports, where it could be sold for top dollar."[21]

[17]Young's speech in the Salt Lake City Bowery, July 28, 1861, cited in Rable, *God's Almost Chosen Peoples*, 78.

[18]Ibid., 158.

[19]"Celebration," address by John Taylor, *DN*, July 10, 1861, 4/1, 8/1.

[20]Young to H. B. Clawson, July 26, 1861, BYLC, CR 1234 1, box 5, vol. 5, 845; Maxwell, *GGSL*, 102–103.

[21]Boone, "Church and the Civil War," 128–29.

In several letters to his trusted leaders, Brigham Young expressed anger that Union troops, distrusting Mormons' allegiance, had destroyed eighty wagons with 160 tons of guns and ammunition rather than bequeathing them to Utah's territorial militia. He bitterly prophesied the Union soldiers' fate: "They have burned, or otherwise destroyed what they could not take, sell, or waste and are now on their way to hell in the States where they also will be wasted, burned, and destroyed."[22]

Mormonism's founder, Joseph Smith, had prophesied in 1832 of a war that would begin in South Carolina and "terminate in the death and misery of many souls," and Mormons awaited an outcome they considered foretold, when they would take command of government, regain possession of the lands they had lost in Missouri and Illinois, and prepare for the return of Christ to the earth.[23] Their second prophet, Brigham Young, said as the war was raging: "The men of the South pray to God for the destruction of the men of the North; the men of the North beseech God to bring destruction upon the men of the South; I say amen to both prayers."[24]

In the books he authored or in newspaper articles or private ledgers, Baskin left no record of his opinion of the Mormons' nonparticipation in the conflict. It was a war in which more than 3 million men served, and in which the 752,000 who died, when added to untold thousands of wounded and missing, far surpasses the numbers lost in all of the nation's other wars combined. Based on recent studies of deaths proportional to population, the cited number of deaths would translate into 7.5 million American men dying if such a war were fought in the present time. The number of white women widowed in the war is estimated at 200,000.[25] Through all this the people in Utah Territory remained untouched, protected in their isolated mountain valleys.

The Civil War was the "crossroads of our being" as a nation, wrote historian Shelby Foote. It is an astonishing fact that the central event

---

[22]Young to H. B. Clawson, July 26, 1861, BYLC, CR 1234 1, box 5, vol. 5, 845.

[23]Bushman, *Rough Stone Rolling*, 191–92; Long, *Saints and the Union*, 19, 30.

[24]"Goodwin, "Mormon Situation," 758. The *Union Vedette*'s version said: "The North prays that their swords may strike into the heart of every rebel, and I say Amen; and the South prays that the North may be cut down on a thousand battlefields, and again I say Amen." *UV*, January 16, 1865, 2/2.

[25]Recent studies have estimated the total number of deaths to be far higher than previously set, ranging from 650,000 to 850,000. Hacker, "A Census-Based Count of the Civil War Dead," 310–11.

of American history, the cataclysm engulfing twenty million people, was for the Mormons less than a raindrop in comparison with an unrelenting, four-year hurricane of death and destruction that enveloped the majority of the nation. It may have been more than serendipity that Utah became Baskin's western home. Here he was on safe ground; there would be no need to defend the reasons for his inaction in the war or to discuss with Mormons the issue of slavery. There existed in Utah entirely different but equally profound subjects of contention regarding the right of a state to be free of federal oversight. The issues of theocracy and polygamy would demand much of Baskin's energy during his life in Utah.

3
Arriving in Utah

*We should come home from adventures, and perils, and discoveries
. . . with new experience and character.*

HENRY DAVID THOREAU

W HEN ROBERT BASKIN ARRIVED IN AUGUST 1865, HE
was one of fewer than three hundred non-Mormons in
Utah Territory among a Mormon population estimated
at sixty-five to seventy thousand.[1] Baskin leaves no comment on his
minority status but describes moving promptly to prepare for law practice by studying Utah's territorial statutes. His attention was caught by
several unique 1852 territorial legislative provisions. The first was that
Utah's citizens were provided with the option of making no payment
to a lawyer for any professional services rendered.[2] More significantly,
only laws passed by the territorial legislature were valid, while laws
and legal precedents arising outside Utah Territory could not be cited
in Utah courts, and references or rulings based on English common
law could not be employed.[3] As Bigler and Bagley noted: "Cut down
at a stroke were two pillars of the American judicial structure—legal
precedence and common law."[4]

---

[1] Dwyer, *Gentile Comes to Utah*, 26; data also extrapolated from the 1860 and 1870 census figures. Gen. Patrick Connor's estimate of Gentile numbers in 1865 was 1,500. *WOR*, ser. 1, vol.
50, part 1, 1184–86.

[2] This law reflected Brigham Young's utter disdain of lawyers, a sentiment he frequently
expressed from the pulpit.

[3] Baskin, *REM*, 5–6; An Act in Relation to the Judiciary, Sec. 1 (1852).

[4] Bigler and Bagley, *Mormon Rebellion*, 48.

The suspicion attached to Baskin in Ohio that he had participated in packing a grand jury with Democrats makes it ironic that the third aberration he noted was Utah's provision for procuring grand and petit juries. The law stipulated: "From the *assessment roll* of the county, a list containing the names of at least fifty *men, residents* of the county," were eligible to serve.[5] Limiting the list to male taxpayers and residents of permanence almost ensured that jurors would be Mormon. With the exception of two or three urban areas where the scant numbers of non-Mormons lived, jury packing with Mormons would be automatic throughout Utah Territory. Impaneling could be delayed if the fifty names were exhausted during the term of court, for no cases could be brought to trial until and unless more names were drawn. The act was formed "with a view of making it impossible to impanel any but a jury composed of Mormons," wrote Baskin.[6]

Baskin's final observation concerned the priority of jurisdiction to the local, Mormon-dominated probate courts in matters of civil and criminal actions. The probate judge for each county was to be elected by the Mormon controlled legislature and commissioned by the governor, LDS Church president Brigham Young. This was a subversion of the 1850 act of Congress organizing the territory, which had placed such jurisdiction in the supreme and district courts of the territory.[7] Concurrent jurisdiction with district courts was not an ordinary responsibility of probate courts in other states and territories. This anomaly prevented enforcement of federal law and hampered the administration of justice in Utah Territory and would be a festering sore with the non-Mormons until corrected by the 1874 Poland Act. Mormons, however, considered it a necessary safeguard against alien judges, who were thought to unfairly rule against them.[8]

Noting these peculiarities, Baskin continued his study of legal stat-

---

[5]Baskin, *REM*, 7; italics added.

[6]Ibid., 7–8.

[7]Ibid. The 1852 action to give probate courts jurisdiction was taken because most appointed federal officers had fled the territory, fearing for their lives at the hands of Mormons. Allen, "Unusual Jurisdiction," 132.

[8]The Poland Act restricted probate courts to matters of estates and guardianship, giving district courts exclusive jurisdiction for all suits over $300. It abolished the offices of territorial marshal and attorney. Juries were drawn by the district court clerk in alternation with the probate court, selecting names until two hundred were called, presumably with equal numbers of Mormons and non-Mormons. The U.S. marshal drew jurors from these two hundred. Probate courts retained concurrent jurisdiction with the district courts over divorce until 1887. Firmage and Mangrum, *Zion in the Courts*, 148.

utes and was admitted to the Utah Territorial Bar in May 1866. In early 1867 he entered a partnership with attorney Stephen DeWolfe, an active Mason who had been in the Salt Lake valley for some time. In fact, DeWolfe was the prosecuting attorney in the unsuccessful 1859 attempt by Judge John Cradlebaugh and U.S. marshal Peter K. Dotson to bring the Mountain Meadows murderers to account.[9] DeWolfe had briefly served in 1861 as Utah's territorial secretary, appointed by Acting Governor Francis H. Wootton, but he declined to stay in the position, saying he could not conscientiously serve under Wootton's administration.[10] Well acquainted with events in Utah, DeWolfe edited the non-Mormon newspaper begun by Kirk Anderson, the *Valley Tan*.[11] As DeWolfe's partner, Baskin had ready access to the details available from DeWolfe of the many other murders committed throughout the territory and of Cradlebaugh's 1859 investigation of the mass murder of Arkansas travelers at Mountain Meadows.

FREE AND ACCEPTED MASONS IN UTAH

Excluded from brotherly ties within Mormon groups, non-Mormon men sought comradery in fraternal organizations in territorial Utah. With time, a variety of societies were established: the Independent Order of Odd Fellows, the Caledonian Club, the Knights of Pythias, the Improved Order of Red Men, the Knights of Honor, the Sons of Saint George, and the Irish-American Society.[12] The earliest and by far the most influential of these societies was the Free and Accepted Masons, with whom Baskin associated.

"Friction" and "conflict" were the applicable terms describing the interaction between the Mormons and the Masons.[13] Disputes began in Illinois, where Hyrum Smith was a Master Mason before the LDS Church was organized; Joseph joined many years after Hyrum. These

---

[9]Lyman, *Amasa Mason Lyman*, 293–94.

[10]David Calder to Brigham Young, June 4, 1861, BYLC, CR 1234 1, box 5, vol. 5, 798–99.

[11]The Baskin-DeWolfe office was one door "west of the City Drug Store and opposite Wells Fargo." *SLTel*, January 7, 1867. The term "Valley Tan" originally applied to leather *tanned in the Valley* and was later applied to other local products. Even the poteen was designated "Valley Tan Whiskey." The non-Mormons appropriated the term to name the paper; its first publication appeared on November 5, 1858.

[12]"The Fraternal Societies," *SLT*, March 24, 1893, 7/1.

[13]"Utah at no time in its history has offered conditions favorable to the establishment and development of the Masonic Fraternity," wrote Samuel Henry Goodwin, a leading historian of Utah Freemasonry. Goodwin, *Freemasonry in Utah*, 5.

two, together with large numbers of LDS followers formed several Masonic Lodges in Nauvoo and other cities during the Illinois expansion of the LDS Church. There were more than 1,600 Mormons in the Illinois lodges, when the combined number of non-Mormon members numbered barely 150. Under urging from LDS leaders, growth of the Masons became so rapid that initiating ceremonies were shortened and did not follow Masonic protocol. The supervising Masonic bodies declared the Mormons' Masonic Lodges clandestine and voided their dispensations. Brigham Young ended Mormon participation in Nauvoo lodges in April 1845.[14] However, some Mormon leaders, Young included, considered themselves Master Masons long after emigrating to Utah. Portraits from as late as 1854 show Young with the Masonic compass and square prominently displayed on his shirt.[15]

The formation of Masonic lodges in the territory originated with the federal troops stationed at Camp Floyd after the Utah War. They applied for a dispensation, and the Rocky Mountain Lodge No. 205, of Missouri Registry, was instituted in 1859 as the first Masonic Lodge in Utah. Short-lived, it surrendered its charter in 1861 when the post was disbanded and its troops went east with the Civil War's outbreak.[16]

In November 1865 a group of non-Mormons in Salt Lake City petitioned the Grand Lodge of Nevada for a dispensation to form a new lodge. This was granted on January 25, 1866, but the Grand Master "attached to the Dispensation an edict requiring the 'Lodge to exclude all who were of the Mormon Faith.'"[17] The petitioners objected, not because they wished to admit Mormons, but on the grounds that they, rather than distant members, should decide admissions. Another application was made, and Mount Moriah Lodge No. 2 was given its dispensation from the Grand Lodge of Kansas in November 1867 and received its charter November 1868.[18] Baskin was initiated into Mount

---

[14]Kenneth W. Godfrey, "Freemasonry in Nauvoo," www.lightplanet.com/mormons/daily/ history/1831_1844/nauvoo_freemasonry_eom.htm, accessed March 2012. For a modern study of Freemasonry and Mormonism, see Homer, "'Similarity of Priesthood in Masonry,'" 1–116.

[15]Holzapfel and Shupe, *Brigham Young*, 108, 118–19, 121, 124–25; M. R. Werner, *Brigham Young*, 192.

[16]Clark and Hanson, *History of Wasatch Lodge Number One*, 2.

[17]Gooding, *First 100 Years of Freemasonry in Utah*, 5.

[18]No Baskin names are found recorded in the lodges of Highland County, Ohio. Les Brower, Past District Deputy Grand Master, 7th Masonic District of Ohio, e-mail message to author, November 2009.

Moriah Lodge No. 2 in Salt Lake City on March 23, 1869, and was raised on May 31, 1869.

Another group of Masons in Salt Lake grew impatient with waiting to hear from Kansas and petitioned Montana. They were Stephen DeWolfe; Reuben Howard Robertson, a lawyer with whom Baskin would later coauthor the Cullom Bill; and Obed Franklin Strickland, who was destined to be a Utah associate court justice. The dispensation for Wasatch Lodge was received from the Grand Lodge of Montana No. 22 on October 7, 1866, and contained no clause restricting admissions of Mormons.[19]

Although no Salt Lake City lodge had official rules excluding Mormons, exclusion existed from the lodges' beginnings and persisted for many years. The Grand Master of the Utah Lodge, Joseph Milton Orr, wrote to Mormon men in 1877: "You cannot enter our lodge rooms—you surrender all to an unholy priesthood. You have . . . sacrificed the sacred obligations of our beloved Order and we believe you would do the same again. . . . Such a wound as you gave Masonry in Nauvoo is not easily healed, and no Latter-day Saint is, or can become[,] a member of our Order in this jurisdiction."[20]

By 1880 Baskin was made the Worshipful Master of Mount Moriah Lodge, and in 1881, while he was Grand Orator, two Mormon men applied for admission. John Peter Sorenson, a Danish convert and polygamist, made application in 1879. Near the same time, George Aaron Goodrich, a Massachusetts-born Mormon convert and polygamist from Utah's Morgan County, applied. The requests were referred to Baskin for a ruling. In January 1882, Baskin's jurisprudence committee ruled against Goodrich and further recommended that "the Grand Secretary be instructed to prepare a circular letter setting forth the facts and grounds of the decision."[21] Therefore, on May 10, 1882, Grand Secretary Christopher Diehl wrote a circular, a copy of which was mailed to every Grand Lodge throughout the globe, saying:

> [Freemasonry] recognizes the right of every Craftsman to join any church, . . . and demands of him only that he shall admit the theological

[19]Clark and Hanson, *History of Wasatch Lodge Number One*, 3, 8, 11.

[20]*Proceedings of the Grand Lodge of Utah, 1877*, 11–12.

[21]Freemasons, Grand Lodge of Utah, "Report of the Jurisprudence Committee on Masonry and Mormonism," in *Proceedings of the M. W. Grand Lodge of Ancient Free and Accepted Masons of Utah, at Its Special Communications* (Salt Lake City: Tribune Printing and Publishing Co., 1882), 44, 46, http://books.google.com/books?id=pg0vAAAAYAAJ, accessed November 2009.

belief taught on the threshold of our sacred Temple, and further, *that he must be loyal to the Government under which he lives, and yield a willing obedience to all its laws,* the Masons in Utah contend that the latter important prerequisite is wanting in the Mormons, because one of the[ir] chief tenets . . . is Polygamy, which a United States Statute has declared to be a crime. . . . All [Mormons] believe it to be a revelation of God, and consequently all of them . . . by the laws of our country, [and] the decisions of our courts, . . . [are] guilty. . . . Hence every disciple of . . . the Mormon doctrine . . . is barred out of our Lodges.[22]

Exclusion of Mormons became official Masonic policy in Utah in 1925: "A member of the Church of Jesus Christ of Latter-day Saints, commonly called the 'Mormon' church, is not eligible to become a member of any Lodge F. & A. M. in this state."[23] This exclusion persisted until rescinded by the Grand Lodge of Utah in 1984. Not until 2008 did the Grand Lodge of Utah elect its first Mormon as its Grand Master.[24]

In Baskin's telling, the Masons' antipathy toward Mormons was primarily related to polygamy and to Mormons' failure to heed federal law. Baskin also held that Mormon rites had been altered to include oaths not found in Masonic sources. As evidence, he cited an oath of obedience to Mormon church laws over U.S. laws and an oath of vengeance on the U.S. government for the deaths of Joseph and Hyrum Smith.[25] In *Reminiscences*, Baskin published a detailed account of Mormon temple rites that included these two oaths, attributing his source as former church member Caroline Owens Miles. Besides the account by Miles, Michael W. Homer notes the publication of secret ceremony details on at least seven occasions in the *Salt Lake Tribune* over a thirty-year period.[26]

---

[22]Italics in the original. Hogan, "Mormonism," 293.

[23]Signed by W. I. Snyder, P.M., in *Proceedings of the Most Worshipful Grand Lodge of Utah, 1924*, 82. See also Dern, *Proceedings of the Grand Lodge of Utah, 1925*, 65.

[24]Glen A. Cook, Sr., is the first Mormon to hold the Utah post.

[25]Baskin, REM, 98–99. The Law of Retribution (Oath of Vengeance) was first administered in Nauvoo and was included in the endowment ceremony until February 1927, according to historian H. Michael Marquardt. The target of vengeance may have changed over time. Joseph Smith, speaking to Stephen Markham of his premonition of being killed, extracted a promise that "my loyal friends will avenge my blood, that you and your posterity after you will not rest until *the last member of this mob is killed.*" Cited in David John Buerger Papers, box 27, folder 9. Marquardt cites Increase Van Deusen's writing in 1847: "We will avenge the blood of Joseph Smith *on this Nation.*" Marquardt, pers. comm., October 2011. By the time of the Civil War, the vengeance was meant to be directed against the nation's entire population.

[26]Homer, "Similarity of Priesthood in Masonry," 60–62.

In Baskin's time, Mormons were fully aware that most of the non-Mormon men working against them over polygamy and church control of government were dedicated Masonic brothers.[27] Opposition moved from ideological into the political sphere as the Liberal Party grew in strength and numbers, and its political agenda could be advanced in lodge meetings. In 1890 the Masons were finally able to assert: "The body politic, that has for forty years misruled our rich and fair territory and stood in the way of progress[,] will crumble down."[28]

Baskin's association with the Masonic Order and its precepts was lifelong. He was appointed Deputy Grand Master pro tempore in the Grand Lodge of Utah from November 1879 to November 1880. He was elected and served as Worshipful Master of Mount Moriah Lodge No. 2. Additionally, he was Grand Orator in 1879–81, was Grand Chaplain in 1882, and throughout served on a number of standing committees in the Grand Lodge of Utah. At his death, his funeral was conducted in the Masonic Temple, according to Masonic ritual, and attended by several Masonic brothers.[29]

MARRIAGES, DIVORCE, AND UNCERTAINTY

What is known of the woman who became Robert Baskin's only wife is sparse. She first appears in Utah records on August 17, 1867, when Mormon bishop Frederick Kesler, returned to his ranch near the Great Salt Lake and entered in his journal: "I went to my ranch & found all well, also found a Mrs. Stafford there that bin very Badly hurt while traveling North in the stage."[30]

In late August or early September 1867, Judge Elias Smith recorded in his personal journal: "I went out to F. Kesler's Ranch near Black Rock with R. N. Baskin, Esq., to administer an oath to Mrs. Spafford [*sic*], a lady who had been injured by the upsetting of a coach belonging

---

[27]Prominent examples include Parley Lycurgus Williams, superintendent of schools; George R. Maxwell, land office registrar and U.S. marshal; Cyrus Myron Hawley, associate court justice; and Clarence Emir Allen, named by Baskin as the father of public education in Utah; Patrick Lannan, businessman and *Salt Lake Tribune* editor and owner; and Nathan Kimball, surveyor general for Utah.

[28]Homer, "Similarity of Priesthood in Masonry," 67, citing the 1890 *Proceedings of the Grand Lodge of Utah*, 15.

[29]Historical details of Utah's Masonic Lodges were provided by Aaron E. Saathoff, Past Worshipful Master, Wasatch Lodge No. 1, 33rd Degree Scottish Rite Mason, and Past Potentate of El Kalah Shrine in Salt Lake City.

[30]Frederick Kesler Papers, August 17, 1867, 150.

to Wells Fargo & Co. She is commencing a suit for the procurement of a divorce from her husband."[31]

On September 24, 1867, a $3,000 personal injury settlement by Wells Fargo to Mrs. Olive Stafford was entered in the Third District Court.[32] On October 29, 1867, a woman identified as Mrs. Olive L. Stafford appeared in the probate court of Judge Smith, with a well-composed request for divorce and restitution of her maiden name, Olive L. Gardner.[33] Declaring she had been for "some time" a resident of Utah, she stated that she had been married on December 10, 1865, to one Eli F. Stafford, who quickly became "a habitual drunkard" and who "without reasonable cause has absented himself from your petitioner for more than one year last past." Mrs. Stafford also stated that he was "without the reach of the process of this court." Her request was immediately granted.[34]

On November 27, 1867, the *Union Vedette* reported that Olive Gardner had repudiated the first court settlement and was moving against Wells Fargo for an award of $50,000.[35] The Third District Court docket for January 6, 1868, reveals that Olive L. Gardner, represented by the law firm of Baskin and DeWolfe, entered suit for damages against Wells Fargo and Company.[36] Wells Fargo hoped to prove Olive was not married in September 1867, making the settlement on that date binding. Had she remained married, the settlement would have been void, since Utah law said that married women could not act alone in a binding contract. In February 1868 the jury ruled for the plaintiff, finding her, at the time of the settlement, still legally married to Stafford, thereby invalidating her acceptance of the $3,000 settlement. The jury awarded her new damages in the amount of $12,000.

---

[31]Thomas, *Elias Smith's Journal*, vol. 2, October 29, 1867. This date is almost certainly an error, and the visit was likely earlier.

[32]Records of the Third District Court, Salt Lake City, Utah Territory, ser. 01649, reel 1, Utah State Archives, Salt Lake City.

[33]The place of her marriage to Stafford was not included in the petition. Baskin was later accused of aiding her divorce proceedings. Townsend, *Mormon Trials*, 17.

[34]Salt Lake County Probate Court Records, ser. 373, reel 17, box 12, folder 97, Utah State Archives, Salt Lake City; Thomas, *Elias Smith's Journal*, vol. 2, 1863–74. Olive almost certainly had heard of the divorce mills in Utah and was probably one of the first clients of Judge Elias Smith, who made such divorces into a profitable enterprise.

[35]According to the *Vedette*, Olive was bedbound, and its pessimistic report added, "It is probable that her injuries may prove fatal." "Heavy Suit," *uv*, November 26, 1867, 3/1; "The Stafford–Wells Fargo Suit," November 27, 1867, 3/1.

[36]Third District Court Case Files, ser. 9802, reel 10, box 3, folders 39 and 40.

By July 30, 1868, Olive and Robert Baskin were not yet married, for Kesler's papers again name the woman who remained a visitor in his household: "Mother is still taking Care of Mrs. Stafford[, who is] feeling as well as could be expected."[37] Details of Olive's prior marriages, the courtship of Olive and Robert, and the place and date of their marriage are unknown. By the best inference, Robert Baskin married Olive Lavinia Gardner in the latter half of 1868, very likely in September; their twenty-year marriage seemed tranquil, and Baskin was devastated by her death and the deaths of their three daughters.

THE IMBROGLIO

Baskin's temper, uncharacteristic of his otherwise calm demeanor, was illustrated in a brief court encounter in 1870 with Judge Cyrus Myron Hawley. Hawley arrived in Salt Lake City in June 1869 as a newly appointed associate justice in the Second District Court and was soon also engaged as an active Mason. Shortly he joined several non-Mormons, including Baskin, in Liberal Party membership, working against the seating of George Q. Cannon in Congress.[38] Baskin and Maxwell had appeared before Judge Hawley in late November as prosecutors of several Mormon men accused of violating Governor John Wilson Shaffer's prohibition of Mormon Militia marching.[39] Less than a month later, on a different case, Baskin had a strong flare against Hawley's in-court ruling. Baskin threw a paper to the floor and "ground it with his boot-heel into an inoffensive tobacco quid." The judge, who "respects himself and his rulings," threatened Baskin with a fine." Baskin retorted, "Go ahead with your fine! . . . you're of no account." Baskin was fined $100 for contempt and ordered to spend ten days at Camp Douglas, an extraordinary move for one professional man against another. As author George Alfred Townsend reported, "Baskins [*sic*] twitched the order out of the Judge's hands and said that being an 'old granny' the Judge should forthwith be kicked down stairs. At this Baskins threw open the door to expedite the descent of the vulnerable man, and rushed upon him. . . . The Marshal interposed . . . and Baskins went to camp in custody. . . . Judge McKean

[37]Frederick Kesler Papers, July 30, 1868, 159.
[38]Maxwell, *GGSL*, 172.
[39]The so-called Wooden Gun Marching Episode. See Maxwell, *GGSL*, 153–54.

let Baskins out on *habeas corpus* in four days, and Baskins disdained to pay his fine."[40] The *Salt Lake Herald* gave each man a share of disapproval: "It is painful to think of a member of the bar treating a man who holds so high and dignified an office as a Federal Judge, in such a disgracefully contemptuous manner; and it is still more painful to think that the Territory has a Federal Judge who cannot command more respect." The editor lamented that Baskin, "a man whose legal knowledge is undisputed, . . . was conveyed . . . to Camp Douglas like a felon."[41] Baskin's recent testimony before Congress, in which he had declared that the scheme concocted by Hawley and other non-Mormons to have all land north of the forty-first degree of latitude ceded to the Idaho Territory was a "harebrained idea," was very likely the unacknowledged irritant between the two.[42]

During November and December, the Baskins were negotiating the purchase of a plot of land from Daniel H. Wells. The property was "on the hill just north of President Kimball," according to Wells's intermediary, Amos Milton Musser. His letter to Brigham Young in Saint George suggests that Olive was not entirely pleased with Baskin's investments: "Mrs. Baskin is yet undecided about purchasing the place; her husband thinks it is too small. . . . Her liege lord, (in whom I don't think she has unlimited confidence) she tells me he is investing largely in mining stocks, an enterprise she regards as speculative and very uncertain."[43]

THE TEST CASE THAT WASN'T:
THE REYNOLDS PRECEDENT

In the late summer of 1874, the Poland Act returned control of Utah courts to federal hands. George Reynolds, then personal secretary to Brigham Young, was arrested for polygamy. Tried and found guilty in December 1875, Reynolds was fined $500 and sentenced to two years of hard labor in the Utah Territorial Penitentiary.[44] Within these bare facts is a robust story of another Baskin-versus-Mormon struggle.

[40]Townsend, *Mormon Trials*, 10; "Fined and Imprisoned for Contempt of Court," *SLT*, December 21, 1870, 1/1. Townsend repeatedly misspelled the surname as "Baskins."

[41]"The Legal Imbroglio," *SLH*, December 23, 1870, 3/3.

[42]Madsen, *Corinne*, 75.

[43]Musser to Young, December 8, 1870, Brigham Young Collection (LDS History Library, Salt Lake City), MS2736, box 12, folder 4.

[44]"Polygamy," *SLT*, December 11, 1875, 4/2.

Reports by Mormon leaders, especially those of George Q. Cannon and Orson F. Whitney, claim that the arrest and trial of Reynolds were preplanned events, done by bilateral agreement. The reports allege a purpose of having the case reach the U.S. Supreme Court, for Mormons were confident that the high court would vindicate them and establish that polygamy fell under the aegis of religious freedom.[45] Both Baskin, who was intimately involved as a trial observer, and Marshal Maxwell, who was a participant and published his record of the events, denied that the matter was prearranged as a trial case. Details provided by Maxwell in 1879 clearly disproved any intent on the part of Mormon leaders to instigate the suit.[46] Maxwell recalled that a Mormon from Ogden, Utah, one James Horrocks, appeared in the marshal's office in 1874 with a complaint over remarks on polygamy made by George Reynolds in a speech recently delivered in the Tabernacle. When Horrocks's testimony was presented to the grand jury, an indictment for Reynolds's arrest was issued. Five years later, when the Supreme Court decision was finally rendered, Maxwell documented in the *Salt Lake Tribune* the trial details and the role of Deputy Marshal Arthur Pratt in securing the second wife's testimony. Maxwell said he pursued the publication of the information "to refute the lies which the Church organ is disseminating in the community in regard to this being a test case, and also the flagrant misstatements" of Cannon in a letter to Pres. Rutherford B. Hayes.[47]

Under oath in court, Daniel H. Wells and Mormon apostle Orson Pratt both testified they had no knowledge of the alleged second marriage of Reynolds. Maxwell was immediately concerned that the case was therefore lacking proof. Baskin secured a subpoena for the plural wife and instructed Maxwell and Arthur Pratt to bring the witness to the courthouse as quickly as possible. In ten minutes the two brought the second wife into court by a side door, where she could be seen by the entire audience. As the second Mrs. Reynolds was revealed, consternation flitted visibly through the Mormon crowd. Under oath the polygamous wife's testimony was Spartan and on point: "I was married to George Reynolds in the endowment house in this city in August last by General Wells. Mr. Orson Pratt was present [and] . . .

---

[45]Whitney also insisted that a pretrial agreement of no punishment was violated by federal officials. Whitney, *HOU*, 3:47–50.

[46]"That Test Case," *SLT*, June 28, 1879, 4/3.

[47]Marshall Maxwell's role in the trial is treated in Maxwell, *GGSL*, 199–202.

I have lived with George Reynolds ever since our marriage."[48] Wells refused to answer several questions put to him, because he considered "the keys and powers and mysteries of the church" were being invaded. As a result he was sentenced to forty-eight hours in the penitentiary. The city experienced these hours as potentially explosive, with intemperate talk by both Mormons and non-Mormons.

Baskin had no official role in the trial but attended it as an observer, hosting the visiting Assistant Secretary of the Interior Benjamin Rush Cowan, who had come to Salt Lake City to learn more about "the affairs of Utah." In a letter to the *Cincinnati Commercial,* Cowan recounted Baskin's role in securing the verdict. Following the second wife's testimony, Baskin reported giving a note to prosecuting attorney William Carey that read: "Do not give the case to the jury tonight, but dismiss them to their homes until morning." Baskin reasoned that Cowan's high position in the administration was well known to Mormon leaders. Having heard testimony that required a verdict of guilty, the Mormon jurymen would be flummoxed over their instructions—or intentions—to bring a verdict of innocent. Baskin predicted that, during the night, instructions would be circulated to bring a guilty verdict, lest Cowan report an improper acquittal and cause "an outrage which might justify the government in instituting more vigorous steps for the suppression of polygamy."[49] The next day, an all-Mormon jury of twenty-three men entered a guilty verdict.[50]

Preplanned or not, the verdict in the Reynolds case was appealed to the U.S. Supreme Court, and in January 1879 the court's ruling corroborated the position that non-Mormons had held for some time—that religious *beliefs* were protected under the First Amendment, but religious *practices* arising from those beliefs were subject to law. The case is cited to the present as a precedent.[51]

"They say that they made a case to test the constitutionality of this law. Does not that imply an intention to yield the point if the decision

---

[48]Baskin, *REM*, 61–72. Arthur Pratt, Orson Pratt's son, shared his mother's opposition to polygamy, and that may explain his willingness to assist the prosecution even though he was an apostle's son.

[49]Ibid., 66–67.

[50]Baskin noted that a grand jury of twenty-three members was improper. An appeal was entered and the judgment reversed. An immediate second indictment was brought with fifteen jurors, and Reynolds was again convicted. Ibid., 63. Reynolds was defended by Parley Lycurgus Williams, Baskin's friend and fellow Mason.

[51]Ibid., 62; Bigler, *Forgotten Kingdom,* 305; *Reynolds v. United States,* 98 U.S. 145 (1879).

should be against them?" reasoned Baskin. "The decision was against them, but they still insist that the law is unconstitutional, and have continued to treat it as void," he added.[52] Mormons were as shocked at this Supreme Court decision as the non-Mormons had been at an earlier case in which the nation's highest court ruled that criminal issues in Utah were within the jurisdiction of the territorial officers. In 1872, *Englebrecht v. Clinton* had invalidated 130 pending actions of the district courts. Predictions circulated that the *Reynolds v. United States* decision would deal polygamy a lethal blow, but other federal laws would be needed to accomplish that, and their impact on polygamy would not be felt for more than a decade.

GRIEF OVERWHELMING

Shortly after the Reynolds case, Baskin left for Washington to lobby against a petition scheduled to arrive with a delegation of Mormon women, many of whom were polygamous wives. Their petition sought statehood for Utah and the overturn of the 1862 Morrill Anti-bigamy Act. It was mid-December 1875 when Baskin received a telegram calling for his "immediate attendance at Salt Lake City."[53] Health problems were the apparent reason for the telegram, for shortly after the New Year's celebrations of January 1876, the Baskin family was beset with concern when five-year-old daughter Stella was stricken with scarlet fever.[54] Lamentably, the child's infection "assumed a malignant form," and she died on January 7. "It is a matter of profound regret to announce the serious indisposition of Mrs. [Olive] Baskin when her soul is overwhelmed with grief, but we hope to be able to chronicle her speedy recovery."[55] The Baskin household was not a cheerful one during the winter season of 1875–76.

---

[52] Baskin, *REM*, 70.

[53] "From Washington, Marginal Notes," *SLT*, December 17, 1875, 4/2.

[54] The death warrant gives her name as Della Baskin, but an *S* inserted between the given name and the surname is consistent with a middle name, Stella, by which she is identified in the *Salt Lake Tribune*.

[55] "Condolence," *SLT*, January 9, 1876, 4/1. According to the *Tribune*, Della Stella Baskin was born in Chicago on July 10, 1870, and the family was living in the Eighteenth Ward of Salt Lake City at the time of her death. The funeral took place in the family home, with burial at Mount Olivet Cemetery.

4

A Theocratic Society

*In a theocratic system, God's will renders obsolete
the imperfect human covenants on which social order depends.*
DAVID L. BIGLER

W HAT ELEMENTS CAN EXPLAIN THE EMERGENCE OF
an isolated, closed society facing poverty, deprivation, and
near extinction in 1846 to a society able to engage the full
power of the United States in 1857 in its first civil war? What accounts
for the transformation whereby the same society, only four years later,
contemptuously decried the parent federal government's struggle for
survival in a full-scale, cataclysmic war? The conventional answer
from the Latter-day Saints has been that they were uniquely chosen,
directed by God, held together by restored Christian principles, given
endurance fueled by faith, and guided by prophecy and divine revelation. Another answer is that unity, dictatorship, control, violence, and
force have explained other such immense societal transformations.
Robert Baskin's experience in Utah led him to the latter explanation.

Joseph Smith's violent nature, and that of Mormon society under
the Zion's Camp, the Danites, the Nauvoo Police Force, and the
Council of Fifty, is extensively documented.[1] Yet historians would be
hard-pressed to contend that a dictatorship in Nauvoo was preplanned.
Brigham Young may not have had a preplanned goal of establishing
a theocratic monarchy in the West when he organized the faithful to
leave Illinois by crossing the frozen Mississippi River in January 1846.

---

[1] Quinn, "Culture of Violence."

An ardent observer would find it equally difficult to deny that Smith did exactly that in Illinois, and that Young did so in the Great Basin.

Illinois governor Thomas Ford described Nauvoo as "a government within a government, [with] a legislature with power to pass ordinances at war with the laws of the State; courts to execute them with but little dependence upon the constitutional judiciary, and a military force at their own command."[2] "What also infuriated their [Nauvoo] neighbors . . . was their denial of the most basic liberty imaginable: freedom of thought," wrote Nathan O. Hatch. Joseph Smith "demanded the strictest loyalty" to his commands as he moved the Saints "toward greater intellectual isolation."[3] With control unequivocally its outcome, Mormons created a secret society of two hundred to five hundred oath-bound members in Missouri in 1838. The initial purposes of the Daughters of Zion, later called the Danites, were "to intimidate apostates into leaving Mormon society; to enforce obedience . . . ; and to influence state and county elections." Excesses soon included burning farmhouses and barns, killing cattle and horses, and setting small villages on fire.[4] Murders were alleged at their hands, and they became Joseph Smith's secret police force in Missouri and Nauvoo. First coined by Joseph Smith in 1844, the term "theodemocracy" meant a society in which "God and the people hold the power to conduct the affairs of men in righteousness." When used by Brigham Young, it meant "people ruled by their united voice, without a dissension; in learning what is for the best and unitedly doing it." He added, "This is true Republicanism."[5] With allusion to God, equality, and majority rule, the term "theodemocracy" softened and made palatable the real level of control held by LDS leaders.[6]

U.S. president William J. Clinton, in his 1997 inaugural, observed: "For the very first time in all of history, more people on this planet live under democracy than dictatorship."[7] If dictatorships have been prevalent and long enduring, review might identify a justification of the totalitarian state that developed, first under Smith in Nauvoo's city-state, then under Young in the inhospitable West. "If not justified, at least understandable," cautions historian Will Bagley, adding

---

[2]Ford and Milton, *History of Illinois*, 2:66.
[3]N. O. Hatch, "Mormon and Methodist," 76.
[4]Bennett, Black, and Cannon, *Nauvoo Legion*, 62, 75.
[5]Joseph Smith, "Globe"; B. Young, "Government of God," 855–58.
[6]George Davies proposed the term "materialistic theocracy" as appropriate to describe Utah society. Davies, "History of the Presbyterian Church."
[7]"Bill Clinton's Second Inaugural Address," http://en.wikisource.org/wiki/Bill_Clinton%27s_Second_Inaugural_Address, accessed April 2012.

the qualifier that dictators often germinate from leaders who were, in the beginning, working for a greater good, for a cause higher than a personal one.[8]

In the Roman Empire, dictatorship was an accepted, legal expediency in establishing stable leadership during a time of emergency or crisis. One man was appointed temporarily, holding absolute power for a fixed period, with a resumption of republican rule after the crisis had passed.[9] If dictatorship under such circumstances can be legitimate—even preferable—the assassinations of brothers Joseph and Hyrum Smith that launched the Mormon people into profound crisis made subsequent dictatorship understandable. Without shelter, faced with starvation, they found their survival imperiled. Under Young's leadership, with precious few dollars drawn from donations by wealthy British converts, sympathetic Americans, and the U.S. government salaries of the men of the Mormon Battalion, they struggled westward. Even after their arrival in Salt Lake, Mormons needed, moreover *required*, an unflinching governance to form them into a self-sufficient community in a desolate desert. All Saints, irrespective of their social strata—from the "first wagon" LDS Church leaders to the "last wagon" lesser members—started from scratch.[10] Survival required unity, for they were isolated from mainstream America not only geographically but also societally, by their religious beliefs and by social and economic practices. Undisciplined, untidy democracy and a random, laissez-faire economy would have failed them. Saints would have been lost to the promises of the Pacific Coast or the sparkling gold in the rocks of the Sierra Nevada, or to the allure elsewhere of fertile soil, clear water, and abundant grass.

Ten Years of Control and the Reformation

Foremost in the Saints' purpose was the responsibility to gather in Zion, to convince all who would listen that the Kingdom of God and Christ's gospel had been restored and the millennium and the end of times were

---

[8]Will Bagley, pers. comm., March 2010.

[9]Essential to a "republican government" is the proscription against hereditary monarchs and aristocracies. James Madison said the purpose of the Guarantee Clause of the U.S. Constitution was to "defend the system against aristocratic or monarchical innovations." Madison also named a second essential element in a republic: "the delegation of the government . . . to a small number of citizens elected by the rest." Madison, *Federalist Papers*, no. 10.

[10]Arrington, *From Quaker to Latter-day Saint*, xvii.

nigh.[11] Therefore, control was primary; dissent, potentially catastrophic. Incrementally, democracy disappeared and free agency atrophied. From their labors, the desert produced, and if they did not dissent, Mormons prospered, along with Brigham Young and his theocratic oligarchy. In 1847 Young said that if given ten years unmolested, he would have his people and his Kingdom of God solidly ensconced.[12] Unity was served serendipitously by the hostile words and actions of federal officials sent to the territory in the decade of the 1850s. During this time Asa Cyrus Call wrote, "The voice of Brigham is the voice of God."[13]

In 1851, newly arrived territorial supreme court justice Perry C. Brocchus spoke from the pulpit at Young's invitation. Brocchus undiplomatically railed against Young's consignment of President Zachary Taylor to hell for having denied Utah statehood. Brocchus further incensed the Saints over the "impurity" of their polygamy. Of his remarks, Young resentfully recalled, "If I had but crooked my little finger, he would have been used up; . . . the sisters alone felt indignant enough to have chopped him to pieces." After leaving Utah in fear of being killed, Brocchus said the Mormon Church was "controlling the opinions, the actions, the property, and even the lives of its members; usurping and exercising the functions of legislation and the judicial business of the Territory, organizing and commanding the military; disposing of public lands; [and] coining money . . . [with] obedience to the councils of 'the Church,' as paramount."[14] As with Brocchus, Young laid the threat of death on Governor Alfred Cumming, saying: "Toe the line and mark by the law, and do right or I shall crook my little finger, and you know what will come then."[15]

In his first annual message to Congress in December 1857, President James Buchanan wrote that Young's power was "absolute over both church and state" and "there no longer remains any government in Utah *but* the despotism of Brigham Young."[16] In 1849 Young's instructions

---

[11]As Eric Hoffer observes, "Those who would transform . . . must know how to kindle and fan an extravagant hope. It matters not whether it be hope of a heavenly kingdom, of heaven on earth, of plunder and untold riches." Hoffer, *True Believer*, 9.

[12]"The day I entered the Salt Lake valley 24 July 1847, I remarked, 'If the devils will let us alone for ten years, we will bid them defiance,'" said Young. Van Wagoner, *CDBY*, July 24, 1847, 1:233. Ten years later he added, "God is with us, and the devil has taken me at my word." Schindler, *Orrin Porter Rockwell*, 248.

[13]Asa C. Call, "From Utah, Great Salt Lake City," *National Era*, January 23, 1851, 5:212.

[14]Neff, *HOU*, 172, 174–75.

[15]Van Wagoner, *CDBY*, 5:1882.

[16]Richardson, *James Buchanan*, 31.

were vivid and blunt: "If you catch any man or boy stealing your property, shoot him dead on the spot, and all this people will say, Amen."[17] Young labeled judges William W. Drummond and George P. Stiles as guttersnipes, mountebanks, and evil critics obstructing God's plan. In barely a month's time territorial governor John W. Dawson's alleged moral improprieties so enraged the Mormons that he was brutally beaten, probably castrated, and barely escaped Utah alive. U.S. surveyor David H. Burr, true to his name's connotation as an irritant, insisted that federal land laws should trump land practices adopted by Mormons.[18] He left Utah with his adult son, fearing death at the hands of Mormons. Shortly after Cumming was installed as governor, Judge Delana R. Eckels wrote to his friend Secretary of State Lewis Cass, saying: "Brigham Young is *de facto* Governor of Utah whatever Cumming may do *de jure*. His [Brigham's] reign is one of terror."[19]

Concluding that his people's afflictions at the hands of government were God's punishment for straying from their restored religion, Young enlisted fiery orator Jedediah Grant to sound the tocsin. From pulpits across the territory came the sounds of the battue. For lesser sins, repentance and rebaptism might suffice, but for some sins, atonement by shedding blood was required. Grant, arguably Brigham Young's Torquemada, waxed allegorical in his call for violence: "*I wish . . . the people of God might lay the axe to the root of the tree. . . .* Putting to death the transgressors *would exhibit the law of God, no matter by whom it was done.*"[20] While Salt Lake City's mayor in 1856, Grant described the punishment awaiting those who brought prostitutes to Utah; he would "make holes through such miserable, corrupting rascals."[21] Orson Pratt advised the death penalty as appropriate for both men and women for prostitution.[22] Salt Lake's police magistrate, Jeter Clinton, said of

---

[17]Van Wagoner, *CDBY*, 1:339.

[18]Within a month of their arrival in Utah, Mormons had performed their own land surveys; many had farmed ten years on land they considered theirs.

[19]Eckels to Cass, n.d., State Department Letter Books, 1853–59, cited in Lamar, *Far Southwest*, 308.

[20]Thomas B. H. Stenhouse, *Rocky Mountain Saints*, 304; italics in the original.

[21]J. M. Grant, *JOD* 3 (1856): 232.

[22]Orson Pratt, *JOD* 7 (1859): 251, cited in Nichols, *Prostitution, Polygamy, and Power*, 26. Ironically, Pratt's first wife, Sarah Marinda Bates Pratt, ever against polygamy, admitted the need "to conceal from my neighbors and from church authorities" that she taught her children "never to espouse the Mormon faith." She added, "Many a night . . . I have locked the door, pulled down the window curtains, . . . and talked to them in whispers for fear that what I said would be overheard." "Orson Pratt's Harem," *NYH*, May 18, 1877, 2, cited in Bergera, *Conflict in the Quorum*, 224.

prostitutes and their customers: "Take a double barreled shotgun and follow them, shoot them to pieces; and if you do not overtake them before they get to their haunts or dens, go in and kill them both."[23] The record suggests that the most severe fanatics could be identified by their exceptionally clear conscience over the taking of life.

Young's message was similarly violent: "If he wishes salvation and it is necessary to spill his blood upon the ground in order that he be saved, spill it."[24] Young continued the theme: "There are sins that the blood of the lamb, or a calf, or of a turtle dove cannot remit, but they must be atoned for by the blood of the man."[25] In his message to George Q. Cannon, then on assignment in San Francisco, Young took pride in his labors: "The Territory . . . has taken an emetic and the way Lawyers, Loafers, Special Pleaders, Apostates, Officials, and filth has [*sic*] been cast out, is a caution to all Sinners that here they would be in the wrong pew."[26]

Apostates were especially repugnant to Mormon leaders in Illinois, and in Utah, Young continued to place them in the crosshairs: "Disturb not this community, or else you will find judgment is laid to the line." Ominously, he added, "Remember, you are not playing with shadows, but it is the voice and the hand of the Almighty you are trying to play with."[27]

Violent preaching was reaching its zenith, yet many faithful Mormons were oblivious to the fear and the need for secrecy that others, weaker in the faith, experienced from the threats of the Reformation. Judge Elias Smith failed to identify the reasons for the wholesale, secretive exodus he was observing in the spring of 1857: "Apostates [are] leaving the city constantly . . . [,] some of them with Handcarts, . . . before their nearest neighbors know they are thinking of going or that they are tired of Mormonism. A curious spirit seems to actuate them, and I am not sure but some leave without knowing they are going one hour before starting, not knowing what ails them, what they want, where they are going, nor what for."[28] Even Brigham Young's son characterized the reformation period as a "reign

[23]"Sermon Delivered by Dr. Jeter Clinton," *Mormon Expositor* 1, no. 1 (1875).

[24]Brigham Young, *JOD* 4 (February 8, 1857): 219.

[25]"Discourse by President Brigham Young," *DN*, October 1, 1856, 3/3.

[26]Young to Cannon, July 4, 1857, BYLC, CR 1234 1, box 3, vol. 3, 690.

[27]Brigham Young, *JOD* 1 (March 27, 1853): 84, cited in Aird, Nichols, and Bagley, *Playing with Shadows*, 6.

[28]Thomas, *Elias Smith's Journal*, vol. 1, April 16, 17, 1857.

of terror."[29] Formerly a dedicated Saint, Thomas B. H. Stenhouse later admitted, "The Reformation was the outburst of the worst elements of fanaticism—a fanaticism at once blind, dangerous and terrible, but at the same time the natural result of the teachings of the Tabernacle."[30]

Union officer William E. Waters made his observations about the Mormons and their leonine leader:

> A more . . . conscientious people are not to be found, nor a people so completely controlled by the will of one man. Brigham Young is worshiped as a god and . . . the Mormon Church is ultimately to cover . . . the whole world. . . . They are taught that the Government is the enemy of the church as are all individuals not within her pale. . . . [N]othing that the Prophet requires is considered too great a sacrifice and nothing . . . is regarded as other than a virtue if enjoined by him. They consider that they are doing God service in murdering . . . women and children or becoming the assassin in the dark hour of night.[31]

CONDITIONS IN 1865

At Harvard Law School, Baskin undoubtedly encountered new ideas and terms, but even in such a cosmopolitan atmosphere, it is unlikely that the phrase "totalitarian state" or "dystopian society" reached his ears. His first law partner, Stephen DeWolfe—the fourth and last editor of Utah's first non-Mormon newspaper, the *Valley Tan*—certainly made observations that would have identified the existence of such a state. Baskin clearly asserted, "Before the completion of the Union Pacific railroad it was very hazardous for an apostate to leave the Territory with his family and property."[32] Just months before Baskin's arrival in Utah, Bishop Edwin D. Woolley exhorted his Thirteenth Ward members to deadly violence: "Our streets are now filled with whores, thieves, gamblers, pimps, etc. The only way to purify it is to drive them out. Tear down their houses and send them where Gebow and his gang . . . went . . . [,] so that they would not come again, and God would have been with us. . . . We will clean, purify and wash the 13th ward of all damnable sinners. Amen."[33] Years later, the

---

[29]Brigham Young, Jr., Diary, December 15, 1862, cited in Bigler and Bagley, *Mormon Rebellion*, 95n4.

[30]Thomas B. H. Stenhouse, *Rocky Mountain Saints*, 292.

[31]Waters, *Life among the Mormons*, 195.

[32]Baskin, *REM*, 154.

[33]"The Word of God as Preached in Great Salt Lake City," *UV*, January 7, 1865, 2/5–3/1.

son of Utah Supreme Court chief justice Charles S. Zane observed that so innocuous a decision as to leave membership in a congregation was treated as a crime: "Apostasy from the church was an unforgivable crime, yet the steadfast courage of certain apostates will always remain an inspiring lesson in human fortitude."[34]

Had Baskin been given a list of required ingredients for a police state, he would have been able to observe most to be present in the Mormon oligarchy. Excesses present in Mormon culture from the Illinois period worsened drastically during the "Reformation" and the Utah War and continued in some degree until the death of Brigham Young in 1877, and arguably beyond.[35] Many non-Mormons left testimony that mail was intercepted, read, even copied or destroyed. "No letters deposited in the post office, by either gentiles or Mormons, ever left the valley without its contents being known," wrote Oregon-bound emigrant Jotham Goodell of his danger-filled, oppressive layover in Utah in the winter of 1850–51.[36] Indian agent Jacob Holeman hand-carried his 1852 letter to the non-Mormon mail post at Fort Bridger. Its contents told of white men's participation in Indian attacks on emigrant trains. Caution was employed, for he suspected that the white men in the attacks were Mormons who would read his mail.[37] On August 30, 1856, surveyor David H. Burr placed a letter to federal officials in Salt Lake City's mail. It reported the severe beating of his employee Joseph Troskolawski by William Adams Hickman and two others. The same day, a letter was sent by Brigham Young to Representative John M. Bernhisel, forewarning him of Burr's report of the incident. Clearly Utah's federal mails were not secure from Mormon inspection.[38] Another letter by Burr in 1857 to the U.S. land office, charging Brigham Young with "extensive depredations upon the public lands," was answered instead by faithful Mormon and acting U.S. attorney Hosea Stout and territorial marshal Alexander McRae. It said Burr would "not be permitted to write such letters, declaring that all [of Burr's] letters would be examined," and if unfavorable to the

---

[34]Zane, "Rare Judicial Service," 91.

[35]Townsend, *Mormon Trials*, 46.

[36]Bigler, *Winter with the Mormons*, 78, 78n10, 79. As another example, intimate details of Judge W. Drummond's life found in a May 1857 letter written by William Ivins Appleby could have been known only by means more intrusive than violating personal mail. "Judge Drummond Used Up," *Millennial Star* 19, no. 26 (June 27, 1857).

[37]Bigler and Bagley, *Mormon Rebellion*, 57.

[38]Young to Bernhisel, August 30, 1856, BYLC, CR 1234 1, box 3, vol. 3, 39.

Mormons, they would not leave the territory.[39] Mail was not secure in May 1861 when Brigham Young's scribe at the time, David O. Calder, opened Stephen DeWolfe's letter declining an invitation from Utah's acting governor, Francis H. Wootton, to become the acting territorial secretary. Before placing it for Pony Express mailing, Calder shared the letter with William Clayton and sent a copy to Brigham Young, who was then on a tour of the southern settlements.[40]

In March 1864, prior to Baskin's arrival in Utah, an unidentified convert to the LDS Church from Scotland wrote a letter home that was published in the *Dundee Advertiser* and republished in the *Daily Union Vedette* in Salt Lake City. He questioned rhetorically: "Is it holiness to say the end justifies the means, and that the big men are the only judges of right and wrong, as is always done? . . . To have every one a spy upon another, . . . that he might not breathe even to a friend of his crushed hopes, which might in time, by accumulation, get up such a revolution that would hurl the chiefs and prophets from their thrones, and show the poor and honest fanatics how they have been imposed upon?" The Scotsman reported the "breakup of letters at the Post Office, so that they might know all your communications with the outer world, and make it all but impossible to leave the territory if you were dissatisfied."[41]

Eveline Brooks Auerbach's Jewish family considered returning to California after "they had seen such hard times while in Salt Lake and lived in fear of their lives."[42] Austin and Maria Ward, visitors to Utah, observed that the pendulum of assassination might swing both ways: "Brigham Young would be a dangerous enemy, and many fearful though secret crimes have been imputed to him. . . . Perhaps the greatest evidence that these reports are not without foundation is afforded by the fact, that he is so afraid of assassination as to be unpleasantly suspicious of strangers."[43] By 1862 Colonel Connor's observations were similar to those of other non-Mormons, for he wrote: "The federal officers are entirely powerless, and talk in whispers, for [fear of] being overheard by Brigham's spies. Brigham Young rules with despotic sway[,] and death by assassination is the penalty of disobedience to his

---

[39]Bigler and Bagley, *Mormon Rebellion*, 52.

[40]Calder to Young, June 4, 1861, BYLC, CR 1234 1, box 5, vol. 5, 798–99.

[41]"Mormonism as Seen by a Scotchman," *Dundee Advertiser*, March 2, 1864, reprinted in *UV*, May 5, 1864, 1/2.

[42]Ogden, *Frontier Reminiscences*, 52.

[43]Ward, *Male Life among the Mormons*, 297.

commands."[44] Connor's concern for his and his family's safety led to their leaving Utah in April 1867.[45]

Life among Utah's Mormons was monitored, if not controlled, as power went downward by ecclesiastical organization. At the top was the president, then the First Presidency, the Twelve Apostles, the Seventies, the stake presidents, and the bishops. "I wish the bishops had eyes like an eagle and [would] not let a man be . . . in your ward whom you do not know," said Young in 1854.[46] Beginning in 1857, ward teachers visited each Mormon family and reported their findings to the bishop of the respective ward. Monthly visits could be solely in the family's benefit or could operate as thinly disguised monitoring.[47] Information picked up from ward teachers and from his extensive mail correspondence to and from Mormon leaders provided the "threads" Young boasted about in 1857: "I am watching you. Do you know that I have my threads strung all through the Territory, that I may know what individuals do?"[48] "No Pope in Rome, no Czar in Moscow, no Caliph in Bagdad ever exercised such power as the Mormons conferred on Brigham Young," said Presbyterian leader William Hepworth Dixon.[49] Young himself acknowledged his paramount role when he said in 1844, "There never was a prophet on the earth that dictated to the people, but he dictated their temporal affairs as well as spiritual."[50] In 1862 the marital dispute of an elder of Spanish Fork needed no court or legal counsel when it was summarily ended by Young's letter to the local bishop, instructing him to present the wife with a bill of divorce: "Let her have her things and keep her child, . . . and [you] ascertain whether it would be right for the wife to have any share of . . . property."[51] "I have been your dictator for twenty-seven years—over a quarter of a century I have dictated this people," he told the Saints in 1871.[52] Speaking in Salt Lake City's Third Ward in 1874, he repeated, "The man that dictates the spiritual kingdom of God, must dictate the temporal affairs[;] it can not be otherwise."[53]

[44]Connor to Maj. R. C. Dunn, Assist. Adjutant Gen., San Francisco, September 14, 1862, *wor*, ser. 1, vol. 50, part 2, 119.

[45]Madsen, *Glory Hunter*, 169–70.

[46]Van Wagoner, *cdby*, 2:780.

[47]Beadle, *Life in Utah*, 381.

[48]Brigham Young, *jod* 3 (October 8, 1855): 122.

[49]William Hepworth Dixon, *New America*, 1:245, cited in Stewart, "Pioneer Work," 194.

[50]Nauvoo Conference, October 6, 1844; Van Wagoner, *cdby*, 1:54.

[51]Young to A. K. Thurber, *bylc*, cr 1234 1, box 6, vol. 6, 321.

[52]Young, *jod* 14 (August 13, 1871): 205.

[53]Van Wagoner, *cdby*, June 21, 1874, 4:3034.

Immense power resided in the hands of Brigham Young and the LDS Church in Utah. Until 1858 all laws passed by the territorial legislature were subject to Young's approval as governor before they would take effect. He was supreme in granting pardons for offenses against the territory and reprieves for acts against U.S. laws; his commission was required for all officers appointed to territorial office.[54] The church was incorporated under the terms of the 1851 assembly of the "state" of Deseret. This action was adopted into law by the Utah territorial legislature in 1855, thus granting the LDS Church the ability "to acquire and sell property, regulate marriages, register births and deaths, and make all laws, rules, and adjunctions it deemed necessary. It was not subject to legal review: "Having been legally endowed with all necessary powers, the church was . . . freed from petty legal challenges. Armed with these powers, it became deeply involved in members' economic lives." In addition, the church "held a major portion of the Mormons' collective wealth."[55] The trustee-in-trust for the LDS Church was embodied in his person, making him the exclusive controller, if not owner, of church property. His hand also controlled the Perpetual Emigrating Fund, for he was its treasurer.

Many church leaders simultaneously served as policemen and judges or occupied a civil post. Information efficiently flowed upward and instructions downward. As president of the Church of Jesus Christ of Latter-day Saints, Young was its "Prophet, Seer, and Revelator," a monarch with lifelong tenure. Chairman of the Council of Fifty, he was the ordained King, Priest, and Ruler over Israel on Earth.[56] In Utah he was simultaneously the superintendent of Indian Affairs, Utah Territory's governor, the commander in chief of the Utah Territorial Militia, and the trustee-in-trust for the financial holdings of the LDS Church, needing to give only a simple fillip to see immediate response. President of the United Order in All the World, Wherever Established, was another title applied during one period of his endeavors.[57] James Street, who was well acquainted with Young from their work together on completion of the transcontinental telegraph,

---

[54]These powers were stipulated by federal law in the Organic Act of 1850, "An Act to Establish a Territorial Government for Utah."

[55]Firmage and Mangrum, *Zion in the Courts*, 251–52.

[56]The Council of Fifty, a secret theocratic society originated by Joseph Smith, continued under Brigham Young and John Taylor and had it last known meeting on October 9, 1884. Quinn, *Mormon Hierarchy*, 726.

[57]Masthead, *DN*, October 14, 1874, 9/1.

wrote to Samuel Clemens in 1861 that Mormons "maintain a sem-blance of republican form of government, but the petrified truth is that Utah is an absolute monarchy and Brigham Young is king."[58]

Nominating meetings or nomination ballots for input by the public at large were nonexistent. Decisions of who would run for election were made in closed meetings of the Mormon priesthood. From these, a ballot of People's Party candidates for territorial offices was formed, then published in the *Deseret News*. When Brigham Young offered Thomas L. Kane, his friend and benefactor from the Mormon Battal-ion days, the position of Utah's territorial representative to Congress in 1854, he assured the Philadelphian of his election, because the peo-ple "will vote as they may be counseled."[59] Less than a year later Young was confident that Dr. John M. Bernhisel would, for the third time, be unanimously elected to this post and that the brethren of Davis County were instructed to elect John D. Parker as their county representative.[60] Similarly, non-Mormon judge John F. Kinney was assured of election in 1863 as Utah's congressional representative.[61] Instructions would go forth that LDS Church members should vote to "sustain" by unanimous acclimation the officers selected by the men of the priesthood.[62] "The Mormon women cared but little for the privilege of voting and cast their ballots just as their Bishops directed," said Wilfred Munro from his 1871 observation.[63] In 1872, with Gen. George R. Maxwell running against Cannon, Young sent unequivocal voting instructions to all LDS bishops and stake presidents: "Be awake and prepared for the Coming Election[;] vote for . . . George Q. Cannon Delegate to Congress with all your strength and *cast not a single vote for any other Candidate* and use every exertion to poll a strong unanimous vote."[64] Former territorial governor George L. Woods had this to say of Utah voting schemes: "It is a common thing to see a Mormon priest with 6, 8, 10 & some-times more wives and concubines go to the polls to vote together."[65]

[58]Twain, *Roughing It*, 101.

[59]Young to Kane, October 30, 1854, BYLC, CR 1234 1, box 2, vol. 1, 722–27.

[60]Young to Orson Spencer, July 31, 1855, BYLC, CR 1234 1, box 2, vol. 2, 260–62; BYLC, CR 1234 1, box 2, vol. 2, 284.

[61]"Affairs in Utah," *NYT*, August 18, 1863; ibid., August 30, 1863.

[62]Jack, "Utah Territorial Politics," 2:518; Young to Bernhisel, March 22, 1862, BYLC, CR 1234 1, box 6, vol. 6, 186.

[63]Munro, "Among the Mormons," 229.

[64]Cooley, *Diary of Brigham Young*, 11; italics in the original.

[65]Recollections of George L. Woods, unpublished manuscript, Bancroft Library, University of California, Berkeley, cited in Prior, "Civilization, Republic, Nation," 298.

In 1862 a territory vote was completed on a provisional state constitution to accompany another request in Washington for statehood. With pride, Brigham Young informed Representative Bernhisel, "Returns have been received from all the Counties except two; without those two, over 11,000 votes were cast without a single vote 'against' the Constitution."[66]

When Elias Lacy Thomas Harrison, one of the spiritualists associated with William S. Godbe, was on trial for apostasy before the LDS High Council, he questioned whether it was "apostasy to differ honestly with the measures of the President." George Q. Cannon's answer was, "It is apostasy to differ honestly with the measures of the President." Daniel H. Wells confirmed Cannon's remark, adding that "we might as well ask the question whether a man had the right to differ honestly with the Almighty." The *Utah Magazine* reporter explained, "Thus the doctrine was unqualifiedly asserted that the Almighty and the Priesthood, so far as its [the church's] official dictates were concerned, were to be accepted as one and the same thing, on pain of excommunication from the Church."[67]

Godbe added to Harrison's words, saying,

> [Mormon leaders] claim the prerogative of absolutely dictating the people as to where they shall live, and what they shall do, what they shall eat, and what they shall drink, what they shall accept as true and what they shall reject as false, and this assumption of priestly power goes as far as to determine what we shall *think* . . . for as is well known they are visited by teachers, who as a class, are made up of our most faithful men, who are themselves compelled to put such inquisitorial questions as will force [those] questioned . . . to a truthful avowal of their view."[68]

Young claimed the "right to dictate about everything connected with the building of Zion, yes even to the ribbons women wear."[69] David Prior, in his article on the reconstruction of "Mormon Utah" following the Civil War, points out that many outside the territory alleged that the theocratic despotism "the Mormon Church had created in the territory . . . was a monstrosity not only for its particular religious doctrines, but also because it eroded the distinction between church

---

[66]Young to Bernhisel, March 22, 1862, BYLC, CR 1234 1, box 6, vol. 6, 186.
[67]"An Appeal to the People," *Utah Magazine*, October 30, 1869, 406.
[68]"A Card by W. S. Godbe" *Utah Magazine*, October 30, 1869, 409.
[69]Brigham Young, "Discourse," *JOD* 10 (February 3, 1867): 210.

and state and concentrated power into the hands of a power-hungry, aristocratic priesthood."[70]

Nearly one hundred years after Governor Ford's observation that Nauvoo was "a government within a government," western historian Wallace Stegner, in a letter to friend and fellow historian Dale Morgan first put on paper that Mormons in Utah operated what approximated a police state:

> More and more I come to a condition of astonishment at the parallelism in methods between Utah in the early days, and any totalitarian state today. The whole thing is there—private army, secret police, encirclement myth, territorial dynamism, self sufficiency, chosen people, absolute dictatorship operating through party rule, group psychology, esoteric symbols and distinguishing uniforms (garments), New Order and all.[71]

Morgan responded with interest, adding that "there are even more parallels." As an example, he noted that "the Mormons . . . also experimented with price control and wage control," apparently referring to the restrictions applied to purchasing only from Zion's Cooperative Mercantile Institution or other Mormon-owned sources.[72] He could also have commented on the communal works exemplified in temple building and on the communalism of economic practices of the United Order of Enoch, the latter an egalitarian effort that was short-lived.[73] Morgan softened his evaluation, cautioning that "in any study of the Mormons as an American dictatorship, . . . due weight must be given to the conditioning influence of the American frontier." He recalled that the Mormons had experienced "the psychology of dispossession" and the stresses of their danger-filled years of mass migration into the untouched, undeveloped resources in the Great Basin.[74] When Stegner was later interviewed by distinguished western historian Richard Etulain, he again touched on control in Utah: "The theocracy in Utah was a police state with a secret police and all the rest of it, which most

---

[70]Prior, "Civilization, Republic, Nation," 296.

[71]Stegner to Morgan, November 24, 1941, in P. Stegner, *Selected Letters of Wallace Stegner*, 326.

[72]In addition, tithing was automatically subtracted from the pay of Utah Central and Utah Southern Railroad employees. "Tithing Exactions," *SLT*, December 12, 1877, 4/2.

[73]Joseph Smith began communal experiments while the Saints were in Ohio, and they were tried again in Utah by Brigham Young.

[74]Morgan to Stegner, December 3, 1941, Dale Lowell Morgan Papers, microfilm, roll 6, 1122–23.

[Mormons] won't grant. If they do grant, they just sort of wave it away, cover it over with dead leaves. But it's a very early example of a theocracy ruled by priesthood."[75]

Conformity was promoted by the physical unity of Mormon villages, where homes were clustered in a central location and the people churched together, kept watch on one another, and left the communal core only to labor on their peripheral farming plots.[76] There were military and police forces, secret assassins with total allegiance to the monarch, and terrorist tactics. Since there were no public schools, classes were held in Mormon church buildings and taught by Mormons, using Mormon scripture for curriculum. There was a single political party, surveillance of the voting process by numbered ballots, an all-embracing ideology, and means of mass communication. There was restriction of free discussion and criticism. Control and limitations were placed on entry and exit across geographical boundaries of Utah Territory.[77]

A totalitarian state also demands the revision of the past. Mormon historian Orson F. Whitney published Brigham Young's revision of the Mormon Battalion history, which deliberately distorts the Mormon men's volunteer service into an unreasonable demand forced upon the Mormon people, to their detriment.[78] The tragic fiasco of the starving, late-arriving Martin and Willie 1856 handcart companies, which resulted in the suffering and death of hundreds, was lost in its transformation into a faith-promoting tale of courage and endurance. The Mormon leaders' several prophecies of good weather, promises of safe passage, and the organizational errors of the failure are all but forgotten. In 1861 Young instructed George Q. Cannon, then in charge of the LDS Saints in Liverpool, England, to destroy, or sell as wastepaper, all volumes of the prophet Joseph Smith's history written by Mother Lucy Smith.[79] In 1865 Young commanded that all copies of her accounts then held by the Saints in Utah be given to him or burned.[80] The events of the Mountain Meadows murders continue to be revised.

---

[75]W. Stegner and Etulain, *Conversations with Wallace Stegner*, 105–106.

[76]The "New Jerusalem" model. See Maxwell, GGSL, 133.

[77]The most extreme limitation took place in September 1857 when Young declared martial law, with a "permit" from him required to enter or leave Utah.

[78]Baskin, "The Mormon Battalion," RCSW, 4–9. In an 1856 address, Young claimed that Missouri senator Thomas Hart Benton had the "authority and privilege to gather the troops in the U.S. and to slay this people if 500 men did not go." Van Wagoner, CDBY, 2:1156.

[79]Young to Cannon, May 15, 1861, BYLC, CR 1234 1, box 5, vol. 5, 790–91.

[80]Van Wagoner, CDBY, 4:2274.

The shock experienced by Peter McAuslan, an "unexceptional" Mormon convert from Scotland, is laid out by biographer Polly Aird, as McAuslan came to recognize the undeniable climate of fear created by violent preaching, intrusive interrogation, condoning of murder, harassment of dissidents, and secret paramilitary networks within an enforced "culture of impunity and silence."[81] Other men, similarly on the lower rungs of the priesthood ladder, confirmed McAuslan's experiences. Samuel Knight, an acknowledged participant in the 1857 Mountain Meadows murders, testified that his instructions to do the killings "could not be disobeyed without imperiling his own life."[82] Philip Klingensmith, a witness in the first trial of John D. Lee, made the same report—that not following the authorities risked death at their hands.[83] James McGuffie, a former southern Utah Mormon, put Brigham Young into layman's terms: "He was God on earth; he got the word of God and gave it to the people."[84]

Even Mormon men of long service experienced punishment if they differed with the those high in the priesthood. Young abruptly dismissed George D. Watt, his personal scribe of sixteen years, when Watt had the temerity to press for fair pay for his work. Biographer Ronald G. Watt says plainly of Young, "No one ventured any opposition to his decisions."[85] On the conflict that existed between Mormon apostle Amasa Mason Lyman and Young that led ultimately to Lyman's excommunication and estrangement from the LDS Church, historian Edward Leo Lyman says, "The central issue—beyond doctrine—was Young's apparent expectation that opposition to him of whatever kind was automatically an error."[86] When Amasa Lyman was planning to travel north to visit Salt Lake City, William Shearman, one of William Godbe's associates, "had wanted to telegraph Lyman to take the stagecoach . . . to reach the city in time." However, Shearman cautioned, "'the difficulty [of] how to do so with safety to yourself' had been a problem."[87] Another Godbeite, Eli B. Kelsey, spoke of Brigham Young's rule: "The constitution of the Mormon Church is eminently democratic, but the impress of Brigham Young

---

[81]Bolton, review of *Mormon Convert, Mormon Defector*, 271.
[82]Cited in Bagley, *BOP*, 407.
[83]Transcript of the First Trial of John D. Lee, 1:60.
[84]Testimony of James McGuffie, cited in McMillan, *Inside of Mormonism*, 34.
[85]Watt, *Mormon Passage*, 229.
[86]Lyman, *Amasa Mason Lyman*, 388.
[87]Ibid., 426–27.

upon the system in his rule of over twenty years, has been semi-barbaric in character and has changed the system into an unmitigated priestly despotism."[88] On his April 1873 arrival in Salt Lake City, district court judge Jacob Smith Boreman observed that Young "gave his attention mostly [to] temporal affairs," where the people "appeared to look to him with fear and as if he were an iron ruler."[89]

Brigham Young's death did not end comments over his resort to violence. The following was occasioned by the disrespect of tearing down the rock wall that surrounded his home: "Brigham was a tyrant and a coward, and . . . he feared assassination, not because there was any danger, but because the consciousness of his own ability to utilize secret murders, made him eternally suspicious."[90] Ten years after Young's death, Utah Commission members described the conditions of control they observed: "In the church government[,] obedience is exacted from every member." In moving from one ward to another, the bishop's approval was required. Permission to marry was required from the bishop, and every person "must hold himself ready, irrespective of personal considerations, to leave his home to go as a missionary to other lands, and he must also be ready to remove his family and effects to such place as the heads of the church may direct him to go."[91] Many non-Mormons warned Territorial Supreme Court justice Charles S. Zane during his 1884–88 tenure that his life was in danger, but he dismissed the idea. Apparently the elder Zane never knew that, as his son had arranged, "the two well-dressed men, who almost every night seemed to be strolling up the street after him, were a pair of cool-headed faro dealers of accurate shooting proclivities, who had assumed the duty of taking care that the judge suffered no harm."[92] As late as 1892, *Salt Lake Tribune* editor Charles C. Goodwin, speaking before the Republican National Convention in Minneapolis, Minnesota, said, "Formerly men who differed from the Mormons were killed, if the Mormons had dared."[93]

---

[88]Testimony before William P. Appleby, Register in Bankruptcy, District of Utah, January 23, 1873, Frank Herman Jonas Papers, MS 641, box 156, folder 6. Kelsey also said he "had not seen any indication God had ever acknowledged Young as prophet, seer, and revelator, or even that [Young] had ever yet himself claimed such a status." Lyman, *Amasa Mason Lyman*, 417.

[89]Arrington, "Crusade against Theocracy," 8.

[90]"A Token of Disrespect," *SLT*, November 28, 1878, 4/3.

[91]Utah Commission, *Report of the Utah Commission to Secretary of the Interior*, 6.

[92]Zane, "Rare Judicial Service," 93.

[93]"Republican National Convention," *DN*, June 11, 1892, 20/1.

Did the actions of a theocracy have any impact on non-Mormons, who were not directly subject to its power? John Hanson Beadle's 1870 analysis stated: "[Gentiles] are subjected to all the annoyances of petty tyranny; . . . in their business and social life they are constantly subjected to the secret espionage of the Church." Beadle continued: "[Non-Mormons] are hampered in business by church hostility and the imposition of excessive taxes; . . . friends and fellow-countrymen have been secretly murdered, and the Church prevents them from obtaining justice; in short, they are exposed to the tyranny of an unopposed majority . . . controlled by a small and compact hierarchy, working out its Star-chamber decrees against liberty by secret and . . . irresponsible agents."[94]

As Beadle explained, "If polygamy were blotted out to-morrow, we could never admit Utah [as a state]," for government by church was far more disturbing than the practice of plural marriage. "It is this that grinds the feelings of American citizens, not polygamy," he asserted.[95] Robert Baskin confirmed that the Mormon people "are honest in their conviction, in sticking to their Theocracy." But he also noted, "When you apply the same review to their leaders . . . you must come to the conclusion they are dishonest. Instead of being 'profitable to this people' they have taken advantage of the confidence reposed in them and turned it against the people and in favor of themselves."[96]

These were the dire conditions in Utah that led Robert Baskin to enlist William McGroarty, George R. Maxwell, Patrick Connor, and scores of other non-Mormons to form the Liberal Party, dedicating themselves to making Utah a better place for its citizens, and making statehood for Utah possible by eliminating theocracy and polygamy through legal means.

---

[94]Beadle, *Life in Utah*, 400.
[95]Ibid., 400–401.
[96]"City News, Ratification Meeting," *SLT*, July 31, 1872, 3/3.

5

A Climate of Violence

Victory attained by violence is tantamount to a defeat, for it is momentary.
MAHATMA GANDHI

THE MURDER OF JAMES MONROE SERVES AS AN EXAMPLE of the disabling of justice by Utah's denial of common law that Baskin discovered in his study of the territorial statutes. Monroe was said to have seduced one of polygamist Howard Egan's wives; the woman gave birth to a child said to be Monroe's, and in 1851 Egan killed Monroe. At Egan's trial, presided by Judge Zerubbabel Snow, Mormon apostle George A. Smith's closing argument held that it was lawful for Egan to kill Monroe, as the act fell not under "English common law" but under "mountain law," wherein the verdict was appropriate and immediate punishment applicable. Egan was acquitted.[1] Very similar was the murder of non-Mormon Dr. John M. Vaughn, shot in 1851 by Madison Hambleton at Manti, Utah. Hambleton had married a nineteen-year-old as his second wife, and not long after, Vaughn was alleged to have seduced Hambleton's thirty-three-year-old first wife. The murder occurred after church, witnessed by the people, but at court Brigham Young appeared and pronounced, just as had George A. Smith, the homicide as justified.[2] Historian Kenneth Cannon reports that five other men, in addition to Egan and Hambleton, received immunity under mountain common law after shooting or killing men who had seduced one of their female

---

[1]Firmage and Mangrum, *Zion in the Courts*, 217.
[2]Bigler and Bagley, *Mormon Rebellion*, 41.

relatives. The five perpetrators named were William Hughes, John J. Baum, James Hall, William Hobbs, and Wilford H. Halliday.[3]

Other threats of violence came from the highest level, as when Lt. Col. Edward J. Steptoe departed for California in 1855 with as many as one hundred single and married Utah women under his protection. Young vowed: "Let the women be ever so bad, so help me God, we will slay them."[4]

Shortly after arriving in Utah, Baskin observed that murders could be committed with perfect immunity under the conditions then existing. In the opening pages of his first book, he describes several murders. The first was the slaughter of two men in Summit County in the summer of 1867. Isaac Potter, Charles Wilson, and John Walker were apostate Mormons with sullied records of arrests for theft.[5] Arrested anew for cattle stealing, they were not tried in court but were marched from the Coalville school building that had held them prisoner. Near the town's edge, Potter was downed by a shotgun blast, and the job finished by slicing his neck. Wilson fled but was killed as he reached the Weber River. Walker was wounded but escaped and found his way to refuge at Camp Douglas. Before a grand jury, Walker identified the perpetrators, but their arrest was farcical; en route to prison to await trial, the men simply lifted the armed but unresisting Mormon guard from the wagon and drove away. Prior to the trial, Walker disappeared, never to be seen again, and ten Summit County men he had cited went free.[6]

Baskin took up the case of Squire Newton Brassfield, a non-Mormon teamster who had courted and married the estranged wife of a Mormon man then absent from Utah. Thereafter he was arrested for theft of the former husband's property. Walking beside a territorial marshal after his court appearance in April 1866, Brassfield was shot by an assassin "who fled in the direction of the Salt Lake Theatre." Despite a reward of $4,500, no arrest was ever made.[7] The "publicly expressed opinion of certain Mormons in this city" was that Brassfield

---

[3]K. L. Cannon II, "'Mountain Common Law,'" 308–27.

[4]Kelly and Birney, *Holy Murder*, 119.

[5]Isaac Potter was named as a Sanpete County cattle thief. J. A. Peterson, *Black Hawk War*, 38.

[6]Baskin cited nine men as perpetrators of the murders: Arza Hinkley, James Mahoney, Mahonri Cahoon, Thomas Dodson, Joshua Wiseman, and John Stanley, together with Alma, Edmund, and Hyrum Eldredge. The cooperative driver lifted out of the wagon was Mormon faithful John D. T. (David Thompson) McAllister. Baskin, *REM*, 9–13.

[7]Baskin, *REM*, 16; Dwyer, *Gentile Comes to Utah*, 47–48, 47n62; S. H. Goodwin, *Freemasonry in Utah*, 10.

had been "justly punished" for "meddling with their women" and that "Gentiles would be served in the same way if not careful."[8]

THE FLOW OF BLOOD

The release of John G. Ambrose and Thomas Betts on Christmas Day 1856 from the Utah territorial prison prompted a letter from Brigham Young to Aaron Johnson, the twelve-wife bishop of Springville, Utah, stating that caution must be employed lest the two steal church-owned horses on their journey south to California. Young was clear that if thievery should occur, "we do not expect there would be any prosecutions for false imprisonment or tale bearers left for witnesses." Young warned that the Mormons should "have a few men that can be trusted on hand, and make no noise about it and keep this letter safe." According to historian Ardis Parshall, it was shortly thereafter when three men traveling with John Tobin, a Mormon in ill favor with Brigham Young, were ambushed on the Santa Clara River.[9] Tobin's group was mistaken for that of Ambrose and Betts, who had decided to accompany the mail train. Tobin and the others survived despite more than fifty bullet holes in the bedding in which they were wrapped.[10] Evidence pointed to a party of Mormons from Parowan under orders from Mormon leader Isaac C. Haight. In his confessions, John D. Lee named Joel White and John Willis as shooters, acting on orders from "authorities in Salt Lake City."[11]

Bishop Johnson dealt more surely with the apostate William R. Parrish, whose membership in the LDS Church dated to Nauvoo times. Parrish planned to leave Utah with his two sons, with California as their goal. On March 15, 1857, the elder Parrish and one of his sons were killed near the city of Springville, along with Gardner G. "Duff" Potter, a conspirator mistaken for the second Parrish son. The Parrish-Potter murders were never investigated by LDS Church authorities.[12]

---

[8]"Utah," *NYT*, April 27, 1866; "Letter from Utah," *Boston Daily Advertiser*, November 19, 1866.
[9]Parshall, "'Pursue, Retake, and Punish,'" 64–86.
[10]In August 1861, Young ordered it published in the *Millennial Star* that Tobin had been cut off and forbidden from being accepted into church membership. Young to Lyman, Rich, and Cannon, August 25, 1861, BYLC, CR 1234 1, box 5, vol. 5, 873.
[11]Lee, *Mormonism Unveiled*, 279.
[12]Aird, "'You Nasty Apostates, Clear Out.'" In 1871 Johnson was arrested, indicted, and released on bail but was freed as a result of the 1872 U.S. Supreme Court decision *Clinton v Englebrecht*.

Judge Elias Smith dismissed them as merely an "internal row."[13] Judge John Cradlebaugh's 1859 investigations in a Provo court for these— and other murders—were hamstrung by grand jury failures to indict and by Mormons hiding the suspects. Murders in the area convinced Peter McAuslan and twenty-nine other Mormons that they should leave central Utah for California under military protection, reports biographer Polly Aird. McAuslan observed that apostates were done away with "faster than a murderer or an adulterer."[14] Hosea Stout stated the obvious: "The fire of the reformation is burning many out who flee from the Territory afraid for their lives."[15]

The *Salt Lake City Directory* published a report about the 1857 murders of "two Irishmen, teamsters, discharged at Fort Bridger from the employ of Messrs Russell, Majors, and Wadell." The two had attempted to make their way to California and were "murdered four miles below Fillmore City." The directory also described the case of Franklin McNeil: "In the winter of 1857 and 58, . . . [he] was incarcerated . . . for no other crime than being an American citizen. Mr. McNeil sued Brigham Young for false imprisonment, on the 2nd of August. The day preceeding [*sic*] the appointed time for trial he was called to the door of his boarding house and shot down. He died of his wounds next morning, and thus the suit was abated."[16] The *Valley Tan* reported the 1858 murder of Jacob Lance, a man arrested at Lehi on a charge of rape. Lance was murdered while confined and under guard. Notably, Lance was a Mormon who apostatized in 1856 and was planning to leave for California.[17] En route from California to Illinois, non-Mormon Henry Forbes was killed near Provo in January 1858, shortly after arriving in Utah. Suspected of the murder was Mormon elder Parshall Terry, seen riding Forbes's horse and sporting his revolver. Joseph Bartholomew, Wilber J. Earl, and Sanford Earl were also suspects, but no inquest was held, and no criminal investigation ever took place.[18]

In February 1858, Henry Jones, about twenty years old, was at home in Salt Lake City, where, according to Hosea Stout's recounting, men

---

[13]"Court Doings at Provo," *DN*, April 6, 1859, 1/1.

[14]Aird, *Mormon Convert, Mormon Defector*, 175–76, 176n16, 178, 249.

[15]Brooks, *On the Mormon Frontier*, 625.

[16]Owens, *Salt Lake City Directory*. Judge Cradlebaugh also confirmed McNeil's murder. "How President Buchanan Suppressed the Rebellion in Utah," *Ohio State Journal*, April 3, 1860, 1/1.

[17]"To the Editors of the Valley Tan," by "Veritas," *Valley Tan*, November 19, 1858, 2–3/1.

[18]Aird, *Mormon Convert, Mormon Defector*, 206–207.

disguised as Indians pulled "him out of bed with a whore and castrated him by a square and close amputation." In April several Mormon men from Payson, Utah, approached the crude dugout where
Hannah Gailey Jones Hatch and her son Henry had moved after his
castration. Entering the hovel, they killed the mother; Henry briefly
escaped but was soon killed, and both were entombed when the structure's roof supports were knocked away.[19]

In August 1859 William Adams Hickman was credited with killing
C. M. Drown, who had brought suit against Hickman for an unpaid
$480 promissory note. In court, Drown obtained a judgment; days
later, when he and his friend Josiah Arnold stopped in Salt Lake City,
Hickman, with seven or eight other men, rode up to the house and
called for Drown to come out. Drown refused, whereupon the men
dismounted, broke down the doors, and shot both Drown and Arnold.
Drown died the next morning, and Arnold a few days later.[20] Hickman confessed to Baskin that "he personally knew of thirteen persons
. . . murdered, some of them by him, and others by various Danites."[21]

In 1859 N. L. Christianson, a city policeman, was arrested and
charged with murdering Andrew Bernhard, a deaf boy. Judge
Charles E. Sinclair recorded simply, "No inquest was ever held."[22] In
1861 a letter from Brigham Young told Edwin Watts of Provo that
his killing fourteen-year-old Levi York for stealing should not result
in any "loss of blessing" or punishment, since those who would steal
knew the "risk of meeting with serious accidents."[23] In the Tabernacle
in 1862, Young expanded York's example to a principle, saying: "Let
every man in this Territory be a vigilant officer, and, when a thief is
found in the act of stealing, take him, dead or alive."[24] In April 1861 a
letter from Young and Daniel Wells provided license to kill to the men
commanding the "out" phase of two hundred wagons headed to Flor-
ence, Nebraska. Tempting for thieves was a cargo of 150,000 pounds
of flour. With the trails "infested with travelers . . . seeking prey,"

---

[19]Rumors of incest and a child of the union circulated. George W. Hancock and seven other
Mormons were indicted for the murders in August 1859 but were never brought to trial. Ten
years later Hancock was convicted of the murder; on appeal a new trial was scheduled but
never carried out. See ibid., 217–19.

[20]Owens, *Salt Lake City Directory*; Mortensen, "Elias Smith," 137.

[21]Baskin, *REM*, 150.

[22]Owens, *Salt Lake City Directory*. The 1860 federal census lists N. L. Christianson as aged
thirty-one, born in Denmark, married with three children, and a farmer in Sanpete County.

[23]Brigham Young to John Young, April 3, 1861, BYLC, CR 1234 1, box 5, vol. 5, 740.

[24]Van Wagoner, *CDBY*, 4:1944.

Brigham's son Joseph W. Young was instructed to form *"vigilance committees* in *weeding out and cleansing your camps from all such noxious vermin"* before thievery occurred, and to "have no misgivings about *putting the law of right in force against . . . all workers of iniquity."*[25] Years after its occurrence, Martin Douglas Wardell testified in court that he had seen the death penalty inflicted on a man named Green in 1862. Traveling with three wagons loaded with merchandise, Green had just gotten into bed when he was pulled out of his wagon by eight Mormon teamsters of the William H. Dame Company, and his throat was cut. One of a group took Green's belt containing $5,000.[26] And in a 1862 threat to a wayward sister in Provo, Brigham Young warned Mrs. M. Hildreth "not to sell property willed to the children of her first husband, . . . nor to follow any man out of this Territory, . . . for most excellent reasons that you already are or should be fully aware of."[27]

In Sanpete County, notorious for its violence, Mormons led by Manti's bishop Warren S. Snow castrated Thomas Lewis "in a brutal manner[,] Tearing the Chords right out." Lewis was in custody for sex crimes. When Brigham's older brother John Young disapproved, the Prophet reported that thousands would be made eunuchs "in order for them to be saved in the Kingdom of God."[28] Massacres of Indians by whites, and of whites by Indians, in Sanpete County spawned the Black Hawk War, with untold hundreds of brutal deaths tallied in its course from 1865 to 1872.[29]

Lifelong Guilt and a Quest for Justice

When Gen. Patrick Connor was transferred to his new assignment in March 1865, non-Mormons were left without the protection and oversight they had enjoyed from his presence, beginning when he and the California Volunteers arrived in October 1862. Within a month of his leaving, an apostate Mormon who had renounced polygamy and

[25]Young and Wells to Joseph W. Young, April 29, 1861, BYLC, CR 1234 1, box 5, vol. 5, 774; italics added.
[26]Trail excerpt, William H. Dame Company, 1862, in *SLH*, November 18, 1889, 8. Among the Mormon teamsters, Wardell named W. D. Williams, Joseph Collett, Dave McBride, Mark Surridge, George Snyder, and John W. Young.
[27]Young to Hildreth, April 18, 1862, BYLC, CR 1234 1, box 6, vol. 6, 215.
[28]Bigler and Bagley, *Mormon Rebellion*, 113.
[29]Young guarded news of the war's numerous grisly events, fearing intervention by federal troops. J. A. Peterson, *Black Hawk War*.

joined a splinter group of former Mormons—called Josephites because
of their devotion to Joseph Smith's interpretations—wrote of escalat-
ing intimidation. Planning to leave the territory, R. W. Atwood wrote
to Connor:

> [Among the people,] fear . . . has . . . returned, and they are afraid of
> being placed in greater bondage than ever. Heavy threats are made by
> Brigham and his colleagues against those who dare to differ from him
> in sentiment. Dark deeds are contemplated and enacted. . . . Brigham
> instituted a military law . . . and commanded the bishops . . . [that]
> none of his people [were] to be allowed in the street after 10 P.M.; [he]
> also organized a strong police force in every ward . . . to patrol night
> and day, and the people are under greater surveillance than ever. . . .
> The attempt that has been made to assassinate Mr. Maloney.[30]

Atwood's observations were confirmed by Camp Douglas's commander, Lt. Col. Milo George, who wrote that "a system of espionage
and insolent interference with the affairs of individuals not belonging
to the Mormon Church has been organized in Great Salt Lake City
. . . by direction of Brigham Young, and others of the church authorities" and that "there has been shown such a disposition to violence . . .
that citizens, considering their lives in danger, have called upon me for
protection."[31] Connor responded, "I regret that Utah is taken out of
my command. I pity those poor fellows who, relying upon my promise
of protection, have declared their independence of Brigham."[32]

In August, the month of Robert Baskin's arrival in Utah, Capt.
George F. Price, acting adjutant general at Fort Laramie, wrote Gen.
Granville M. Dodge: "When the news went to Utah that the sin-
ridden Territory was cut off from . . . the direct influence of General
Connor, there went up a great cry of rejoicing from the polygamous
traitors. They indulged in all manner of threats, and warned gentiles
to leave; that they could not hunt for gold and silver any longer."[33]

It was in this time of threatened and real violence that the murder
of Baskin's friend and client Dr. John King Robinson took place. This
was an unmistakable confirmation of the insecurity of life for non-
Mormons in Utah, and the consequences of the event rested painfully
on Baskin for the remainder of his life. Robinson, a retired assistant

---

[30]Atwood to Connor, April 26, 1865, in *WOR*, ser. 1, vol. 48, part 2, 219–20.
[31]George to Capt. George F. Price, May 4, 1865, in ibid., 315–16.
[32]Connor to Gen. G. M. Dodge, July 21, 1865, in ibid., 1113.
[33]Price to Dodge, August 15, 1865, in ibid., 1187–88.

surgeon formerly with the California Volunteers, had been discharged in December 1865. He remained in Utah and in March 1866 married Ellen "Nelly" Kay, the daughter of former Mormon stalwart, alleged henchman for hire, and apostate John Kay.[34] An intimate friend of Rev. Norman McLeod, who himself had survived an 1865 attempt on his life, Robinson attempted to gain title to eighty acres of land that included Warm Springs, a bathing resort whose natural spring water was desirable.[35] He was planning construction of a hospital, with its warm waters a recuperative feature, but the land was claimed by Mormon leaders for the City of Salt Lake. The acreage claimed was, as with most of the Mormon claims for city boundaries, far in excess of that allowed by federal land statutes.[36] Robinson was warned by non-Mormon friends that to contest this property would put his life in jeopardy, a caution underscored when "a crowd of men with axes broke the windows, doors, and fixtures of a building belonging to him." When Robinson approached Baskin for legal counsel in obtaining title, Baskin minimized the danger, saying "he did not believe it possible anywhere in the United States that a citizen would jeopardize his life by applying to the courts of his country for an adjudication of his rights."[37] Unfortunately, Baskin lacked the level of concern held by Robinson's friend Capt. Stephen E. Jocelyn, also of Connor's Volunteers, who predicted violence "in a letter to the *New York Tribune* ten days previous." No one "knew on whom the blow would descend," Jocelyn wrote, and "many of those who believed or knew themselves under ban took extraordinary precautions to meet the threatened danger." Speaking of Robinson, Jocelyn said, "Not three days before his foul murder, he expressed to me a sense of the danger he felt himself exposed to in attempting, single-handed to fight the Mormon authorities of Salt Lake City."[38] Robinson certainly knew that only

---

[34]Kay's apostate status is cited in Ogden, *Frontier Reminiscences*, 51. A polygamist Mormon, Kay had been a territorial marshal, but in 1859 Judge Delana R. Eckels and Marshal Peter K. Dotson refused to appoint him as a deputy, for he was a "notorious Mormon"—i.e., he did whatever Mormon leaders asked. Alexander, *Brigham Young*, 22. Sarah Kay Crosby, Ellen's sister, lived with the Robinsons and verified the testimony of other witnesses at the inquest.

[35]George Price wrote to Dodge on August 21, 1865: "Mormons tried to murder Rev. McLeod, Christian minister now teaching in Salt Lake City, but failed." Price to Dodge, in *WOR*, ser. 1, vol. 48, part 2, 1199–1200.

[36]Salt Lake City lacked a legal boundary claim until November 1871. Maxwell, *GGSL*, 138.

[37]Baskin, *REM*, 13.

[38]"Affairs in Utah, Dr. Robinson's Assassination," letter of S.E.J., *Chicago Republican*, January 4, 1867.

two weeks earlier the *Union Vedette*'s fiery, anti-Mormon editor in chief, Isaac Mellen Weston, was taken at night by Mormons, brutally beaten, and warned he had six hours to leave the city.[39]

Seven years old at the time, Eveline Brooks, who lived with her family at the corner of Main Street and Third South, gave an account of Dr. Robinson's murder: "At midnight, he was called up to attend a man who was supposed to be injured. Just as he left his house he was hit on the head by a blunt instrument and then shot: Mother and Father jumped out of bed, as did we children too; . . . *Mother was sure of one of the criminals but dared not tell*."[40] Fear of violence "seized the whole non-Mormon community," she explained. Non-Mormons laid Robinson's death on the doorstep of Brigham Young, a charge supported by the fright experienced by the Brooks family, at risk for being able to identify one of the killers. Jocelyn's record also substantiates the fear felt by other witnesses to the killing: "Witnesses were unwilling to identify [the attackers] without adequate assurance of safety, for fear their own lives would pay the forfeit."[41] The *Union Vedette* noted that the people's fright that ensued after this blatant butchery on a moonlit night in a city of twenty thousand people went virtually uninvestigated.[42] *News* editor Albert Carrington published a damage control piece, saying: "The history of the States . . . furnishes a record of violent deeds. . . . It has been with gratification and an allowable pride that we have pointed to the rare occurrence of similar acts in this Territory."[43] Incongruous to this allegation was the note on an earlier page reporting that "Gen. Connor, formerly commanding in Utah, telegraphs from Salt Lake that the Gentiles are panic stricken, and advises the Rev. Norman McLeod not to return."[44] Connor and McLeod had recently testified before a House committee that armed assassins had violated the sanctity of "our place of worship" and that

---

[39]Weston was attacked on October 3. He refused to leave, and it was he, along with Dr. Anderson and Captain Jocelyn, who carried Robinson's body home. "News from Salt Lake City," *NYH*, October 19, 1866, 1/4. Weston later had an illustrious career in Michigan.

[40]Ogden, *Frontier Reminiscences*, 51; italics added.

[41]Jocelyn had witnessed Robinson's death: "I was by his side only a few minutes after he was struck down—held his hand and felt the last faint pulse that flitted from his heart."

[42]"The Murder of Dr. Robinson," *UV*, October 24, 1866, 2/1. Judge Titus's review of the legal issues in Robinson's contest was carried in the *Deseret News* two days after Robinson's death. "Legal Ruling," *DN*, October 24,1866, 5/1. However, the murder was not reported in the *News* until October 31. "Murder," *DN*, October 31, 1866, 5/1.

[43]"Deeds of Violence," *DN*, October 31, 1866, 4/1.

[44]"By Telegraph," *DN*, October 31, 1866, 1/3.

"law abiding citizens are threatened even by Brigham's police." In fact, McLeod did not return to Utah for six years.[45]

Even distant newspapers, such as the *Springfield* (*Mass.*) *Republican*, sounded their concern: "The alarm spread among the anti-Mormon citizens of Salt Lake City by the shocking assassination of Dr. Robinson was even deeper than was obvious. Gentile fears extended to the federal judges, the district attorney and the U.S. marshal, with Gen. Connor, now a private but conspicuous citizen. One or all are felt to be marked for the next blow from the secret assassins in the interest of the Mormon hierarchy." The report added that Gentiles thought LDS president Johnson to be indifferent to their danger.[46] Samuel H. Goodwin, a Utah Masonry historian, also left a record of Robinson's murder:

> The entire community was terribly excited. . . . [A] reward amounting to nearly $7,000 was offered for the arrest of the murderers—Brigham Young's name headed the list of subscribers. . . . Some time later when certain Mormons were arrested . . . Brigham published his withdrawal of the $500 he had subscribed. . . . The community was terrorized for no one knew what he might be the target of an assassin's bullet; men who had never done so before, armed themselves; respectable citizens declined to use the sidewalks when going home at night, but walked in the middle of the streets carrying a revolver in their hand.[47]

Baskin, who wrote that seven people "were participants in the murder," noted, "It is evident that they had previously met and deliberately agreed upon the manner in which it was to be accomplished."[48]

City coroner Jeter Clinton asked Chief Justice John Titus and Associate Justice Solomon P. McCurdy to assist in an inquest. The committee included two Mormons—Seth M. Blair, previously the U.S. attorney for Utah, and Hosea Stout, former head of the Mormon police in Nauvoo. The non-Mormons were Judge Charles Hempstead, former editor of the *Union Vedette*, and John B. Weller, former governor of California. It was learned that none of the eight city policemen or the numerous volunteer policemen searched for the perpetrators or investigated the crime scene. Robinson's gold watch, his pocketbook,

[45]Bigler, *Forgotten Kingdom*, 272–73.
[46]"Affairs in Utah: The Gentiles Panic-Stricken and Over-awed," *Springfield (Mass.) Republican*, November 28, 1866.
[47]S. H. Goodwin, *Educational Bulletin*, 6–7.
[48]Baskin, *REM*, 13–16.

and other valuables were untouched.[49] In the end, Governor Weller's words left no doubt as to where he believed ultimate responsibility for the grisly murder lay:

> The founder of the Christian religion preached good will amongst men . . . "Blessed," said He, "are the peace-makers." Did He not teach obedience to law and respect to the powers that be? Did He not say "thou shalt love thy neighbour as thyself? Did He not say "love your enemies and pray for those who despitefully treat and persecute you? . . . *How inconsistent are these sentiments, promulgated by our illustrious Savior, with the doctrines taught by the . . . prophet in the tabernacle.*[50]

Despite a $9,000 reward, despite several members of the city police force later being charged with the crime, and despite the presence of thirty-six appointed policemen in every ward in Salt Lake City to monitor the city at night, no one was ever convicted of Robinson's murder. Notably, Baskin's name was not among the contributors to the reward, but he carried for his lifetime the desire to bring to justice those responsible for this crime.[51] Baskin's long-held emotion over Robinson's death stemmed from his sense of guilt for the grave mistake of assuring the doctor that he would not incur any personal risk in seeking legal remedy for his claim.

Other unsolved murders of non-Mormons were thought—but never proved—to be instigated at the hand of Mormon rulers around this period. Thomas Coleman, possibly a witness to Dr. Robinson's attack, was killed and castrated December 1866.[52] In 1873 John Howath, formerly a soldier at Camp Cameron near Beaver, Utah, was killed in an ambush as he walked across the common field of the city. He also had filed on land claimed by Mormons.[53]

In *Reminiscences*, Baskin writes of the 1857 murders of the Aiken party and, using Hickman's confession, details the death of Horace Bucklin, one of the Aiken group who was known at the time to Baskin and Hickman only as a man named Buck. Allegedly under orders from Brigham Young, Hickman lured "Buck" and co-perpetrator John

---

[49]The city policemen named in the *Union Vedette* were Andrew Burt, Henry Heath, William Hyde, Joseph Hyde, Grant Livingston, Charles Ringwood, and officers Dewey and Calder. "Coroner's Inquest over the Body of Dr. J. K. Robinson," *UV*, October 26, 1866, 2/2.

[50]Baskin, *REM*, 108; italics added.

[51]"Reward for the Apprehension of the Assassins of Dr. Robinson," *DN*, October 31, 1866, 5/3.

[52]Maxwell, *GGSL*, 124, 124n26, 125.

[53]Ibid., 124–25.

Chapman to the area of the Hot Springs, where Hickman abruptly shot Bucklin in the head. Death was assured with a knife as Bucklin lay on the ground.[54] David Bigler's recent research has clarified that the Aiken party consisted of six men from California who traveled to Utah, hoping to turn a profit dealing with army troops then marching toward Utah. The executions "ordered by Mormon leaders and carried out by church members in central Utah," says Bigler, "are a haunting reminder of the . . . absolute power Brigham Young exerted over the lives of all who entered the territory."[55] A visitor to Camp Douglas, William Waters, also gave his observation of Utah's violence: "If Brigham Young tells a saint to murder his son, or his enemy as a sacrifice, that saint tells us he would do so. Where is greater infatuation than this? or where more dangerous power in the hands of one man?"[56]

Baskin reports a lengthy 1872 confession by William Adams Hickman to a number of murders.[57] One victim was frontier trader Richard Yates, killed during the 1857 Utah War. Yates was reported to have gunpowder, lead, and firing caps for sale to the highest bidder, be it the U.S. Army or the Mormon Militia. Under suspicion that he was a disloyal spy, he was arrested and placed in Hickman's custody. In Echo Canyon, Hickman received the message from Mormon Militia commander Daniel Wells that Yates "ought to be killed." When Yates fell asleep that evening, Hickman, in the company of Hosea Stout, approached Yates, and "his brains were knocked out with an axe." A gold watch and $900 were taken, and the body was buried in a grave hidden by a campfire placed over it. Hickman claimed he gave the booty directly to Brigham Young.[58]

Baskin relates the murder of the non-Mormon lawyer Jesse Thompson Hartley, who married a Mormon woman named Bullock and became familiar with the Mormons. Alleging the Mormon authorities' murder of California-bound immigrant David Hull, Hartley pleaded in a September 1853 letter to fellow Mississippian Jefferson Davis that Utah was unsafe for Gentiles, that the "general govern-

[54]Baskin, *REM*, 150–51; Bigler and Bagley, *Mormon Rebellion*, 235, 235n8. Chapman escaped and fled to California, where his murder was unrelated to Utah events.
[55]The eight perpetrators were Orrin Porter Rockwell, John Lott, John Murdock, Homer Brown, Abraham Wollf, Miles Miller, John Kienke, and Sylvanus Collett. Bigler, "Aiken Party Executions," 457.
[56]Waters, *Life among the Mormons*, 196.
[57]Baskin, *REM*, 36–37.
[58]Hilton, *"Wild Bill" Hickman*, 77–78; Bigler and Bagley, *Mormon Rebellion*, 220–21.

ment laws" were defied.[59] Davis was "a powerful member of President Franklin Pierce's cabinet," and Hartley asked him "to work to remove Young as governor, bring in federal men to run the territory and courts, and use U.S. troops already in the West to implement this change."[60] Given that the mails were monitored, it is no surprise that Hartley's letter never reached Davis. Speaking at the semiannual LDS Church conference, Brigham Young arose, and his vatic voice singled out Hartley as dross, saying, "He ought to have his throat cut." Shortly thereafter, Hickman, in the company of Mormon elders George Boyd and Orson Hyde, shot and killed Hartley as he crossed a creek on horseback.[61]

"Man of God, Son of Thunder"

Robert Baskin entered the infamous name of scapegrace Orrin Porter Rockwell only once in his description of Utah murders, when he reported that the Aiken party members "were murdered by Rockwell and his ever-ready assistants."[62] Rockwell's reputation as a Mormon gunman began in May 1842, when he shot, and narrowly missed killing, ex-governor Lilburn W. Boggs for having issued an order to the Missouri Militia to "exterminate" the Mormons in their insurrection. Among others, Rockwell was suspect in the attack on John Tobin, the brutal slaying of Henry Jones and his mother in Payson, and the killing of Dr. Robinson.

Allegedly, Rockwell acted only on instructions from Joseph Smith and later as Brigham Young's apparatchik, but he occasionally freelanced.[63] The death of John Gheen with a dead-center, forehead shot in September 1859 was ruled a suicide, despite the lack of powder marks on his skin and the inconsistent entry wound. Thomas B. H. Stenhouse reported Gheen's death as "blood atonement" for a prior murder. In fact, Gheen had shot and killed Lilace W. Conditt in Council Bluff, Missouri, in April 1848 for trespassing. Charged with murder, Gheen was not convicted. He emigrated to Salt Lake City, set up a butcher shop,

---

[59]Hartley to Davis, September 26, 1853, Brigham Young Collection (LDS History Library, Salt Lake City), MS1234, box 23, folder 2.

[60]Marquardt, *Coming Storm*, 5–7.

[61]Baskin, *REM*, 152–54.

[62]Baskin, *REM*, 151. In the subtitle of his biography of Rockwell, Harold Schindler referred to him as "Man of God, Son of Thunder."

[63]Bean, *Destroying Angels of Mormondom*.

and was alleged to have asked for blood atonement.[64] In 1878 Samuel D. Sirrine insisted Rockwell had killed Gheen, and recent research shows that Rockwell's younger brother, Merritt, was married to Martha Conditt, the daughter of the murdered Conditt.[65] Thus Gheen's killing is almost surely one of Rockwell's freelance actions, done at personal motive. No civil authority questioned the story of suicide, despite evidence to the contrary, nor did the coroner hold an inquest.

On another front, Brigham Young was implicated in a counterfeiting venture involving Myron Brewer and David McKenzie. McKenzie was arrested by Marshal Peter K. Dotson in May 1859 with more than $16,500 in new bills manufactured for Utah War debts.[66] Brewer and a "handsome scoundrel" named Robert Keith "Joachim" Johnson, who had threatened to kill a Mormon editor, were both cut down in May 1860 in Salt Lake City by balls and buckshot from a shotgun, a weapon combination known to be a Rockwell favorite. An inquest concluded that the two had simultaneously killed each other. That would have been a remarkable feat, for each to have fired a shotgun at exactly the same instant, especially since both were armed only with revolvers. No charges were ever filed. Of the event, Judge Elias Smith made a bland note in his diary: "Killed by some persons unknown."[67]

Marvin Oats, a teamster, stopped on a cold January day at the Hot Springs Brewery Hotel, an establishment located on the road connecting Great Salt Lake City and Lehi and owned in part by Rockwell. Armed only with a knife, Oats engaged Rockwell, whom he did not recognize; the altercation ended as the bartender placed a pistol against Oats's head. Escorted out, Oats went on his way. Rockwell saddled up smartly, caught Oats in his wagon, and felled him with one shot to the chest. An investigation followed, and Rockwell was "honorably acquitted." A bizarre *Deseret News* report said, "The result seems to have given general satisfaction to all parties."[68]

In another incident, brothers Kenneth and Alexander McRae, accused of robbing emigrant traveler John Love, were stopped in August 1861 in Emigration Canyon by a sheriff and his deputies. According

[64]Gheen's death is described in detail by Schindler in *Orrin Porter Rockwell*, 299–301.
[65]Lilace W. Conditt was also known as Amos W. Conditt. Details of Gheen and the Conditt family were supplied to the author by Dr. Don Maxwell, Jr., of Oklahoma City, August 2010.
[66]Fry, *Peter K. Dotson*, 5.
[67]Schindler, *Orrin Porter Rockwell*, 306–308, 308n31; Bigler and Bagley, *Mormon Rebellion*, 348, 348n49; Mortensen, "Elias Smith," 156, 156n21. McKenzie was tried, found guilty, and served time in prison.
[68]"Another Man Killed," *DN*, February 1, 1860, 4/1.

to Rockwell biographer Harold Schindler, "When they ignored the command, the two boys were gunned down." Sirrine named Rockwell as the trigger man, but Judge Elias Smith entered in his diary the innocuous phrase "killed after they were arrested in an attempt to escape."[69] Lot Huntington, charged among other crimes with the beating of departing Governor John Dawson, was killed by Rockwell in Rush Valley during "an attempt to escape." Two of Huntington's associates, Moroni Clawson and John P. Smith, met a similar fate the next day near Salt Lake City's Townsend Hotel. Once again Judge Smith entered the familiar note "in an attempt to escape . . . both were shot and killed."[70] However, Thomas Stenhouse reported the event differently: "It was believed that the prisoners were walking in front of the officers when the latter quietly put their revolvers to the back of their heads and 'stopped them.'"[71] With the deaths of Huntington, Clawson, and Smith, any opportunity for official inquiry as to Mormon leaders who might have had a role in Dawson's near assassination also died.

Sparse evidence now exists to tie the many murders to Mormon leaders' control. One bit of substantiation is the anecdotal deposition of Mary Ettie V. Smith, who attested to a murder planned at the highest level in Utah. She was present, she said, "when Brigham Young, General Wells, and John and Wiley Norton . . . adopted a plan for the murder of Wallace Alonzo Clarke Bowman." She reported that "Norton and James Ferguson shot . . . Bowman, in Salt Creek canyon."[72] Though it likely did not apply to Bowman, the eminent George Q. Cannon gave this remarkably blunt message from the pulpit in 1869: "We close the door on one side, and say that whoredoms, seductions and adulteries must not be committed among us, and we say to those who are determined to carry on such things, we will kill you."[73] At the time he made this threat, Cannon was one of the Twelve Apostles and the editor of the *Deseret News*.

Camp Floyd's post–Utah War troops brought lawlessness and violence apart from that attributed to Mormon factions. As Schindler notes, "Loud, profane soldiers, arm-in-arm with camp followers and civilian teamsters, now caroused the streets." The *News* contended that "more blood had been shed and more murders committed in the

---

[69]Schindler, *Orrin Porter Rockwell*, 312–13; Mortensen, "Elias Smith," 265.
[70]Mortensen, "Elias Smith," 347–48.
[71]Thomas B. H. Stenhouse, *Rocky Mountain Saints*, 592n.
[72]Green, *Fifteen Years among the Mormons*, x–xii.
[73]*JOD* 14 (1872): 58.

eight months since the Expedition's arrival . . . than in the previous nine years."[74] Stenhouse also alluded to troops when he reported,
"During the summer and fall of 1859 there was a murder committed in
Salt Lake City almost every week, and very rarely were the criminals
brought to justice."[75]

Violent means were still being implemented in the spring of 1877,
when respected and experienced *New York Herald* reporter Jerome B.
Stillson experienced two attempts on his life. Stillson earned these by
his investigative journalism while touring the southern settlements
of Utah near the time of John D. Lee's execution. Interviewing witnesses, including Brigham Young, he gathered facts concerning the
Mountain Meadows murders that were published in the *Herald*. This
brought about widespread speculation that charges against Mormon
leaders for the crimes would be forthcoming. As Stillson was returning from Camp Douglas after dark one night, his carriage was fired
upon, but he was unharmed. Several days later he again escaped death
when he was attacked as he opened the door of his room at the Walker
House; the knife used was deflected by his metal suspender buckle.[76]
Robert Baskin acted as Stillson's counsel and adviser when the city's
leadership resorted to the inexplicable tactic of convening a semifor-
mal investigation on whether Stillson's story was truthful, rather than
investigating the matter as a crime. Baskin insisted that no man guilty
of falsehood could have gone through such a thorough inquisition
without betraying signs of confusion.[77]

Confirmation from Unexpected Sources

The contention that the lives of those who sinned or dissented could
be in mortal danger was supported in a conversation between Robert
Baskin and William S. Godbe, a quite unlikely source for such a confirmation. Godbe, who had been a prominent Mormon, simultaneously the husband of several wives, and a prosperous merchant and
drugstore owner, was held in high regard. With a group of bright,
educated businessmen and professionals who met to explore the intellectual reaches of spiritualism, Mormonism, and economic progress,

---

[74]Schindler, *Orrin Porter Rockwell*, 297.
[75]Thomas B. H. Stenhouse, *Rocky Mountain Saints*, 417.
[76]"Attempted Assassinations," *SLT*, June 1, 1877, 4/2; "Take That, You Handsome Son of a Bitch,"
    SLH, June 1, 1877, 1.
[77]"Blood Atonement," *SLT*, June 2, 1877, 4/2.

William S. Godbe. Salt Lake merchant, spiritualist, free thinker, and founder of the *Utah Magazine*, Godbe was excommunicated by Brigham Young, largely for criticizing Young's limiting economic policy. *From the Alta Club Photographic Collection of Special Collections Department of the J. Willard Marriott Library, University of Utah in Salt Lake City.*

Godbe questioned the theoretical and practical pronouncements of Brigham Young, including his anti-mining stance and his narrow views on the economy. The "Godbeites" held that mining exploration and extraction of Utah's metals and ores should be not only allowed but encouraged. For his dissension Godbe was excommunicated, along with several other Godbeite men.[78] Not long afterwards, Baskin was inspecting, for possible rental, a home owned by Godbe. Noting heavy irons bars on the ground-level windows, Baskin commented that the bars "express more forcibly than words can do, that you have jeopardized your life by apostasy and that you are guarding against murderous assaults by the Danites." Godbe replied laconically: "Yes, that is the reason why I barred that window."[79] Godbe experienced no assassination attempt or back-alley bludgeoning, but he received punishment of a different sort. A manuscript given to Baskin by one of Godbe's sons details the Mormon efforts toward his financial destruction. Godbe wrote: "In ninety days . . . 'there wouldn't be a grease-spot' left of me and to carry out that prediction the Zion Drug Store was started, and I found the competition too severe for me, and [I] was forced to close. . . . [I]nstead of being worth at least $100,000 . . . I found myself owing that much . . . and paying interest at . . . $1000 a month." Henry W. Lawrence, another Godbeite, suffered a similar financial fate after his excommunication.[80] E. L. T. Harrison

[78]Campbell, *Establishing Zion*, 321–24.
[79]Baskin, *RCSW*, 26.
[80]Baskin, *REM*, 80, 81.

felt threatened as well. Harrison was an architect, a businessman, a copublisher (with Godbe) of the *Utah Magazine* (which morphed into the *Salt Lake Tribune*), and a fellow traveler with Godbe in their disputes with Young. Under oath Harrison admitted he feared retribution following his own excommunication: "I was in some apprehension about my personal safety. That lasted for about a year or two. . . . I did[,] on a number of occasions, take precautions for my safety."[81]

EUPHEMISMS FOR MURDER

The Zeitgeist of violence is further illustrated by the array of Mormon euphemisms for murder.[82] Intemperate and inflammatory, they were not simply street jargon; many were used from the pulpit. The people needed no ecclesiastical dictionary to understand the meaning of these terms: "appointed";[83] "cared for";[84] "castout and trodden under foot of men";[85] "circumcised below the ears";[86] "clean, purify and wash";[87] "cleansing the inside of the Platter first";[88] "cut him off—behind the ears" or "cut off just below the ears";[89] "cut off" or "cut him off";[90] "dirty job";[91] "dose of rope";[92] "forfeited his head";[93] "have his tail cut off two inches below his ears";[94] "help him";[95] "helping those who need help";[96] "hewn down";[97] "hogholes would be stopped up with

[81]McMillan, *Inside of Mormonism*, 50.
[82]Euphemisms for castration were also in use, such as "mutilated" and "qualified for the office of chamberlain in the King's palace." Bagley, "Conan Doyle Was Right," 7.
[83]Thomas B. H. Stenhouse, *Rocky Mountain Saints*, 471.
[84]"*New York World* Interview with Bill Hickman," in MacKinnon, *At Sword's Point*, 305.
[85]Quinn, "Culture of Violence," 22.
[86]Brooks, *On the Mormon Frontier*, 241.
[87]Bishop Woolley, "The Word of God as Preached in Great Salt Lake City," *UV*, January 7, 1865, 2/5–3/1.
[88]Meaning that apostates were to be killed before non-Mormons. Aird, *Mormon Convert, Mormon Defector*, 178.
[89]Quinn, *Mormon Hierarchy*, 247; Hickman, *Brigham's Destroying Angel*, 15–16.
[90]Ekins, *Defending Zion*, 230; David H. Burr to Thomas Hendricks, March 28, 1857, in Buchanan, *Utah Expedition*, 118–20.
[91]Lee and Bishop, *Mormonism Unveiled*, 158.
[92]Brigham Young to George A. Hicks, February 16, 1869, BYLC, CR 1234 1, box 8, vol. 11, 303; "Some Startling Facts," *SLT*, August 21, 1874, 2/2–3, cited in Bigler and Bagley, *Innocent Blood*, 266, 269.
[93]Hansen, *Quest for Empire*, 79.
[94]Brigham Young, quoted in "Brigham Up to His Tricks," *SLT*, September 9, 1875, 4/3.
[95]Brigham Young, *JOD* 4 (February 8, 1857): 219.
[96]Thomas B. H. Stenhouse, *Rocky Mountain Saints*, 467.
[97]Brigham Young, "The Necessity of the Saints Living Up to the Light Which Has Been Given Them," *JOD* 3 (March 2, 1856): 226; Jedediah M. Grant in the LDS Tabernacle in Salt Lake City, March 12, 1854, in Thomas B. H. Stenhouse, *Rocky Mountain Saints*, 304.

them";[98] "hoisted them down the stairs";[99] "the job reported on and approved";[100] "judgment shall be laid to the line and righteousness to the plummet";[101] "killed by Indians";[102] "laid by the heels";[103] "leave them where they will be safe";[104] "nepo" or "nepo'd";[105] "over the rim of the basin";[106] "pickled down in Salt Lake";[107] "pilot them over the troubled waters of the Styx";[108] "puke them with a dose worse than lobelia";[109] "pulling hemp by the neck";[110] "put away";[111] "put him where the dogs cannot bite him";[112] "put out of the way";[113] "the risk of meeting with serious accidents";[114] "salted down" or "saved him;"[115] "send him duck hunting";[116] "sending him to hell";[117] "sent home by a short cut";[118] "sent over the rim" or "send them where Gebow went;"[119] "sent to hell across lots";[120] "sent up the pocket of the Lord";[121] "separating the tares from the wheat";[122] "severed windpipe";[123] "sheared down";[124] "shot while trying to escape";[125] "shut off his wind";[126]

[98]"Testimony of Alvira L. Parrish and Orrin E. Parrish and Confession of AbrahamDurfee," *Kirk Anderson's Valley Tan*, April 19, 1859, cited in Bigler and Bagley, *Mormon Rebellion*, 110.

[99]Bishop Woolley, "The Word of God as Preached in Great Salt Lake City," *UV*, January 7, 1865, 2/5–3/1.

[100]"*New York World* Interview with Bill Hickman," 305.

[101]Kelly and Birney, *Holy Murder*, 119.

[102]Ibid., 104.

[103]F. J. Cannon and Knapp, *Brigham Young*, 281.

[104]Kelly and Birney, *Holy Murder*, 86.

[105]The word "open" spelled backwards, referred to opening body cavities and filling them with stones, thereby preventing the corpse from surfacing. MacKinnon, *At Sword's Point*, 55, 303.

[106]Lee, *Mormonism Unveiled*, 255, 284.

[107]Bigler, *Winter with the Mormons*, 80–81.

[108]"Utah Polygamy and Its Fruits," *Milwaukee Sentinel*, April 23, 1860, 3/2.

[109]Hansen, *Quest for Empire*, 117.

[110]John M. Bernhisel to Brigham Young, December 17, 1857, cited in Bigler and Bagley, *Mormon Rebellion*, 268.

[111]Philip Klingensmith's testimony at the John D. Lee trial, quoted in Baskin, *REM*, 111.

[112]Schindler, *Orrin Porter Rockwell*, 37.

[113]Lee and Bishop, *Mormonism Unveiled*, 158; Green, *Fifteen Years among the Mormons*, 77.

[114]Brigham Young, to John Young, April 3, 1861, BYLC, CR 1234 1, box 5, vol. 5, 740.

[115]Lee and Bishop, *Mormonism Unveiled*, 159; Alfred Henry Lewis, "The Viper on the Hearth," *Cosmopolitan*, vol. 50, no. 4, March 1911, 444.

[116]Brigham Young, quoted in Bigler, *Winter with the Mormons*, 49–50.

[117]Quinn, "Culture of Violence," 25.

[118]*New York Evening Post*, November 7, 1867, in Baskin, *REM*, 15.

[119]"The Word of God as Preached in Great Salt Lake City," *UV*, January 7, 1865, 2/5–3/1.

[120]Brigham Young, *JOD* 3 (1856): 83, 317; 5 (1858): 78; Baskin, *REM*, 100.

[121]Hilton, *"Wild Bill" Hickman*, 77.

[122]Kelly and Birney, *Holy Murder*, 23.

[123]Bagley, *BOP*, 114.

[124]Beadle, *Life in Utah*, 178,

[125]Mortensen, "Elias Smith," 265.

[126]Lee, *Mormonism Unveiled*, 255.

"slipped his wind";[127] "speedily reaped the fruit such sowing is apt to produce";[128] "stop a man's breath";[129] "summary citation to meet the future";[130] "sweeten you up right suddenly";[131] "tail cut off below the ears";[132] "take care of that man";[133] "take other measures to accomplish the object desired";[134] "take out and lay aside";[135] "time to remove them";[136] "to be wasted" or "wasted";[137] "used up";[138] "where the crows could not find him";[139] and "wipe out" or "wipe me out."[140]

This collection of more than sixty everyday euphemisms for the killing of human beings seems incongruous as originating from men who claimed divine intervention as the source of their restored Christian religion. The term that historian Michael Quinn coined is apt, for this was indeed "a culture of violence."[141]

As Baskin and Others Saw It

Baskin had no doubt "that the high priesthood of the Mormon church were the actual rulers of Utah, . . . that the government established by the Organic Act existed in name only; [and] that the priesthood claimed to be divinely authorized to rule the members of the Mormon

---

[127]Quinn, "Culture of Violence," 23.

[128]"The Killing of Brassfield," *DN*, April 12, 1866, 4/2.

[129]Bigler, *Winter with the Mormons*, 75.

[130]"Killing of Brassfield."

[131]Brigham Young, April 13, 1857, cited in McMillan, *Inside of Mormonism*, 79.

[132]"Gilbert Morse: A Mountain Meadows Witness Whom the Court Needed Not," *SLT*, September 28, 1876, 4/2.

[133]"*New York World* Interview with Bill Hickman," in Mackinnon, *At Sword's Point*, 305.

[134]Brigham Young to Charles N. Smith, September 19, 1876, BYLC, CR 1234 1, box 10, vol. 14, 513.

[135]George A. Hicks is quoted as saying that if he did not stop singing a ballad about Mountain Meadows, "some of Lee's boys were to take me out 'and lay me aside.'" Bagley, *BOP*, 258.

[136]Quinn, *Mormon Hierarchy*, 245.

[137]Lee and Bishop, *Mormonism Unveiled*, 159.

[138]Baskin, *REM*, 152; Hilton, *"Wild Bill" Hickman*, 85.

[139]Bushman, *Rough Stone Rolling*, 337.

[140]David H. Burr to Thomas Hendricks, March 28, 1857, in Buchanan, *Utah Expedition*, 118–20, cited in Bigler and Bagley, *Mormon Rebellion*, 112.

[141]As Quinn wrote, "LDS leadership . . . created a culture of violence with sermons, congregational hymns, newspaper editorials, and patriarchal blessings invoking memories of past persecution, while urging vengeance against Mormonism's enemies and 'blood atonement' against the wicked." Quinn, "LDS 'Headquarters Culture,'" 149. Quinn states that for at least a decade after 1847, murder, castration, and beheading were punishments imposed on Mormon men and women for sexual sins. Quinn, *Mormon Hierarchy*, 241–61; Quinn, "Culture of Violence," 16–28.

church in all matters, temporal and spiritual."[142] Aird's review emphasizes the episode in which Brigham Young lifted his right arm to the square, and the stones of the Mountain Meadow monument were immediately leveled by his devoted followers.[143] In 1912 octogenarian Julia F. Thompson told Baskin that, years before, she had heard Mormon militiaman William H. Dame say: "If you wives and sisters in passing by, see the head of a husband or brother upon the street, you must not ask any reasons. It is none of your business."[144]

If murders of apostates and objectionable non-Mormons diminished or stopped after the death of Brigham Young, control by ecclesiastical thews and sinews continued well into the twentieth century. Although Frank Jenne Cannon was not impartial, his 1911 historical account, published during the rule of the sixth LDS president, Joseph F. Smith, said that the Mormon people "live under an absolutism": "All direction, all command, comes from the man at the top. It is not a government *by* common consent, but a government *of* common consent—of universal, absolute and unquestioning obedience—under penalty of eternal condemnation threatened and earthly punishment sure."[145]

Robert Baskin was well placed to observe the violent context, the totalitarian-like state created by men who truly believed that its origins were in revelations from God and that they need answer only to God's law. The return of Christ to the earth was imminent, the Saints testified. Mormons believed that they themselves were uniquely responsible to ready the world for that event, that the one and only true church, the Church of Jesus Christ of Latter-day Saints, had been reestablished on the earth for that purpose. To some of the Mormons, accomplishing God's ends justified what others would consider heinous crimes. With the paucity of admissible evidence, the conclusion emphasized by Ronald Walker, Richard Turley, and Glen Leonard in their account of the Mountain Meadows murders has application: "Context is the historian's best friend."[146]

---

[142]Baskin, *REM*, 17.

[143]Aird, review of *Innocent Blood*, 255.

[144]Baskin, *REM*, 109.

[145]O'Higgins and Cannon, *Under the Prophet in Utah*, 318–19; italics added. Cannon and Joseph F. Smith were long-term bitter enemies. K. L. Cannon II, "Wives and Other Women," 74, 94–95.

[146]R. W. Walker, Turley, and Leonard, *Massacre at Mountain Meadows*, xiv.

6

The Combative Years

The government at first was a pure theocracy.
To cause that to change . . . has been the work of the bench and the bar.
CHARLES C. GOODWIN

BASKIN DID NOT EXPERIENCE THE PUBLIC OUTRAGE THAT arose from the few non-Mormons in Utah in 1857 who knew of the facts of the massacre at Mountain Meadows. He did not witness the Mormon conflicts with federal authority that led to the march of the Utah Expedition troops in 1857–58. He was still in Ohio but well aware that the Mormons were the only citizens in the nation who were not overwhelmed with the Civil War's exigencies. The war's end and the Republican administration's ability to refocus some attention on "the Mormon problem" coincided with Baskin's arrival in Utah. The middle months of 1865 also marked an increase in violence and threats against non-Mormons following Gen. Patrick Connor's departure to the Department of the Plains. From the time of the Civil War's end, a waxing and waning staccato of ongoing philosophical, social, and practical conflicts existed between the Mormon leadership and the non-Mormons. Non-Mormon influx increased with the 1869 transcontinental railroad's completion, aggravating the friction. Even the apparent divestment by the LDS Church of its albatross of polygamy in 1890 did not bring peaceful coexistence. Non-Mormon persistence and Mormon resistance continued through Utah's achievement of statehood in 1896 and lasted until plural marriage finally ended about 1910.[1]

---

[1]Seventy years of Mormon civil disobedience began when Joseph Smith took plural wives in Nauvoo and did not end until 1910. G. D. Smith, *Nauvoo Polygamy*; Hardy, *Doing the Works of Abraham.*

When Baskin arrived in Utah, he did not qualify for inclusion in the "Utah Ring," a pejorative term coined by Mormons to describe the federal appointees sent by President Ulysses S. Grant following the Civil War. Most were Republicans and war veterans. Union men far outnumbered Confederates, and many of both groups were lawyers. Only one of these features—being a lawyer—applied to Baskin, who was a Democrat, had not served in the war, and had come voluntarily among the Mormons for his own very private reasons. Joining efforts against the "twin evils of theocracy and polygamy" did qualify Baskin to be among those the Mormons despised, as he participated with individuals of "the Ring" in many of their moves against the two practices.[2]

In June 1869, five weeks after the railroad was linked at Promontory, Gen. George R. Maxwell arrived in Utah as the registrar of land, to provide Utah's people with the type of land ownership that citizens of other states and territories enjoyed.[3] As the land register, as the U.S. marshal, and as a deputy attorney, Maxwell would repeatedly join efforts with Baskin, making both of them castigated members of the Ring.[4] Until Maxwell's death in 1889, they worked together, albeit intermittently, to delay statehood for Utah until the territory could qualify by eliminating polygamy and by accepting the same republican rule of other territories. The two men would cooperate in efforts to secure legislation, to challenge the seat of Utah's congressional representatives, to bring justice for the murders of Mountain Meadows, and to change Utah's voting abuses. Arriving on the same train as Maxwell was another lawyer who would trouble the Mormons and have his difficulties with Baskin as well. Cyrus Myron Hawley, appointed as an associate justice of the Second District Court, was the former partner of Illinois's anti-Mormon senator, Lyman Trumbull. Despite some friction between Baskin and Hawley, the three worked with a common purpose to bring Utah into compliance with federal laws.[5]

---

[2]Brigham Young was incensed that federal appointments went to men outside Utah rather than to residents of the territory. However, the same practice was followed in other states and territories, with the positions often awarded as political plums for past service.

[3]Survey and land development issues are treated in Maxwell, *GGSL*, 117–26.

[4]George Alfred Townsend, of the *Cincinnati Gazette*, placed thirteen men in rank order as "Federal Enemies of the Saints." Number one was Judge James B. McKean, with Baskin and Maxwell as numbers two and three. Townsend, *Mormon Trials*, 16–18.

[5]Maxwell, *GGSL*, 128. Hawley shared Trumbull's antipathy of Mormon practices and brought twenty-two years of Chicago law experience to his new location in Utah.

THE CULLOM BILL OF 1870

Brigham Young reacted with anger to the 1870 Cullom Bill. He insisted it was not written by Illinois congressman Shelby Moore Cullom but "concocted in Salt Lake City by a pettifogger named Baskin." Young wished Baskin to be given some inconsequential "lick-spittle" federal job in Utah so that Mormon women could "show him his walking-papers in the shape of a forest of broomsticks."[6] Young was correct about the Cullom Bill's authorship, for its writing was an accomplishment from which Baskin derived a substantial measure of fulfillment.

Baskin explained his motivation: "As I had mentally resolved while looking on the mutilated body of my murdered client, Doctor Robinson, to do all that I possibly could do to place in the hands of federal authorities the power to punish the perpetrators of such heinous crimes, I drafted the Cullom bill."[7] Baskin was aided by fellow lawyer and fellow Mason Reuben Howard Robertson, together with other unnamed Utahans, in drafting the legislation that would be introduced to Congress with Cullom's sponsorship.[8] The bill was early in a series of many federal acts that would be forged to attempt to end theocracy and polygamy in Utah.[9] The 1862 Morrill Act had been ignored by a federal government consumed by Civil War.[10] The Wade Bill was introduced in 1866 by Ohio senator Benjamin F. Wade, the Ashley Bill in 1869 by Ohio representative James Ashley, and the Cragin Bill in 1867 by Senator Aaron Harrison Cragin of New Hampshire. The Cragin Bill was withdrawn in favor of the Cullom Bill, whose provisions were severe: probate courts would be denied criminal jurisdiction, and believers in polygamy would be excluded from jury duty in polygamy trials.[11] Wives could testify against husbands charged with polygamy.

---

[6]Young to William H. Hooper, January 11, 1871, BYLC, CR 1234 1, box 8, vol. 11, 951.

[7]Baskin, *REM*, 28.

[8]Reuben Howard Robertson, of Iowa, was a Mason before joining Wasatch Lodge in Salt Lake City, where he served twice as Worshipful Master. He was interred at Mount Olivet Cemetery, not far from the plot he kindly gifted to Gen. George R. Maxwell.

[9]Coincident with the Cullom Bill, Senator William M. Stewart's bill would have reduced the land size of Utah, just as the Ashley Bill would have done. "Another Slice off Utah," *DN*, February 9, 1870, 11/1. Neither bill would have affected theocracy or polygamy.

[10]Young was arrested on March 9, 1863, when U.S. marshal Isaac L. Gibbs served a warrant charging violation of the Morrill Act. Journeyman O. P. Rockwell and four other Mormon men posted Young's $2,000 bail. Schindler, *Orrin Porter Rockwell*, 333.

[11]Modified somewhat, the Cragin Bill was reintroduced in the Senate on December 4, 1871, after the Cullom Bill died. "A Bill to Aid the Execution of the Law against Polygamy," *DN*, December 27, 1871, 4/1.

Polygamists could not hold public office, and a variety of fines were stipulated. Polygamist men would be compelled to support children of their marriages, and the federal marshal could call on U.S. soldiers when needed. Baskin insisted that had the severe Cullom Bill's provisions become law, republican rule and statehood for Utah would not have required twenty years of piecemeal federal legislation.[12]

Baskin was in Washington in February 1870 to testify before the Senate Committee on Territories, regarding the Cullom bill. The *Defiance Democrat* of Ohio reported Baskin's reply when asked what would happen in Utah if the bill passed: "Brigham Young would oppose it with a strong hand, but . . . I do not think he would resort to open violence. . . . He would threaten it . . . [and] come to the verge of it; then he would go down. . . . [The bill] would break up the concentration of power that now exists in Utah. Brigham is now as absolute as the Czar of Russia. . . . He controls everything, religious and secular."[13]

In the debate of Cullom's proposed legislation, the nation's leaders called for action. Vice President Schuyler Colfax was critical of the Mormon position: "The Mormons claim the benefit of every law they see fit to approve . . . and trample under foot such other laws . . . as they see fit to reject." Was the authority of the nation or the authority of Brigham Young the supreme power in Utah, Colfax asked, and did the laws of the United States or those of the Mormon church take precedence?[14] Hamilton Ward, a Republican from New York, spoke in Cullom's favor, taking a hard line against his colleagues: "Had you enforced the laws of the country against Utah years ago, you would not have had this terrible power confronting you at this moment."[15]

Others came to the Mormons' defense. Despite having been excommunicated the previous October, William S. Godbe, a Mormon with several wives, claimed receipt of divine instruction regarding the future of Mormonism. As a result he traveled to Washington in early 1870 to work against Cullom. In interviews with Colfax and Grant, Godbe "pleaded for kindly treatment of the Mormon people by the general government."[16] Franklin H. Head, superintendent of

---

[12]Baskin, *REM*, 31.

[13]"Abolition of Polygamy in Utah," *Defiance (Ohio) Democrat*, February 26, 1870, 1/3.

[14]"The Mormon Question by Vice President Colfax," *New York Independent*, reprinted February 9, 1870, *DN*, 5/1.

[15]Poll, "Political Reconstruction of Utah Territory," 114.

[16]Cited in Van Wagoner and Walker, *A Book of Mormons*, 96.

Indian Affairs, and transport mogul Alexander Majors were among those who appeared before the House Committee on Territories and spoke against the bill's provisions. Majors refuted the allegations of violence in Utah, for "he felt as safe in Salt Lake City as in any place in the world."[17] To the contrary, J. Wilson Shaffer's letter to Secretary of State Hamilton Fish, written within two weeks after arriving in Utah as its newly appointed governor, said that "unless something like the Cullom or Cragin Bill passes, the U.S. officers will be powerless."[18]

Cullom Means War

Newspapers in February 1870 anxiously warned that another civil war would erupt if the Cullom Act became law. The *New York World* was blunt: "*This bill means war. . . .* Fifteen years ago, when the Mormons had less than a quarter of their present strength, they showed their entire readiness to fight for their system. . . . Mormons can give us a very disagreeable, a very wearisome, and tremendously expensive war . . . of not less than two hundred millions of dollars."[19] Other publications carried a similar message; it escalated into a chorus from the *Journal of Commerce*; the *Times*, the *Atlas*, the *World*, the *Globe*, and the *Evening Press* of New York; the *Age* of Philadelphia; the *Boston Traveller*; Portland's *Oregonian*; Baltimore's *Sun*; and the *Cincinnati Commercial*. As one New York newspaper repeated the theme: "If the Cragin or Cullom bills pass, war with Utah will be the result. . . . The question for the American people is, whether they are willing to carry the sword and fire into the beautiful Salt Lake valley and leave it a scene of desolation and death."[20] The *Cincinnati Gazette* added, "Polygamy will die sooner than we could kill it with an army of a quarter of million. Let us not give it new life by watering it with blood."[21] The composed calm of the *New York Times* cautioned: "We

---

[17]"Testimonies before the Committee on Territories," *DN*, March 23, 1870, 8/1. The firm of Russell, Majors, and Waddell had been a major transporter of Mormon goods. In the 1857 Utah War, thousands of pounds of gunpowder, secretly placed in their wagons, was supplied to Mormons of the Nauvoo Legion.

[18]Shaffer to Fish, April 1, 1870, cited in Bigler, *Forgotten Kingdom*, 285–86.

[19]"The Danger of War in Utah," *New York World*, reprinted in *DN*, February 23, 1870, 12/1; italics in the original. Lyman reports that the *New York World* was not among those papers whose editorial opinions could be purchased. Lyman, *Political Deliverance*, 84.

[20]*Globe* and *Evening Press*, reprinted as "The Press on Utah Affairs," *DN*, March 2, 1870, 1/2.

[21]Reprinted as "The New Crusade," *DN*, March 9, 1870, 12/2.

have tried the strong arm already with no good result. . . . Our present finances do not warrant it, and . . . no true interests of the country require it."[22] Nevada's representative, Thomas Fitch, courting Mormons' favor, gave the same warning: "The Mormons would regard the passage of this bill as a declaration of war. . . . It will add millions to the debt and thousands to the muster role of the nation's dead."[23]

Did the theme of war arise from serious, profound concern, or was it a scare tactic, the result of Mormon influence—and money— applied in the right places to provoke a degree of public panic in order to defeat the legislation before Congress? The combative tone of the Mormons' spokes piece, the *Deseret News*, insisted Mormons would not capitulate: "Coercion by bullet and bayonet will never induce the people of Utah to forsake the principles . . . of their religion."[24]

With four damaging sections removed, the Cullom Bill passed the House on March 30, 1870.[25] It languished in the Senate Committee on Territories and died there. Biographer Matthew Grow suggests that Brigham Young's friendship with Thomas L. Kane was influential, for Kane wrote, "I can kill the Bill in the Senate," and Kane's "interventions with President Grant and several senators 'greatly relieved' his [Young's] mind."[26] Some thought railroad lobbyists and sympathetic southern interests responsible; Baskin's opinion was that Senator James Nye of Nevada, the committee's chair, had intentionally not allowed it to leave his committee, to benefit fellow congressman Thomas Fitch in making his mark as a pro-Mormon politician.[27] Historian Will Bagley contends that Nye was simply corrupt and for sale.[28] Baskin also asserted that a number of men of Salt Lake City who should have aided the bill's passage were frightened by threats made by Mormon leaders. According to Baskin's account, a group of non-Mormons, whom he apparently presumed to be Master Masons because they met in the Masonic Hall, drafted a resolution of protest and forwarded it to the Mormon delegate, George Q. Cannon, who used it to

[22]*NYT*, January 27, 1870, reprinted as "The Press on Utah Affairs," *DN*, March 2, 1870, 1/2.

[23]Baskin, *REM*, 48–49.

[24]"The Press on Utah Affairs," *DN*, March 2, 1870, 1/2.

[25]"Action by the House on the Cullom Bill," *DN*, March 30, 1870, 5/3.

[26]Kane to Young, March 20, 1870, cited in Grow, *"Liberty to the Downtrodden,"* 259.

[27]Baskin, *REM*, 48–51. Fitch either lied or knew nothing of the man when he argued that the Cullom Bill was unnecessary because "that great Mormon leader, Brigham Young, . . . will strangle polygamy by a revelation." *DN*, March 9, 1870, 5/1.

[28]Bagley, *BOP*, 283.

advantage.[29] In this matter Baskin was in error, for it was not the Masonic element but the Godbeites, several of whom were polygamists, who asked Congress to modify the act to exempt those marriages that had taken place prior to its passage. Maxwell, who was sympathetic, also urged moderation and wished to have "the land and disenfranchising clauses so modified as not to injure any who were disposed to be loyal to the government."[30]

KICKING A HORNET'S NEST

In August 1870, James Bedell McKean arrived from New York to become Utah's Territorial Supreme Court justice and Third District Court judge. McKean admitted he felt "called" by President Grant to bring Brigham Young and the Mormons to account.[31] At the resignation of Charles Hempstead in August 1871, McKean appointed Robert Baskin to serve as the U.S. attorney ad interim.[32] In a span of days in October 1871, the team of McKean, Baskin, and Maxwell made three unprecedented moves against the Mormon leadership.[33] LDS Church president Brigham Young was arrested for lewd and lascivious cohabitation. In addition, a young Mormon man, Thomas Hawkins, was tried for adultery, based on a Utah territorial law written by Mormon legislators, and found guilty on October 28. And Brigham Young and three others were arrested for murder.

---

[29]Baskin, *REM*, 56.

[30]Whitney, *HOU*, 2:433–38.

[31]One author quotes McKean: "The mission which God has called upon me to perform in Utah, is as much above the duties of other courts and judges as the heavens are above the earth, and whenever and wherever I may find the Local or Federal laws obstructing or interfering therewith, by God's blessing I shall trample them under my feet." Hilton, *"Wild Bill" Hickman*, 124.

[32]Capt. Charles H. Hempstead, the first editor of the Camp Douglas newspaper *Union Vedette*, had been appointed U.S. attorney for Utah in 1870. When McKean was made chief justice, Hempstead's load increased and he resigned, saying that the fees were a "mere bagatelle" and that "any respectable attorney . . . would receive a fee . . . exceeding . . . my annual salary for four years." Urged by President Grant to stay on, Hempstead agreed to remain for a time, but resigned several months later, joining Patrick Connor in mining ventures. Bigler cites fear of Mormon violence as motivating his withdrawal. Madsen, *Glory Hunter*, 110; Cresswell, *Mormons and Cowboys*, 81–82; Bigler, *Forgotten Kingdom*, 290.

[33]George C. Bates brought charges of judicial corruption against McKean, asserting that Baskin's appointment was illegal. Baskin insisted that Revised Statutes, Sec. 1875, allowed appointments to U.S. attorney and U.S. marshal. Baskin, *REM*, 38. McKean was vindicated, and the Baskin and Maxwell appointments were confirmed. Alexander, "Federal Authority versus Polygamic Theocracy," 91–101.

Baskin realistically feared that arresting the most powerful man in the territory on a murder charge was likely to stir his followers to violence. This supposition proved correct, as it was soon reported in the *Salt Lake Tribune*:

> A prominent lawyer's wife became a little disturbed when she saw two wagons loaded with armed men drive past her, and hearing . . . crazy zealots exclaim: "Damn old Baskin! We'll hang him to a telegraph pole! We'll make the hell hounds of the ring squeal!" During the lady's drive, she met other wagons coming in from the country, the occupants all showing excitement, and some . . . threatening death to the Gentiles.[34]

Baskin reasoned it safer to deal with the Hawkins case first. Since plural marriages were not recorded publicly, conviction for marrying more than one woman was nearly impossible. Baskin and Maxwell were able to secure a guilty verdict on the charge of adultery, based on its definition in Section 32 of the 1852 Utah Territorial Code and the testimony of Harriet Hawkins, the first wife. She told of having been married in England, with a happy relationship for a number of years, until her husband brought into their home another woman, whom he claimed to have married as a second wife. She described how, through a thin curtain, she could hear the sounds emanating from the carnal union of her husband and his new wife in the bedchamber the three occupied. Ironically this first conviction for polygamy in Utah was based on a law against bigamy passed by Mormons in their territorial legislature.

On October 2, 1871, U.S. marshal Mathewson T. Patrick served a warrant of arrest to Brigham Young on the count of lewd and lascivious cohabitation. This was followed, on October 28, with another arrest warrant against Young, together with Salt Lake City mayor Daniel H. Wells and Mormons Hosea Stout and William H. Kimball, for the 1857 murder of Richard Yates.[35] On November 18, 1871, three indictments appeared in the Third District Court's criminal docket: *The People v. Wm. Adams Hickman*, for murder; *The People v. Brigham Young, Daniel H. Wells, Hosea Stout, William Adams Hickman, and Joseph A. Young*, for murder (of Yates); *The People v. Brigham Young, Wm. A. Hickman, Morris Meacham, Simon Dalton, George D. Grant,*

---

[34]"A Few Questions Answered," *SLT*, October 30, 1875, 2/1.
[35]Baskin, *REM*, 39–41; Maxwell, *GGSL*, 146–47.

O. Porter Rockwell, and William Kimball, for murder (of "Buck," now identified as Horace Bucklin).[36]

In *Reminiscences,* Baskin recorded in detail that Hickman came to him asking for professional representation, out of fear of being killed by his former Danite associates. Hickman confessed to killing Yates, who sold supplies to the U.S. troops headed to Utah, since Mormons considered this activity to be treason during the Utah War. Hickman insisted he killed Yates on orders from Mormon leaders. Baskin described writing the details of several interviews with Hickman, and finding no contradictions among the versions, he was "satisfied that Hickman told me the truth." Hickman consented to testify before the grand jury. Baskin placed this confession "in the hands of Major Hampstead, who was the United States district attorney," but Hampstead did not act on the evidence.[37] It was at this time that Hempstead resigned and Baskin was appointed, circumstances that support Bigler's claim that Hempstead feared Mormon reaction.

By December 1871, Baskin's efforts against Young had earned him the lashing tongue of George Alfred Townsend, also known in the trade as "Bobster" and "Gath." In an article appearing first in the *Omaha Herald* and reprinted in the *Deseret News,* Townsend wrote with a certain élan: "The leading half of this split pea in office is one Baskin[,] . . . known by his . . . uncombed 'sorreltop,' chin shrubbery of the same burnt hue, bran-spattered countenance, . . . and features of that lank, cadaverous cut which betoken hunger for a double deal, supplemented by that twitching snarl of the upper lip which proves the Darwinian theory developed as far as a canine standard." Gathering invective, Townsend attacked Baskin's professional qualifications: "He is not accused of any learning in the law, but every time he opens his tobacco-stained lips he pleads guilty to a fresh murder of the King's English." It was clear that Townsend, from southern Ohio, knew of Andrew West's death in his encounter with Baskin: "The fellow is currently reported to have fled from Ohio for Ohio's good and his own immunity from the punishment which commonly follows ——, though committed, as report credits him with averring, in self defence."[38] Townsend saved some of

---

[36]Hilton, *"Wild Bill" Hickman,* 127; Bigler, "Aiken Party Executions," 465.

[37]Baskin, REM, 36–37.

[38]"A Rattling Review of Affairs in Salt Lake," *Omaha Herald,* reprinted in DN, December 6, 1871, 3/1. Omitting the word "murder" or "homicide" or "manslaughter," Townsend apparently wished the reader to supply a term.

his criticism for McKean, charging that his motives were political. The possibility that McKean might "wake up to a senatorship at Washington," Townsend pronounced, "brightens an horizon above which his sun will never rise."[39]

The Mormons' response to the indictments against Brigham Young for murder was debated at a meeting held at Jeter Clinton's ranch, near the shore of Great Salt Lake. Young and other church officials convened "to decide whether his arrest should be resisted by armed force." Choosing flight rather than fight, Young went on a journey to southern Utah for the protection of his health.[40] The proceedings of the case of *The People v. Brigham Young, Sr.* went on despite his absence, with Baskin and Maxwell representing the people against a defense team of at least nine lawyers. By teams, they were Fitch and Mann; Hempstead and Kirkpatrick; Snow and Hodge; and former U.S. attorney Hosea Stout with A. Miner and Leonard Young.[41] The defense alleged that the charge of lascivious cohabitation had an ulterior purpose: "A system is on trial in the person of Brigham Young." Judge McKean had, in fact, readily admitted that the case would more appropriately be named *Federal Authority v. Polygamic Theocracy.* The Mormons' sharp retort was it should be named *The Utah Ring of Imported Officers v. Religious Liberty.*[42]

The Third District Court in the spring of 1872 was located on the second floor of a stable, with activity proceeding against Hawkins, Hickman, and Young. Mormon dignitaries George Q. Cannon and William Hooper, along with Thomas Fitch, headed to Washington with a petition for Utah statehood, backed by a mandate approved by thousands of Mormons in a February mass meeting. Non-Mormons drafted their opposing petition, asking Congress to withhold statehood for several reasons: "Citizens of Utah entertain doctrines antagonistic to the fundamental ideas of free government. . . . They believe in one supreme political as well as religious head, whose word . . . is superior to all law and civil authority, and even to the Constitution."

---

[39]Ibid. Townsend also added a similar, disparaging description of George R. Maxwell. GGSL, 311–12.

[40]Baskin, REM, 55–56. Argument erupted in court over the amount of appropriate bail for Brigham Young and whether it would be forfeited on Young's failure to appear. See Maxwell, GGSL, 160–61.

[41]"Third District Court," DN, October 18, 1871, 1/2.

[42]"Plea in Abatement in the Case of the People vs. Brigham Young," DN, October 18, 1871, 12/1. Brigham Young returned to Salt Lake City in January and was under house arrest until released by the Englebrecht ruling of April 1872.

The petition's framers cautioned that "any offers for the surrender of polygamy are . . . for the purpose of obtaining possession of the powers and machinery of government in the Territory, and freeing them from the supervision and control of the General Government."[43]

Baskin was a featured speaker at a mass meeting at the Liberal Institute supporting the anti-statehood memorial.[44] The *New York Times* reported: "An immense meeting of citizens opposed to the admission of Utah as a state was held. . . . Hundreds of ladies were present."[45] Baskin and other Liberal Party members traveled to Washington, warning the administration of the disastrous consequences that Mormon control by virtue of statehood would bring to non-Mormons living in Utah.[46]

On March 29 a Philadelphia newspaper incorrectly reported that the U.S. Supreme Court had sustained McKean's jury impaneling in a federal court in the Englebrecht case.[47] Within two weeks the decision in *Clinton v. Englebrecht* was correctly reported, and all the court proceedings against Hawkins, Hickman, Brigham Young, and his minions were stopped.[48] This April 15, 1872, ruling concluded that jury selection should have been done in district courts according to the requirement of territorial laws, not according to the federal selection processes set forth by the acts of Congress, as McKean, Baskin, and Maxwell had interpreted. Non-Mormons were thunderstruck. It would be two years before *Clinton v. Englebrecht* would be reversed by the Poland Act's provisions.[49]

McKean explained the impact of this ruling to Col. Henry Andrew Morrow of Camp Douglas: "Two years ago, numerous witnesses under oath charged several men, then and now policemen of this city, with the atrocious assassination of Dr. J. King Robinson, but . . . I have never been able even to put them upon their trial. Mr. Zerubbabel Snow, though never appointed by the Governor, claims to be Territorial Attorney General of Utah, and he would claim the right to appear

---

[43]"Memorial to Congress," *SLT*, March 28, 1872, 2/2.

[44]"Mass Meeting To-Night," *SLT*, March 27, 1872, 2/1.

[45]"Utah, Anti-State Meeting in Salt Lake—Denunciation of Church Influence," *NYT*, March 30, 1872.

[46]Lyman, *Political Deliverance*, 18.

[47]"The Press of the Situation in Utah," *Philadelphia Press*, reprinted in *SLT*, March 29, 1872, 2/3.

[48]Schindler, *Orrin Porter Rockwell*, 280n42.

[49]Baskin and Maxwell were counsel for Paul Englebrecht and two other men in their attempt to recover an award and damages for the destruction of their stores. The Englebrecht ruling invalidated hundreds of pending actions and left district courts almost powerless. See Maxwell, *GGSL*, 160–62.

as public prosecutor, if Clinton, Burt, or Smith were arraigned before me."[50] The shock of non-Mormons was expressed by the *New York Times*: "A hundred thousand . . . gathered from both continents with no elements of unity or homogenity [*sic*], save their strange faith, have, through the silent but relentless power of the Courts, gained a victory over forty millions of people."[51]

The arrest of Brigham Young for lascivious cohabitation and murder was very damaging for Judge McKean, for he had already been deemed overzealous in his opposition. A surprising editorial piece written with carefully measured tones appeared in the *Deseret News* in 1871:

> If the United States desires to wage war upon Mormon polygamy, let it be done in an open and dignified manner, and not in the pettifogging style which has thus far characterized the prosecutions in Judge McKean's court. . . . No good citizen . . . can have any sympathy with polygamists. It is a doomed institution, and it must disappear from our social system; but all good people are interested in having its destruction brought about by methods . . . so ordered that the judgment of the civilized world shall approve them.[52]

Baskin personally urged McKean to caution, but McKean was relieved of his appointment via an abrupt telegram from President Grant in March 1875, around the time the judge imprisoned Brigham Young for failure to pay fees related to his divorce from Ann Eliza Webb Dee Young. Certainly the 1871 charges against the "Lion of the Lord" contributed to the dismissal.[53] The reasons for McKean's removal were complex and not fully known, but he was judged as intemperate in moving against Young, a man whom, whatever his faults, many held in respect for his accomplishments in colonizing a huge span of western America.[54] Baskin's 1871 view of McKean does

---

[50]"Another Crusade Dodge," *DN*, February 11, 1874, 1/3. The reference is made to Jeter Clinton, Andrew Burt, and Lot Smith.

[51]"The Mormons," by "J. L. H.," sent from Salt Lake City on April 20, published in *NYT*, April 29, 1872.

[52]"Editorials, Mormon Question," signed "F," *DN*, November 8, 1871, 4/2.

[53]"Prometheus Bound," *SLT*, March 13, 1875, 2/1.

[54]Thomas Alexander claims that McKean's censure of Salt Lake City lawyer George E. Whitney, brother-in-law to both U.S. Supreme Court associate justice Stephen J. Field and Wisconsin senator Timothy O. Howe, was the event inciting McKean's discharge. Alexander, "Federal Authority versus Polygamic Theocracy," 96–97. Jacob Smith Boreman corroborated this, asserting that Field and Howe petitioned Grant for McKean's removal while Grant was preoccupied over matters of Southern reconstruction. Arrington, "Crusade against Theocracy," 33–35. Grow admits that in April 1871 Young asked Thomas Kane to work in Washington for McKean's replacement, but indicates Kane "advised a different strategy." Grow, *"Liberty to the Downtrodden,"* 260–61.

not reflect the complexity of the interactions that befell the man, for he said simply: "Judge McKean was both upright and intelligent, and has been derided by . . . fanatical polygamists because, under his decisions in the Englebrecht and Hawkins cases, they could no longer violate with impunity the law of Congress against polygamy."[55] That the Baskin and McKean family burial plots are adjacent in the Mount Olivet Cemetery may be the most accurate available measure of their mutual admiration.

"Feeing" against Legislation

April 1872 found the Voorhees anti-polygamy bill in the Senate Judiciary Committee, and Baskin and McKean were in Washington, working to support it. George Q. Cannon, Utah's congressional representative, was fearful, for if the bill "or any like it" were to pass, Mormon polygamists would be "launched again upon a sea of troubles." In a letter to Daniel H. Wells, Cannon left unequivocal evidence that Mormons did not rely solely on strength of argument to ward off damaging legislation. Cannon wrote: "[It would] be well for us to fee some of the members of Congress, for them to stay proceedings on this infamous Bill. . . . We think its defeat is important, and we think we can defeat said Bill by giving a few thousand dollars. . . . If you (the brethren) wish us to do this, it would be well for you (bro Wells) to arrange . . . with Kountze Bro's. at New York, depositing the money with them in my name."[56] With funds available to Cannon for bribery, and with a willingness from those in Salt Lake City to put money to such use, it was not surprising that the Voorhees proposal failed—as did many bills directed at the "Mormon problem."

Jurisdiction in Utah's Courts—The Poland Act

Twenty-six lawyers of the Utah Territorial Bar—including Baskin—met in March 1874 to construct a memorial to the U.S. Senate and House of Representatives in support of legislation coming before the two bodies. They testified that the administration of justice in Utah was in utter chaos, unable to bring to trial those accused of crimes, and

[55]Baskin, *REM*, 52.
[56]George Q. Cannon to Daniel H. Wells, April 16, 1872, cited in Bigler and Bagley, *Innocent Blood*, 309–10.

that civil cases involving property worth millions of dollars were without action. They assured Congress that those desiring legislation were not irresponsible troublemakers or promoters of their own interests but men who had the urgent interests of the territory in mind. Imploring Congress to action, they wrote: "Life and property in Utah are without the protection of the civil government, so far as courts might give that protection. Wherefore, your memorialists pray your Honorable body to enact . . . provisions of the bills now pending . . . to remedy the evils complained of."[57] Among its provisions, the Poland Bill would restrict local probate courts to matters of divorce, estates, and guardianship, removing all civil, chancery, and criminal jurisdiction to federal courts and federal officers. The act would also give district courts exclusive jurisdiction for all suits over $300, while abolishing the locally appointed offices of territorial marshal and territorial attorney.[58]

In spring and summer of 1874, Utah's U.S. marshal Maxwell and U.S. attorney William Carey traveled to Washington to personally lobby members of Congress for the Poland Bill's passage. Although he did not identify them by name, George Q. Cannon was openly attempting to undermine the lobbying efforts effectively put forth by Maxwell and Carey: "We have had the United States marshal . . . on the floor of this House . . . doing all in his power to push forward this bill . . . [and] the United States district attorney stealing on this floor . . . for the same purpose[,] . . . constantly pressing upon members of the Judiciary Committee, upon members of the Committee on the Territories, and upon gentlemen who are not on either of those committees the passage of this bill."[59]

Unlike most of his non-Mormon colleagues, Baskin did not consider the Poland Act the best, or the only, way to deal with court control by Mormons, and from 1872 he had pursued a different pathway, aiming for a Supreme Court ruling. In a probate court in Salt Lake City, he represented a party in a case designated as *Ferris v. Higley*. The dispute was a relatively minor one that resulted in a judgment of $1,000. In the probate court's decision, Baskin saw an opportunity to send the question of jurisdiction in Utah's courts to the U.S. Supreme Court. He sought a precedent-setting opinion that would reverse *Englebrecht v.*

---

[57]"A Lawyers' Memorial," *DN*, March 11, 1874, 8/3.
[58]Poland Act of 1874, 18 Stat. 253.
[59]"The Poland Act, 1874," http://law2.umkc.edu/faculty/projects/FTrials/mountainmeadows/polandact.html, accessed April 2012.

Clinton, which placed jurisdiction in jury selection with local probate courts, requiring that they be impaneled according to territorial law. *Ferris v. Higley* was appealed to the district court and then sent by writ of error to the U.S. Supreme Court.[60] The high court's ruling, finally made in October 1874, concluded: "The [1852] act of the Territorial legislature conferring general jurisdiction in chancery and at law on the Probate Courts *is, therefore, void.*"[61]

The relationship of the Poland Act and *Ferris v. Higley* is puzzling.[62] Why did the Supreme Court rule in *Ferris v. Higley* in October if Congress had removed general jurisdiction from the probate courts by the Poland Act in the previous June? Since the 1872 initiation of Utah's court action of *Ferris v. Higley* preceded the effective date of 1874 for Poland Act, the act evidently made the *Ferris v. Higley* decision nugatory before it was rendered.

In *Reminiscences*, Baskin addressed the issues of whether all the decisions made by the probate courts over the twenty-two years prior to *Ferris v. Higley* (and the Poland Act, although Baskin did not name it) were void. He showed no reluctance to raise the issue when he boldly stated that from the time the legislature acted in 1852 "the probate courts continued to exercise illegally [their] general, civil and criminal jurisdiction." It was his further legal opinion that "practically all the legal business . . . transacted in the probate courts of the Territory," and therefore "all the judgments and decrees rendered in said courts were void."[63] If Baskin's interpretation of the after-the-fact application of *Ferris v. Higley* had been the prevailing judiciary opinion, it would have resulted in a judicial circus with all convictions, rulings, and even executions during that period void. Chaos would have ensued in Utah Territory. Baskin appears guilty of legal error, for Section 3 of the Poland Bill said: "All judgments and decrees heretofore rendered by the probate courts which have been executed, and the time to appeal from which has by the existing laws of said Territory expired, are hereby validated and confirmed."[64]

At a personal level, any retroactive extension could have opened

---

[60]Baskin, *REM*, 59–60.

[61]*Ferris v. Higley*, 87 U.S. 375; italics added.

[62]Legal opinion regarding the implications of *Ferris v. Higley* and its relationship to the Poland Act was kindly provided by Salt Lake City attorney Kenneth L. Cannon II.

[63]Baskin, *REM*, 59.

[64]The Poland Bill, Sec. 3, in *Compiled Laws of Utah, 1888*, 1:104. Orson Whitney did not pass up the opportunity to point out Baskin's error. Whitney, *Popular History of Utah*, 294n.

Baskin to criticism by the Mormons, since the divorce Olive Lavinia Gardner Stafford obtained in Utah, clearing the way for her marriage to Robert Baskin, would have been void if *Ferris v. Higley*, rather than the Poland Act, had been held applicable. Olive Baskin could then have been charged with bigamy for living as the wife of and bearing three children with Baskin while she had not been legally divorced from her first husband.[65] Baskin left no record that this possibility came to mind.

The Poland Act's passage was aided by Utah bar association members, including Maxwell and Baskin, together with many influential non-Mormons. Ann Eliza Webb Dee Young, divorced wife of Brigham Young, influenced thousands in presentations on the Chautauqua Circuit. In the nation's capital, William Horace Clagett of Montana, Samuel Augustus Merritt of Idaho, and Pennsylvania's James Scott Negley all worked with Luke Poland of Vermont for at least two years. Poland explained the background of his involvement: During 1872 he was in Utah for professional reasons and made the acquaintance many members of the Utah bar. In consequence of these friendships, the gentlemen made their appeal to him. He said he had, "to a considerable extent," prepared the Poland Bill and had introduced it and urged its passage.[66]

Gone, said the *Salt Lake Tribune*, was "the judicial blockade that effectively stayed the arm of justice in Utah for many years."[67] The U.S. marshal now had the power to summon juries and execute all processes issuing from the federal courts, and the U.S. district attorney had the power to prosecute criminal cases arising in these courts. "Polygamy and Murder No Longer Justified," trumpeted the *Tribune*.[68] The most notable immediate outcome of the Poland Act was the impaneling of a grand jury to address the 1857 killings at Mountain Meadows. Seventeen years late, arrest warrants were issued for nine southern Utah men. The arrest and trial of Mormon leader John Doyle Lee at Beaver, Utah, would again unite the efforts of Robert Newton Baskin and George R. Maxwell.

---

[65]Baskin was criticized by the Mormons for helping Olive Gardner Stafford obtain a divorce in a Utah probate court while believing that such authority should not be in the probate court's jurisdiction.

[66]"Poland Act, 1874."

[67]"The Day of Jubilee," *SLT*, June 24, 1874, 1/2.

[68]"Ad Majoriam De Gloriam," *SLT*, June 24, 1874, 1/3.

BASKIN AS A LADY'S MAN

According to historian Jeffrey Nichols, Kate Flint, an entrepreneurial woman, first opened a house of prostitution in Corinne about 1870, anticipating that business would arise upon completion of the transcontinental railroad near that city. By 1872 Flint moved her operations to Commercial Street in Salt Lake City. On August 29 ill-reputed Salt Lake policeman Jeter Clinton, only days fresh from his stay in the Utah Territorial Penitentiary under charges of the murder of John Banks, called together a crew of the unquestioning faithful, composed of Andrew Burt, John D. T. McAllister, Brigham Y. Hampton, Charley Crow, and Bill Hyde. Armed with the authority of his office and the support of Mormon leaders, Clinton was bent on unleashing his hatred of prostitution. It was an assignment very much like that carried out on Paul Englebrecht's liquor store, with the complete destruction of the store and its contents. Allegedly under instructions from the city council but, according to the *Tribune*, on the direction of Brigham Young, Clinton and his deputies destroyed the furniture and other possessions of Flint and Cora Conway, her partner.[69] Another similarity followed when Flint and Conway, like Englebrecht, hired Robert Baskin in a suit for damages. Claiming losses of more than $9,000, the women sued for triple damages, but the trial awarded Flint only $7,000 and Conway $3,700. By the time the case was appealed to the U.S. Supreme Court and completed five years later, Clinton and friends had declared bankruptcy, and with the death of Brigham Young a month earlier, they had no source of money. Coming against the city, Baskin and his clients faced Mayor Feramorz Little, who was not impartial, for his mother was Susan Young, a sister of Brigham Young. A many-wife polygamist, Little had married Fannie Maria Decker in 1846; she was the sister of Lucy and Clara Decker, both wives of Brigham Young. Conflict of interest also arose from Little's 1858 marriage to Julia A. Hampton, the younger sister of one of the accused, Brigham Y. Hampton. The mayor was compelled to turn to city funds and awarded $3,400 to Flint and $2,600 to Conway.[70] Protecting the legal rights of the city prostitutes was unlikely to endear Baskin to either Mormons or non-Mormons, but he did not shirk the task.

---

[69]Nichols, *Prostitution, Polygamy, and Power*, 27–30.
[70]Flint v. Clinton, case no. 554, Third District Court Files, 1877; "Come Down!" *SLT*, September 21, 1877, 4/5.

7

"The Canker Worm of Their Souls Ever Since"

Those who can make you believe absurdities can make you commit atrocities.
VOLTAIRE

*The poet's imagination can not picture, nor the historian's pen describe,
the slaughter of the emigrants.*
ROBERT N. BASKIN

ON HIS ARRIVAL IN UTAH, ROBERT BASKIN FOUND IT beyond belief that the killing of at least 120 Arkansas emigrants eight years earlier had been "ordered by Mormon officials and carried out by a militia force of Mormons." However, this was the assertion of virtually all non-Mormons he met in Salt Lake City.[1] Baskin was soon convinced by discussion with Stephen DeWolfe, who, as editor of the *Valley Tan*, had published articles on the Parrish, Jones, and Aiken murders in central Utah and on the Mountain Meadows murders.

DeWolfe's articles had earned him a visit by several Mormons, including the city's mayor, Abraham O. Smoot, and headed by Dr. Jeter Clinton, police magistrate and Mormon tough and enforcer. Clinton threatened DeWolfe's life, pending a retraction.[2] Hardly cowed,

---

[1]Baskin, *REM*, 83.
[2]"Affairs in Utah," *NYT*, March 2, 1860. Clinton was alleged to have killed apostate John Banks by pithing his spinal cord; he was also implicated in the death of Dr. John King Robinson and in other murders.

DeWolfe published further: "There is incontestable proof that men have been murdered in this Territory whose death was . . . decided upon in meetings over which a person holding a high position in the Mormon church presided." He offered "not a word of retraction." Shortly thereafter, Arthur Stayner, Brigham Young's tithing clerk, entered the law office. With uplifted hands and in the name of Jesus Christ, Stayner pronounced a curse upon DeWolfe. According to the journalist, the curse was "from head to toe and wound up by cursing my powers and parts of procreation, at which I took him by the collar and ejected him." Baskin's decision to join DeWolfe in a law partnership was influenced by DeWolfe's resolve in facing down Mormon threats.[3]

Any administration of justice to the perpetrators was long delayed. Federal judge John Cradlebaugh attempted to bring southern Utah men to trial in 1859, but marshals were unable to serve any of forty warrants. All those named in indictments were forewarned and scattered into hiding. As late as 1873, Judge Jacob Smith Boreman noted that it was widely known that a number of the Mormon militia leaders were hiding out of the territory, yet the Mormon territorial legislature refused funds for the pursuit and arrest of any residing outside the territory.[4] Now empowered by the provisions of the Poland Act, where exclusive jurisdiction for criminal cases was remanded to Utah's district courts and federal judges, U.S. marshals regained exclusive authority in criminal matters and could make arrests and belatedly deal with the crimes.

Baskin was convinced that the Mountain Meadows killings had been orchestrated by Brigham Young and his cabal, but it was not until 1875, eighteen years after the fact, that John D. Lee was prosecuted for murder by Baskin and William Carey before Judge Boreman's Second District court in Beaver, Utah.[5] Even in Jefferson County, Ohio, the delayed judicial process in Utah was newsworthy: "Years have passed since a party of emigrants . . . were murdered in cold blood at Mountain Meadows in Utah. . . . [S]ubsequent developments leave no doubt that the whole slaughter was planned and perpetrated by the Mormons themselves."[6]

---

[3]Baskin, *REM*, 83–84.

[4]Even after Lee's trials, Boreman continued seeking federal funds for the capture of fugitives outside the territory. Arrington, *Crusade against Theocracy*, 16–17.

[5]Maxwell, *GGSL*, 207–17.

[6]"Twenty Years Ago, the Great Mormon Crimes at Mountain Meadows—Will the Murderers Ever Be Brought to Justice?" *Steubenville (Ohio) Daily Herald and News*, October 20, 1874, 1/4.

PROSECUTOR IN THE FIRST LEE TRIAL

It was more than momentary shock at the deceit surrounding the Mountain Meadows murders that led Robert Baskin to suspend his law practice and appear in the district courtrooms of Beaver, Utah, in 1875. His motive was to see justice done, most particularly to Brigham Young, whose hands he saw as incarnadine with unequivocally held responsibility. In addition he sought recognition that innocent young children had unjustly been provided no care or compensation by the people who made them orphans.[7] Baskin drafted a congressional bill proposing that a quarter section of public land be awarded to each survivor of the massacre. Introduced by an Arkansas representative, the bill did not reach passage.[8]

As with the murder of Dr. Robinson, Mountain Meadows was a lifelong concern to Baskin. Years after the Lee trials, Baskin indefatigably pursued facts about the massacre. In 1912, at age seventy-five, he interviewed an eighty-two-year-old former southern Utah resident, Mrs. Julia F. Thompson, and recorded her account of the times and of George A. Smith's preaching disfellowship for any Mormon aiding the Arkansas group.[9]

In the spring of 1875, Robert Baskin was approved by U.S. attorney general George H. Williams to assist Utah's federal attorney William C. Carey in the prosecution of John D. Lee.[10] Jabez Gridley Sutherland and former U.S. attorney George Caesar Bates, together with Enos D. Hoge, Wells Spicer, William W. Bishop, and John McFarlane, were bundled as Lee's defenders, courtesy of LDS Church funding by Brigham Young.[11] Bagley suggests Young's confidence that he could control the outcome of the trial was a "disastrous miscalculation," for it again brought "the story of the massacre and all its horrors to a national audience."[12] Then as now, the journalist's

[7]Baskin, *REM*, 135. While researching the Luttrell Bill, Baskin unearthed proof that others had been concerned with the children's welfare: an 1860 Senate bill granted land to the massacre's surviving children. Unable to find the bill's author or fate, he assumed it had originated with an Arkansas or Texas senator. "Washington," *SLT*, April 5, 1876, 4/3.

[8]Baskin, *REM*, 141.

[9]Ibid., 109. Census records for 1910 confirmed that Julia Thompson, age eighty, was widowed and living with her daughter. Thompson died in 1916 and was buried in Mount Olivet Cemetery.

[10]Baskin, *REM*, 56–57. D. P. Whedon was also a member of the prosecution panel. Maxwell, *GGSL*, 215n33.

[11]McFarlane was also William Dame's attorney and an eyewitness to the massacre. Bagley, *BOP*, 298. Enos D. Hoge, from Illinois, had been appointed associate justice to the territory's supreme court on July 27, 1868; he would later join Baskin as his law partner.

[12]Bagley, *BOP*, 291.

instincts dictated that if it bleeds, it leads. Intense interest in the trail was acknowledged by *Salt Lake Tribune* editor Frederic Lockley, in Beaver preparing daily reports for his editorials. He observed that the town was "full of strangers" and "hard-pressed to provide rooms for all the lawyers, soldiers, and curious outsiders."[13] A *Tribune* article virtually shouted that the trial had "more than a local interest": "IT IS NATIONAL."[14]

Baskin's involvement resulted, in part, from concern over William Carey's ability to compete against the army of astute lawyers hired by Mormon money. Several July letters from Lockley to his wife reveal the anxiety also held by Marshal Maxwell and non-Mormons among the nearby mine workers regarding Carey's legal skills. "It is firm that Carey is not the right man. . . . Sutherland carries too many guns . . . and will be apt to head him at every point." Lockley wrote that Maxwell had brought word that "miners in Star district will to-day petition Carey to associate one or two able lawyers with him in the prosecution, they offering to pay the expenses."[15] Lockley was influenced by an earlier episode in which Carey's allegiance was also brought into question. When asked by a book vendor for his opinion of textbooks best suited for the schools of Utah, Carey responded he would need to consult with Hiram B. Clawson, Brigham Young's son-in-law and business manager and the former head of the Mormons' retail store, ZCMI. The *Tribune* concluded that Carey was "owned, body and soul by the Mormon Church and carried in the breeches pocket of Brigham Young."[16] Four days after expressing his doubts, Lockley wrote again to his wife, relieved that Carey would have assistance: "Baskin's appearance upon the scene is our salvation. He tells me Carey wrote to him to come. . . . Without this able and fearless attorney, the prosecution would have made a complete failure of the trial."[17] Baskin arrived in Beaver on the torrid summer day of July 18, 1875. He was described by the *Tribune* as the "distinguished criminal

---

[13]Ibid., 300.

[14]"The Butcher Lee," *SLT*, January 22, 1875, 4/2; capital letters in the original. In his closing statement Carey claimed that the murders were of "odious repute all over Europe." "Equal and Exact Justice," *SLT*, August 4, 1875, 2/1.

[15]Lockley to Lockley, July 17, 1875, Frederic E. Lockley Papers. George Q. Cannon's letter to Brigham Young assessing Carey as not "vindictive" may have been a coded opinion that Cannon considered Carey a weak opponent. Cannon to Young, December 10 and 12, 1872, Brigham Young Collection, cited in Bagley, *BOP*, 282.

[16]"Owned by Brigham," *SLT*, April 29, 1876, 4/2.

[17]Lockley to Lockley, Beaver, Utah, July 22, 1875, Frederic E. Lockley Papers.

lawyer" from Salt Lake City, preparing for "the most important criminal case ever tried in the United States."[18]

Lockley had difficulty finding time for sharing Baskin's energy. Each
evening, the persistent, motivated Baskin was so "full of the Lee trial
that we talk it over till 12 every night." Lockley added, "He says he has
waited ten years to see this day."[19] From when he first heard the details
of the massacre from DeWolfe, Baskin was "convinced of the complicity of the Mormons" and "made a memorandum of the facts and the
names of the participants, as from time to time I learned them." In
Reminiscences, Baskin repeatedly entered fifty-two as the number of
white participants.[20] However, only nine men were ordered arrested.[21]

U.S. marshal George R. Maxwell and his deputies served 260
subpoenas to 160 individuals as suspects or witnesses, as Carey and
Baskin prepared the prosecution.[22] Lee's trial began on July 23, 1875,
and the *Tribune* forewarned its readers, "It is not likely a verdict will
be found."[23] A number of the witnesses had been participants in the
killings. One such, Joel White, was brought in by Bill Hickman, who
was described by the *Tribune* as Maxwell's chief of staff.[24] Evidence
of the national publicity the trial generated was the report of witness
Philip Klingensmith's testimony published in Steubenville, Ohio: "I
met Ira Allen and he said that the emigrant's doom was sealed and the
die cast for their destruction. . . . Higbee had command. . . . [I]t was
the Nauvoo legion, organized by tens and hundreds. They marched
in sight of the emigrant train, and Lee went out with a white flag."[25]

On July 27, Baskin and Sutherland became engaged in a "keen
encounter" over the wan defense paraphrased as "the Indians made us
do it." According to Sutherland, the massacre was perpetrated by the

---

[18]"The Lee Trial," *SLT*, July 19, 1875, 1/3.

[19]Lockley to Lockley, Beaver, Utah, July 26, 1875, Frederic E. Lockley Papers.

[20]Baskin did not cite fifty-two names. The number "fifty-two" in *Reminiscences* may have been
given Baskin by Lee or derived over time by Baskin's own tally. Bigler and Bagley cite the
number of white perpetrators at seventy; Carleton's report gave the number as fifty or sixty.
Bigler and Bagley, *Mormon Rebellion*, 172, 176.

[21]The nine were John Doyle Lee, William Horne Dame, Isaac Chauncey Haight, John Mount
Higbee, Philip Klingensmith, William Cameron Stewart, George Washington Adair, Jr.,
Samuel Jewkes, and Ellott Willden.

[22]Maxwell, *GGSL*, 215.

[23]"The Lee Trial," *SLT*, July 23, 1875, 1/6.

[24]"Obedience to Counsel," *SLT*, July 31, 1875, 4/2. A brief time before, Hickman had been freed
from prison by the Englebrecht decision; he was appointed by Governor Emery to assist
Maxwell, including the transfer of Lee to the territorial penitentiary. Maxwell, *GGSL*, 222–24.

[25]"By Telegraph: A Tale of Horror," *Steubenville Daily Herald*, July 24, 1875, 1/4.

Indians, who "were the masters of the situation, and compelled the whites to take part in the butchery by threats." Baskin countered "with abundant authority to sustain his view," that even if such a preposterous assertion were true, it could not justify unlawful killing. Baskin insisted, on the authority of English jurist William Blackstone, that "a man under duress is not justified in killing an innocent party, because his social duty requires him to give up his own life rather than take the life of an unoffending person."[26] Wells Spicer's defense blamed the victims and held that rash acts of Arkansas people had led to the emigrants' deaths, since "a state of war existed in Utah . . . with vast armies . . . approaching to exterminate the Mormons."[27]

Sutherland asked Judge Boreman to allow the depositions taken in Salt Lake City from Brigham Young and George A. Smith to be telegraphed and introduced into evidence. "I will make a showing that they are unable to make that journey," offered Sutherland. Baskin immediately answered, "We are able to make the showing that they are able." Baskin held that Brigham Young feigned invalidism, lest he be subjected to the incisive questions Baskin would ask in an intense, probing cross-examination in Beaver.[28] A physician's affidavit was sent, stating that the two witnesses were unable to travel. Depositions taken in Salt Lake City were sent to Beaver, but Boreman denied the motion to place such ex parte material into the court record as evidence. Carey exposed the ruse, observing that, with proper notice, depositions from Young and Smith could have been taken in Salt Lake City, with Carey and Baskin present for cross-examination.[29] George A. Smith's plea of ill health was not far from the mark, for two months later he died of heart failure.

Lockley was impressed with Baskin's handling of the trial, reporting to his wife: "[He] has done nobly, as he always does when he is working for the people. In his argument he intends to make a scathing arraignment of Brigham Young."[30] Baskin compared the John D. Lee trial with the *Dred Scott* case, in which Scott was more than a symbol, but "the whole system of negro slavery was involved." So it was with the Mountain Meadows affair: "In as much as this crime was

---

[26]Fielding and Fielding, *Tribune Reports*, 133–34.

[27]"The Lee Trial," *SLT*, July 30, 1875, 1/2.

[28]For an account of Young's vigorous life while alleging to be an invalid, see Maxwell, *GGSL*, 215n30.

[29]Transcript of the First Trial of John D. Lee.

[30]Lockley to Lockley, Beaver, Utah, July 31, 1875, Frederic E. Lockley Papers.

concocted by the leaders of the Mormon Church . . . I am willing to accept . . . that it is the Mormon Church that is now on trial."[31] In his five-hour closing-argument marathon, Baskin aimed less at Mormon Militia major John D. Lee, in the defendant's seat, than at the militia's highest commander, who was not present:

> I arraign Brigham Young as an accessory of the massacre, because considering the power he had over his people, no man . . . would have dared . . . such a heinous scheme, if he hadn't the direct or implied sanction of the head of the church. . . . I not only arraign Brigham Young as accessory . . . but also as having violated his oath of office in failing to do what both his official duty and the common dictates of humanity required of him, which was to prevent the little children who were saved from being robbed; to have the property of the emigrants collected and sold and the proceeds appropriated to the nurture and education of those children.[32]

Those doing the killing were members of both the LDS Church and the Utah Militia, formerly called the Nauvoo Legion when the Saints were in Illinois. There is no surprise that neither of the two stake presidents, William Dame and Isaac Haight, convened a church court to investigate themselves and their neighbors. Neither would Utah Militia officers Colonel Dame, Major Haight, and Major Lee, commanding Companies A to H of the Iron County Brigade, investigate themselves in a military court. If Brigham Young and Daniel H. Wells, commanders at the highest level of Utah's territorial militia, had any genuine interest in seeing justice done for the victims, they held the authority and the responsibility to do so, reasoned Baskin.[33] In his summation, Baskin charged that this critical omission on Young's part remained as the most potent argument for his complicity and cover-up: If the killings had been done by southern Utah militiamen gone rogue, countermanding or exceeding the authority and

---

[31]Arrington, "Crusade against Theocracy," 43n60.

[32]Baskin, *REM*, 135. Baskin's report that Young was "beyond doubt the leading instigator of the massacre" appeared in California newspapers—e.g., "The Utah Massacre: The Closing Argument," *Alta California*, August 6, 1875. The Arkansas group was an argosy, sailing on the grass sea, well stocked with clothing, arms, weapons, gold, and livestock. Polly Aird suggests that their commodities—all desperately needed by Mormons preparing for war—were among the Mormons' objectives. Aird, review of Bigler and Bagley, *Innocent Blood*, 259.

[33]Walker, Turley, and Leonard's book, *Massacre at Mountain Meadows*, perpetuates the conclusion that local men, acting in their military and ecclesiastical roles, did so without Brigham Young's permission or knowledge. Their book does not deal with the many years of the camarilla's cover-up.

instructions given them by superior officers, an emergency military tribunal should have been immediately convened. "Common humanity" demanded that Young, Wells, and the Militia leadership should have had the "hearts of men" and arrested those who led the massacre, "tried them by drumhead court-martial and . . . blown them away at the mouths of muskets." Baskin asked, "Why was it not done?"[34]

Baskin focused on Brigham Young for another reason as well: he anticipated the outcome of the trial already fixed, admitting: "If any one of this jury is a member of the Mormon church, I don't expect any verdict. . . . [If he wears the endowment garments and] took an oath of obedience and laid down his individuality, no evidence can . . . induce such a man . . . to find a verdict of guilty, and I do not expect it."[35] Baskin's assessment was accurate. Nine jurors—eight Mormon men and one ex-Mormon—stood for acquittal, and three non-Mormons voted for conviction. The *Tribune* observed, "More evidence was disclosed in the jury room by Mormon jurymen, who 'never heard of the massacre,' than was elicited on the witness stand."[36] A deadlocked jury resulted in a mistrial and failure to convict.[37] The *Tribune*, not surprised by this outcome, saw in it a potential advantage: "The trial will . . . demonstrate the futility of applying the ordinary methods of administering justice in a community which refuses to recognize the principles upon which all law is based."[38] Lockley added, "We are all hoping this will be the result, as the attention of the whole country is directed to this trial. . . . [I]t will render the insufficiency of the Poland bill so manifest, that Congress cannot fail to give us additional legislation."[39]

The failure of the jury to reach a verdict of conviction led to howls from newspaper editors across the United States. These articles included one penned by Ann Eliza Webb Dee Young, Brigham Young's whilom wife, who charged that "The blood of murdered Americans and their wives and daughters and little ones that cries out vengeance has been spit upon by the remorseless despotism that rules

---

[34]Transcript of the First Trial of John D. Lee. Baskin's words "drumhead court-martial" and "blown them away" suggest he was alluding to the well-known British practice in India regarding those found guilty—in an immediate on-the-field trial—of the barbaric killing of women and children. Punishment was also immediate: they were secured over the cannon's mouth, or a few feet in front, when it was then fired.

[35]Baskin, *REM*, 135–36.

[36]"The Verdict," *SLT*, August 8, 1875.

[37]For other details of Lee's first trial, see Maxwell, *GGSL*, 207–22.

[38]"Brigham's Great Crime," *SLT*, August 7, 1875, 2/2.

[39]Lockley to Lockley, Beaver, Utah, July 31, 1875, Frederic E. Lockley Papers.

Utah."[40] Drawing criticism that the prosecution did not try John D. Lee, Baskin admitted to the charge: "The Mormon Church was on trial. . . . I do hold Brigham Young responsible; I do hold the system which . . . distinctly teaches . . . and practices the shedding of human blood to atone for real and imaginary offenses. I hold, I arraign this iniquitous system, and the leaders of the church."[41]

Apostates' Fear of Retribution

The end of the Lee trial left the non-Mormons of Beaver feeling threatened. They petitioned Utah's governor, George W. Emery, and Gen. Cuvier Grover for an increase in troops at nearby Camp Cameron, stating this was needed for "the well-being and safety of the loyal citizens of Southern Utah."[42] They reasoned: "We deem it highly essential to the safety of our people that the garrison be increased. . . . [The] infantry would be powerless . . . in the mountains. One or two good cavalry companies would accomplish more than all the infantry put together." Behind their concern was that "Haight, Higbee, Stewart, and a number of other Mountain Meadows murderers are yet fugitives in the mountains about Cedar City and St. George." Their petition further emphasized, "We are greatly in the minority and were it not for the presence of the military, *we would not be safe in the enjoyment of life, liberty, or property*." This *Tribune* report, signed by an apostate Mormon, G. W. Crouch, added that all non-Mormons of the area signed the petition, at least all those who were able to get "sight of it."[43] This plea for federal protection gives evidence that a climate of violence still existed in Utah in 1875.

The Church Stiffs Its Enigmatic Lawyer

The role of George Caesar Bates on Lee's defense team is as convoluted and puzzling as Baskin's is straightforward. Born in New York,

---

[40]Lockley, *Lee Trial!* 53–64.

[41]Arrington, "Crusade against Theocracy," 43n60.

[42]Grover, from Maine, was an 1850 graduate of West Point. During the 1857–58 Utah War, he served as a captain at Camp Scott in the Tenth Infantry under Colonel Johnston. He lost one arm in a Civil War battle in 1864.

[43]"Troops for Beaver," *SLT*, September 7, 1875, 4/3; italics added. Crouch, a schoolteacher, his wife, Elizabeth C., and their daughters, Nancy and Eleanor, are listed in the 1870 census with a note "am" in the margin, identifying them as apostate Mormons. Other names are marked with the letter *g*, identifying the individual as a "Gentile."

Bates followed a legal career as a U.S. attorney in Michigan. There he prosecuted James J. Stang—a former Nauvoo Mormon who had vied with Brigham Young for leadership after Joseph Smith's death—for counterfeiting and other federal charges. Bates then went to Chicago, where his office and books were destroyed in the city's catastrophic fire in 1871.[44] A December 1871 letter from Hiram B. Clawson to Brigham Young reported that Clawson and Charles H. Hempstead had discussed Bates's qualifications and had been assured by Bates that he had "no prejudice or hatred for the Mormons." After Clawson's approval, Hempstead had telegraphed Bates: "By all means accept appointment and come as soon as possible." Clawson added, "[Members of] the Ring were ignorant of Bates['s] whereabouts and did not look for him until the last of the week. On . . . the day set apart for [Brigham Young's] . . . trial, Baskin appeared in Court, took the Oath and at once assumed the duties of his office."[45] On appointment as U.S. attorney to Utah, he required a $500 advance for transportation to Salt Lake City. Another letter from Hiram Clawson to Brigham Young said "The change . . . will be a change for the better. I have some good reasons for saying this."[46] Bates received approval from Attorney General Amos T. Ackerman to hire Robert Baskin to assist in the murder prosecution of William Adams Hickman. When Bates let the action lie fallow, Baskin implied bribery as the cause, in light of Bates's sympathy with the Mormons, whereupon Baskin resigned his assistant attorney position.[47] President Grant asked for Bates's resignation and replaced him with William Carey, whereupon Bates appeared opposite Baskin and Carey on the Mormon payroll to defend Lee. Historian Hubert Howe Bancroft states plainly the lawyers representing Lee were also "the attorneys of the first presidency," and Baskin confirmed their paymasters with equal simplicity: "They were not employed by Lee."[48] In his papers, Judge Boreman relates an

---

[44]The 1870 federal census for Illinois, Cook County, Chicago, First Ward, lists George C. Bates, age fifty-five, born in New York, a lawyer, with property evaluated at $10,000; he lived alone with a doctor, a publisher, and an architect as neighbors.

[45]Clawson to Young, December 11, 1871, CR 1234 1, box 34, folder 3, reel 46, LDS Church History Library.

[46]Clawson to Young, November 15, 1871, CR 1234 1, box 34, folder 3, reel 46, LDS Church History Library.

[47]Evidence at Lee's first trial embarrassingly revealed that while he was the U.S. attorney, Bates had also made a brief, desultory attempt to bring action against the Mountain Meadows perpetrators.

[48]Baskin, *REM*, 114.

incident wherein Bates, without the knowledge of Sutherland, proposed that William Stewart, John M. Higbee, and Isaac Haight would present themselves if Boreman would promise to immediately release them on bail. Infuriated at the legal chicanery, Boreman threatened Bates's disbarment but in the end only fined him $50.[49]

Following the Beaver mistrial, Bates returned to Salt Lake City and within months was discoursing as though he had converted into the priesthood. In Mormon meetings he preached that "all the Gentiles who have come to Utah . . . are hoodlums of the most disreputable character, seeking to provoke trouble and then fatten upon the spoils." He implored the sisters "not to patronize the Gentile schools for their little dears might be contaminated by the hoodlums, imported from Babylon."[50] Bates may have been seeking absolution for his letter to the *Salt Lake Tribune*, written during the period he served on Lee's defense team in the first trial. In it, he gave up the names of the murderers, admitting that "the massacre was consummated by [George A.] Smith, Haight, Higby [*sic*], Lee, and Bill Stuart [*sic*]."[51]

In April 1877 a district court petition was entered, bringing up another call for Bates to be disbarred. He was charged with unprofessional conduct, dishonorable propositions for business, and rascally professional relations. Bates was to explain his connection with the clandestine divorce business in Utah, recently exposed by the *Tribune*, which accused him of misusing a surname so divorce-related mailings coming to his office would be disguised.

In 1877 Sutherland transferred his portion of fees owed him for the Lee trial to Bates, who asked Baskin and DeWolfe to bring suit against Young as the trustee-in-trust for the church "to recover for the services so performed, as payment of a large portion thereof had been refused by Brigham."[52] The *Tribune* cited $5,000 due Bates.[53] LDS Church attorneys denied the complaint on grounds that the legislation incorporating the church did not grant the authority to employ the two men. Bates instructed Baskin to move against Young, not as trustee, but as personally responsible. Baskin reports: "I drew a complaint, as requested, and sought Mr. Bates . . . but instead of finding

---

[49]Arrington, *Crusade against Theocracy*, 31–32.

[50]"The Rev. George Caesar," *SLT*, December 8, 1875, 2/1.

[51]"Letter from Geo C. Bates," *SLT*, August 7, 1875, 4/5.

[52]Baskin, *REM*, 113.

[53]The sum was for services between August 17, 1875, and May 20, 1877. "Sacrilege," *SLT*, August 16, 1877, 4/2.

him, I ascertained that he had entered into a written marriage contract with a 'doctoress,' and that they had left the Territory."[54] Young's
death in August 1877 ended Bates's colorful pursuit of life with the
Saints. By June 1880 he had repaired to Leadville, Colorado, to reap
the rewards of litigating in the boom of Babylon's silver mining; he
was married, living alone in a hotel and listing his occupation as an
attorney.[55] Bates did not find the Lion of the Lord to be a grateful or
generous paymaster, and LDS Church attorneys found legally plausible
reasons to deny payment for his services.

LEE'S SECOND TRIAL

Lee was held at the territorial prison in the period before his second
trial in Beaver.[56] All his visitors brought a similar message: admit all,
name the other perpetrators, and make a self-serving bargain with the
prosecution. But to all he answered, "I would never PurJure Myself to
get out," adding, "& thus we parted."[57]

In September 1876, Lee again faced Judge Jacob Smith Boreman,
but William Carey and Robert Baskin were no longer the prosecution
team. Newly appointed U.S. attorney Sumner Howard was assigned
to the task, with assistance from attorneys Presley Denney and
Enos D. Hoge. Maxwell was replaced by Marshal William Nelson,
and Lee's lawyers were now William W. Bishop, Wells Spicer, and
J. C. Foster. Jury selection lasted only an hour. Prosecuting attorney
Howard skirted prosecutorial misconduct by peremptorily challenging every non-Mormon candidate. The astonishing result was a jury
intentionally packed with Mormons, accomplished by the non-Mormon prosecuting attorney. Howard then gave surprising notice that
Philip Klingensmith, the star witness of the first trial, was in Salt
Lake City but would not testify.[58] The first witness was Daniel H.

---

[54]Baskin, *REM*, 114.

[55]From the 1880 federal census for Leadville, Colorado.

[56]Lee had been released on $15,000 bail, supplied by William Hooper. Hooper withdrew his
   bail bond just before the start of the second trial, sending Lee back to prison—an unmistakable sign the climate had changed.

[57]Cleland and Brooks, *Mormon Chronicle*, 376–77.

[58]Also not called was Gilbert Morse, Lee's brother-in-law and an apostate Mormon who had
   moved to California in 1861. He was to tell of Lee's role and to testify that the responsibility
   "rests morally upon every man who holds the Mormon Priesthood." "Gilbert Morse," *SLT*,
   September 28, 1876, 4/2.

Wells, of the triumvirate presidency of the church.[59] According to Judge Boreman, Wells made neither complaint nor comment on the seating of an all-Mormon jury but "located himself in a place facing the jury so that the jury could see him." Boreman judged Wells was asked no relevant questions and struck his testimony, confiding in his journal that Wells's appearance was "to let the jury see that the church was on the side of the prosecution."[60] In the first trial, which lasted thirteen days, not a single Mormon appeared for the prosecution. In this second trial, Jacob Hamblin, among several other Mormon witnesses, experienced a remarkable recovery of memory and speech and provided explicit testimony of Lee's butchery.[61]

Baskin was one of the many to cry foul at the second trial's proceedings. While convinced of Lee's guilt, Baskin was adamant a verdict should not be found by elements outside the evidence or by a jury intentionally packed with Mormons under church instructions to bring a guilty verdict. It is likely that Enos Hoge shared his detailed knowledge of Sumner Howard with Baskin during the time of their later partnership, for in his memoirs, Baskin wrote: "I have not the least doubt . . . Brigham Young entered into an arrangement with District Attorney Howard, that a Mormon jury should be impaneled to convict Lee . . . [a]nd that he [Howard] should exonerate the authorities of the Mormon church of complicity in the massacre."[62] Boreman added corroboration when he recorded: "It began slowly to dawn upon the minds of the people that Howard had made some kind of deal with the heads of the church, whereby witnesses who had been hiding were brought forth and their tongues loosened."[63] In his summation

---

[59]"Territorial Dispatches: The Lee Trial," *DN*, September 20, 1876, 12/2.

[60]Arrington, "Crusade against Theocracy," 42–43.

[61]Laban Morrill, James Haslam, Joel White, Samuel McMurdy, Nephi Johnson, and Samuel Knight are named as witnesses by Bagley, *BOP*, 304. See also "Territorial Dispatches: The Lee Trial," 12/1. Testimony also implied that Lee was a rapist.

[62]Baskin, *REM*, 136.

[63]Arrington, "Crusade against Theocracy," 43. Howard remains an elusive character. After his Utah post, he returned a wealthy man to Flint, Michigan, where he practiced law and was elected to the legislature. In December 1883 he was considered for appointment as chief justice of Utah Territory, prompting Utah attorneys to file a protest resolution: "We cannot believe that a candidate for so high a position, whose reputation was so bad as that of Howard while United States Attorney for Utah, should receive Executive favor." "Protest of Utah Lawyers," *NYT*, December 8, 1883. In Prescott, Arizona, in 1884, he practiced law, was a territorial supreme court justice, and dealt harshly with Mormons. After serving as Prescott's mayor in 1887–88, he returned to Flint, where he died. See also Bigler and Bagley, *Innocent Blood*, 317–20.

Boreman pronounced the massacre was the "result of A VAST CON-
SPIRACY, extending from Salt Lake City to the bloody field."[64]

The affidavit of Brigham Young taken when he was claiming to
be an "invalid" was introduced even though it was not evidence but
ex parte testimony. Over the objections of his defense counsel, Lee
insisted Young's affidavit be admitted. The affidavit was incredulous,
with Young reporting that he knew only vaguely of the Arkansas
company; that he heard of the attack only some later time, from a
"floating rumor"; that he did not instigate an investigation and seek
trial because a new state governor was to be installed; and that he
could not find the critical letter in which he had given written instructions to George A. Smith, who was to meet with Cedar City and
other southern Utah Mormons to relay Young's wishes to them.[65]

Baskin saw the second trial as an attempt by Young to place materials in the public record refuting his own responsibility. Local editors
and journalists elsewhere did not accept Young's plea of innocence,
and another rondo of negative publicity resounded through the
nation's newspapers. "It is adding insult to injury for a man in Young's
position to affront the intelligence of the nation with so bald and so
puerile a tissue of flummery as this. . . . [I]t affords cumulative proof
that he possessed the necessary authority on the premises," said the
Sacramento Record. The *St. Albans Advertiser* of Vermont added, "The
transparent hypocrisy of the entire affidavit is the strongest evidence of
Brigham's complicity in the whole business." The *Leavenworth Commercial* had a similar opinion: "The Mormons are making a desperate
effort to clear Brigham Young of the Mountain Meadows massacre,
but they will never succeed in convincing the world that the old sin-
ner was not guilty of participation in the preliminary to that human
outrage, nor that the work of butchery was not perpetrated with his
sanction, if not by his positive command." The *Indianapolis Herald*
also had its say: "There can be little doubt that Brigham Young is the
arch-fiend who planned and directed the atrocity, and we hope that
the investigation will be prosecuted and every Mormon concerned
in the massacre, from the highest to the lowest, is hung."[66] And in
Helena, Montana, the *Herald* said, "No one who knows the extent of

[64]Fielding and Fielding, *Tribune Reports*, 243; capital letters in the original.
[65]Baskin, REM, 115–17.
[66]Cited in Fielding and Fielding, *Tribune Reports*, 194.

his power . . . can doubt for a moment that this massacre lies at his door, either as a result of his direct order, or at least the natural and necessary result of his teachings."[67] The *Salt Lake Tribune* noted that, in stark contrast, the newspapers of the Mormon Church "have no word of denunciation for the perpetrators of the Mountain Meadows Massacre."[68]

Lee's second trial lasted only six days. The all-Mormon jury brought a unanimous verdict of first-degree murder. He was sentenced to death; he unsuccessfully appealed and was executed by firing squad at the Mountain Meadows site on March 21, 1877. "Unique in the annals of American jurisprudence as examples of jury tampering" are the trials of John D. Lee, "first to exonerate the defendant, then to convict him for the same crime," say the historians of the Mormon rebellion.[69]

In his *Reminiscences*, Baskin devotes more space—sixty-six pages— to the Mountain Meadow massacre than to any other single topic. He records little of Carey, Maxwell, or Judge Boreman but stresses the atmosphere of violence and killing in Utah during the period. Eleven pages are taken to establish that secret Mormon temple and Endowment House ceremonies included an oath to obey the laws of the Mormon church in preference to those of the nation. The penalty—acted out in the ritual—for violating this oath was having one's throat cut from ear to ear. A second oath promised to avenge "the blood of the prophets," with the associated penalty being disembowelment.[70] Many examples from the sermons of Brigham Young and others contain threats of death to sinners, for the blood atonement of sins. Suppose, said Young, "you found your brother in bed with your wife and put a javelin into both of them? You would be justified, and they would atone for their sins and be received into the Kingdom of God."[71] "Rather than that apostates should flourish here, I will unsheath my bowie knife, and conquer or die. Now, you nasty apostates, clear out, or judgment will be put on the line, and righteousness to the plummet," Young cried.[72] "Live here, then, you poor, miserable

---

[67]Baskin, *REM*, 127–28.

[68]"Is the Mormon Church Guilty?" *SLT*, August 7, 1875, 4/2.

[69]Bigler and Bagley, *Mormon Rebellion*, 359.

[70]Confusing to the reader, Baskin cites the testimony of men questioned about Mormon temple practices in 1889, thirteen years after Lee's trial.

[71]Van Wagoner, *CDBY*, 2:1064.

[72]Ibid., 2:642. Note Young's allusion to Masonic symbols in his tirade against apostates.

curses, until the time of retribution, when your heads will have to be severed from your bodies," he threatened.[73] Baskin concluded that the oaths administered in the secret ceremonies of the Mormons initiated and nourished the spirit of violence that had its gruesome climax at Mountain Meadows. He maintained:

> [The killings] were inspired by the throat-cutting sermons and oath-bound covenants of the Mormon church. . . . To call an organization in which such sermons were tolerated, and . . . perpetuated in its official publications, the "Church of Jesus Christ of Latter-day Saints," is a disgraceful profanation of the sacred name of Jesus Christ. These disgusting sermons . . . not only emphasize the absurdity of his assumption of divine agency, but resemble the ravings of a vicious lunatic, and are such as no Christian would deliver.[74]

One hundred fifty-six years after the crime, despite Baskin's reports, despite many professional-quality publications, the degree of responsibility of LDS Church president Brigham Young for the deaths of more than 120 children, women, and men, the failure to provide for the orphans, and the cover-up that lasted almost two decades remain matters of intense opinion and continued controversy. It is as true today as when Thomas B. H. Stenhouse recorded it in 1873 in his history of Utah that "the people were horrified at the deed, and it has been the canker worm of their souls ever since."[75] This pivotal chapter in the history book of the Utah Territory and the Mormons remains open and unfinished.

---

[73]Ibid., 3:1011.
[74]Baskin, *REM*, 110.
[75]Thomas B. H. Stenhouse, *Rocky Mountain Saints*, 358.

8

The Year of the Prophet's Death

A man's dying is more the survivors' affair than his own.
THOMAS MANN

RIGHAM YOUNG'S FINAL MONTHS OF LIFE WERE NOT A crescendo of triumph and victory but a compendium of troubles. Even in April 1876, Young's son Oscar reported his father to be "broke down," saying he "would never be a well man again." Young's ill health on New Year's Day 1877 required that he be carried in a sedan chair as he dedicated the lower story of the St. George Temple.[1] Affected by the tidal wave of negative journalism that followed the farcical trials of John D. Lee, Lee's sacrificial execution, and Lee's published confessions, Brigham Young was no longer the huffing Lion of the Lord but more of an aging lion pacing ground kept painfully hot by mounting criticism. Also troubling was the public's overwhelming opinion of his complicity in the bloodbath at Mountain Meadows, and that punishment was meted to only one man as a disingenuous move to appease the public's demand for justice. On the day Young was attending the St. George Temple's final dedication, the *Salt Lake Tribune* published the *Chicago Inter-Ocean*'s appraisal of him as a remarkable benefactor to his church, but a man whose most monumental failure could not be ignored:

---

[1]Bagley, *BOP*, 322.

[Although he is] suffering from physical infirmities, and troubled beyond measure with cares, anxieties, and assaults from all quarters . . . I doubt if the worst enemies of Brigham Young can deny but he is a man of great energy, determination of purpose, and natural executive ability. . . . The worst thing that lays against him is the insinuations of . . . being a party in the awful business for which he [Lee] suffered death. . . . [T]he plain duty for Brigham Young to retrieve his reputation with the world is now to . . . bring the men . . . engaged in the massacre, to judgment, and facilitate the . . . punishment . . . they deserve.[2]

In April the *Dayton Democrat* of Ohio said of Young: "The presumption of his guilt does not rest merely on Lee's confession . . . but also on the nature and constitution of the Mormon hierarchy and the position of Brigham Young as its directing head. It is one of the most absolute despotisms that ever existed."[3] The *New Orleans Picayune* added, "Young himself is not too old nor too exalted in position to escape the full consequences of complicity, if it be proven that he was connected with it."[4] The *Sharon Springs (N.Y.) Gazette* concluded, "It is not easy to believe otherwise than that Young was the real author of the crime. He was more than king among his people. His subordinates would hardly undertake so foul a deed without his order."[5] Nebraska's *Kearney Press* contributed its opinion: "If his [Lee's] confession is to be believed, Brigham Young is as guilty as himself; for, although Young took no part in the actual butchery, it was done at his instigation and with his connivance."[6] "Not all the rain 'in the sweet heaven,' . . . nor all the witnesses from Adam down to the present hour, could wash away the Prophet's guilt and prove him innocent of the hellish deed at Mountain Meadows," wrote the *San Jose (Calif.) Herald*.[7] Similar castigations of Young were found in the *Alta California*, the *Frankfort (Ky.) Yeoman*, the *Norristown (Pa.) Herald*, and the *Detroit Post*.

Jerome B. Stillson, the *New York Herald* journalist whose investigative travels through southern Utah settlements earned him two attempts on his life, headed this report: "Lee's confession, made in view of death, . . . so plainly incriminates Brigham Young as to leave

---

[2]*Chicago Inter-Ocean*, March 31, 1877, reprinted in "A Father to This People," *slt*, April 8, 1877, 1/6.
[3]"Mormon Record of Blood," *slt*, April 11, 1877, 3/2.
[4]Ibid.
[5]Ibid.
[6]Ibid.
[7]Ibid.

no doubt on the mind of the unprejudiced reader that the Mormon leader was cognizant of that horrible slaughter and a party to it."[8]

Young met other stresses during this time, such as the settlement of Ann Eliza Webb Dee Young's divorce action; the brouhaha over Governor Emery's failure to canvass the election results before awarding the election certificate to George Q. Cannon; Baskin's follow-up contention of Cannon's seat; the combined efforts of federal officials and non-Mormons working with Senator Isaac Christiancy to pass anti-polygamy legislation; attempts by enigmatic lawyer Sumner Howard to try those of the Utah Militia responsible for the 1862 deaths of apostates Joseph Morris, Bella Bowman, and John Banks; and complaints that Sumner Howard and U.S. marshal William Nelson had removed the evidence of Brigham Young's culpability from the pretrial records.

That spring, two sons of John D. Lee were allegedly caught in Young's bedroom, leading to a rumor, later discredited, that they were attempting to poison Young.[9] In May, Jerome Stillson boldly asked Young to supply the 1857 letter delivered by James Haslam from the Mormon men at Mountain Meadow asking for instructions on how the emigrants were to be treated. Stillson also requested Young's letter of reply. Young was not accustomed to such impertinence, and that may explain the two attempts made on Stillson's life.[10] Undeterred, the *New York Herald* published in mid-August that Young "now lives in fear of being indicted and tried for murder," suggesting that safety demanded him to use "a part of his great fortune to buy lands in the northern states of Mexico, and remove his people thither in a body."[11]

Contrary to the contention of Young's poor health was his travel to Cache, Juab, and Sanpete counties to organize stakes of Zion. "Your father's health is good," George Reynolds told Willard Young.[12] Barely two weeks before the Prophet's death, a letter to one of Young's sons

[8]Ibid.

[9]Bagley, *BOP*, 322.

[10]"Attempted Assassinations," *SLT*, June 1, 1877, 4/2.

[11]"A Suggestion to Brigham Young," reprinted in *SLT*, August 15, 1877, 3/2. The *Wilkes-Barre Record* and the *Richmond Enquirer* agreed that the *New York Herald* research into Mountain Meadows would result in Mormon convictions. *SLT*, June 6, 1877, 1/5. In July, Young wrote to Elder J. Z. Stewart, questioning the suitability of land, water, timber, and settlements in the northern Mexican state of Coahuila. Young to Stewart, July 13, 1877, BYLC, CR 1234 1, box 10, vol. 14, 994.

[12]Reynolds to Willard Young, July 3, 1877, BYLC, CR 1234 1, box 10, vol. 14, 974.

said, "Your father's health is good and his spirits are buoyant. I don't know that I ever saw him look or feel better."[13]

However, on August 23, 1877, Young experienced the onset of painful abdominal cramping, followed by nausea and vomiting. His deterioration continued, with abdominal pain, nausea, vomiting, and diarrhea caused by what some historians have labeled perforated appendicitis and peritonitis.[14] Relief by death came to the omphalos of the Mormons' world as he lay in bed on August 29. The family of John D. Lee may have taken some measure of comfort when the monarch's demise came as Lee had predicted. Not long before his execution Lee said: "If I am guilty of the crime for which I am convicted, I will go down and out and never be heard of again. If I am not guilty, Brigham Young [who bears the responsibility and guilt for the murders, was the unstated implication] will die within one year! Yes, within six months." As Will Bagley notes, Lee's family considered this a prophetic utterance; John D. Lee was executed on March 21, 1877, and Brigham Young died five months and eight days later.[15]

In the *Tribune*'s judgment there was "not much sorrow" in evidence at Young's funeral service in the Mormon Tabernacle: "Aside from a few relatives of the deceased, no great demonstrations or sorrow were noticeable, other than the natural soberness of demeanor due even on the smallest occasions of this character and which death should ever evoke." The service was described as overlong. "Many became wearied at the protracted length of the Tabernacle services, abandoned their stations and went home," the *Tribune* observed, "but an immense concourse witnessed the whole gloomy ceremonies from beginning to end."[16]

Judge Elias Smith entertained a grandiose view of Young's impact outside Salt Lake City, for he said: "No person on the earth was more universally known than he, and his departure from this earthly state of existence will be an event that will to a great extent be felt by millions

---

[13]James Jack to W. L. Young, August 13, 1877, BYLC, CR 1234 1, box 15, vol. 22, 867.

[14]Among abdominal conditions of sudden onset causing peritonitis and death in a man of seventy-seven years, perforated diverticulitis of the colon is statistically far more likely than acute appendicitis. Appendicitis can occur at any age, but its incidence falls significantly after age fifty-five, when acute diverticulitis increases in incidence. Sepsis from unsterile catheterization of the bladder has also been implicated as a possible cause of Young's death. Rumors and speculation about poisoning persist.

[15]Bagley, *BOP*, 319n63.

[16]"The Funeral," *SLT*, September 4, 1877, 1/1.

of the human race in all quarters of the globe, and thousands . . . will lament the termination of his labors."[17] For thirty years he served as the head of the nation's most despised religion, yet he left a record of temporal accomplishments as a banker, merchant, farmer, and legislator whose "ability, will, and determination overcame mighty obstacles, surmounted grave perils, and outwitted and overthrew many powerful enemies."[18] Nearly four hundred settlements were begun west of the Rockies; he amassed an estate with a value estimated in the double-digit millions and pushed the building of telegraph and railroad lines, recognizing that they were the soon-to-be-profitable technological advancements of his era. In the opinion of the *Deseret News*, "No earthly potentate ever reigned more fully in the hearts of his people than did President Brigham Young."[19]

Black Flowers for the Bier

Baskin did not leave any record of praise or criticism occasioned by Brigham Young's death, but the criticism of the man's legacy began immediately in the national press, and much of it was reprinted by the *Tribune*.

> *San Francisco Chronicle*: "It was a long, eventful, and marvelous life considering the surrounding conditions of it . . . from poverty and obscurity to the ruler of millions. . . . The Mormon Prophet had everything to make and to mold not merely out of new and unfavorable material, but with the spirit of the age all against his enterprise."[20]

> *Eureka (Nev.) Republican*: "If any man ever deserved wholesome punishments at the hands of a lawful tribunal, that man was Brigham Young. Nor does his death atone for the heinous crimes perpetrated in Utah Territory during its settlement by the Mormons. There are scores of blood stained villains of the Mormon faith who should keep him company through the medium of the gallows. Not all the briny waters of the Great Salt Lake would wash the blood-stains from Utah's soil. . . . [H]e has fomented treason and raised troops to fight the Government; he has opposed free schools and popular education; he has inhibited free religious worship; he has circumscribed the privileges

---

[17]Thomas, *Elias Smith's Journal*, 3:1875–88.
[18]"Death of President Young," *slh*, August 30, 1877.
[19]"Last Moments of President Brigham Young," *dn*, August 31, 1877, 2/2.
[20]"Press Remarks," reprinted *slt*, September 4, 1877, 3/2.

of citizenship; he has prevented free speech and tried to muzzle a free press."[21]

Chicago Inter-Ocean: "The time was when Brigham Young was the idol of his people. His word was law and his advice was implicitly obeyed, but in the last few years he has fallen off in these particulars. He has made many mistakes, unlike himself, and has blundered in many ways. His Order of Enoch enraged many of his best friends, and the persistent determination to keep Cannon in Congress injured his power in many respects."[22]

Gold Hill (Nev.) News: "He has done much of good as well as much of evil to this country. Now . . . he has gone, and is powerless to do any more harm."[23]

Sacramento (Calif.) Union: "Brigham Young is dead, and he died full of years and of crimes, in his bed. . . . [H]e was a man of very remarkable ability, and in weighing the black deeds that stain his name it is necessary also to reckon the many evidences his career affords of mental power and administrative capacity. . . . By introducing terror and superstition, by practicing at once the arts of modern civilization and the devices of medieval tyranny, he succeeded in establishing a compact, self supporting bigoted and disloyal community. . . . [H]e mercilessly removed all suspected persons from his path. Treason against the Church was a capital crime, and the penalty was executed with all the most awe-inspiring accessories of midnight murder. . . . [I]t must be admitted he was a man of mark, a natural leader of men, and possessing capacities which under better cultivation might have made him an honor to the country that now looks askance upon his bold but lawless career."[24]

Indianapolis Sentinel: "The imagination is taxed to comprehend the facts. He built a city, subdued a wilderness, and in defiance of almost insurmountable obstacles organized not only his church, but society. In Utah he became an absolute ruler. The Czar of Russia was less absolute. In arrogance of power he defied the United States, and ruled his realm with more than Eastern despotism. . . . Cities rose as if by magic. Manufacturers flourished, and, remote from civilization, the most difficult problems of civilization were successfully worked out. . . . His word was law, his will supreme. . . . [He] made himself immensely rich. He lived in luxury."[25]

---

[21]Ibid.
[22]Ibid.
[23]Ibid.
[24]Ibid.
[25]Ibid.

Stockton (Calif.) Independent: "The pangs of sorrow felt for the loss of a leader by a people of such coarse moral fiber as the Mormons, will find immediate, healthful vent in an hour's blubbering, while the more refined portion of mankind will have no tears of regret over the demise of a man who has expended the energies of his life in an endeavor to lower the standards of morality."[26]

San Jose Mercury: "Dead, in Salt Lake City, . . . Brigham Young, prophet, high priest of the Mormons, bigamist, murderer, enemy of the American Government, in his seventy-seventh year. . . . An American, he was a disgrace to the country. We have no tears to shed in his demise."[27]

Beaver Square Dealer (Beaver City, Utah): "The eagle eye had lost its fire, and the shrill notes of his voice that was wont to permeate from wall to wall of the Great Tabernacle had become broken and faltering. It is not unjust nor unkind to say that the last half dozen years of the Prophet's life added nothing to his former work. And it seems a misfortune that nature does not know enough to take care of her children when their work is finished."[28]

Virginia Enterprise: "Unfortunately, he had not a thought which was not selfish, not a desire which was not unhallowed. To hold his followers around him, he misled them to their basest passions, and robbed them year by year in the name of the Lord. To carry out his purposes he not only did not shrink from crime, but organized it as a revelation from Heaven. He has planted a plague spot in the depths of our continent from the first, and to the shame of our Government has darted the highest laws of our country, and has left as a legacy, thousands of depraved men and defiled women. There is hardly a doubt that he was equally implicated with Lee, Dame, and the rest in the murders of Mountain Meadows. . . . The death of such a man should cause no regret."[29]

Springfield (Mass.) Republican: "It was a rare combination of qualities that made up the man—Yankee shrewdness, tireless energy, executive powers of the highest type, religious cunning, and iron will, a merciless heart. There can be no moral doubt that he was the real author of the Mountain Meadows Massacre."[30]

Philadelphia North American: "No grave could be dug deep enough to hide the mass of corruption or prevent it from still being a stench in

[26]Ibid.
[27]Ibid.
[28]Ibid.
[29]Ibid.
[30]"Death of Brigham Young," *Springfield (Mass.) Republican*, August 30, 1877, 4/2.

the public nostril. While the evil that men do lives after them, it is certain that no good has been interred with the bones of the Mormon despot."[31]

Philadelphia Times: "He was a man of uncommon energy with a will of iron, a wonderful talent for organization, a personal magnetism, and above all, ambitious. His idols were fame, wealth, and power. He believed in destiny. The religion of Mormonism was one of the instruments with which he carved his way to power."[32]

New York Post: "In one respect he was a vulgar cheat, of course. In his character he was essentially coarse and brutal, without refinement, without culture, without the finer instincts of men. He gave free rein to the worst passions of his own nature, and made the worst passions of other men his tools. Yet he was a man of almost unbelievable force of character of a certain kind. . . . He established himself as a despot, and drew willing subjects from all parts of the world."[33]

New York Herald-Tribune: "[He was] nothing but a cunning, clever old rascal, and no prophet at all. . . . [He has] gone with his bloody hands beyond our jurisdiction. . . . Sham as he was, he made big figure in the world. He was a Yankee Mohammed, and American aristocrat. He founded a kingdom within a republic and wielded a power such as no civilized king enjoys."[34]

New York Times: "The Mormon community of Utah has been in reality an autocracy. Brigham Young has held in the hollow of his hand the happiness, fortunes, and destinies of his people. . . . [T]he Mormon community has been . . . as completely autonomous as it could have been if it had been isolated by wide seas from the rest of mankind. . . . Young gained an ascendency over his people which has scarcely a parallel in modern history. It is possible that some of them hated him; it is certain they all feared him. . . . [H]is will and purpose have dominated all the councils of the theocracy from 1848 until now. . . . Cruel, bloody and vindictive though this man doubtless was, he must be credited with the possession of abilities of a superior order." The *Times* continued, "Not only things secular, but things spiritual, were ever rendered subordinate to the purposes of his own unholy ambition, his own sensualities, and his own enrichment and self-aggrandizement. The prosperity of Utah was encouraged and fostered, because it added

---

[31]"Brigham Young," *Philadelphia North American*, September 4, 1877, 1/1.
[32]Stout, *HOU*, 1:91.
[33]*New York Post*, untitled, undated, cited in Malmquist, *First 100 Years*, 48.
[34]"Brigham Young," *New York Herald-Tribune*, August 30, 1877, 4/2.

to his vast accumulated wealth; the property of the Mormon Church was carefully tended and nurtured, because its prosperity tended to the achievement of the same ends. Selfish, sensuous, and avaricious, Brigham Young could be and often was audaciously cruel; frequently betraying the spirit of a murderer, even if not following this brutal example."[35]

Historians Gary Bunker and Davis Bitton read the materials published after Young's death and concluded: "His death was seized upon by newspapers and illustrated weeklies as an occasion . . . not for measured evaluation, but for written and artistic satire. Humor and ridicule were the dominant tones in the public media's coverage of Young's death."[36] If humor and artistic satire is found in these accounts, it is well hidden.

Historian Hubert Howe Bancroft gave Young this modest measure: "Esteemed by his followers as an angel of light, and considered by his foes as a minister of evil, an imposter, a hypocrite, a murderer, he was in fact simply an enthusiast, a bigoted and egotistical enthusiast, as the world believes, but a practical and foresighted man, one who by his will, ability, and intuitive knowledge of human nature fitted to combat the difficulties that beset each step in his path of life."[37]

Fifteen years after Young's death, the anniversary of his birthday occasioned the recognition by the *Deseret News* of how the man, so great in its eyes, was seen so critically by others. Prejudice was at the heart of their disdain, the newspaper voice of the Mormons continued to insist: "The recognition of the worth of Brigham Young, outside of the community of the Latter-day Saints, was comparatively meagre during his lifetime. This ungenerous lack of appreciation for a great man was due to ignorance of the work he accomplished, and perhaps to a still larger degree to unreasoning prejudice."[38] John Hanson Beadle recorded that Young admitted to a lesser role than other titles

---

[35]"Death of Brigham Young: The Mormon Prophet's History," *NYT*, August 30, 1877. Many severely castigating evaluations were published across the nation. Among the scores of similar newspaper reports and editorials that could be cited are these: "Death of Brigham Young," *Princeton (Minn.) Union*, September 7, 1877, 2/3; "Mormon Rule a Failure," *Wichita City (Kans.) Eagle*, September 20, 1877, 1/5; "Death of Brigham Young," *Walhalla (S.C.) Keowee Courier*, September 6, 1877, 1/6; *NYTrb*, September 12, 1877, 4/4; and "Brigham Young," *Boston Daily Advertiser*, August 31, 1877, 2/2.

[36]Bunker and Bitton, "Death of Brigham Young," 358.

[37]Bancroft, *HOU*, 673.

[38]"Brigham Young's Birthday," *DN*, June 4, 1892, 20/1.

paid him: "When speaking of the vote of each semi-annual conference indorsing him as a prophet, he said: 'I am neither a prophet nor the son of a prophet, but I have been profitable to this people.'"[39]

To the present hour the name "Brigham Young" remains, in the minds of most non-Mormons outside Utah, indelibly linked with many wives and the practice of polygamy. The passage of years has dulled the memory of the oftentimes crude, rustic, barnyard language in his sermons, of his calls for the shedding of blood, for violence and vengeance. The LDS Church website currently insists Brigham Young "encouraged excellence and refinement in every aspect of life."[40]

The Baskins, Judge Smith, and Utah's Divorce Mills

In July 1877 a Saint Louis newspaper exposed the reprehensible divorce mills existing in Utah's probate courts, resulting from misapplication of its liberal divorce law. The article described the case of a man in Indiana who had been granted a Utah divorce, but neither the man nor his wife had ever lived in Utah. The man was indicted for bigamy, since the divorce from his first wife was not recognized in Indiana, and his second marriage was therefore illegal.[41] The charge of laxity of a residence requirement in Utah's divorce law was merited; the applicable statute, which dated from March 1852, said: "If the court is satisfied that the person so applying is a resident of the Territory, *or [merely] wishes to become one*; and that the application is made in sincerity and of her own free will and choice . . . , the court may decree a divorce from the bonds of matrimony . . . for any of the following causes[:] . . . adultery . . . willful desertion . . . absenting himself without a reasonable cause for more than one year."[42] Also listed were commission of a felony, "inhuman treatment so as to endanger the life of the defendant's wife," and the parties' inability to live in peace and union.

A Salt Lake County grand jury was convened by U.S. attorney Sumner Howard to investigate the issue. Its September report summarized a six-month investigation of divorces granted in the Salt Lake

---

[39]"Late Head of the Mormon Theocracy and Priest of Polygamia," *Cincinnati Daily Gazette*, August 31, 1877, 1/1. See also Van Wagoner, *CDBY*, 4:2201.

[40]"Brigham Young, 2nd President of the Church," LDS Church History, www.lds.org/church history/presidents/controllers/potcController.jsp?leader=2&topic=facts, accessed April 2012.

[41]"Utah Divorces," *St. Louis Republican*, reprinted in *SLT*, July 3, 1877, 1/3.

[42]*Compiled Laws of the Territory of Utah* (1876), 375–76 (para. 1151); italics added.

City probate court of Judge Elias Smith and his clerk and son-in-law, Dirk Bockholt.[43] In 80 percent of the three hundred divorces granted in a one-year period, both parties in the petition were nonresidents of the territory and thus beyond the court's jurisdiction. The report noted that 42 percent of the divorces were granted within a week of application. Many were for individuals who never appeared in court, merely having submitted letters to Bockholt. It was also charged that Judge Smith, and some lawyers, required out-of-state residents to respond within a time frame that was impossible. The grand jury found that in many instances all of the court's proceedings were recorded only in the handwriting of Judge Smith, indicating he was both the judge and the attorney of record of his own court.[44]

This furor over the legal status of Utah divorces likely generated some apprehension for Robert and Olive Baskin. There were several striking parallels with the 1867 divorce granted to Olive Lavinia Gardner Stafford: her divorce was obtained in Judge Elias Smith's probate court; she stated that she was a resident of the territory; the only handwriting of the court record was Judge Smith's; the partner in the divorce was not present; and the reason for the divorce was that her husband had absented himself for more than one year. Although no legal counsel represented her, the facts, so economically and succinctly presented, were exactly those required by the 1852 territorial law, suggesting, as Mormon critics accused, that Robert Baskin had assisted Olive in the preparation of her divorce plea.

The evidence suggests that Judge Smith had begun his lucrative divorce business much earlier than the 1877 report of its discovery, with Olive Lavinia Gardner Stafford being one of his early clients.[45] As noted previously, suspicion also attaches to Smith's court in that case, because no mention was made of the whereabouts, the custody claim, or even the existence of Lila, the child born to Olive before her marriage to Baskin.[46]

---

[43]The probate court judgeship was an elected position. Therefore, those who held the office were almost uniformly Mormon men concurrently holding a church leadership position. "The Grand Jury," *SLT*, September 27, 1877, 2/2.

[44]"Utah Divorces!" *SLT*, September 27, 1877, 4/2. The same report was also published by the *Deseret News*: "Divorces in the Probate Court," *DN*, October 3, 1877, 12/1.

[45]However, the *News* claimed that "it is but very recently that any attempts have been made to take advantage of the loophole to be obtained by wresting and perverting that one phrase of the law." "Divorce," *DN*, October 3, 1877, 8/2.

[46]Judge Smith is known to have dealt with the question of child custody and support in other divorces coming before his court, and custody issues were within the probate court's jurisdiction.

Bogus divorce mills in Utah were not limited to Smith's court. In fact 250 or more divorces had been granted in Beaver, mostly for parties in the eastern states, for which the "Probate Judge and County Clerk" had realized about $6,500, and the newspaper publisher had made about $1,000.[47] The probate court of Box Elder County also was said to be "deep in the slime," and the number of divorces granted in Kane County was said to be eighty.[48]

The grand jury investigation of probate court divorce practices created further ammunition for the non-Mormon position that judicial practices in Utah were faulty and needed federal correction.[49] In 1876 Brigham Young, in a letter to high-ranking Mormon apostle Lorenzo Snow, had recognized the divorce mills as pernicious, saying, "The greatness of the injury . . . is almost inconceivable, and . . . . granting of these divorces is not only a wrong to the partners of those making applications, it also jeopardizes the liberties and rights of the entire people." Young warned that probate courts would be denounced "as unworthy to have the power they wield," and he instructed Snow to "take the necessary steps to put an end to all such transactions for the future."[50]

The year of the Prophet's death was a very active one for the non-Mormons of Utah, and a very difficult one for Utah's Saints. But even more difficult years lay ahead for polygamy and the Mormon theocracy, now without the commanding, leonine presence of President Brigham Young at its head.

---

[47]"Beaver," *slt*, November 27, 1877, 4/3; "Divorce Business in Southern Utah," *slt*, November 28, 1877, 4/3.

[48]"These Divorce Doings," *slt*, September 28, 1877, 2/1; "The Divorce Business in Southern Utah," *slt*, November 28, 1877, 4/3.

[49]In October, U.S. attorney general Charles Devens wrote to Sumner Howard about this matter, directing him to draw up appropriate legislation to be submitted to Congress. Devens to Howard, October 4, 1977, U.S. Department of Justice, Files Relating to Utah 1855–1912, MS 18871, box 1, folder 7, item 20, p. 447.

[50]Young to Snow, November 7, 1876, BYLC, CR 1234 1, box 10, vol. 14, 644.

9

Elections, Challenges, and Ill Winds

*An election is coming. Universal peace is declared
and the foxes have a sincere interest in prolonging the lives of the poultry.*
GEORGE ELIOT (MARY ANN EVANS)

ROBERT BASKIN WAS ONE OF THREE MEN OF UTAH'S LIB-eral Party who challenged, on four separate occasions, the qualifications of preeminent Mormon politician George Q. Cannon to sit as the territorial delegate to Congress. The first unsuccessful challenger was Gen. George R. Maxwell in 1872. Baskin's two unsuccessful attempts followed his defeat in the elections of 1874 and 1876, and the final contest came from Allen Green Campbell after his defeat by Cannon in 1880. Valid citizenship, a basic requirement for service in Congress, was contested in all but the first of the challenges. Cannon's multiple wives and allegiance to the LDS Church, superseding that to the U.S. government, were also part of the enduring controversies between the non-Mormons and Cannon.

CANNONS FROM LIVERPOOL
Cannon was no easy target for Baskin and Liberal Party contestants. Apart from Joseph Smith and Brigham Young, "no one surpassed [Cannon] as a leader, shaper, and defender of nineteenth-century Mormonism," said historian-biographer Davis Bitton.[1] He was the

---

[1]Bitton, *GQC*, ix.

friend and confidant of Brigham Young and, for forty years, an LDS Church apostle. After Young's death, Cannon remained in the inner sanctum of Mormon power as counselor in the triumvirate First Presidency of the LDS Church to three of its presidents: John Taylor, Wilford Woodruff, and Lorenzo Snow. Cannon's entire adult life was unswervingly spent as the paladin of the LDS Church, especially outside Utah.

"The Cardinal," "the Mormon Richelieu," "Judas George," "Smoothbore," "British Mountain Howitzer," "Oily Gunman Cannon," and "the Premier" were other epithets used by non-Mormons and anti-Mormons to describe him in the sometimes lacerating language of the *Salt Lake Tribune*.[2] All were apt, for George Q. Cannon was for many years an enormously powerful personage, "second only to Brigham Young in prominence in nineteenth-century Mormon Utah."[3] "Outside Utah, Cannon and Mormonism were almost synonymous," says Bitton.[4] In his eight years as Utah's territorial representative, Cannon was an extraordinarily influential nabob, fighting anti-Mormon legislation in the halls of Congress and through his widely spun network of social contacts in Washington. He was personally acquainted with the presidents and many other powerful men of the time.

Like many of Utah's immigrants, Cannon was a British convert. Born in Liverpool, Lancashire, England, in 1827, he was baptized into the LDS Church at age thirteen. He and his family sailed for the United States in 1842, and he arrived in the valley of Salt Lake in October 1847. Eventually Cannon was husband to six wives, who bore him thirty-seven children.[5] His polygamous marriages were a relatively easy target for Maxwell, Baskin, and Campbell in challenging his qualifications for Congress, because they were illegal after the 1862 Morrill Anti-bigamy Act. Allegations that Cannon lacked citizen status was more difficult to make stick.

---

[2] The *Tribune* added another phrase: "The greatest and smoothest liar," a play on Young's humor that the best of all categories could be found among Mormons, including liars. "Took His Peaches," *SLT*, November 24, 1878, 4/2; "Salt Lake County Returns," *SLT*, November 7, 1878, 4/3.

[3] K. L. Cannon II, "Wives and Other Women," 71.

[4] Bitton, *GQC*, xii.

[5] Cannon also adopted five children born to Caroline P. Young Croxall; in 1881 he adopted Karl Quayle Cannon, the illegitimate son of Franklin Jenne Cannon and Maud Baugh. Bitton, *GQC*, 463–64; K. L. Cannon II, "Wives and Other Women," 85.

Territorial and Federal Requirements for Naturalization

The three requirements for naturalization against which all Utah immigrants were measured came from the territorial statutes, including Sections 2165 and 2170. Section 2165 stipulated that a candidate for naturalization "shall declare on oath . . . two years, at least, prior to his admission, that it is *bona fide* his intention to become a citizen of the United States."[6] The applicant was required to appear in a territorial district court or supreme court and also declare "that he absolutely and entirely renounces and abjures all allegiance and fidelity to every foreign prince, potentate, state, or sovereignty."[7] This was to be signed by the district court clerk and filed in the permanent records. The second and third requirements—on the length of residency and that the years must be contiguous—are found in Section 2170: "No alien shall be admitted to become a citizen who has not for the *continued* term of *five* years next preceding his admission resided within the United States."[8] For those applying from a territory, *one year* of residency was required.[9]

The federal requirements were generally similar to those of the territory, but with three additions. First, the oath of intention was to be filed three years before admission, not two. The second specified that the applicant "has behaved as a man of good moral character," and the third that "the oath of the applicant shall, in no case, be allowed to prove his residence."[10] An 1824 federal statute eliminated the requirement to make a personal appearance for the declaration of intent prior to naturalization.[11]

Cannon's Timeline

The timeline of Cannon's life is critical in answering the question of whether his citizenship was legally acquired. At the time of his arrival in 1847, Mexico ruled and owned the western land occupied by the Saints. From the 1848 Treaty of Guadalupe Hidalgo to September 1850, when Utah Territory was formed, the Mormon people

---

[6]*Compiled Laws of the Territory of Utah* (1876), Sec. 2165, 57.
[7]Ibid., 58.
[8]*Compiled Laws of the Territory of Utah* (1876), Sec. 2170, 60; italics added.
[9]*Compiled Laws of the Territory of Utah* (1876), Sec. 2165, 58; italics added.
[10]Enacted April 15, 1802, 2 Stat., 153 (USHS, PAM 1647).
[11]Enacted May 24, 1824, 4 Stat., 69 (USHS, PAM 1647).

occupied U.S. land but were not residing in a named state or territory. George Q. Cannon arrived in the Great Basin in October 1847 and was sent by Brigham Young in October 1849 to labor in the gold fields of California, which had not yet been granted statehood.

Cannon departed California from the port of San Francisco on November 22, 1850, on the ship *Imaum of Muscat*, bound for the Sandwich Islands.[12] After a voyage of approximately two weeks, he arrived on or about December 12, 1850.[13] Without returning to the United States, Cannon served as an LDS missionary in the islands until he left Honolulu on July 28, 1854, on the *Polynesia*, arriving in San Francisco on August 12, 1854.[14] For nearly four years he had no residency in either the United States or Utah Territory, nor did he file an oath of intent in any U.S. court. On his return to California in the fall of 1854, Cannon assisted Apostle Parley P. Pratt with his autobiography. Leaving California, Cannon arrived in Salt Lake City on November 28.[15] His first few days of December in Salt Lake City were not likely to be incorrectly remembered. He claimed to have been granted citizenship on December 7. This amounted to three months and twenty-two days of residence in the United States or one of its territories immediately preceding that date. On December 10, Cannon married his first wife, Elizabeth Hoagland.[16] In April 1855, Cannon was called to return to California to again assist Apostle Pratt and to publish the *Book of Mormon* in Hawaiian.[17]

From a comparison of naturalization requirements with his personal history, it is unequivocally clear that Cannon did not, on December 7, 1854, meet the requirements of residency within the United States or the residency requirement for Utah Territory, and he had not entered a proper preceding declaration of intent in a Utah or California court. Legal and political wrangling over Cannon's citizenship would set two Utah governors at odds and continue as a battle between non-Mormons and Mormons until 1881.

---

[12]California received statehood on September 9, 1850.

[13]George Q. Cannon, "Sandwich Islands Mission," DN, March 14, 1855, 17/1. Bitton supplies the names of the vessels but gives December 12, 1850, as the date of leaving and December 24, 1850, as the arrival date in the Pacific islands. Bitton, GQC, 2.

[14]Bitton, GQC, 31.

[15]Ekins, *Defending Zion*, 34; Bitton, GQC, 2, 31, 69–70, 193. See also U.S. Third District Court, Naturalization Index, Salt Lake City, MIC 12, reel 2, Utah State Archives.

[16]They were married by Brigham Young in the home of the bride's father.

[17]Bitton, GQC, 72.

ELECTIONS AND CHALLENGES

Cannon's political career could be said to have begun in May 1862 when he was elected by the territorial legislature, along with William H. Hooper, to be the senator of a hoped-for new western state. Cannon traveled to Washington from his post in Liverpool on Brigham Young's call, but senators and representatives were too preoccupied with the disaster at Shiloh and the other disturbing matters of the second year of the Civil War to address Utah's bid for statehood. Elected to the office of secretary of state in the nonexistent state of Deseret in 1865, Cannon found a more substantial political path in 1872 when he was made the People Party's choice for Utah's congressional seat. He was opposed by the Liberal Party candidate, Gen. George R. Maxwell, who was then the land registrar. The outcome—Cannon's 20,969 votes to Maxwell's 1,942—was no surprise, but, undeterred, Maxwell and the Liberals moved on to their primary objective: to contest Cannon's seat and publicize Mormon opposition to federal laws and defiance of representative government principles. As required by statutes, Maxwell's challenge appeared in the public news, listing the issues on which Cannon should be disqualified: numbered ballots were used in the election, allowing voter intimidation; voting precincts in mining areas were willfully denied; only those who paid taxes were allowed to vote; Cannon lived openly with four women in violation of the Morrill Act; his oath of allegiance to the LDS Church superseded his allegiance to the U.S. laws and government. Despite intensive lobbying by Associate Justice Cyrus Myron Hawley, Judge William Carey, and others, Maxwell's challenge was not successful. Bribery on Cannon's part was implicated.[18] Notable by its absence in Maxwell's challenge was the question Cannon's citizenship.

In 1874 Robert Baskin was the Liberal Party's choice to run against incumbent Cannon. In a ratification speech, Baskin directed his remarks specifically to the Mormons in the audience. He spoke of freedoms that they did not enjoy, including voting rights: "Every time you vote you represent a principle, and this you must do without suffering dictation from any man."[19] He asked the Saints if they had received return on their tithing and other monies contributed to their

---

[18]"The General Protests," *slh*, October 31, 1872, 2/3; U.S. Congress, House, *George R. Maxwell vs. George Q. Cannon: Papers in the Case.*

[19]"Freedom in Utah," *slt*, July 29, 1874, 4/2. Ballots were marked with identifying numbers, ensuring identification of each person's vote.

church-run government: "You have paid your city taxes for years, and what have you to show for your money? . . . Do we have free schools . . . as is done in every other State and Territory?" Brigham Young had established free schooling for his own children, but what of the "man who earns his pittance by hard toil?" asked Baskin.[20] He continued the same theme, noting the people had contributed for the Salt Lake temple "enough to build a second St. Peter's, and the Priesthood have grown rich by it." The temple fund, the tithing fund, and the perpetual emigrating fund "were drained from the pockets of all" while many of them lacked life's necessities.[21]

The *Tribune* praised Baskin's anti-theocracy activities, including the arrest of Young for murder and for cohabitation. It recognized Baskin's service to widow Sarah Ann Cooke in her fight with Young over ownership of her home after her husband, a policeman, was killed in the line of duty.[22] Referring to the attempts by the non-Mormon "Committee of Forty-Five" to secure release of the city financial records, it added, "Our city masters have for years been squandering the public revenues and refusing to account for the large sums of money they have misapplied." Baskin secured a peremptory mandamus from the district court, ordering the production of the public accounts.[23]

The *Deseret News* responded sarcastically, taking in jest the voice and stance of the Liberals and thereby ridiculing them: "We 'Liberals' number . . . about one-tenth of the population of Utah . . . [and] ought to have all the offices in the Territory. . . . [A]fter you 'Mormons' have cleared about the brush, built the bridges, killed the snakes, tamed the red men, conquered the soil, built up houses and public buildings, organized society, framed the laws, [and] beautified the country . . . we, being new-comers, ought to step in and enjoy it."[24]

Marshal Maxwell organized his deputies on Election Day under the provisions of a federal law—the Bayonet Rule, or the Force Act—passed

---

[20]Ibid.

[21]Ibid. Many issues addressed by Baskin were included in Governor George L. Woods's January address to the legislature. "Governor's Message," *DN*, January 14, 1874, 4/1.

[22]Cooke later opened a school for girls in the Fourteenth Ward and headed the Women's National Anti-Polygamy Society. Scott, "Widow and the Lion," 189–212.

[23]"Our Delegate to Congress," *SLT*, July 29, 1874, 2/1. Baskin and forty-five citizens repeatedly petitioned Mayor Wells for the city financial records. They claimed that non-Mormons, at one-sixth of the population, were paying one-half of the taxes. "The Committee of Forty-Five," *SLT*, April 2, 1874, 2/1.

[24]"Liberal Logic," *DN*, August 12, 1874, 3/2.

during Reconstruction to assure people's voting rights when candidates to national offices were to be elected. Under this law, local authority was temporarily suspended and U.S. law took precedence. Maxwell hired extra men, mostly non-Mormons, to supervise the election process, but Mayor Wells and Police Chief Alexander Burt opposed the federal efforts and hired extra city policemen, mostly Mormons. When the voting site doors were inexplicably closed at noon, rioting broke out between the two police groups. The mayor had his clothing torn; serious injuries were sustained by both groups. Maxwell took control and with his deputy marshals arrested Burt, Dr. Jeter Clinton, and police officers Brigham Y. Hampton, Charles Ringwood, and J. Livingstone.[25]

Cannon's victory was again very lopsided, with 24,863 votes against Baskin's 4,518. Baskin contested Cannon's seat on grounds not unlike several Maxwell had raised: membership in a church that sanctioned plural marriage, with two of his marriages performed after the 1862 federal law prohibiting it, and his binding allegiance to a theocracy.[26] Baskin, the compulsive researcher of legal statutes, now formally contended that Cannon had not lawfully become a U.S. citizen. Cannon responded that he had appeared in the First District Court of Salt Lake City on December 7, 1854, had sworn allegiance to the United States, and had received a certificate of naturalization that remained in his possession.[27]

As a result of Baskin's challenge of Cannon's seating, testimony was taken in a January 4, 1875, inquest in Salt Lake City at notary public James Nathan Kimball's office. Baskin acted as his own counsel, with Jabez G. Sutherland representing Cannon. Five witnesses were called, including Albert Carrington, who in 1855 had been a *Deseret News* editor, and James McKnight, also a *News* employee. Both were asked about a report dated March 7, 1855, from George Q. Cannon, published in the *News* on March 14. In this updated history of the Sandwich Islands Mission, Cannon said he had left the United States on November 22, 1850, and remained in the islands until being released from the mission on July 24, 1854, and embarking for California "soon

---

[25]The Bayonet Rule episode is covered in Maxwell, GGSL, 202–204.

[26]Cannon ignored references to the 1862 Morrill Act but argued that the April 1874 House bill disbarring polygamists from Congress had not yet become law, and grand jury indictments in Utah against him were in abeyance.

[27]Bitton, GQC, 191–92.

after."[28] Other witnesses were asked about Salt Lake County court records.[29] Presumably, the newspaper article content and the text of the court records were submitted by Kimball to authorities in Washington.[30]

Late in January the House Committee on Elections voted that Cannon was "unworthy to occupy a seat in the House of Representatives" and that he "be expelled therefrom." To the utter surprise of Cannon's opponents, the newly arrived Utah governor, Samuel Axtell, issued Cannon the certificate of election that the previous governor, George L. Woods, had denied him. However, the committee bill to expel Cannon failed to come before the House of Representatives for its required vote, and Cannon was seated. If the testimonies taken by Kimball arrived in Washington, they and further pursuit of the question of Cannon's citizenship seem to have lapsed back into shadow.[31]

Early in 1876 Baskin was in Washington working for passage of a bill introduced by Michigan senator Isaac Christiancy that would prohibit Mormons from serving on juries in Utah. This prompted Cannon to say, "My contestant is here and busy as he can be in arousing hatred against Zion by his slanders and calumnies."[32] Testifying before the House Committee on Territories, Baskin delivered what Cannon described as "a bitter, malignant argument against Utah," citing such actions as blood atonement, incest, women driven from the harems in droves to the polls, and a reign of terror and blood.[33] To Baskin's allegation that opponents of the LDS Church were killed, Cannon responded that Baskin was a "living refutation of the falsity" of his argument: "For nine years he has been a resident of the Territory and one of the worst enemies of the people there. Yet he has not been assassinated."[34] Cannon's remarks to Congress may have been prompted by an underlying concern, and Bitton clarifies its likely cause: Baskin had carefully "examined the naturalization books in the Utah [district] court and found no entry for Cannon."[35]

---

[28]"Sandwich Islands Mission," *DN*, March 14, 1855, 17/1.

[29]The others were John H. Beadle, William Jarman, and William N. McCurdy.

[30]U.S. Congress, House, *Papers in the Case of Baskin vs. Cannon.*

[31]Bitton, *GQC*, 195.

[32]Journal of George Q. Cannon, February 25, 1876, cited in Bitton, *GQC*, 198n133.

[33]Bitton, *GQC*, 198–99.

[34]Cannon to Brigham Young, March 23, 1876, cited in Bitton, *GQC*, 199n137. Baskin replied to this and other such comments by saying: "My assassination . . . would have strengthened the Liberal cause and intensified the conflict." Baskin, *Reply*, 26.

[35]Bitton, *GQC*, 199.

Against all odds, Baskin tried a second time to overturn Cannon's limber in the 1876 election. The *Tribune* offered a familiar warning: "Let the electors of Utah remember that in voting for Apostle Cannon, they vote for an avowed opponent of free schools, a man who condemns public improvements, . . . a law-breaking polygamist, living in open adultery with four wives, and an unnaturalized alien."[36] Speakers derided Cannon as "a tyrant and a minion of tyranny who would dwarf and fetter the mind instead of enfranchise and enlighten it."[37] Fiery rhetoric did not win the day, as Baskin was again swamped, garnering 3,833 votes to Cannon's 21,101.

Shortly thereafter, on a summer evening in August 1877, an encounter between Robert Baskin and U.S. attorney Sumner Howard involved Cannon. Baskin had delegated some portion of the challenging of Cannon's citizenship to Howard. The animated scene described by the *News* reporter of their meeting near the post office illustrated that Baskin not only possessed a short temper but was capable of using his polished cane, his Irish shillalah: "District Attorney Howard and Attorney R. N. Baskin had an 'uprising.' . . . [F]ailing to convince each other by the peaceful means of logical reasoning, [they] resorted to the knock down style of argument, fists and canes being the implements of war brought into requisition."[38] Word circulated that the subject matter leading to the fight was Howard's mishandled attempt to challenge Cannon's naturalization certificate.[39] The question extended nationally, for the *Rocky Mountain Christian Advocate* of Denver, Colorado, reported: "If the Courts decide that Geo. Q. Cannon has never been naturalized, and is not a citizen of the United States, then R. N. Baskin will represent Utah in Congress."[40] Howard had written on May 1 to U.S. attorney general Charles Devens regarding his plan to cancel Cannon's citizenship certificate, giving the several supporting reasons for the move and asking for instructions on how to proceed.

---

[36]"Liberal Ticket," *SLT*, November 2, 1876, 2/1.

[37]"Liberal Meeting," *SLT*, November 2, 1876, 4/4.

[38]"Animated Scene," *DN*, August 15, 1877, 7/4.

[39]Also at issue between the two was Howard's criticism of Baskin's conduct of Lee's first trial, and the praise given Howard for the second trial. "Sufficient credit has not been given . . . to the talent, courage, and perseverance of Sumner Howard . . . for the part taken by him in bringing to justice the leader of the Mountain Meadows massacre. The duty was not an easy one, but he went through it with equal firmness and ability. . . . Howard . . . should have all the credit to which he is honestly entitled," said the *New York Sun*, reprinted in *DN*, June 6, 1877, 16/2.

[40]"Religious Papers Should Tell the Truth," *DN*, May 9, 1877, 8/2.

Devens replied on May 10, "Cannon has been the Delegate . . . for two or three Congresses. The House of Representatives has recognized his citizenship by twice awarding his seat as a Delegate. He has . . . been treated as a citizen of the United States by two at least of my predecessors. . . . I very much doubt whether it is judicious to . . . deprive him of the rights and privileges of citizenship. My predecessors have not thought it proper to take such steps and I am disposed to concur with them."[41] Howard replied again, indicating his intent to travel to Washington to personally discuss the matter, after Devens's wrote to him on May 17: "No action taken concerning Cannon until your arrival for consultation."[42] Howard was involved at the time with grand jury calls for criminal investigation in several deaths during the Morrisite rebellion. The sharp personal confrontation between Baskin and Howard in August very likely resulted from Howard having not gone to Washington after all to obtain Devens's support. The *Tribune* offered its opinion that Devens considered the "government," and not Cannon, responsible for the defect in the record of Cannon's naturalization.[43] Presumably "government" was a reference to the person of Judge Leonidas Shaver, in whose court Cannon's certificate had been entered on the records, even though Cannon had not met the eligibility requirements.

Ill Winds

If the winds of 1877 blew ill for the Mormons with the death of Brigham Young and the public castigation of his reign, the winds of ill fortune in 1878 were equally as bad but shifted to pummel the non-Mormons.[44]

---

[41]U.S. Department of Justice, Files relating to Utah, 1855–1912, MS 18871, box 1, folder 7, item 20, p. 263. Devens's predecessors who were apparently contacted regarding Cannon's citizenship were George Henry Williams, 1871–75; Edwards Pierrepont, 1875–76; and Alphonso Taft, 1876–77.

[42]U.S. Department of Justice, Files relating to Utah, 1855–1912, MS 18871, box 1, folder 7, item 23, p. 270. Devens would shortly serve an important role for the government in the polygamy case *Reynolds v. United States*, 98 U.S. 145. His argument was persuasive. "Washington: The Reynolds Case before the Supreme Court," *SLT*, November 1878, 4/2.

[43]"Cannon's Case," *SLT*, October 18, 1877, 4/2. Another account, consistent with Devens's letters, was that Howard "brought an undertaking into the Third District Court" requiring Cannon to "prove his citizenship." "Time to Be Moving," *SLT*, October 23, 1877, 2/1.

[44]The year 1878 began with the resignation of U.S. attorney Sumner Howard. Devens thanked Howard for "the efficiency and fidelity" he had shown. U.S. Department of Justice, Files relating to Utah, p. 647. By the end of March, Howard was running for Congress from Flint, Michigan.

Governor Emery's siding with Cannon by secretly signing his certificate of election, acquittals in several murder trials, a brutal street attack on a *Tribune* reporter, the desultory progress in Congress of the Luttrell Bill with its attempt again to prevent polygamy—all made 1878 a difficult year for Baskin, the Liberal Party, and the non-Mormons of Utah.

Under pressure from non-Mormons over the numbered ballots, and under threat of more stringent legislation on voting via the Luttrell Bill, Utah's legislature passed some token features of improvement in February, including the outlawing of marked ballots.[45] However, in the session's closing minutes, Mormons outmaneuvered the non-Mormons by attaching amendments that seriously abridged the non-Mormon vote. These included limiting admission to voting sites, requiring property ownership, payment of taxes, and a residency period. Before the Liberal Party knew the amended bill's provisions, it was passed. Governor Emery signed it, shocking and infuriating the non-Mormons, who felt the bill demanded his veto because it removed voting privileges for a substantial portion of Utah's people.[46]

Before Congress, Cannon asserted that the Luttrell Bill, then under their consideration, was now unnecessary, since the changes needed in Utah had been enacted by the territorial legislature and signed into law by the governor.[47] The *New York Times* agreed with the *Salt Lake Tribune* that the election law passed in the Utah legislature was "entirely different" from the one that George Q. Cannon had previously described before the House Committee on Territories. The holder of the *Tribune*'s editorial pen was sharp with regard to the bill's unfair provisions: "A Danish girl . . . is qualified for a voter on the day of her arrival by going through the Endowment house and being sealed to a man that owns a dog upon which he paid taxes, [though he is] . . . a pardoned felon."[48] Also included in the legislature's actions—and signed by Emery—was a bill taxing unpatented mining properties, which non-Mormons said were government owned and not subject to taxation.[49] At a Liberal Party meeting several non-Mormon leaders, including Patrick Lannan, Henry W. Lawrence, and Baskin, each

---

[45]Representative John King Luttrell, was a Democrat from California.
[46]"The Election Law," *slt*, February 24, 1878, 2/1.
[47]"Utah Election Law," *nyt*, February 24, 1878, reprinted in *slt*, March 9, 1878, 2/2.
[48]"The Election Law," *slt*, March 3, 1878, 4/5.
[49]"Inspired Legislation," *slt*, February 26, 1878, 4/5.

spoke vehemently, particularly against the election bill.[50] As the *Tribune* reported, Baskin "stepped upon the stand amid the wildest and most enthusiastic cheers . . . [and,] in an able speech, tore the Election bill to pieces."[51] Non-Mormons, livid over Emery's siding with Mormon leadership by not vetoing the bill, anointed him with the pejorative title of "Elder Emery."[52] In their view, the bill gave the Mormons total control of the election process and disenfranchised every miner in the territory.[53] Baskin, Maxwell, and Judge J. C. Hemingray all traveled to Washington to push harder for the Luttrell Bill's passage, which would have corrected the loss of voting rights for non-Mormons.[54]

Realizing that the outcome was predetermined, the Liberal Party decided, in a drastic step, to boycott the 1878 elections, a first in Utah political history. The *Tribune* gave its assessment of the situation: "With the whole machinery of the election in the hands of bishops and other orders of the priesthood, with the suffrage conferred upon women who are made a privileged class of voters, and a public sentiment so debased that the grossest frauds are connived at, any attempt to record an opposition vote would be futile."[55] August and November elections went to the Mormon candidates by default.[56] Incumbent Cannon, "the bulwark of polygamy in Congress," ran without opposition.[57] The *Salt Lake Herald* confirmed the low spirit and apathy over the election: "No apparent interest has been taken[,] . . . one side resting serenely in the knowledge that it will be successful."[58] The count gave 14,221 votes for Cannon and eight write-ins for Baskin.[59] Baskin

---

[50]Non-Mormons' regard for Emery was further lowered by his starting a butcher shop that competed with Patrick Lannan's Empire Market and an abortive attempt to start his own newspaper, known in its short run as the *Whistle*. "G. Wash.," *SLT*, March 14, 1878, 4/2; "It Was a Whistle," *SLT*, March 20, 1878, 4/5.

[51]"Liberal Meeting," *SLT*, February 28, 1878, 4/2.

[52]"A Deserving Elder," *SLT*, March 6, 1878, 4/3; "Washington—The Sub-committee Will Report Luttrell's Bill," *SLT*, March 6, 1878, 1/6; "Grandmother's Admission," *SLT*, March 6, 1878, 2/1.

[53]"The New Election Law," *DN*, February 27, 1878, 9/2.

[54]"The True Inwardness of the Utah Election Act," *SLT*, March 8, 1878, 2/1; "Utah Election Law," *SLT*, March 9, 1878, 2/2.

[55]"A Fraudulent Election," *SLT*, November 6, 1878, 2/2.

[56]"Liberal Meeting," *SLT*, February 28, 1878, 4/2; "Utah in Congress, *SLT*, June 5, 1878, 2/2; "Waiting for Victory," *SLT*, August 4, 1878, 2/2; "The Election," *DN*, November 13, 1878, 1/4; "Utah in Congress," *SLT*, June 5, 1878, 2/2; "The Utah Election Law," *SLT*, June 26, 1878, 2/2.

[57]"An Electoral Farce," *SLT*, November 7, 1878, 2/3.

[58]"Editorial," *SLH*, November 5, 1878.

[59]Utah Territorial Papers, 1850–1902, Executive Proceedings, March 12, 1877–December 31, 1888, microfilm A-873, roll 1.

may have enjoyed a hearty laugh when Tooele County returns showed that Salt Lake City's notorious madam, Miss Kate Flint, had managed to pull sixteen write-in votes to Baskin's four.[60]

Because it was known that Cannon would be unopposed, Governor Emery, unbeknownst to Baskin, mailed Cannon the official certificate of election in March. This resulted in Baskin's missing the thirty-day deadline to contest the seat.[61] Baskin immediately wrote to Washington, explaining Emery's action and his own intention to again challenge Cannon's citizenship and qualifications. It was learned later that the letter was "lost" in the mail or in the clerk's office in Congress—alternatively, it may never have left the Utah post office.

By late March it was clear that the Luttrell Bill would not be presented for a vote in that House session.[62] Even those outside Utah placed the blame on Governor Emery, whose administration was said to have been "a conspicuous and humiliating failure."[63] Non-Mormons, in and out of Utah, called for Emery's removal.[64] In May, Baskin returned to Utah, and with Baskin absent from Washington, Cannon continued his attempt to convince the committee that the Luttrell Bill was not needed.[65] A fusillade of contrary articles followed in the *Tribune*.[66]

In July the plot hatched by Cannon and Emery was exposed: Emery signed a territorial law that permitted the positions of territorial auditor and treasurer to be elected, ensuring that Mormons would fill the positions and thus control the territorial finances. Emery also signed the highly partisan and faulty territorial election bill; he next sought federal remuneration of $1,121,000 for earlier Black Hawk Indian War

[60]Utah Territorial Election Papers, 1876–79, Marriott Library, JS, 3, U8, A361.

[61]"Governor Emery," *SLT*, March 13, 1878, 2/2.

[62]"Governor Emery's Treachery," *SLT*, March 20, 1878, 1/1; "The Election Law," *SLT*, March 21, 1878, 2/1; "Utah in Congress, *SLT*, March 21, 1878, 2/2.

[63]"Mr. Luttrell's Bill," *Philadelphia Record*, reprinted in *SLT*, March 27, 1878, 1/7.

[64]"Washington—They Also Go for G. Wash's Diminutive Head," *SLT*, March 28, 1878, 1/4. Gen. Patrick Connor was suggested as a replacement appointee. "General Patrick E. Connor," *SLT*, March 23, 1878, 2/1; "Receipt of Conscience Money at the Treasury," *SLT*, March 24, 1878, 1/4; "Which of the Twain?" *SLT*, March 29, 1878, 2/2; "Governorship of Utah," *SLT*, April 6, 1878, 4/4; "The Trio," *SLT*, April 25, 1878, 4/6.

[65]"Our Prospects in Congress," *SLT*, May 3, 1878, 2/1; "Washington," *SLT*, May 3, 1878, 4/2; "Utah in Congress," *SLT*, June 5, 1878, 2/2.

[66]"Utah Election Bill—The Christiancy-Luttrell Bill at Last on the Calendar," *SLT*, June 25, 1878, 1/4; "Good News from Washington," *SLT*, June 25, 1878, 2/2; "The Utah Election Law," *SLT*, June 26, 1878, 2/2; "An Ignorant Suffrage," *SLT*, June 30, 1878, 2/2.

expenses. In return, it was alleged that efforts would be made to place Emery as Cannon's companion delegate to the Senate.[67] Cannon was also said to have been at the heart of an ambitious plan with Committee on Territories chair J. Proctor Knott of Kentucky, Representative Benjamin Joseph Franklin of Missouri, and other Democrats to have five thousand Mormon colonizers sent to each of the territories of Arizona, New Mexico, and Wyoming.[68] These territories would each be divided into two smaller territories and, along with Utah and Idaho, would be admitted as Democratic states, delivering ten new Democratic senators (with Emery as one) to achieve a long-enduring control in the Senate.[69]

Around this time it came to light that Baskin and Hemingray had been unable to find in the clerk's office Baskin's notice contesting Cannon's seating, despite Baskin's insistence he had written and mailed it himself. "That an official document should miscarry in the mail is remotely possible, but the chances are a million to one against it," said Baskin. "By such means Mr. Baskin has been fooled in the contest, and Cannon is still allowed to misrepresent this Territory in Congress," lamented the *Tribune*.[70]

When Emery overgraciously approached Baskin to justify the conduct that had led to the governor's pejorative title "Elder Emery," Baskin's retort evidenced his short temper: "D——n your politeness. I only ask you to perform your duties properly."[71]

Lost Heart and Hope

In the fall of 1878, *Tribune* editor Frederic Lockley wrote the first of two letters to former vice president Schuyler Colfax bemoaning the state of depression and defeat he saw among the non-Mormons. In October he reported: "The non-Mormons of Utah have lost heart and hope. . . . We have asked the removal of Governor Emery and Chief Justice [Michael] Schaeffer . . . and men have gone . . . before the President [Hayes] . . . but they have been put off with a jaunty

---

[67]"A Million Steal," *slt*, July 11, 1878, 4/2.
[68]New Mexico's governor was now Samuel Axtell, the Mormon-favored ex-governor of Utah, who could be counted on to cooperate with Cannon.
[69]"A Nice Scheme," *slt*, November 1, 1878, 3/1.
[70]"Utah Statehood—A Plot Exposed," *slt*, July 12, 1878, 2/2.
[71]Ibid.

indifference. . . . I regret that such apathy should exist in the mind of my fellow citizens but there is a limit to human endurance."[72]

An episode of lawlessness, reminiscent of that which accompanied the Reformation, did not help the dejected tenor of Lockley and the non-Mormons. John C. Young, a nephew of Brigham Young, former Mormon turned reporter for the *Tribune*, was attacked as he left work. Three men surprised him as he reached the street and one "dealt him a heavy blow on the bridge of his nose with what he supposed to be brass knuckles." Young was treated by Dr. Thompson, who indicated something more than brass knuckles was used in the assault.[73]

Lockley's November letter to Colfax gave vent to continuing frustration, for all seemed "discouraged and the money is not coming forth. Mine owners are here temporarily and their business is to make money. They care nothing of the political situation and furnish neither moral or material support."[74] The *Tribune* observed, "The Mormons have planted colonies in Wyoming, Idaho, Arizona and New Mexico, and now hold the balance of power . . . , being able to dictate the policy of their delegates. . . . The New Mexico colony . . . received great encouragement through [Governor] Axtell . . . but their designs . . . are becoming more apparent."[75] With Utah in under Mormon control, and three other territories virtually so, Lockley warned that "a dangerous power is growing up right in the heart of the Republic."[76]

The Liberal Party boycotting an unwinnable election, the territorial governor siding with the Mormons, judges seemingly exhibiting overt Mormon bias, officials in Washington remaining unresponsive, lawlessness and physical assaults of apostate Mormons occurring in the streets, murderers going unpunished, the Luttrell Bill stalling in Congress, LDS Church expansion spreading through the West—all seemed contributory to the low spirits of Utah's non-Mormons in 1878.

---

[72]Lockley to Colfax, October 21, 1878, MS A 1508, vault 08/07/89 C, USHS Archives. Schaeffer's disapproval arose from his decree that the marriage between Brigham Young and Ann Eliza Webb was "void, and all orders for temporary alimony not them complied with, [are] null and void." Schaeffer also absolved Utah Militiaman Robert Burton of killing of Bella Bowman and Jeter Clinton in the death of John Banks at the Morrisite Rebellion. Near this time Baskin appeared in the U.S. Supreme Court's fall term representing Sarah Pratt, the wife of Orson Pratt, and mother of deputy Arthur Pratt over land title taken by Brigham Young after Sarah separated from her husband. *Cannon v. Pratt*, 99 U.S. 619 25 L.Ed. 446.

[73]"Thuggism," *SLT*, November 14, 1878, 1/5. John C. Young served as a *Tribune* reporter in Cedar City during the Lee trial.

[74]Lockley to Colfax, November 26, 1878, MS A 1508, vault 08/07/89 C, USHS Archives.

[75]"Mormon Colonies," *Eureka (Nev.) Sentinel*, reprinted in *SLT*, November 15, 1878, 3/1.

[76]Lockley to Colfax, November 26, 1878.

IO

Lying for the Lord

No legacy is so rich as honesty.
WILLIAM SHAKESPEARE

A FTER ASCENDING TO THE LDS CHURCH PRESIDENCY, John Taylor appointed George Q. Cannon in October 1880 as his first counselor. In the election a month later, Allen Green Campbell, a non-Mormon whose wealth came from Utah's Horn Silver Mine, ran against Cannon for the position of congressional representative. Campbell was well known in Beaver, Utah, but less well known among Salt Lake City residents.[1] Again the vote imbalance favored the People's Party candidate, and, confident in the anticipated victory, Mormons held not a single political meeting. "That fact alone proves all that we allege to be true . . . the Church party is a pure theocracy," said Judge John R. McBride.[2] By a margin little different from those earlier—18,568 to 1,357—the Liberal Party's Campbell was defeated. And again the issue of Cannon's citizenship involved the governor of Utah, when Eli Murray, in deference to the non-Mormons' claim that Cannon was an alien, sided with them and awarded the election certificate to Campbell as "the person, being a *citizen* of the United States, having the greatest number of votes."[3]

---

[1]Campbell came to Utah in 1857 with Johnston's troops and later went to Montana, where he was successful in mining, before returning to Utah. Though he lost the election, he was lauded by his party for being instrumental in Cannon's unseating. "He ran merely to vindicate a principle and as a protest against what he looked upon as a defiance of law on the part of the majority here," wrote newspaperman Charles C. Goodwin in *As I Remember Them*, 291.
[2]"Liberal Rally," *SLT*, November 2, 1880, 4/2.
[3]B. H. Roberts, *Comprehensive History of the Church*, 2–20; italics added.

John Q. Cannon, George's son, wrote in his journal: "Father approves of any honorable method to checkmate the governor. I yesterday brought up from the farm Father's certificate of naturalization which has the seal of the court on it, also an endorsement on the back telling where it is recorded. I have not let anyone see it yet."[4] Three weeks later, the younger Cannon added a note saying that he had given to prominent Mormon newspaperman John T. Caine his "father's certificate of naturalization[,] as he thought it might be needed in Washington."[5] On February 8, 1881, Arthur Thomas, acting governor of Utah Territory, overrode Murray's previous action and granted a certificate of election to Cannon as "the *person* who received the greatest number of votes."[6] The investigations that followed Governor Murray's withholding, and Acting Governor Thomas's granting, of the election certificate continued the battle over the validity of George Q. Cannon's citizenship.

Third District Court Testimony in 1881

Allen Campbell's contest of Cannon's congressional seat led to an extensive investigative hearing in 1881 in Utah's Third District Court, conducted by its supreme court chief justice, John A. Hunter.[7] From approximately eighty-five pages of testimony, portions relevant to the question of Cannon's citizenship are distilled in the following.

Certificate of W. I. [William Ivins] Appleby in the United States First District Court for the Territory of Utah.[8]

---

[4]John Q. Cannon Diary, January 17, 1881. John Q. Cannon, son of Elizabeth Hoagland Cannon, gives no specific indication in his diary as to whether he knew the certificate was fraudulent, but the reason for his need for secrecy is unclear.

[5]Ibid., February 25, 1881. At this time John Q. Cannon was a *Deseret News* editor. On June 4 the younger Cannon entered a note about "a man named Gibson of Ogden, to whom Father had telegraphed to come down to testify in his case," but on the next day he added, "The man Gibson called today, but as it is too late to do any good, he went home." A. M. Gibson, an Ogden businessman, later testified against passage of the 1887 Edmunds-Tucker Bill championed by Robert Baskin.

[6]U.S. Congress, House, *Cannon vs. Campbell: Testimony and Papers*, 388/67; italics added. Citations of this work are from the executive record, pp. 322–407 inclusive, with page numbers within documents (hereafter cited as *Cannon-Campbell*, record page number/internal document number).

[7]Hunter was chief justice of the territorial supreme court from 1879 to 1884. His records on Cannon were submitted in 1882 to the House Committee on Territories and published in the records of the Forty-seventh Congress. In the hearing, Campbell was represented by George Sutherland and John R. McBride; Cannon was represented by Arthur Brown.

[8]William Ivins Appleby, a dedicated Mormon, was the Eastern States Mission president in 1846, and a Camp of Israel clerk and journalist in October 1849. A three-wife polygamist

Be it remembered that on the 7th day of December, A.D. 1854, George Q. Cannon, a subject of Queen Victoria, made application and satisfied the court that he came to reside in the United States before he was eighteen years of age; and thereupon the said George Q. Cannon appeared in open court and was sworn in due form of the law, and on *his oath did say that for three years past it has been his bona fide intention to become a citizen* of the United States, and . . . thereupon the court being satisfied *by the oaths of Joseph Cain and Elias Smith, two citizens of the United States, that the said George Q. Cannon for one year last past has resided in this Territory; and for four years previously thereto he resided in the United States*; . . . whereof I have hereunto subscribed my name and affixed the seal of said court.[9]

   (L.S.)[10]   W. I. Appleby, Clerk[11]

Conflicting testimony from Henry G. McMillan, deputy clerk of the Third District Court, and clerk E. T. Sprague followed. McMillan testified he was unable to find any record of George Q. Cannon's citizenship in the period of October 6, 1851, to December 4, 1855, in either the First or Third District Court records.[12] Sprague testified to the existence of a Third District Court certificate of authorization of citizenship for George Q. Cannon on "page 585" of the court records, dated December 7, 1854.[13] Two conflicting records were presented and shown to Sprague. The first was marked as Exhibit F. The second, named

---

with eighteen children, he was a University of Deseret regent in 1850. Bancroft, *HOU*, 709n76. In May 1857, Appleby sent a letter to William Drummond, citing intimate details of Drummond's life that, if true, could have come only from intrusive personal investigation. "Judge Drummond Used Up," written May 19, 1857, published in the *Millennial Star* 19, no. 26 (June 27, 1857). Close to Jedediah M. Grant, he was nominated in 1857 by Brigham Young for territorial office and was coeditor of the *Mormon*, a New York City newspaper that defended Mormonism. He worked with Thomas Kane in the Utah War and relayed reports to Young from New York in April 1857 of Gen. Winfield Scott's orders to Gen. William S. Harney to move 2,500 troops on the Oregon Trail from Fort Leavenworth to Fort Laramie. In the fall of 1857 Young instructed Appleby, among others, to procure powder and lead for Utah and to work to get Saints back to Salt Lake City. Mackinnon, *At Sword's Point*, 127–28, 277–80.

[9]Appleby incorrectly cites the First District Court and refers only to Cannon's intent to make a declaration, not to his having made it or to a written record of it. He also cites only four years of residence, not the required five. Italics added.

[10]The initials signify Leonidas Shaver as the judge of record, but the notation does not establish Shaver's presence.

[11]*Cannon-Campbell*, 338–39/17–18.

[12]Ibid., 361–62/40–41, dated May 18, 1881. Apparently McMillan was instructed to search the records of both district courts because of the inconsistent citation of the court in which the naturalization had allegedly taken place.

[13]Utah State Archives, U.S. Third District Court, Naturalization Index, Salt Lake City, MIC 12, reel 2, vol. A [poorly legible], p. 285 [not 585].

Exhibit G, was purportedly a certificate of Cannon's naturalization; however, it was described as discolored, smaller by one-fourth than other certificates, and with "its appearance [having] quite a different look," and it lacked the court's seal but had the initials "L.S."[14]

When Elias Smith, about age seventy-seven and the judge of Salt Lake County's probate court, was sworn as a witness, he admitted that George Q. Cannon had been in Sandwich Islands—Hawaii— from approximately 1850 to 1854 and had been in Utah about ten days prior to his naturalization. On cross-examination the question was posed, "Were you asked whether Mr. Cannon had resided in the United States for five years preceding his application?" Smith's answer was oblique: "I wish to tell the circumstances how I knew it."[15] To the next question—"You were aware that at the time of this application for naturalization he had not lived in this country even for the year next preceding?"—Smith's answer was again evasive: "I knew the circumstances just as I have stated."[16]

Notary public A. S. Patterson introduced the First District Court record for December 7, 1854, signed by Judge "Leo Shaver," showing that the only matters before the court for that day were for R. T. Burton's entry of subpoenas for pending cases and Dimick B. Huntington's appointment as Indian interpreter.[17] McMillan certified the foregoing as a "*full*, true, and correct copy of the original journal or minute-book entries of the first judicial district court on the 7th day of December, 1854, as the same appears on page 216 of the journal of the said court, now in my possession."[18]

INVESTIGATION CONCLUSIONS

When the complaint by Campbell and the testimony filed by U.S. district attorney Philip T. Van Zile reached Congress, the lengthy

---

[14]*Cannon-Campbell*, 365–66/44–45. Sprague was recalled and asked to compare Exhibit G with Exhibit Z. He responded that in Exhibit G were the words "Queen Victoria," while in Exhibit Z were the words "Victoria, Queen of Great Britain and Ireland." *Cannon-Campbell*, 377/56. The testimony did not clarify whether one—or neither—of the differing records was the correct or original one.

[15]Ibid., 371/50.

[16]Ibid., 372/51.

[17]Ibid., 381/60. A microfilm record of the court entry is found in Utah State Archives, Naturalization Case Files, 1850–1915, ser. 3562.

[18]*Cannon-Campbell*, 381/60, dated May 18, 1881; italics added.

hearing record described above was entered into the record. Chief Justice John A. Hunter's conclusion relative to Cannon's qualification for citizenship was that "the witnesses named in the pretended certificate of naturalization . . . knew that said George Q. Cannon had not resided within the Territory of Utah, or within the jurisdiction of the United States, for the time required . . . and said certificate and said pretended testimony recited in said certificate was false."[19] The complaint went on to state "[that court clerk W. I. Appleby,] on his own motion and without any authority from said court or its judge, did make out and issue said certificate to said defendant, and that the same is false and fraudulent, and that any and all claims to citizenship based thereon are a fraud upon the laws and upon the United States."[20] Campbell's request had been to ask the court to "adjudge and decree" that Cannon was not a U.S. citizen and had not ever been naturalized according to law and, further, that "the certificate of naturalization, or pretended naturalization, now held by said Cannon, dated 7 December 1854 . . . be adjudged fraudulent and void, and be annulled."[21] On October 31, 1881, Chief Justice Hunter made a final ruling:

> [Given] that from the facts stated . . . , which are admitted by defendant's demurrer, that there is no record of defendant's naturalization, and *that no proceeding for that purpose ever took place in court*; and that the certificate held by defendant as *a certificate of naturalization was obtained by fraud*, and *has been fraudulently used*, and is void on its face, in not professing to be the copy of a record and not certifying a regular naturalization, and therefore there is no sufficient cause shown for annulling it, it is ordered that the said demurrer be, and the same is hereby, sustained, and that the complaint be, and is hereby, dismissed.[22]

When the legal jargon is simplified, it means that Hunter ruled that the certificate was fraudulent and void, but his court could not meet the third part of the plaintiff's request to annul the naturalization certificate, because the certificate was invalid from its beginning.[23] As late as 1890 the fraudulent nature of Cannon's citizenship was still the subject

---

[19] Ibid., 399–400/2–3.
[20] Ibid., 400/3.
[21] Ibid.
[22] Ibid.
[23] Biographer Bitton agrees the certificate could not be annulled, since it was never valid. Bitton, *GQC*, 250. Hunter was asked by Cannon's supporters in 1881 to revise his ruling but refused to do so. *GQCJ*, November 1, 1881, cited in Bitton, *GQC*, 505.

of contentious debate between the *Deseret News* and the *Salt Lake Tri-bune*. The *Tribune* asserted: "We established at the time that it was impossible for Mr. Cannon to become a citizen regularly . . . because he had not been in the country long enough. We showed that just exactly such certificates were given indiscriminately throughout the Territory by a clerk who went on a mule to naturalize people for a fee."[24]

SUPREME COURT LAW RAISED

Following the 1881 investigations, several Privileges and Elections Committee members of the 47th Congress weighed in on certain points of law regarding whether Cannon was an unnaturalized alien. Samuel Henry Miller (R-Pa.) reasoned that the certificate of citizen-ship had been "issued by a court of competent jurisdiction" and "signed and sealed by the court issuing it." He added, "The adjudication of this question has never been opened or reversed by any judicial tribunal having constitutional and legal authority to open and reverse it."[25] Miller did not address why the evidence presented in Utah's supreme court to Chief Justice Hunter and entered into federal records did not fulfill the requirements to which he alluded.

Any opportunity for a charge of fraud against Cannon, Appleby, Cain, and Smith for the December 1854 entry into the Utah court records was lost when Judge Leonidas Shaver died suddenly under unusual circumstances. According to reports, Shaver complained of an earache one evening but took his usual late supper and sat comfort-ably in his chair afterward, smoking. He was found dead in bed the following morning, June 29, 1855. Mayor Jedediah M. Grant's inquest into Shaver's death, and the *Deseret News* report of it, were unusually detailed, "for the consolation of his . . . relatives," explained the news-paper. Dr. William France and Indian agent Dr. Garland Hurt testi-fied that Shaver had complained of ear pain and they had planned to examine him but had not done so. At the inquest the two men probed the ear canal for softened bone and concluded that death was due to an ear abscess with rupture into the brain. No autopsy was done. Dr. France indicated that he—like Shaver—was a user of opium, but that

---

[24]"Cannon's Citizenship," *SLT*, August 11, 1890, 4/1.
[25]U.S. Congress, House Committee on Elections, *Cannon vs. Campbell: Contested-Election Case*, 23 (USHS, PAM 1647) (hereafter cited as *Cannon-Campbell Contested-Election Case*).

overdose or withdrawal was an unlikely cause of death. Four Mormon men (Almon W. Babbitt, W. C. Staines, Robert T. Burton, and William Ivins Appleby) gave strange testimony about the body position, saying it was the position "he always lay and slept in," adding the puzzling phrase "they having been much with him." It is particularly noteworthy that premonitory signs or symptoms of a bacterial brain or middle ear infection (headache, fever, seizures, disorientation, dementia, vomiting, weakness, paralysis, stroke, prostration, coma, hearing loss or deafness, or visual or speech impairment) were not mentioned in any testimony.[26] Grant directed Babbitt, Judge Zerubbabel Snow, and George A. Smith to draft a resolution honoring Shaver.

At the closed-casket funeral at the Council House, supreme court justice John F. Kinney's eulogy admitted that some of Shaver's decisions were "adverse . . . to the wishes of the church and community." Apostle Orson Pratt spoke at length, and mourners were asked to wear black armbands for thirty days. Mayor Grant was thanked for his "energetic arrangements" for Shaver's funeral and for "taking charge of his remains" for burial. No lesser official than President Brigham Young offered the prayer at the start of the funeral possession, which was headed by city marshal Jesse C. Little. A battalion of Life Guard troops of the Utah Militia, headed by Major Burton, was next, followed by the Nauvoo Brass Band. In the procession were Brigham Young, congressional delegate John M. Bernhisel, the district and probate court judges, and Utah bar members. George A. Smith spoke a graveside prayer.[27] The *News* also published a tribute to both Judge Shaver and the recently deceased Judge Lazarus H. Reid, for they had "innately pursued" a course that was "kind, affable, dignified, consistent, and upright."[28]

The ostentation, praise, and generosity given to Shaver's legacy by numerous high-ranking Mormons were severely incongruous, more like those given at the death of a distinguished Mormon hero than for a non-Mormon judge whose decisions were "adverse" to LDS Church interests. Rumors circulated that Shaver had been exceedingly "social" with "the brethren" but had been poisoned because of some "difficulty

---

[26]It is highly improbable that an indolent, low-grade, bacterial middle ear infection would produce sudden death, especially in the absence of any of the accompanying signs or symptoms listed.

[27]"Death of the Honorable Leonidas Shaver," *DN*, July 4, 1855, 4/1, 5/1–4.

[28]"The Late Judges Reid and Shaver," *DN*, July 4, 1855, 5/4.

with Brigham Young."[29] Suspicion was laid out in Mary Ettie V. Smith's account:

> I knew Judge Shaver well, and recollect the circumstances of his death.
> . . . There were a great many things connected with the trouble between
> him and the Prophet[,] . . . much more than has yet been disclosed.
> . . . The Heads of the Church made a great show of having the case
> investigated, by which they made it appear that the Judge died of some
> disease of the head. . . . But I heard the Prophet say . . . Judge Shaver
> knew a great many things he did not wish to come to the knowledge of
> the Government in Washington. . . . *He was unquestionably poisoned.*[30]

U.S. surveyor general David H. Burr also attested to Shaver's death by poisoning.[31]

Shaver's silence in death—from natural causes or otherwise—shielded Cannon, for the judge could never be questioned about the court record. By 1880 both Joseph Cain and W. I. Appleby were beyond questioning, also silent in death.

Representative Ferris Jacobs (R-N.Y.) agreed that "the judgment of naturalization cannot be attacked collaterally."[32] The minority report emphasized a number of precedent-setting decisions by the territorial supreme court, among them that the Utah records, having been entered, were in themselves indication that the court had been "satisfied." The report also alluded to "calamities to which . . . immigrants would be exposed if the validity of their naturalization should be made to depend upon the accuracy or regularity of the official works of clerks of courts" and stated: "It is well settled (in McCarthy *v.* March, 1 Seld., 263) that the judgment of the court admitting the alien to become a citizen is conclusive proof that the prerequisites of the law have been complied with."[33]

---

[29]Shaver and Reed were said to have delivered some "favourable speeches" after they replaced Justice Perry C. Brocchus and the other judges who left Utah in fright. Thomas B. H. Stenhouse, *Rocky Mountain Saints*, 279.

[30]Green, *Fifteen Years' Residence with the Mormons*, 247; italics in the original.

[31]Burr to Hendricks, March 28, 1857, in Buchanan, *Utah Expedition*, 118–20. William W. Drummond made the same assertion of poisoning, but Mormons considered him untruthful. Drummond to Black, March 30, 1857, in Buchanan, *Utah Expedition*, 118–20, cited in Bigler and Bagley, *Mormon Rebellion*, 112–13.

[32]*Cannon-Campbell Contested-Election Case*, 27–28.

[33]Ibid., 57–60. Other committee members included William H. Calkins (R-Ind.), Augustus H. Pettibone (R-Tenn.), Ambrose A. Ranney (R-Mass.), and Gibson Atherton (D-Ohio).

"The Lie Passed into History
and Became Truth"

William Ivins Appleby—with the collusion of Cannon, Judge Elias Smith, and probably Joseph Cain—entered into the court records a certificate of citizenship that was fraudulent, for Cannon did not meet the three basic requirements.[34] The Utah court records were entirely void of any action by Judge Shaver on December 7, 1854, other than appointing Dimick B. Huntington as interpreter to the Indians. Chief Justice Hunter concluded that the meeting described by Appleby's entry, in which Cannon, Cain, and Smith testified before Judge Shaver as to Cannon's whereabouts, had never taken place.

Despite years of wrangling, despite the official challenges by Robert Baskin and Allen Campbell, despite Chief Justice Hunter's ruling based on abundant evidence that Cannon had never qualified to be a citizen in 1854, despite the fraudulent entry—or double entry—made in the Utah court records, the U.S. House Committee on Elections in March 1882 ruled that earlier territorial supreme court precedents required that Cannon be considered a citizen. Congress immediately moved to disqualify George Q. Cannon from his seat representing Utah Territory, on the basis of his bigamous marital or cohabiting relationships addressed by the March 1882 Edmunds Act.[35] Cannon returned to his LDS Church service. Campbell was not awarded the seat, however, and it went unfilled until the election of monogamous Mormon John T. Caine.

Cannon represented Utah Territory from 1873 to 1881, in the Forty-Third, Forty-Fourth, Forty-Fifth, and Forty-Sixth Congresses. During his entire tenure in Washington, he worked diligently, with unwavering financial support from Utah, to defeat or derail numerous federal acts against theocratic rule, polygamy, and the application of federal land laws in Utah. To the Mormon theocracy's delight, the Logan, Nelson, Browning, Julian, Wade, Cragin, Ashley, Cullom, Stewart, Clagett, Voorhees, Merritt, Frelinghuysen, McKee, Luttrell, Christiancy, Woodburn, Hailey, and Cullom-Struble bills—variously directed toward polygamy, voting practices, court jurisdiction, and matters where Mormons were considered recusant to federal

---

[34]The quotation that is this section's subhead is from Orwell, *1984*, 46.

[35]Firmage and Mangrum, *Zion in the Courts*, 161. Cannon made a personal appeal to Vermont Republican George Edmunds to moderate his bill but was coldly rebuffed. Bitton, *GQC*, 252.

law—were never enacted.[36] In large measure, many, if not most, of these defeats were the result of Cannon's influence. Although considered by Mormons as victories at the time, enactment of one or more of these bills could have led to Utah receiving statehood much earlier than 1896. During all his years serving in Washington, Cannon held only a fraudulently obtained certificate of citizenship, yet he burked all attempts to reveal that fact. He held offices in which he was, in Congress's own term, a "usurping interloper." If biographer Davis Bitton is correct, that at life's end Cannon "had a clear conscience," it must also be true that he had either a selective memory or an ability to stringently compartmentalize his dissembling of the truth of the events surrounding his dishonestly obtained citizenship.

---

[36]Historian Howard Roberts Lamar claims that Cannon did little else in Congress than fight legislation: "While most territorial delegates were busy scrounging for appropriations, the Utah representative was busy defeating anti-polygamy bills or holding off the American land laws. As a result, Utah got a minimum of federal funds throughout the territorial period." Lamar, *Far Southwest*, 333.

II

The Tide against the Mormons Strengthens

There is a tide in the affairs of men,
which, taken at the flood, leads on to fortune.
WILLIAM SHAKESPEARE

AN UNSTATED "I TOLD YOU SO!" EXISTS IN ROBERT Baskin's recounting of why he did not give his greatest vigor to the passage of the 1874 Poland Act or the 1882 Edmunds Act. Baskin stubbornly maintained that if his Cullom Bill had become law in 1870, Utah's Americanization would have been accomplished much earlier. Piecemeal legislation—like the Poland and the first Edmunds Bill—would never have been needed, he insisted.[1] Yet Baskin and others were infused with renewed purpose in the final months of 1885 and early 1886. "[The Mormons'] political institution must be broken first, and polygamy would soon follow," he told the *New York Times*.[2] Baskin would soon be the principal proponent of the most severe legislation ever enacted against the theocracy in Utah.

On January 8, Senate Bill 10, labeled "the New Edmunds Bill," was reported favorably from the Senate Judiciary Committee and was scheduled for hearings in the House Judiciary Committee.[3] In Utah,

---

[1] Baskin, *REM*, 31, 173.
[2] "The Situation in Utah," *NYT*, March 23, 1886; "The Tucker-Edmunds Bill," *DN*, January 12, 1887, 12/5.
[3] The bill had been favorably reported by the Senate Judiciary Committee in 1884 but disappeared until December 1885, when it was reported out. Lyman, *Political Deliverance*, 34.

Charles C. Goodwin, *Salt Lake Tribune* editor
and Liberal Party member. *From the Alta Club
Photographic Collection of Special Collections
Department of the J. Willard Marriott Library,
University of Utah in Salt Lake City.*

Governor Eli Houston Murray refused to sign several bills passed by
the Mormon-controlled legislature, and for these refusals, which were
added to six years of disagreements with the Mormons, they called for
his "decapitation." He had been a "terror to the Mormon polygamists"
and "they one and all detested him," observed an Ohio newspaper.[4]
To Mormons he was "Gov. Whiskerando," a disparaging reference to
his luxurious black beard.[5]

On March 15 a polyglot of non-Mormons, mining men, merchants,
bankers, and attorneys convened to discuss Murray's plight and other
important Utah matters. Baskin was elected to represent Liberal
interests for the remainder of the Forty-ninth Congress, and Nevada's
Woodburn Bill was to receive their "hearty support."[6] Baskin was
authorized to work full-time in Washington on Utah's behalf and to
"urge legislation," presumably advancing the New Edmunds Bill, the
Woodburn Bill, or both.[7]

A March telegram from Interior Secretary L. Q. C. Lamar to
Governor Murray was curt: "The President . . . will be pleased now to

[4]"Removal of Governor Murray," *Newark Daily Advocate*, April 8, 1886.
[5]"Our Chicago Letter," *DN*, May 12, 1886, 2/1.
[6]William Woodburn, a lawyer in Virginia City, served from 1875 to 1877 in the Forty-Fourth
    Congress and from 1885 to 1889 in the Forty-Ninth and Fiftieth Congresses. The fate of the
    named "Woodburn Bill" is lost, its contents presumably incorporated into the Edmunds-
    Tucker Bill and/or into McAdoo, Voorhees, or Van Eaton bills, also introduced.
[7]"Gentile Representative," *SLT*, March 16, 1886, 4/4.

have your resignation."⁸ Despite Liberal Party men's pleas for Murray to fight for his term's remaining two years, he immediately replied: "Hon. R. N. Baskin . . . will proceed to Washington immediately and will on arrival place my resignation in the hands of the President."⁹ Non-Mormons, including those with Park City mining interests, contributed cash to support Baskin's effort in Washington for Murray and for passage of legislation.¹⁰

Baskin traveled to Washington with *Tribune* owner and editor Charles C. Goodwin. Joining them at the last moment was U.S. marshal Frank H. Dyer.¹¹ They planned to aid Baskin and "represent the silver interests" of the territory.¹² Dyer's decision to join Baskin may have resulted from knowing that Edward Payson Ferry was in Washington. Edward and William, brothers of Michigan senator Thomas White Ferry, both lived in Park City and were "deeply engaged in the silver mining business."¹³ The trio stopped in Chicago, whereupon the *Deseret News* correspondent transmitted a farcical message: "The rooms they occupied . . . were disinfected. . . . They carried a suspicious looking box . . . [that] contained the most succulent parts of a 'fatted Mormon' . . . destined to grace the banquet board . . . where Senator Edmunds, Hoar, Cullom, [and] Logan . . . are to be dined on their favorite dish."¹⁴

Baskin's luggage carried something far more substantial, however. Several days before Baskin's departure, Abraham Hoagland Cannon, the third son of illustrious George Q. Cannon, asked district court judge Charles S. Zane if he might make a few remarks before being sentenced on a charge of cohabitation. Abraham explained his

---

⁸Lamar, a Mississippian, was persuaded by George Q. Cannon to see Utah's non-Mormons as analogous to carpetbaggers. They answered that it was the enterprise of non-Mormons that had brought "nearly a hundred million in gold and silver" to Utah from mining. "How the Mischief Comes About," *slt*, April 25, 1886, 2/4.

⁹"Gov. Murray Resigns," *slt*, March 17, 1886, 4/2; "Kicked Out," *dn*, March 24, 1886, 1/3. Lamar treated Murray as a "bitter foe." "Gov. Murray Resigns," *nyt*, March 18, 1886. Highly regarded by others in Washington, Murray had retained his office well beyond the defeat of the Republican administration that appointed him.

¹⁰"To Help Baskin," *Park Record* (Park City, Utah), March 20, 1886, 3/2.

¹¹Dyer was later named the receiver of confiscated lds Church property, where he ran afoul of Baskin.

¹²"The Situation in Utah," *nyt*, March 23, 1886; "Personal Mention," *Park Record*, March 20, 1886, 3/3.

¹³"E. P. Ferry in Washington," *Park Record*, February 6, 1886, 3/3.

¹⁴"Our Chicago Letter," dated March 29, 1886, published in *dn*, May 21, 1886, 2/1.

defiance of the law: "That I now stand before you convicted . . . is due
to the fact that I acknowledge a higher law than that of man, which is
the law of God. . . . I promised to place all that I had, even life itself,
upon the altar, and I expect to abide by that covenant. . . . I hope the
day will never come when I must sacrifice principle, even to procure
life or liberty."[15] As Cannon finished, Baskin called to the clerk: "I
want a certified copy of that young man's speech. Give it in full and
see that it is certified to properly." The *News* reporter instantly recognized Baskin's intent to use Cannon's words "to facilitate and has-
ten hostile legislation."[16] Baskin now carried an official, undeniable
transcript proving the Mormon belief in the supremacy of theocratic
law over U.S. law. This was powerful ammunition for the upcoming
battle in Congress, refuting Mormon contentions that attitudes had
changed. Especially damaging was that the testimony came from the
son of George Q. Cannon, who had for years been paid "a heavy salary to . . . deceive Congressmen as to the real facts," purporting Mormons' subservience to federal authority.[17]

Against Baskin and the new Edmunds Bill was a formidable six-man
group, headed by John T. Caine, Utah's monogamist congressman.
Caine had filled the seat vacated by George Q. Cannon's discharge in
1882. Others of the team were George S. Boutwell, whose past political
positions made an impressive list; Jeff Chandler, of a prestigious Washington law firm; and Joseph A. West, a Utah legislator.[18] Franklin S.
Richards, a Mormon of high professional regard, would argue against
Senate Bill 10 while simultaneously defending Apostle Lorenzo Snow
in three cohabitation charges then before the Supreme Court.[19] Journalists commented that Mormons had "unlimited money" to hire such
lawyers as Chandler and Boutwell. There was "disappointment" that
"a man of Mr. Chandler's standing" would serve in such a role, but

---

[15]"A. H. Cannon Sentenced," *DN*, March 24, 1886, 1/4. Abraham H. was sentenced on the same
day his father, George Q., forfeited bail for failing to appear. "President Cannon's Case,"
DN, March 24, 1886, 9/2.

[16]"A Point for Treason," *DN*, March 24, 1886, 8/1; Whitney, *HOU*, 3:477.

[17]"Mr. Baskin's Appointment," *SLT*, March 17, 1886, 2/3.

[18]Boutwell's record included commissioner of Internal Revenue under Lincoln, secretary of
the treasury under Grant, U.S. representative and senator from Massachusetts, Joint Committee on Reconstruction member, and governor of Massachusetts.

[19]"The Apostle Surrenders," *SLT*, March 13, 1886, 4/6. Richards was successful, for the Supreme
Court ruled that Snow's three indictments would receive only one punishment. Ogden
businessman A. M. Gibson was the sixth member.

"Governor Boutwell's fall to the Mormon level was a shock his moral Massachusetts friends will never recover from."[20]

Several women were present for the battle: Emmeline B. Wells, a "bright and shrewd woman" who was Daniel H. Wells's sixth wife; Mrs. Franklin S. (Emily) Richards; Mrs. S. D. West; Mrs. John T. (Margaret) Caine; and Mrs. Ferguson, the wife of Dr. Ferguson.[21] Women supporting the bill included Caroline Owens Miles, known for her report of Mormon Temple ceremony details, and the colorful Kate Field, for many years a sought-after lecturer whose programs were severely critical of Mormons and polygamy.[22] In a note puzzling for the details it lacked, the *Tribune* said that "it was due more to her than to any other one person that the legislation, which culminated in the Edmunds-Tucker bill, was put in motion in the House."[23]

By April 1886, news of Baskin's efforts had drawn attention even in Utah's southern settlements. The Cotton Mission's Charles Lowell Walker entered in his diary, "A man . . . of bad repute has of late been lobbying Congress to influence them to enact law to disposes [*sic*] us of all our political rights and bring us under the rule of [a] set of adventurers and unprincipled men."[24]

In the House Judiciary Committee only three of the fifteen members were Democrats: the chairman, Virginia's John Randolph Tucker; Vermont's John W. Stewart; and John R. Eden of Illinois. In preparation for testifying before the committee, Baskin made three important visits. The first was to Tucker, with whom he was "well acquainted." Baskin explained the reasons behind Utah's non-Mormons sending him to argue for the bill, and the necessity of "radical and exceptional legislation." Tucker admitted that "he had never, except in a casual way, given any attention to the Mormon question." Reminding Tucker that his "position of chairman now imposed upon him the duty of making a thorough investigation of the subject," Baskin offered to furnish him with needed documents and data.[25] Baskin's visit with Tucker had

---

[20]"Mormons in Washington—the Star Engagement before the Congressional Committee on the Judiciary," *Brooklyn (N.Y.) Eagle*, June 7, 1886, LDS Archives, M243.91, M8654, 1886.

[21]"Capital Pointers," *SLT*, April 24, 1886, 1/4.

[22]"The National Capitol," *SLT*, May 4, 1886, 1/5. Mary Katherine Keemle, known as Kate Field, was famous for her lectures, especially "The Mormon Monster." Iverson, *Anti-polygamy Controversy*, 111.

[23]"Miss Kate Field," *SLT*, April 29, 1887, 2/3.

[24]C. L. Walker, *Diary*, 664.

[25]Baskin, *REM*, 173.

success, for a *Tribune* correspondent observed: "Tucker [was] in the Congressional library to-day studying up the laws of Utah, preparatory to grappling with the Woodburn bill. . . . He tells me that he is surprised to find how very little he knew about the statutes against polygamy. R. N. Baskin, an earnest Gentile from the Mormon Territory[,] was rendering him efficient aid."[26] Baskin's second visit was with President Grover Cleveland, seeking the support implied when Cleveland stated in his inaugural address that "the conscience of the people" demanded that polygamy be eliminated.[27] The third meeting was with Caleb Walton West, Utah's newly appointed Democratic governor, who also wisely had paid his respects to Cleveland.[28] West influenced his fellow Kentuckian John G. Carlisle, Speaker of the House, to facilitate Baskin's receiving speaking time before the committee.[29]

In four hours of testimony, Baskin emphasized that Utah's primary problem was the inextricable fusion of church and state. He pointed out that the Organic Act of 1851, which provided territorial status, contained a fundamental provision: "All the laws passed by the Legislative Assembly and governor shall be submitted to the Congress of the United States, and if disapproved shall be null and of no effect."[30] However, Brigham Young repudiated this requirement and, in reference to common law, deplored that in Utah there existed an "odious, tyrannical, and absurd system of colonial government . . . [that] emanated from the British throne."[31]

Baskin continued his criticism of Utah's church-state amalgam: Included in the territorial act of 1851 was the incorporation of the Church of Jesus Christ of Latter-day Saints, authorizing the church to hold property without limit and to buy, sell, and manage real and personal estate. Unqualified authority to participate in temporal affairs

---

[26]"Capital Pointers."

[27]John S. Scott, a mine owner, accompanied Baskin and likely stressed the benefits that mining had brought to Utah.

[28]"Our Capitol Outlook," *slt*, April 27, 1886, 1/4; "Choice Capital Crumbs: Governor West Has a Talk with President Cleveland; Mr. Baskin Calls on the President," *slt*, April 25, 1886, 1/4. Baskin may have known that the *Omaha Herald*'s George L. Miller had urged Cleveland to treat Mormons kindly. Lyman, *Political Deliverance*, 26–27.

[29]Lyman, *Political Deliverance*, 42.

[30]*Compiled Laws of the Territory of Utah* (1876), 30 (art. 15, sec. 6). In 1866 district court chief justice John Titus documented that Utah's territorial laws had never been submitted to Congress at any time up to 1861. "Legal Ruling," *dn*, October 24, 1866, 5/1.

[31]"Annual Governor's Message," delivered December 11, 1855, *Millennial Star* 18, no. 257, cited in Bigler and Bagley, *Mormon Rebellion*, 83.

afforded the LDS Church an immense income, which supplemented its revenue from tithing. Also included was Brigham Young's appointment as trustee-in-trust of the entire holdings—a position of great wealth that he occupied until his death. Even spiritual affairs were placed under LDS Church control, for "every act, or practice . . . [,] adopted for law, or custom, shall relate to solemnities, sacraments, ceremonies, consecrations, endowments, . . . [that] increase morality, and are not inconsistent with, or repugnant to the Constitution of the United States . . . and are founded in the revelations of the Lord."[32]

Baskin argued that the LDS Church incorporation was adverse to the English laws of mortmain, which prevented land from passing into church possession. He also considered it incredible that territorial laws, particularly those allowing unlimited church ownership of land and property and those relating to the territorial control of spiritual affairs, had never been submitted to or approved by the U.S. Congress. Since all else had failed, Baskin held it critical that the provisions of the 1862 Morrill Act, which dissolved the corporation of the LDS Church, be recast and the property accumulated by the corporation be escheated. Seizure of the financial base would be the key element in bringing Mormon government into compliance with federal law and civil practices, including marriage, Baskin reasoned.[33]

For his efforts Baskin earned the praises of Utah's non-Mormons. The report reached them that the audience remained standing as Baskin closed his argument: "His quiet, earnest manner and manly bearing made quite a favorable impression. . . . The general feeling . . . [is that he] has delivered some hot shot right into the enemy's camp, and has shown the . . . Judiciary Committee a load of paper they are not accustomed to seeing."[34]

In contrast to Baskin's four-hour presentation, five days of Mormon testimony stretched from April 26 to May 5, when summations took place. Jeff Chandler, capable and knowledgeable, spoke for the Mormons, spending an entire day arguing that government had no right

---

[32]*Compiled Laws of the Territory of Utah* (1876), 234 (sec. 3).

[33]In 1880 John Taylor admitted LDS Church ownership of $430,000 in Zion's Cooperative Mercantile Institution's stock, the Deseret Telegraph system, Zion's Bank, the *Deseret Evening News*, the Deseret paper mill, a church farm of over 1,300 acres, street railway stock, stock in the Deseret Bank and other banks, railroad shares and bonds, and a large amount of real estate in Salt Lake City and elsewhere. Utah Commission, *Report of the Utah Commission* (1887), 7.

[34]"The National Capital: Judge Baskin's Able Statement," *SLT*, May 4, 1886, 1/5.

to disestablish a church or interfere with the establishment of religion. Franklin S. Richards opened the second day, angry at Baskin's remark that a new revelation discontinuing polygamy could be readily procured, ordered up from pressure on the Prophet Brigham. Stating that this implied "insincerity on the part of the Mormon people," Richards chided, "Mr. Baskin knows full well that the Mormon people are sincere in their belief in the divinity of this principle." Baskin replied sharply: "Some are sincere believers, and some are hypocrites."[35] Considerable discussion centered on the distribution of proceeds if financial dissolution of the LDS Church were to occur.[36]

The contention that Boutwell was window dressing, appearing for the fee, was validated by his opening statement: "My retainer requires me to state such objections as occur to me."[37] The *Tribune* said of him: "He is too shrewd a man not to know that if the Mormon chiefs would give up what is illegal in their creed and teachings, there would never a word again be heard in Congress on the Mormon question. Yet for money he rushes to the defense of their system."[38] The *Tribune* ventured that the Mormons' goal on the hearing's fourth day was largely to occupy the time, thereby excluding opponents. Discredit on the conduct of Utah judges was attempted, which Baskin capably rebutted. Caine tried to establish that the motivation behind the bill was non-Mormon profiteering by putting church property in the hands of a receiver, for the benefit of "unscrupulous, designing, self-seeking men whose only object is the plundering of my people."[39] As to the matter of Congressional disapproval of territorial legislation, he argued that federal action was lacking, for "Congress . . . reserved the right to disapprove, and if it [had] exercised this power, the acts of the Legislative Assembly disapproved were null and of no effect."[40] Baskin considered Caine's argument to be specious; in Baskin's view, the reason the territorial acts in question had never been disapproved was that they had never been submitted to Congress as required.

On the final day, Baskin did not rehash his previous testimony but "in a quiet, earnest manner" gave "a new story":

[35]U.S. Congress, House, *Arguments against the New Edmunds Bill*, 54.

[36]Ibid., 89–91.

[37]Ibid., 92.

[38]"And Now Boutwell," SLT, May 4, 1886, 2/2.

[39]"The Mormon Problem," speech by Hon. John T. Caine of Utah in the House of Representatives, January 12, 1887 (USHS, PAM 1335).

[40]Ibid.

[He told] of the wonderful natural resources of Utah in climate, minerals and soil, . . . answering numerous questions from surprised committeemen. . . . He gave numerous instances . . . showing the determined purposes of the Mormons to prevent Gentile immigration, showing by statistics that Colorado, and Montana, Territories more recently settled, excel Utah. The statement of the untaxed mineral wealth of Utah made a favorable impression, and the Mormons admit this Gentile enterprise furnished the best market for their farm products.[41]

After listening to five days of testimony against his position and against him personally, Baskin was exhausted, and as he rose to close, supposedly by mutual agreement, Caine, to the "disgust of everyone, again rose for a speech. Baskin . . . seized his hat and cane, saying to the committee, 'Oh, I'm tired of this; I'm very weary,' creating great laughter."[42] The *Tribune* judged Baskin had done his task well, "his arguments having the force of legal ability, and supported by numerous references, which were especially satisfactory to the committee of most eminent lawyers, and which must convince them that there is something in the Mormon Church laws which prevents their harmonizing with the American form of free government, and that legislation is necessary for Utah."[43]

Baskin remained in Washington and in July had another interview with President Cleveland. Of that meeting, Baskin said that Cleveland was "interested in Utah affairs," and Baskin's judgment was that the president "would like to see the Tucker Bill passed."[44] By the end of July, Baskin succeeded in adding $10,000 to Utah's appropriations for apprehending and prosecuting cohabitors. He warned that Mormons were "using all their power" to remove U.S. attorney William H. Dickson and Judge Zane.[45]

Baskin's stay in Washington was interrupted by a telegram calling him to New York City in August, whereupon Washington newspapers shifted focus to the arrival of the Grand Army of the Republic

[41]"Baskin's Good Work," *slt*, May 6, 1886, 1/5. Baskin's comments on mining were on target: there were thirty-four active mining smelters in Utah by 1880, and by 1914 Utah became "the most industrialized state within the interior of the west through processing of ore." Taniguchi, *Necessary Fraud*, 16; Wiley and Gottlieb, "Salt Lake City," 455.

[42]"Baskin's Good Work."

[43]Ibid.

[44]"Tenacious Mr. Baskin," *slt*, July 11, 1886, 1/4.

[45]"Mormon Intrigue," *slt*, July 30, 1886, 1/2. Caine held a lengthy interview with Representative William Woodburn of Nevada, who was now derisively called "Buttermilk Woodburn" by the Mormons. "Our Chicago Letter," *dn*, May 12, 1886, 2/1.

(GAR) delegation, publishing a synopsis of the GAR speeches on the ills of Mormonism.[46] The *Tribune* waxed vehemently critical of J. Randolph Tucker for holding the legislation in committee for four months, accusing him of permitting his brother, Beverly Tucker, to influence the process, resulting in a "manifest neglect of duty." Tucker brought the bill to a hearing only when driven to by an indignant press, the *Tribune* said, charging that Beverly Tucker had been for years "the paid attorney of an organization of traitors against whose lawlessness the bill was aimed" and that almost daily he "was seen in company" of "a chief attorney of this traitor organization."[47]

The *Deseret News* ridiculed Baskin's living high in Washington while achieving only "barren results" and celebrated the becalmed state of the legislation: "The Church was to be robbed of its property[,] . . . the county and precinct officers were to be filled by the anti-'Mormons,' the territorial treasury and offices were to fall into the hands of the ring. . . . They sent their tool [Baskin] to do their dirty work. . . . And now they are flat. They haven't energy enough to curse with their accustomed viciousness."[48]

Growing support for legislation against Mormon theocracy was evidenced by a huge gathering of Civil War veterans in Salt Lake City, attended by Gen. S. S. Burdett, GAR commander in chief; Governor Frederick Robie and Gen. Selden Conner of Maine; Sarah E. Fuller of the National Women's Relief Corps; vocalist Clara Barton; and a host of Utah dignitaries. All spoke at "campfire gatherings," voicing their opposition to Mormon recalcitrance.[49]

Baskin took respite from the inertia afflicting the legislative process for the quiet Salt Lake City wedding of his "beautiful and accomplished" daughter Katherine "Kitty" Baskin to Frank Peyton, an employee of the Denver and Rio Grande Railroad. With only the couple's closest friends attending, they were married in the Baskin home by Baptist pastor Wood. Following a sumptuous wedding breakfast, the couple left by train for their future Utah home in Pleasant Valley Junction.[50]

The bill in Tucker's committee did not come for vote in the fall session, and in December Baskin returned to Washington, accompanied

---

[46]"Judge Baskin," *SLT*, August 7, 1886, 1/4; "The Mormon Lobby," *SLT*, August 14, 1886, 1/4.
[47]"On What Meat Doth This Caesar Feed?" *SLT*, August 10, 1886, 2/1.
[48]"Poor Creatures!" *DN*, August 11, 1886, 9/2.
[49]"The GAR Gush Continues," *DN*, August 11, 1886, 2/1.
[50]"The Peyton-Baskin Wedding," *SLT*, August 31, 1886, 4/5.

by fellow Mason and Liberal Party member Charles Washington Bennett. Before leaving Utah, the two men again sought support from non-Mormons in Park City, where they addressed a crowd of Loyal League members.[51] When asked if he would recommend a non-Mormon boycott of all Mormon enterprises, Baskin answered that it should not be done unless circumstances changed. In the Edmunds-Tucker legislation there was much for which they could all rejoice; it would prove to be an effective measure, explained Baskin.[52] The *News* reported that one man (Bennett) would "pull wires on the Republican wing," and the other (Baskin) would do so on the Democratic side. The "two B's" would "prove no drones" but attempt to babble, badger, banter, bargain, beaver, beg, bicker, bluster, bore, brag, bulldoze, and buzz, and to "bring about the bondage of the many for the benefit of the few," the *News* alliterated.[53]

Brigham's son John W. Young worked in Washington to prevent the legislation's passage, and John Taylor and George Q. Cannon's report was darkly cryptic: "He has done a good work, much of which from its nature can never be known but to a few." He also worked at "concentrating all our influence in business circles in channels that will be most favorable to us," where "our patronage should be so valued . . . they will help us politically."[54] However, as they had done when faced with the sure failure of the 1861 statehood petition, the Mormon leaders acknowledged divine intervention, whether it be for success or failure. In reference to Edmunds-Tucker they wrote to John W. Young, "the Lord had a purpose in permitting this bill to go through. . . . We must acknowledge the hand of the Lord in this."[55]

Knowing of another imminent bill from Idaho's John Hailey for the Americanization of Utah, Caine delivered a four-hour plea against

---

[51]The Loyal League, successor to the Gentile League, had three stated goals:"[to] combine the loyal people of Utah . . . in opposition to the political and law-defying practices of the so-called Mormon Church; to oppose the admission of Utah into the Union until she has the substance as well as the form of republican government; to raise money to maintain agents in Washington or elsewhere to labor for these ends." Larson, *Americanization of Utah*, 208.

[52]"Baskin and Bennett," *Park Record*, March 26, 1887, 3/4. Many of the estimated three to four thousand Loyal League members were associated with the Liberal Party and with Park City mining.

[53]"The Two B's," *DN*, December 1, 1886, 6/1.

[54]Taylor and Cannon to Erastus Snow in Mexico, March 29, 1887, and Taylor and Cannon to James H. Hart in New York, March 31, 1887, both in *First Presidency Letterpress Copy Books*, http://jfs.saintswithouthalos.org/pri/fp_87_03.htm (page discontinued).

[55]Taylor and Cannon to John W. Young, February 12, 1887, *First Presidency Letterpress Copy Books*, http://jfs.saintswithouthalos.org/pri/fp_87_02.htm (page discontinued).

Edmunds-Tucker.[56] Despite the intense Mormon opposition, the Edmunds-Tucker Bill passed the House of Representatives on January 12, 1887. Without President Cleveland's signature, it became law in March 1887. Its first provision validated Baskin's analysis that focus on money and church finances was critical. The Corporation of the LDS Church and the Perpetual Emigrating Fund were dissolved, together with confiscation of the property and wealth of both. The bill also said illegitimate children could not inherit; civil marriage licenses were required; it abrogated the common law espousal privilege for polygamists; it required wives to testify against their husbands; and it replaced probate court judges with federally appointed judges.[57]

If Mormon leaders were on their knees, it was as much in defeat as in prayer, for the restored Kingdom of God on earth was shattered. Ever the defender of polygamy and God's Kingdom, LDS president Wilford Woodruff arguably skirted treason as he saw the law as reason enough for a divine retribution, bringing about "the overthrow & final destruction of the United States government."[58]

BASKIN BATTLES THE
UTAH COMMISSION'S VOTING OATH

Also created by the Edmunds-Tucker Act was the Utah Commission, composed of five men who were appointed from outside Utah and whose primary function was to supervise election returns and issue certificates of election to those lawfully elected. Acting beyond his authority, chair Ambrose Bolivar Carlton drew up the wording of a voter's oath as he interpreted the act's requirements.[59] Carlton's oath included this statement: "And I further swear (or affirm) that I am not a bigamist or polygamist, and that I have not been convicted of any crime under the act of Congress." This elicited an alarmed response from Baskin, Utah legislator John E. Dooley, and Charles W. Bennett,

---

[56]"Injustice and Infamy," *DN*, February 2, 1887, 2–4/1.

[57]Events surrounding Edmunds-Tucker, the Scott amendment, the role of Caine, John W. Young, and Charles Penrose are treated elsewhere. See Bitton, *GQC*, 282–86; Lyman, *Political Deliverance*, 42–46. Mormon defender George Q. Cannon was concerned in fall 1886 and spring 1887 with his son John Q. Cannon's extramarital affair and embezzlement of $11,000 from church funds. K. L. Cannon II, "Wives and Other Women," 77–81.

[58]Woodruff, *Journal*, 8:421, cited in Neilson, *In the Whirlpool*, 64.

[59]After the Mexican War, Carlton had an undistinguished, bland career as an Indiana circuit judge. Monks, *Courts and Lawyers of Indiana*, 2:474–75.

who had spent weeks working in Washington to compose an effectively worded oath. Carlton's wording did nothing to bring about a repudiation of polygamy by Mormons unless they were at the moment personally participating. A man taking the Carlton oath could vote, then immediately take an additional wife. Congress had already prescribed the form of the oath, and Carlton had no authority to alter it, the *Tribune* objected. An oath more pleasing and beneficial to the Mormons could only have been written by the joint efforts of President John Taylor, aided by George Q. Cannon, Joseph F. Smith, and John T. Caine, the *Tribune* added sarcastically.[60]

Baskin sent Carlton the oath that he, Bennett, and others had crafted. It said in part: "I will obey the acts of Congress prohibiting polygamy, bigamy, unlawful cohabitation, incest, adultery, and fornication; . . . I will not hereafter . . . enter into plural or polygamous marriage . . . or cohabit with more than one woman; . . . I will not . . . counsel or advise, any person [to do so.]" Carlton agreed that the oath written by Congress referenced future action, but he insisted this was not allowed by Edmunds-Tucker.[61] Carlton stubbornly held that his appointment as chairman bestowed on him the authority to override the intent of the Edmunds-Tucker Act.

A spate of claims and counterclaims followed, with Baskin, former district attorney Ovando J. Hollister, William H. Dickson, Bennett, and others along with the *Tribune* on one side, contending with Carlton and the *News* on the other.[62] Baskin and five lawyers—Thomas Marshall, Charles S. Varian, Parley L. Williams, Dickson, and Bennett—sent a letter to all county and precinct registrars of Utah Territory. They maintained that, according to the Supreme Court's *Murphy v. Ramsey* decision, Utah commissioners did not have the power to prescribe the oath to be administered, and they offered to defend, free of charge, any election official against whom legal action was brought over Carlton's version of the oath required by the Edmunds-Tucker Act.[63]

---

[60]"An Open Letter to Judge Carlton," *SLT*, April 24, 1887, 2/3.

[61]"Letter from Chairman Carlton," *SLT*, April 24, 1887, 6/2.

[62]"An Open Letter to Judge Carlton," *SLT*, April 24, 1887, 2/3; "The 'Tribune' and the Commission," *SLT*, April 26, 1887, 2/1; "The Conspiracy Develops," *DN*, May 11, 1887, 6/4; "The Latest Test Oath," *DN*, May 11, 1887, 4/5; "The Commission to the Coercion Committee," *DN*, May 11, 1887, 6/2. Hollister, a veteran of the battle at Colorado's Glorieta Pass, became Utah's collector of internal revenue and a part owner of the *Tribune* and was to be the principal speaker at the funeral of Gen. George R. Maxwell in 1889.

[63]"More Registration Outrages," *DN*, May 11, 1887, 4/3.

Carlton claimed that the oaths were already printed and mailed to voting supervisors and there was insufficient time for republication.[64]

Enmity was elevated when Carlton arranged publications in the *Springfield* (*Mass.*) *Republican* and the *Chicago Times* alleging the legal right of the commission chair to write the oath.[65] Carlton described the versions submitted by Baskin and the members of the Loyal League as "an invasion of the prerogative of the Utah Commission."[66] The *Tribune* answered, repeating Baskin's assertion: "The Supreme Court of the United States has distinctly decided that the Commission has no right to formulate any oath; [and that it] has no authority over registrars, and can not in any way be held responsible for their acts."[67]

In the end, Carlton's form of the oath was not changed; clearly Carlton and fellow commissioner John A. McClernand of Illinois were aligned with the Mormons.[68] In their 1887 Utah Commission minority report the two men favored approval of statehood for Utah, but, admitting implicit distrust of the Mormon leadership, they also stood for a constitutional amendment outlawing polygamy.[69]

Statehood Fails Again in 1888

On June 16, 1887, three months after the passage of Edmunds-Tucker, the People's Party, under John T. Caine, called for delegates to convene in Salt Lake City on June 30 to frame a constitution in preparation for statehood. Non-Mormons were very distrustful of this sudden call, following the damages inflicted by Edmunds-Tucker. Mormons, they said, had made no good-faith resolution to abandon polygamy but meant to entrench it by means of the control statehood would bring them. This stance was supported in the majority opinion of the Utah Commission: "If Utah, as a territory, has refused to recognize the force and validity of national laws and decisions of the Supreme Court, can it be reasonably expected, as a State, it will do so?"[70]

---

[64]"The Commission's Reply," *SLT*, April 29, 1887, 4/4.

[65]"Is It More Carlton Dirt?" *SLT*, June 12, 1887, 2/3.

[66]"Dirt in Houses of Pretended Friends," *SLT*, June 29, 1887, 2/2.

[67]Ibid.; *Murphy v. Ramsey*, 114 U.S. 15 (1885).

[68]As a Democrat in Congress in 1860, McClernand had voted against the Nelson anti-polygamy bill directed at the Mormons of Utah Territory.

[69]Whitney, *HOU*, 3:577. Carlton was later hired by the LDS Church to fight the Cullom-Struble Bill.

[70]*Report of the Utah Commission* (1877), 21, 26.

Mormons continued to declare the laws of Congress unconstitutional and continued to claim that enforcement of federal law was persecution: "The only true and rightful government is a theocracy in which the powers of government are derived from God and delegated to ministers, who govern by divine right."[71]

Liberal Party affiliate and Utah Democratic Party chair John B. Rosborough declined the invitation to Democrats' participation in the convention. In a letter to Central Territorial Committee member John R. Winder, Rosborough said: "The control of your [People's] party . . . has stood, for a quarter of a century, and still stands, arrayed against National laws, and used . . . [its] powers to defeat their operation."[72] Republican Party chair William F. James also addressed a letter to Winder declining participation, asking, "Is not this sudden movement for Statehood the last resort of the leaders of your party, to free themselves from the consequences which adherence to their principles have visited upon them . . . , without giving any assurance that your system . . . is to be reformed?"[73] Liberals also did not want to imply any legitimacy by their involvement.[74] The Democrats, Republicans, and Liberals concluded: "The movement for Statehood is a direct fraud. . . . The spirit of . . . Theocracy has not changed in the least since it was intolerable to the men of Missouri and Illinois."[75]

Acting unilaterally, the People's Party convention drafted a proposed constitution. To avoid the pretense that the party represented all the people of Utah, all three non-Mormon parties refused to vote either for or against its acceptance. In this the non-Mormons were deceived, for when the Mormons took their sixth appeal for statehood to Congress, it spuriously appeared unanimous.[76] Again Caine was called on for his leadership, and the proposed constitution was presented to the Senate Territories Committee in February and March 1888. Caine

---

[71]Ibid., 16. On August 23, 1887, seven weeks after the convention drafted a proposed constitution whose provisions deplored polygamy, the Mormon populace feted several polygamists, celebrating their release from imprisonment in defense of the practice.

[72]"On Behalf of Democrats," in Utah Commission, *Utah Statehood*, 7.

[73]"On Behalf of the Republicans," in Utah Commission, *Utah Statehood*, 13.

[74]Lyman, *Political Deliverance*, 48; "Voice of the Non-Mormons," in Utah Commission, *Utah Statehood*, 14.

[75]"Conclusion," in Utah Commission, *Utah Statehood*, 72.

[76]Other difficulties for the Mormon leadership at this time included the death of President John Taylor while still in hiding and still contending, "The Kingdom of God or Nothing." With George Q. Cannon also in hiding and Joseph F. Smith being underground in Hawaii, the First Presidency had not met for nearly three years. Bitton, *GQC*, 287–88.

was supported, as he had been in the Edmunds-Tucker debates, by Franklin S. Richards. Indiana's Jeremiah M. Wilson and Arizona Territory delegates Marcus Aurelius Smith and Curtis Coe Bean also aided the Mormons.[77] Caine and his group were again opposed by Robert Baskin, now joined by Idaho senator Fred T. Dubois. Also in Washington to make their influence felt on lawmakers were John R. McBride, Elisha P. Ferry of Park City, and Patrick H. Lannan of the *Tribune*.[78] All spoke in adamant opposition to statehood. Their arguments focused on bigamy, polygamy, and cohabitation. Baskin pointed out that the Mormons' proposal made bigamy and polygamy forbidden and a misdemeanor but was "totally silent on the offense of unlawful cohabitation."[79] Why would 95 percent of the Mormons vote for the adoption of a constitution containing a clause prohibiting polygamy but with no mention of cohabitation? Baskin asked.[80] To Baskin's mind, the Mormons were cleverly hiding behind a misuse of the terminology, misleading lawmakers. He offered as evidence the declaratory statement the LDS Church published in the *Deseret News*: "Polygamy, in the ordinary Asiatic sense of the term, never was, and is not now, a tenet of the Latter-day Saints. . . . What we claim is that the Mormon system of marriage is, properly speaking, neither polygamy nor bigamy."[81]

Baskin emphasized, "The cohabitation clause of the Edmunds law [is] the only provision punishing polygamic practices that has ever been effective."[82] Lacking any civil marriage records in Utah, the four-man Utah Commission also had difficulty finding a working definition of the conditions of "bigamy" and "polygamy."[83]

Baskin further insisted that polygamy was not the singular issue

---

[77]Brigham's son, John W., telegraphed that he needed $15,000 "for Cullom" and another $10,000 "to make sure of the majority of the committee." Lyman, *Political Deliverance*, 61. Caine also spoke to the House in August and October 1888, his subjects being "Polygamy in Utah, a dead issue," and "Mormon facts vs. anti-Mormon fiction." Whitney, *HOU*, 3:676.

[78]The dates of Baskin's time in Washington are uncertain, for his daughter, Katherine C. "Kitty" Baskin Peyton, suddenly died on February 17, 1888; he almost certainly returned to Utah, but according to congressional records, he was present on Saturday, March 10, 1888.

[79]Baskin, *REM*, 189–90; "Badly Served," *SLT*, October 6, 1888, 2/1; U.S. Congress, Senate, *Admission of Utah*, 81–136.

[80]Utah Commission, *Minority Report*, 35. Evidence later revealed that none of those voting were Mormon polygamists, for they had been disfranchised by the provisions of the Edmunds-Tucker Act.

[81]Cited in Baskin, *REM*, 190.

[82]Baskin, *REM*, 190.

[83]Linford, "Mormons and the Law," 545.

against which laws relating to Utah should be directed, since "the theocratic tenet of the Mormon church is as great [an evil] if not a greater evil than polygamy."[84] Under statehood, theocracy, with all its products, would continue independent of external influence. The *New York Sun* expressed reservations about Utah's statehood that had not been previously identified: a Mormon-controlled state legislature could repeal all anti-polygamy statutes, and the federal government, short of passing a constitutional amendment, would be powerless. In a revised state constitution, Utah's governor would be free to give an outright pardon to any person convicted of polygamy, bigamy, or cohabitation.[85]

Attorney Richards's testimony opened with basic data about Utah's fitness, its population of two hundred thousand people, its financial health (with its only debt being for municipal bonds for irrigation of the city), and an illiteracy rate lower than that of any other territory. He addressed Baskin's criticism of the meaning of the words "bigamy" and "polygamy": "Whatever fine-spun distinctions may have been drawn in this matter . . . I know that they were not present in the minds of those who adopted this constitution."[86] When asked if tithing money was used in support of the poor, he did not answer the question but said, "There are no paupers in the Territory of Utah."[87] Caine made an incredulous assertion that contradicted the basic Mormon conception of the Kingdom of God: "There is not, and never has been, an intention on the part of the Mormons to set up a church establishment or to countenance a union of church and state."[88]

If Caine's testimony had tried the patience of Congress over the Edmunds-Tucker Bill, it was Baskin's "lengthy excursion into the past" over statehood that bored committee chair William M. Springer.[89] Dubois took the floor and told of Idaho's intent to deny statehood and seek governance by a legislative commission. Governor West also spoke, opposing statehood for Utah; his position, succinctly stated, was, "Utah has a theocratic government, while other states and territories

[84]Baskin, *REM*, 187.
[85]"The Constitution Question," *New York Sun*, August 30, 1887, reprinted in *DN*, September 14, 1887, 6/5.
[86]U.S. Congress, Senate, *Admission of Utah*, 4–6, 17.
[87]Ibid., 24.
[88]Ibid., 41.
[89]Lyman, *Political Deliverance*, 61.

have republican governments."[90] Senator Shelby Cullom reported the following from the Committee on Territories: "The Territory of Utah ought not to be admitted into the Union . . . until it is certain beyond doubt that the practice of plural marriage, bigamy, or polygamy has been entirely abandoned . . . and until it is likewise certain that the civil affairs . . . are not controlled by the priesthood of the Mormon church."[91]

The 1887 majority report of Utah Commission was not made part of the hearings in Washington, but in it commissioners G. L. Godfrey, A. B. Williams, and Arthur Lloyd Thomas were harsh regarding Utah's application for statehood: "A republican form of government has not existence in Utah, the church being supreme over all; . . . until the political power of the Mormon church is destroyed, the majority will not yield a full obedience to the laws."[92]

On his return from Washington in February 1889, Baskin again reported: "The committees agreed among themselves that it would not do to report favorably on the Utah admission bill, and it was apparent to the Democratic members that the party could by no possibility be made to unite on it. *This leaves Utah out of the Union for the next four years*, and perhaps by that time the Gentiles will be able to push for Statehood."[93] Once again, statehood for the territory was elusive to capture by the Mormons.

INTRIGUE, BOODLE, AND INDIGNATION

Mormon claims that civil matters were not controlled by the LDS priesthood received a severe blow by the events that followed the arrest of their luminary George Q. Cannon. In 1886, "Wanted" posters were plastered throughout the territory, listing a reward of $500 for Cannon and $300 for John Taylor, the LDS Church president.[94] The higher reward for Cannon's capture reflected his years of prominence in fighting to continue polygamy. Taylor and First Counselor Cannon were both hiding, their arrest sought under Edmunds Act

---

[90]"Governor West's Report," *DN*, November 7, 1888, 2/1.

[91]Baskin, *REM*, 191.

[92]*Report of the Utah Commission* (1887), 29.

[93]"Judge Baskin Feeling Well," *SLT*, February 7, 1889, 4/6; italics in the original.

[94]Samuel H. Gilson, a deputy marshal present at the Lee trial and later in anti-polygamy raids, was the author of reward signs and the sponsor of reward money for Taylor and Cannon. Taniguchi, *Necessary Fraud*, 13.

provisions against bigamy and cohabitation.[95] Cannon was arrested in February 1886 while on a railroad train in Nevada. Jumping from the train, he was soon recaptured. The Salt Lake court set his bail bond at the unusually high figure of $45,000. On release, Cannon jumped bail—as many had predicted—and returned to riding and hiding in the Mormon "underground."[96] He was not seen by Utah's non-Mormons until he presented himself in the Third District Court before newly appointed Judge Elliot F. Sandford on September 17, 1888.[97] Extra guards were stationed about the courthouse, all entering were searched for weapons, and soldiers from Fort Douglas were at the ready.[98] Cannon pled guilty to two separate counts of unlawful cohabitation, but Sandford sentenced him on one count only, and he served only five months in the territorial penitentiary.[99]

Non-Mormons and anti-Mormons were indignant, livid, at the lenient punishment. They considered Cannon, more than any other, to be responsible for preventing the passage of laws to end polygamy and to be the Mormon leader "most influential in advising ignorant men to break the law."[100] Non-Mormons insisted that, in jumping bail, Cannon had become a fugitive from justice, with the loss of all civil rights.[101] They wanted the full punishment of a $500 fine and five years' imprisonment, as stipulated by the Edmunds Act, wherein polygamy was made a felony, for Cannon had entered into another

---

[95]Baskin held that Cannon and Taylor's hiding rather than going to prison for conscience's sake, as they exhorted church members of lesser office to do, "did much to open the eyes of a deluded people as to the . . . folly of . . . resistance to the . . . law." Baskin, *REM*, 218–19.

[96]The *News* justified Cannon's failure to appear by citing a rumor of an intended sentence of life imprisonment, at a distant site, under "unbearable" conditions. "No Victim for the Sacrifice," *DN*, March 24, 1886, 7/3; "President Geo. Q. Cannon's Position," *DN*, March 24, 1886, 8/2. Of the $45,000 bond, $20,000 was contested; the ensuing battle was settled when Congress remitted the contested portion. Baskin, *REM*, 218.

[97]Cannon had been in Topeka, Kansas, having returned from a "visit to the East," reported the *Topeka Dispatch* of August 20, 1888. The paper speculated that when Cannon boarded the train with women presumed to be his wives, they were headed to Mexico, where he and the LDS Church had purchased two hundred thousand acres of land. "More of George Q.'s Withdrawal," reprinted in *SLT*, September 5, 188, 3/2.

[98]Seifrit, "Prison Experience," 223.

[99]Events of Cleveland's removal of Zane and replacement with Sandford, who had promised "a spirit of moderation and kindness," are treated in O'Higgins and Cannon, *Under the Prophet in Utah*, 58–62; and F. J. Cannon and Knapp, *Brigham Young*, 57–60, 70–71, 80–83. Frank J. Cannon cites a fine of $450 with 175 days in prison. See Lyman, *Political Deliverance*, 99–100.

[100]"That Hero and Martyr," *SLT*, September 19, 1888, 2/1.

[101]It was rumored that hundreds of Mormons refused to believe that Cannon had jumped bail. Ibid.

marriage after 1882.[102] A behind-the-scenes prearrangement with Judge Sandford allowed Cannon to enter a compromise plea of two counts of cohabitation, which Edmunds classed as only a misdemeanor, with the punishment for each a fine of $300 and not more than six months in jail.[103] It was widely groused that Cannon had not simply cohabited with women but took six women as his wives, living for periods with each and producing many children.[104]

Those who battled for decades to end the practice of multiple marriages felt that Cannon, the resolute icon for polygamy, deserved far more than a mere token sentence. Punishment should match the crime, and a maximum felony sentence was the proper match, in their opinion.[105] Cannon may have sensed from their anger that he was at personal risk, for he requested immediate sentencing and enactment. Sandford complied, and Cannon was given a courteous, comfortable ride to the prison, guarded by U.S. marshal Dyer and followed by many items for his comfort. [106]

A *Tribune* reporter circulated among the non-Mormons gathered in knots for libations and heated conversation at the Walker House hotel. He sampled the reactions to Sandford's ruling: Col. Enos Wall thought "something was up, and that such maneuvering was not without a *quid pro quo*."[107] Judge John B. Rosborough was "astonished, and hardly knew what to make of it." Ovando J. Hollister said, "The leniency of Cannon's sentence gives color to the general idea that Cannon's action is in pursuance of some covert scheming to advance

---

[102]Gustive Larson, "The Crusade and the Manifesto," in Poll, *Utah's History*, 259. Two of Cannon's marriages were before the 1862 Morrill Act, three after Morrill, and one after the 1882 Edmunds Act.

[103]Laws of the 47th United States Congress, Session 1, Chap. 47, Secs. 1 and 3, March 22, 1882. Sandford chose not to give Cannon two sentences even though he pleaded to two charges of cohabitation covering different time periods. Cannon's brother, Angus Munn Cannon, received the same sentence of a $300 fine and six months' imprisonment for cohabiting with three women. "The Anti-polygamy Law," *NYT*, December 15, 1885.

[104]Despite his 1888 punishment, Cannon subsequently fathered two children by his plural wife Caroline: Anne Y. Cannon was born in 1890, and Georgius Y. Cannon in 1892. Bitton, *GQC*, 464.

[105]George Q. Cannon's five months of prison time was less than the six months given his son Abraham H. Cannon.

[106]Two trips were needed for transporting Cannon's various accompaniments. Seifrit, "Prison Experience," 224.

[107]"The Public Indignation—Salt Lake Stirred Up as It Seldom Has Been—Unanimity against the Deal," *SLT*, September 18, 1888, 4/7. Baskin credited Enos Wall for introducing Idaho's oath legislation.

the Mormon State movement." Dr. John F. Hamilton "was ready to believe that Cleveland would pardon Cannon within sixty days" and thought that "the whole thing was a farce, so far as justice was concerned."[108] Henry W. Lawrence "thought it was a put up job, and a roaring farce."[109] Former chief justice Charles Zane "smiled at . . . [Cannon's] dodge in waiting for a new judge to appear before he gave himself up." Patrick E. Connor was seen sitting alongside Robert Baskin, and "their countenances indicated their ready sympathy with each other." Connor characterized the proceedings as outrageous, as "taking a long step in undoing what it had cost years of struggle to accomplish." The reporter observed: "Baskin had but one opinion. It was short, sweet, and to the point, but unproduceable."[110]

Imprisonment of Mormons for cohabitation or polygamy, John Taylor's death, and dissention over George Q. Cannon's leadership during Taylor's decline all made Mormons dejected. Takeover of church assets and 1888's failure of statehood also took a toll; the tide of Mormon dominance turned.

As the U.S. Supreme Court reviewed the Edmunds-Tucker requirement of a test oath, Baskin and William H. Dickson served as counsel in a Third District case concerning temple oaths taken by Saints. After hearing fourteen witnesses, including apostle John Henry Smith, Judge Thomas J. Anderson concluded: "The evidence . . . established unquestionably that the teachings, practices and aims of the Mormon Church are antagonistic to the government of the United States, . . . and . . . therefore an alien who is a member of said church is not a fit person to be a citizen of the United States."[111] Anderson insisted, "[T]here can be no question but that the church . . . control[s] its membership in temporal as well as spiritual affairs."[112] With this verdict and the Supreme Court affirmation of the Idaho oath, Baskin arrived in Washington in 1890 having written another bill. Confrontation awaited him and Caine over the severe provisions of the Cullom and Struble bills, which called for disfranchisement of *all* LDS Church members.

---

[108]Ibid.

[109]Ironically, Lawrence, previously excommunicated, was selected as receiver of the disincorporated LDS Church after Marshal Dyer's dismissal.

[110]"The Public Indignation"; "That Hero and Martyr." Shortly after this, Connor traveled to D.C. to lobby personally for the position of Utah federal marshal. Madsen, *Glory Hunter*, 257.

[111]"Judge Anderson's Court Decisions," *SLT*, December 8, 1889, 5/1; "A History Making Decision," ibid., 5/3.

[112]McMillan, *The Inside of Mormonism*, 74.

12

Baskin and
Public Education in Utah

*Possibly the gentile victory on the battlefield of education was
the most pregnant of all. . . . [S]chools began the
subtle disintegration of rigid attitudes.*
DALE LOWELL MORGAN

D ISPUTES OVER PUBLIC EDUCATION EXISTED AS ANOTHER
major element of alienation between Mormons and non-
Mormons in Utah. The respective roles of the church and
the state in public education were hotly contested in the latter third of
the nineteenth century, as part of the effort by non-Mormons to move
Utah nearer to social norms. Non-Mormons increasingly pushed for
free public schools comparable to those available to children in other
parts of America.[1] As Utah's non-Mormon population increased,
Episcopalian, Methodist, and Presbyterian missionaries were sent, in
part, to set up private mission schools for stirring Mormons into progressive social action. Mission schools, although not free, were superior to what had been previously available, either free or by tuition.[2]

According to social economist Edward James Blakely, the late
nineteenth century saw public education focused on two primary
objectives. The first was to achieve Americanization, with its emphasis on the values of democracy, love of country, patriotism, and the

---

[1]C. S. Peterson, "New Community," 294. See also Moffitt, *History of Public Education in Utah*.
[2]Tuttle, *Reminiscences of a Missionary Bishop*; Alexander and Allen, *Mormons and Gentiles*,
 111–16.

freedoms that America provided. The second was to provide vocational preparation of students—mostly men—by imparting a base of
knowledge and daily-life skills sufficient to earn a living and to contribute to the betterment of society.[3] Certainly Mormons shared the
second of these educational goals, but limits were in place for exposure
not consistent with their religious views. Despite overriding demands
for mere survival in their initial Utah isolation, Mormons were able,
as early as 1847, to establish common schools in most of their LDS
Church ward houses. However, Brigham Young unequivocally disapproved of the idea that Mormon children's education was the province
of any civic government. "I am opposed to free education as much as
I am opposed to taking away property from one man and giving it to
another. . . . Would I encourage free schools by taxation? No!"[4] Educational practices improved as the Mormons' view of society expanded,
and by 1854 the *Deseret News* reported: "We are commanded to seek
learning out of the best books . . . as we have *the best and most intelligent* set of children in all the earth." Education remained within the
scope of their religion, for the *News* said further, "We are anxious that
they [children] have a fair opportunity to keep the commandments,
and prepare themselves for the greatest possible amount of usefulness."[5] Three years later, Young told his Utah legislature that "each
ward throughout the Territory has provided one or more comfortable
school houses commensurate with the number of pupils to be accom-
modated."[6] His pronouncement was misleading. At the time only a
very small proportion of children were enrolled in the schools or regularly attended them. Even by 1862 only 31 percent of Utah's school-
age youth attended. In the 1886–87 report of Superintendent Parley
Lycurgus Williams, the figure had dropped to 27 percent, with forty-
eight of sixty-four schools reporting they had no school building or
property.[7] In his study of public education, C. Merrill Hough ignored
the non-Mormons' opinion that education at public expense should be
provided for all. "Mormons were not immediately concerned with free

---

[3]Edward James Blakely, "Planning Local Economic Development," presentation, Cornell
University, Ithaca, N.Y., April 30, 2010.
[4]Brigham Young, in Van Wagoner, *CDBY*, 5:3109.
[5]"Schools," *DN*, November 9, 1854, 4/1; italics in the original.
[6]Moffitt, *History of Public Education in Utah*, 27.
[7]Ibid., 264. Williams made no friends among Mormons when he successfully defended Deputy Marshal William Thompson, Jr., in the death of Edward M. Dalton, a Mormon polygamist shot while fleeing arrest in 1886.

Parley Lycurgus Williams, Baskin's friend and fellow lawyer. Williams spoke at Baskin's funeral of their long regard for one another. *From the Alta Club Photographic Collection of Special Collections Department of the J. Willard Marriott Library, University of Utah in Salt Lake City.*

public schools," he wrote, because of their "belief in self-sufficiency, which encouraged each man to assume financial responsibility for his children's education."[8] Classes were most commonly housed in the buildings built for local LDS Church meetings, and their use for any other purpose was controlled by local Mormon leaders, not a pleasing prospect for non-Mormon parents.

Mormon parochial schools aided basic reading, writing, and vocational skills but did nothing to Americanize the Mormon youth. In fact, schools run by the LDS Church taught that all contemporary governments—except that of Utah—failed to meet the most basic requirement of validity: they were not headed by Mormon men of God. Schools were to further the theocratic society established by Joseph Smith, and this policy was continued stringently by Brigham Young. Additionally, Mormons said the textbooks in non-Mormon "institutions of learning" contained "infidelity to God and the mission of our Savior." Textbooks in LDS schools, said the Mormons, "should be the Scriptures of divine truth—The Old and New Testaments, the Book of Mormon, Doctrine and Covenants and other [LDS] standard works, approved by the authorities of the Church." When children's minds were "thoroughly imbued with the principles . . . in those standard works and the oral teachings of inspired men," they asserted, "a

[8]Hough, "Two School Systems in Conflict," 117.

broad and sure foundation is laid, on which we may build up the hope of future usefulness in the kingdom of God."[9] The concept and the benefits of a liberal education were far beyond the pale in this constricted view of education's purpose.

Baskin devotes a substantial portion of *Reminiscences* to the history of the struggle for public schools in Utah. He includes the full text of Clarence Emir Allen's long letter, written in 1911, in answer to Baskin's request to document the happenings in the 1888 Utah legislature when Allen's education bill failed. Allen, a non-Mormon, was a mining executive and a territorial legislator from Bingham, Utah.[10] At the legislative session beginning in January 1888, Parley L. Williams, then territorial superintendent of schools, wanted to introduce a bill he had authored that called for public schools to be independent and nonparochial.[11] At the time, Williams was involved in court, serving as counsel for U.S. marshal Frank H. Dyer, the receiver of LDS Church property and funds seized under the Edmunds-Tucker Act provisions. Thus occupied, Williams asked Representative Enos D. Hoge, a non-Mormon and fellow Salt Lake lawyer, to submit the bill.[12] Hoge, in turn, deferred to C. Emir Allen, presuming that his membership on the House Education Committee would be helpful. Despite Allen's efforts, the bill was overwhelmingly defeated by the solid Mormon voting bloc. Mormon legislators, hoping to tap into the educational monies on their own terms, drew up an alternate bill. Formulated by Apostle Heber J. Grant, it was introduced by Representative James H. Moyle, House Education Committee chair. To no surprise, Moyle's bill sailed through the Mormon-controlled legislature, but it met a stern veto from Governor Caleb W. West. The governor said the bill's objectionable provision was enabling private or denominational

---

[9]"Text Books for Schools," *DN*, August 15, 1877, 9/1.

[10]Born in Pennsylvania, Allen graduated in 1877 from Western Reserve College in Ohio. Moving to Utah in 1881, he taught at the Salt Lake Academy, then pursued mining. Elected to Utah's House of Representatives in 1888, 1890, and 1894, he ran unsuccessfully as a Liberal candidate for the U.S. Congress, against Democrat Joseph L. Rawlins and Republican Frank Jenne Cannon. Admitted to the Utah bar in 1893, he served the Republican National Convention in 1892 and 1896. He then was elected to Congress, serving in 1896-1897. Declining renomination, he returned to mining. He removed to Ohio in 1922 and died in California in 1932. The ashes of Allen and his wife are interred in the grave of their son, Clarence Emir Allen, Jr., in Salt Lake City's Mount Olivet Cemetery. "Clarence Emir Allen," http://en.wikipedia.org/wiki/Clarence_Emir_Allen.

[11]The territorial school superintendent was appointed by the territorial governor.

[12]Hoge would later join Robert Baskin in a law partnership.

schools to share in the public school fund, but it also created an even more serious problem, since it would give "denominational schools . . . the aid of the civil power by the means of taxation to advance the tenets of the [Mormon] church." Rather than enhancing public education, the bill would effectively "destroy the imperfect system of district schools already existing."[13] This first attempt in the territory to provide free public schools ended as a defeat in 1888.[14]

School Monies and Receiver Difficulties

Parley L. Williams and Baskin could not contribute to C. Emir Allen's efforts in the legislature in the early months of 1888, because they were occupied by the ongoing court proceedings over the escheated LDS Church property and funds. Provisions of the Edmunds-Tucker Act called for the seizure of property, corporate assets, the Perpetual Emigrating Fund, and other church funds. A portion of monies so derived was to be designated to benefit public education. Court action on the escheatment started in July 1887.[15] In a mid-November court session U.S. attorney George S. Peters appointed Marshal Dyer as receiver of the property and funds. Anticipating a need for legal advice and counsel, Dyer hired Parley Williams.

The court action seemed to be proceeding smoothly until the session was suddenly interrupted by an unprecedented outburst from the bench. Surprisingly, the outburst came from the presiding judge, Chief Justice Charles S. Zane.[16] After a whispered aside with fellow judges Jacob Smith Boreman and Henry Parry Henderson to discuss Dyer's appointment, "it was apparent that he [Zane] was displeased—highly displeased." To the further surprise of all present, Zane abruptly and uncharacteristically announced, "I want it distinctly understood, . . . that I dissent from this appointment."[17] Charges of fraud came later, when Zane accused Dyer of "hobnobbing with Mormon leaders on

---

[13]Utah Legislative Assembly, House, *House Journal*, 343.

[14]Baskin, *REM*, 198–99.

[15]The divestment of LDS Church property and assets is treated at length in Arrington, *Great Basin Kingdom*, 360–79.

[16]In Illinois Zane had been a close friend of Abraham Lincoln, and a law partner of anti-Mormon hard liner, Shelby M. Cullom.

[17]Peters had already obtained approval of Dyer's selection from the counsel representing both sides. "Marshal Dyer Receiver: Judge Zane Does Not Approve of the Appointment," *DN*, November 16, 1887, 1/1.

the underground" and compromising with them on the property values. Responding to Zane's accusations so occupied Parley Williams that he had no time to devote to the passage of the public school bills then under consideration in the legislature.[18]

Shortly after his court outburst, Zane was dismissed as chief justice by President Grover Cleveland. The reasons for Zane's removal concerned the sentencing of George Q. Cannon and were entirely unrelated to the Marshal Dyer matter. The new appointee, Judge Elliot F. Sandford, relieved Zane on August 28, 1888.[19] No longer a court officer, Zane joined with his son, John Maxcy Zane, and Robert Baskin as trustees to represent the Salt Lake City schools. Wishing to maximize the amount of money for Utah's public school system from the seized LDS Church assets, they charged that Dyer's fees and those of his assistant were "grossly excessive, exorbitant, and unconscionable," constituting fraud, misconduct, and corruption.[20] It was this time-consuming battle over money for public education that prevented Robert Baskin from assisting Allen in the legislative battle over the education bills. The court ruled to investigate the fraud charges against Dyer but declined, at that point, to examine the level of the marshal's compensation. As school trustees, Zane, his son, and Baskin withdrew their charges and explained: "As long as we had some chance of benefitting the common schools of this Territory we thought it our duty to proceed, but we conceive it to be no part of our duties as school trustees to prosecute charges of fraud and corruption against the officers of this Court."[21] According to history written by Baskin's enemy Orson F. Whitney, the two Zanes and Robert Baskin were found in contempt for bringing unfounded complaints before the court. Not only was their well-intentioned effort to gain funds for public schools unsuccessful, but they were allegedly fined court costs.[22]

---

[18]Whitney, *HOU*, 3:661.

[19]Zane's replacement by Sandford was a sub rosa arrangement with President Cleveland to provide a judge who would be lenient when sentencing Cannon for bigamy and polygamy. In June 1889, President Benjamin Harrison dismissed Sandford and restored Zane, an action for which Harrison was criticized. "Why the Utah Justice Was Removed," *NYT*, June 10, 1889.

[20]Whitney, *HOU*, 3:661.

[21]Ibid., 3:662. Dyer was finally awarded $10,000, with $5,500 to Parley Williams and $4,000 to Peters. Other benefits may have accrued, however, for Dyer, Williams, Deputy Arthur Pratt, and Thomas Marshall (all Liberals) quickly took ownership and control of the Salt Lake Gas Company. "Gas Company Directory," *SLT*, March 13, 1890, 5/7.

[22]Whitney, *HOU*, 3:662.

ANOTHER ATTEMPT, ANOTHER DEFEAT

Baskin remained undaunted in wishing to defeat the People's Party candidate and obtain the post of territorial representative to Congress, despite his two earlier losses to George Q. Cannon and the several losses of William McGroarty, George R. Maxwell, and Allen G. Campbell to the People's Party. Under the sponsorship of a group of locally prominent, non-Mormon figures whose political orientation was diverse (Orlando W. Powers, Henry W. Lawrence, Enos D. Hoge, John M. Zane, and Parley L. Williams), the Liberal Party once more drafted Baskin to run against the Mormon incumbent, John T. Caine. On the rain-soaked night preceding the election, the Opera House drop curtain was festooned with a banner that appropriately read: "A Common Peril Unites Us." Baskin spoke of his accomplishments with John Randolph Tucker, of his concern about theocratic rule and indignantly charged that LDS Church leaders had begun using the Democratic Party, to which he held lifelong allegiance, to gain the statehood that had eluded them.[23] Samuel R. Thurman, a Mormon, ran as a "Sagebrush Democrat" but received only 511 votes. Again, voting resulted in a lopsided defeat, with 3,484 votes for Baskin against Caine's 10,127.[24] The *Tribune* appraised it as a dull day, with a very light vote, a "very lame affair."[25]

THE CHILLING PROSPECT OF MORE FROM EDMUNDS

By the beginning of Utah's legislative session in January 1890, C. Emir Allen had advanced to chair the House Education Committee, where he tried once more to move public education legislation forward. Again working with Parley Williams, he introduced two separate bills on education reform, each aimed at creating and supporting public schools. One was shown to the "Sagebrush" representative Thurman of Provo, asking for his support in lower chamber, and the other was shared with Councilman Charles C. Richards of Ogden, seeking his leverage in the upper chamber.

In February the report of territorial school commissioner Jacob S. Boreman drew controversy. Some legislators asked that the report be published only after removing an objectionable paragraph that stated,

---

[23]"Last Night's Big Rally," *SLT*, November 6, 1888, 4/2.
[24]See Lyman, *Political Deliverance*, 102–103; and *Appletons' Annual Cyclopaedia*, 832.
[25]"Our Local Campaign" and "The Election," *SLT*, November 7, 1888, 4/2 and 3/3.

"The authorities of the Mormon Church are inaugurating a system of church schools which are calculated to draw the children of the members of that church away from the district schools." The report further urged that wiser counsels should prevent this and that the American policy of providing free public schools for all should be encouraged and adopted.[26] The charge against the Mormons' plan contained in Boreman's report was roundly denied by the *News*. At this time the Mormons and the non-Mormons ran parallel education systems, with a Mormon commissioner for church education and a non-Mormon territorial school commissioner appointed by the governor.[27]

Both the Allen Bill in the House and one in the upper chamber, sat inert in respective committees, opposed by Mormon majorities, until a shocking news report from Washington was received by Utah's legislators. Allen and Baskin, anticipating the tactic of a blockade, had quietly enlisted the aid of Governor Arthur Lloyd Thomas. The governor personally carried Allen's bill to Washington for submission in Congress by Senator Edmunds, the bête noire of Utah's Mormons because of his Edmunds Act and Edmunds-Tucker Act. Allen announced that Edmunds was ready and willing to submit it for Senate action, an assertion the Mormons vigorously disputed, saying that Edmunds had refused Thomas's request to introduce the bill.[28] However, reports from Washington soon confirmed that Edmunds had indeed submitted the Utah education bill: "The bill introduced by Senator Edmunds today . . . is a most comprehensive measure and with great minuteness provides about all the legislation necessary for the conduct of school affairs in the Territory. One of the objects of the bill is to diminish the Mormon influence."[29] This Edmunds bill would have required an appointed commissioner of schools to supervise education in the counties, with provisions to levy taxation and distribute monies on the basis of the number of children between ages six and eighteen. Each county would have a superintendent of schools appointed by a three-man body composed of the governor, the

---

[26]Former judge Jacob Smith Boreman was appointed in 1899 as the territorial commissioner of schools, a position he held until 1894. Anger at being recently arraigned before Judge Charles Stetson Varian on the charge of cohabitation may have been an additional reason for Thurman's not assisting Allen. Godfrey et al., *Report of the Utah Commission*, 14.

[27]"An Objectionable Paragraph," *DN*, February 15, 1890, 16/3, 17/1; U.S. Congress, Senate, *Hearings before the Committee on Territories*, 4.

[28]"Edmunds' Utah School Bill," *DN*, February 22, 1890, 9/3, 10/1.

[29]"Education for Utah—Senator Edmunds Introduces a Comprehensive Measure," *SLT*, February 12, 1890, 1/6.

commissioner, and the county probate judge. All would answer to the commissioner. Whenever money became insufficient, additional taxes could be levied without approval in Utah's legislature.[30]

Despite John T. Caine's attempts in Washington to block it, the territorial legislators in Salt Lake considered the passage of the Edmunds education bill a risk too high. Suddenly, the two bills of C. Emir Allen's authorship that had been held in committee by Thurman and Richards were fused and promptly reported out. Now named the Collett Bill, for Council Committee chair William G. Collett of Tooele County, "the bill was passed and put into operation throughout the Territory during the year 1890." According to Baskin's summary, education of children in the territory was made compulsory, and city education boards were authorized to submit to the people the question of issuing bonds for school purposes. Under the new law's authority, Salt Lake City was able to place before the public the issuance of bonds of $850,000 for purchasing land and erecting schoolhouses. With support from the Liberals of the city, the bonds were authorized by a "decisive majority of the votes cast."[31]

REFLECTION

Baskin allots the major credit to Clarence Emir Allen, Parley Lycurgus Williams, and a liberal-inclined councilman and Mormon, John D. Peters, and gives lesser credit to himself for the accomplishment that "Utah's free school system is such as any civilized community might well be proud of, and is the boast of the generations of the inhabitants of this State." The laws of 1890 and 1892 provided a uniform system of free public schools throughout the territory, made children's education compulsory, supplied enforcement methods, and included funding provisions. With monies secured from bonds, land was purchased, schools were built, heated, and ventilated, and flagpoles and flags installed. Schools district boundaries were no longer the same as the local LDS ward boundaries.[32] Schools were named for "prominent statesmen, soldiers, men of letters, philosophers, philanthropists, and prominent educators," such as Lincoln, Franklin, and Washington.[33] A

---

[30]Ibid.

[31]Baskin, *REM*, 200–201.

[32]McCormick and Sillito, "Henry W. Lawrence," 228.

[33]"The Board of Education," *SLT*, March 12, 1892, 30/1; March 19, 1892, 31/2; March 26, 1892, 6/1; April 16, 1892, 30/2; May 14, 1892, 30/3; *DN*, August 6, 1892, 30/2.

detailed review of Salt Lake City's progress in public education under
the administrations of Scott and Baskin was published by the *Tribune*.
Each man, while mayor, was simultaneously Board of Education president, and under their leadership in both positions, four "magnificent
school houses were thrown open" and were "at once filled to their full-
est capacity." By 1893, enrollment of eligible students, ages six to eighteen, was at 84 percent, a remarkable figure when compared with the 40
to 50 percent enrollment in New York, Ohio, Indiana, and Illinois in
the same period. All books, stationery, and other articles needed were
furnished to students by the Board of Education. Courses of instruction were set into teachers' manuals, and materials devoted to science
and history were supplied to them. The *Tribune* reported: "Objective
methods of study in arithmetic, language, and science are employed;
principles are reached inductively; and in general, the dogmatic statement of facts by teacher and textbook is made subordinate to their
discovery by the pupil himself, under the guidance and suggestion of
the instructor." The liberal arts were not neglected, for "the choicest of
the English and American classics are read in unabridged form." The
body of teachers and principals numbered 176. "For the study of methods of teaching, the discussion of matters of importance connected
with school work, and the promotion of a professional spirit among
teachers, a regular system of grade meetings" had been set in place.[34]
Henry W. Lawrence, formerly a faithful Saint, later a colleague of
William Godbe's, and a longtime Liberal Party leader, eventually led a
successful effort to allow community groups to meet in the city's public school buildings, a move he thought necessary to reduce Mormon
influence in public education.[35]

Despite his own accomplishments, Baskin insisted that C. Emir
Allen, as he preferred to be called, had earned the title "Father of
Utah's Free Schools," a nomination ignored or forgotten by others
writing about the history of public education in Utah.[36] Baskin also
insisted that recognition was due, not only to Allen, Williams, and

[34]"Public Schools of the City," *SLT*, January 1, 1894, 9/7.

[35]McCormick and Sillito, "Henry W. Lawrence," 236. Students enrolled in public school were
    labeled as Mormon or non-Mormon, a practice that did not end until statehood in 1896.
    White, "Prelude to Statehood," 304.

[36]Baskin, *REM*, 202–204. Despite C. Emir Allen's admirable record of accomplishment, his-
    torian Stanley Ivins identifies him only as an "outsider" and the complicated process of
    securing legislation against Mormon opposition as merely "some jockeying." Ivins, "Free
    Schools Come to Utah," 341.

Peters, but also to former U.S. marshal William Nelson. His name, widely associated with his role as the marshal in the second trial of John D. Lee and the person who conducted Lee's execution in 1877, Nelson was for years a *Salt Lake Tribune* editor.[37] As a Liberal Party candidate, Nelson was elected president of the school board, where he "was most active, persistent and efficient in promoting the interests of the public schools of the city," said Baskin in honoring his colleague, adding that "during his incumbency thirteen modern school houses were . . . erected in the city."[38]

Baskin places into perspective the long divide between Mormons and non-Mormons on the profoundly important issue of schools for public education, observing that "from the organization of the Territory in 1850 until 1890, a period of forty years, no free school law was enacted by the [Utah] legislature" and that "even at that late date it was impelled to act" only by the threat of federal legislation bearing the dreaded name of Senator Edmunds.[39] Mormons wanted no more laws like those of 1882 and 1887 that carried *his* name, for they had broken the unity of church and state and ended their virtual "Kingdom of God" on earth.

---

[37]Undoubtedly, recognition of Nelson's contribution to public education was adversely affected by his being the "sole source of Utah news launched into nationwide circulation through his Associated Press dispatches." George Q. Cannon called him a "champion liar" and complained that his associates worked daily to neutralize Nelson's "batch of inflammatory and lying dispatches." By 1887 John T. Caine asked that church officials contact Associated Press representative William Henry Smith about having Nelson replaced. Lyman, *Political Deliverance*, 33, 70; Mills, "Pushing the Car of Progress Forward," 34–35. Given the antipathy that Nelson generated with his AP dispatches, that he was a longtime Liberal Party man, and that he had served as Utah's marshal and at John D. Lee's execution, it is not surprising that his first act on each day's arrival at the *Tribune* office was to place a pistol within easy reach on his desktop. Malmquist, *First 100 Years*, 245.

[38]Baskin, *REM*, 203. Neither Baskin, Nelson, nor Allen—all non-Mormons—is found in Moffitt's *History of Public Education in Utah*, and Parley L. Williams is mentioned only sparingly.

[39]Baskin, *REM*, 203.

13

Challenge and Controversy

*The ultimate measure of a man is not where he stands in moments
of comfort and convenience, but where he stands
at times of challenge and controversy.*
MARTIN LUTHER KING, JR.

U TAH'S FIRST LEGISLATION INITIATING FREE PUBLIC
schools of quality was passed in 1890 and was accomplished
without Baskin's direct help. His absence from the process
was due, not to lack of desire to be involved or to any hesitation on his
part, but to circumstances beyond his control. In January 1890, Baskin
was eager to cooperate with C. Emir Allen, and they planned to battle
for public schools in the pending legislative session. But personal tragedy intervened.

The weeks prior to the February 1890 elections were "the most
exciting times ever experienced in Utah": "Parades, ratification meetings, display of fireworks, the marching of thousands of men, the illumination of private homes and business houses, the shouts and yells
of enthusiastic men and women made the streets a scene of life and
enthusiasm seldom seen in cities ten times the size of Salt Lake City,"
reported the *New York Times*.[1] Even at seventy years of age, Gen. Patrick Connor played a major organizing role in the Liberals' campaign,
in which he was "everywhere and involved in every detail" in support
of the candidates.[2] Baskin took part in the celebration after the Liberal

---

[1]"Work of Utah Liberals," *NYT*, February 10, 1890.
[2]Connor hoped for a modest retirement income from the military. Madsen, *Glory Hunter*, 263.

Party brought in a clean sweep under manager Orlando W. Powers.[3] George M. Scott, a prosperous hardware merchant, defeated the People's candidate, Mormon businessman Spencer Clawson, to become the first non-Mormon mayor of Salt Lake City. Liberal candidates carried all but three council races, and even these were awarded to the Liberals upon review by the Utah Commission officials.[4] Scores of men, Baskin among them, signed a telegram to notify former Governor Eli H. Murray, then living in San Diego, California, thanking him for the contributions he had made to the end now accomplished.[5]

Baskin, along with other contributors to the victory, was celebrating at the Alta Club late into the evening of Saturday, February 11. Just after midnight he stepped to the telephone at the posh gentlemen's lair to take a call he thought would be a congratulatory one from his wife.[6] The events of the next moments were detailed in the *Tribune*:

> Mrs. Baskin was then apparently as well as ever, and was with her son-in-law, Mr. Peyton, down stairs while she retired. At 12 o'clock she jumped out of bed and called for assistance, exclaiming that she was suffering. Mr. Peyton sent the girl to her assistance, gave what immediate aid he could, and then hurried down town to get the Judge. The two returned from the Alta Club with Dr. Hamilton, but Mrs. Baskin was dead when they arrived. The unfortunate husband is prostrated by the terrible calamity, and scores of friends are extending their sympathy. Mrs. Baskin was born in Canada in 1840, and was Miss Olive Lavinia Gardner where she met Judge Baskin in this city in 1867, in which year they were married. They had three children, but all are dead; the last, Mrs. Peyton, dying two years ago, also from heart disease, which carried off Mrs. Baskin's father. She leaves a daughter by a former husband, Mrs. Lila Jones, who has been wired for in California. The funeral will be held on her arrival.[7]

The following day, a related item appeared in the *Tribune*:

---

[3] The *News* dubbed Powers "Orlando the brave," and Governor West "Caleb the callous." "Our Chicago Letters," *DN*, February 22, 1890, 2–3/1.

[4] "A Clean Liberal Sweep," *SLT*, February 11, 1890, 4/2.

[5] "Gov. Murray Remembered," *SLT*, February 11, 1890, 4/7.

[6] Telephone service began in Salt Lake City in April 1881 by the American Bell Telephone Company; by 1890 there were more than five hundred subscribers. Jay M. Haymond, "The Telephone in Utah," www.media.utah.edu/UHE/t/TELEPHONE.html.

[7] "Death of Mrs. Baskin," *SLT*, February 12, 1890, 4/6. The records for Katherine C. Baskin Peyton list "hemorrhage of the lungs" as the cause of death, suggesting underlying pneumonia or tuberculosis rather than heart disease, as cited by the *Tribune*.

The late Mrs. Baskin was a woman of noble charities, yet she was so quiet about it that the public never accorded the credit due her.[8]

Another sincerely intended note of comfort for Baskin was also found in the *Tribune*:

The whole community will sympathize . . . on the great blow that has fallen upon him. . . . He is an iron man, but his heart is as soft as a woman's, and those kind of people, while giving no sign[,] suffer most.[9]

Even the *Deseret News*, not often gentle in matters relating to Baskin, offered kind words:

Mrs. Baskin . . . was well liked on account of her kindly disposition. . . . [D]eath has made many inroads into [her husband's] domestic circle. . . . "One touch of nature" brings into activity the sympathies of the human heart and subdues, for the time at least, all differences, however wide. We are therefore among those who condole with the chief mourner.[10]

The Reverend R. G. McNece of the First Presbyterian Church recorded in his pocket diary a brief note on the funeral, held February 15, 1890: "This takes away Mr. Baskin's wife and his 3 children[,] leaving him desolate."[11] A large attendance marked her funeral, with "the business and professional part of the city being largely represented," said the *Tribune*. Judge Zane and other prominent city figures were pallbearers. The procession to Mount Olivet Cemetery required more than thirty carriages.[12]

Understandably, Robert Baskin did not attend the boisterous celebration of the Liberal Party that took place on the evening of his wife's interment. Party chair Orlando Powers was feted for his pursuit of purpose: "After working all day he would go and speak often at three or four meetings in the evening. And the only pay he would

---

[8]"City and Neighborhood," *SLT*, February 13, 1890, 4/1.

[9]Untitled article, *SLT*, February 12, 1890, 2/1.

[10]"Mrs. Baskin's Death," *DN*, February 22, 1890, 29/1.

[11]First Presbyterian Church Records, Special Collections, Marriott Library, University of Utah, uu_Acc1049, box 13, folder 2.

[12]"City and Neighborhood," *SLT*, February 16, 1890, 4/1. The Baskin family's sexton records are unclear. Salt Lake City Cemetery records claim Olive's burial but indicate removal in 1917 to Mount Olivet Cemetery, at disagreement with the 1890 newspaper reports. There are no gravestones on the Baskin plot that might give additional information; it appears that Robert, Olive, and one other are interred at Mount Olivet; the burial sites of two Baskin children are unknown.

receive was the good will of his fellow men."[13] Scores of contributors joined Governor Arthur Thomas and the three Utah commissioners, together with Mayor Scott, Chief Justice Zane, Charles C. Goodwin of the *Tribune*, and attorney Charles S. Varian, for food, wine, and a series of toasts to individuals who had worked for the win. Col. Samuel A. Merritt sketched the history of their road to victory, singling out Gen. Patrick Connor, Judge James B. McKean, Gen. George R. Maxwell, and Robert Baskin as pioneers of the efforts that ultimately led to political victories.[14] Powers was awarded $10,000 for his diligence, and he and his wife declared a time for recuperation and soon relocated to San Francisco for a vacation.[15] Newspapermen in that city flocked to interview him on his Utah success.[16] However, lines of jubilation were not uncoiling down the halls at the *Deseret News* office in Salt Lake City, for there the election's outcome and Powers's magnanimous reward were deplored.[17]

Depression Stalks the Man

The severity of the depression and grief that followed the death of Baskin's wife, that emptied him of resolve in working for public education and the Americanization of Utah, can be gauged by his decision to sell his Wood's Cross ranch and his stable of thoroughbred horses. He also made known his intention of selling his home and closing his professional practice in preparation for returning to Highland County, Ohio. Encouraging words from his friends and colleagues were published in the *Tribune*:

> Baskin has . . . sold his farm and horses, and says he wants to sell his home, preliminary to closing up his business and going back to his early home to live. When told that his friends desired him to remain that he might be their first Gentile representative in Congress from Utah, he answered that such an honor would a few years ago have awakened the

---

[13]"The Campaign Workers," *slt*, February 12, 1890, 2/1.

[14]"Banquet to Mr. Powers," *slt*, February 16, 1890, 4/2.

[15]Before the Senate Committee on Territories, Powers testified that $4,000 was given by the Walker brothers, grateful that the value of their properties had increased $400,000 as a result of the election. Fred Dyer was identified as another contributor. U.S. Congress, Senate, *Hearings before the Committee on Territories*, 106.

[16]"The Mormon Defeat," *San Francisco Chronicle*, February 22, 1890, reprinted in *slt*, February 26, 1890, 6/2.

[17]"Statement by Powers," *dn*, March 8, 1890, 26/3.

full measure of his energies and enlisted them all in the work, but now it would really be little more than Dead Sea ashes to his parched lips.

Within the tribute is a description that allows the reader to appreciate the personality of the man now left entirely without family:

> The blows have been thick and heavy . . . and the lion within him which causes him to close his lips and make no complainings against fate, only makes his real sufferings the more severe. Still . . . we do not believe that it will be possible for him to go away with a thought that he is leaving while yet the work which called out the best energies of his manhood remained unfinished. The first effect of a great sorrow is to turn one's thoughts in . . . ; the second is to expand the true heart, to give it a broader fellowship with the world, a gentler patience, a more profound reverence for the commands of duty.

The writer predicted that Baskin would not leave, and wise advice was added:

> We should be glad to see him close up his affairs and give some months to travel; to go where he can catch the voices of waterfalls, or the winds in the forests; where the mountains and the ocean will be reminders to him that all things in nature have their stations. . . . Our excuse for thus bringing up a private citizen's name and discussing his position, is that R. N. Baskin is in one sense public property. . . . The destiny of some at least, is to bear heavy burdens, that the burdens of others may be made lighter, and this was what compelled R. N. Baskin to do for Utah what he has done in the past, what he must still do in the future.[18]

This poignant tribute was reprinted almost verbatim by the *News*, but with a grouchy preamble and conclusion: "It is solely on the ground of his prominence that we . . . [print] the following excerpt, the rhetoric of which is largely inflated. . . . The talk about the delegateship [for Baskin] does not agree with the shouts . . . in favor of Orlando W. Powers, who was paid ten thousand dollars for carrying the late municipal election."[19]

FIGHTING FOR CULLOM AND STRUBLE

However severe was Baskin's situational depression caused by Olive's death following the deaths of their three daughters, he did not sell his

---

[18]"The Calls of Duty," *SLT*, February 27, 1890, 4/4.
[19]"A Remarkable Statement," *DN*, March 8, 1890, 11/1.

law practice, his home, or all of his horses in Wood's Cross. He may
have found release by throwing renewed energies into ownership and
breeding thoroughbred horses, for a featured article in the *Tribune*
several months later noted that he had retained a stallion and four
fillies.[20] Whether his nepenthe from grief was the tribute awarded
him after his wife's death, or his interest in horse breeding, or having extraordinarily important new work in which to immerse himself,
April 1890 found Baskin in Washington at the Fifty-First Congress.
He authored new legislation for Illinois's Shelby Cullom to sponsor in
the Senate, just as he had done at Baskin's request in 1870. Cullom was
a wise choice, for he was both a member of the Senate Committee on
Territories and a close friend and former partner of Baskin friend and
colleague Charles S. Zane. Representative Isaac S. Struble, chair of
the House Committee on Territories, also introduced the bill in that
chamber.[21] Backed by the recent U.S. Supreme Court ruling that sustained the constitutionality of Idaho's disfranchisement law, Baskin
included a similar provision in his legislation for Utah.[22] Idaho delegate Fred Dubois reported news from the LDS Church's latest semiannual conference that the church president was adamant, declaring
that "polygamy was irrevocably fixed upon the Church" and that there
would be "no further revelation" rescinding polygamy, as critics called
for.[23] Governor Thomas was also in Washington to aid Baskin's efforts
for this legislation. Shortly, the *Deseret News* said Baskin "is known
as a bigoted, fanatical, unscrupulous enemy of the Mormon people,"
and recognized that his purpose in Washington was the advancement
of the new Cullom Bill, a product of Baskin's "narrow gauge mind."[24]
    Baskin described the details of the material he placed with Cullom:

> The bill was drawn by me, and provided . . . that no person living in
> plural or celestial marriage, or who taught, advised or counseled any

[20]"Judge Baskin's Horses," *SLT*, September 13, 1891, 3/5. At the October 1890 territorial live-
    stock fair, before Olive's death, Baskin's "Inca" and "Cooley" won gold medals, and "Nellie"
    a diploma. Untitled article, *DN*, October 25, 1890, 17/3.
[21]Baskin, *REM*, 183; Larson, *Americanization of Utah*, 251. Struble was a Republican from Iowa.
    "To Disfranchise the Mormons," *SLT*, April 11, 1890, 1/4; "Senator Cullom's Dose: Heroic
    Remedy for the Desperate Mormon Disease," *SLT*, April 13, 1890, 1/1.
[22]*Davis v. Beason*, 133 U.S. 333. Stripped of excess wording, the decision rested on two basic
    points: bigamy and polygamy were crimes under existing statutes, and the activities cited
    were therefore considered aiding and abetting performance of a crime. Enos Wall was cred-
    ited with introducing the bill in the Idaho legislature.
[23]"Baskin's Latest Bill," *DEN*, April 17, 1890, 8.
[24]Untitled article, *DEN*, April 11, 1890, 6–7.

person to enter into polygamy; or who was a member of, or contributed to the support, aid or encouragement of any organization that taught or sanctioned that practice; or who participated or aided in the solemnization of any polygamous marriage, should vote, serve as juror or hold any office in the Territory.[25]

The *Tribune* rhetorically asked, "Why the Cullom Bill?" In answer to its own question, the editors replied that the LDS Church taught that there was "but one legal government on earth, which is the government of God through His priesthood." The word of the LDS Church First Presidency was "of more binding effect upon any good Mormon than is any law of the United States." It was because "the Mormon people are taught it is their mission to persevere until this Government of the United States shall be overthrown and the government of the Mormon Church shall control the Republic."[26] Another answer to the question could be found in a message sent from Beaver, Utah, regarding the actions of George Q. Cannon, who was deeply involved with LDS Church president Wilford Woodruff, trying to parry the blows against polygamy that were coming with increasing seriousness: "If polygamy is stopped in spirit as well as the letter in this Territory, it shall not be because of the helping influence of George Q. Cannon. . . . [H]e preached continuously from Saturday evening until Monday afternoon, and the burden of his speeches was a recitation of the injustices of the United States Government toward the best people and greatest brains of the Commonwealth." Cannon advised the young Mormon men to go directly into polygamy: "Defy the laws, spit upon the officers—*vox dei, vox populi*," meaning "the voice of God is the voice of the people."[27]

When Baskin and Caleb West rose to speak in support of Cullom-Struble, they faced the now familiar Mormon opposition team of John T. Caine, Franklin S. Richards, and Jeremiah Wilson. Meeting with Struble and members of the Committee on Territories at Washington's Riggs House hotel were Governor Thomas, former governor West, Utah commissioners George L. Godfrey, R. S. Robertson, and Alvin W. Saunders, together with Baskin and Idaho senator Fred Dubois. The Struble Bill was discussed, Struble committed his

[25]Baskin, *REM*, 183.
[26]"Why the Cullom Bill?" *SLT*, April 14, 1890, 4/2.
[27]"Cannon Preaching Polygamy," sent from Beaver, Utah, signed by "Z.Y.X.," *SLT*, April 8, 1890, 2/1.

support, and indeed the bill was favorably reported out of the committee on April 29.[28] With passage seemingly assured, some news that reached Baskin caught him by surprise: "I was informed by Senator Cullom that he had been assured by a delegation of prominent Mormons, that if further action on the bill was delayed for a reasonable time, the practice of polygamy would be prohibited by the Mormon church."[29] Baskin added that he received the same report from Struble, who insisted that vigorous steps would be taken to assure passage of the bill if the Mormons did not move against polygamy soon. Historian Edward Leo Lyman reports that in Salt Lake City some members of the fledgling Democratic Party and some men of the city's Chamber of Commerce were concerned that the Cullom-Struble legislation would disrupt their business relationships and Utah commerce.[30]

By mid-May the prospects for passage were bright, but not settled. Caine arranged with Connecticut senator Orville Platt, now chair of the Senate Territories Committee, for Frank Jenne Cannon to speak before the committee. In addition, Frank J. Cannon went privately to other Senate members, telling them the Mormon Church "was about to make a concession concerning . . . polygamy." He noted, "I told them so in confidence, pointing out the necessity of secrecy, since to make public the news of such a concession, in advance, would be to prevent the Church from authorizing it."[31]

The efforts of Frank J. Cannon and many others working for the Mormon cause were rewarded, and the Cullom and Struble bills were not passed, but as Baskin emphasized, their "pendency forced the issuance of the manifesto."[32] The "Manifesto," as it came to be named, was a proclamation dated September 24, 1890, and printed in the *Deseret News* on October 4. President Woodruff issued a "To Whom It May Concern" letter as an "Official Declaration" in which he denounced

[28]Lyman, *Political Deliverance*, 143.

[29]Baskin, *REM*, 184.

[30]Lyman, *Political Deliverance*, 128–30.

[31]F. J. Cannon and Knapp, *Brigham Young*, 93. The intrigue and complex negotiations that blocked and deferred passage of the Cullom and Struble bills, involving LDS Church president Wilford Woodruff, George Q. Cannon, and his influential friend, Secretary of State James G. Blaine, together with Frank Jenne Cannon, Hiram B. Clawson, and others, are reported in detail in several historical accounts. See Lyman, *Political Deliverance*, 124–49; F. J. Cannon and Knapp, *Brigham Young*, 85–94; and Bitton, *GQC*, 305–307.

[32]Baskin, *REM*, 186.

the practice of polygamy but not the Mormons' theological principle of celestial marriage.[33] Considered by non-Mormons as an unavoidable capitulation to the inevitable, it was—and is—widely considered a divine revelation by faithful Saints. Unappreciated by the non-Mormons was that the Saints wanted to believe, needed to believe, that in giving up the practice of polygamy they were obeying God's newly revealed word, not simply yielding to the imposed law of the land.[34] Of note, the Manifesto was not published as doctrine in the Mormons' *Doctrine and Covenants* until 1908.[35] Modern-day splinter groups, with substantial numbers of men and women, have broken away from the main LDS body as a repercussion of the Manifesto. These groups continue plural marriage in quasi secrecy and live "the Principle."

People's Party Disbands— Baskin Elected to the Utah Legislature

In January 1891 a group of non-Mormons in Ogden concluded that the long-lived anti-Mormon aggressiveness of the Liberal Party was no longer appropriate. In preparation for the upcoming local election, they organized into a Citizen Party, made up of those less aggressive than the early "anti-Ring" Liberal men. Mormons Frank J. Cannon and Thomas D. Dee ran for city council positions on a new Citizen ticket, not under the old People's Party banner. They won and were among seven Citizen Party victors in twenty positions.[36] Very soon an LDS stake presidency from Weber County traveled to Salt Lake

---

[33]"Official Declaration," *DN*, October 4, 1890, 4/1. Announced and affirmed by acclamation of the church body in the October 5 semiannual general conference, it was republished in *DN*, October 11, 1890, 23/3, 24/1. It was at the insistence of Secretary of the Interior John W. Noble that the Manifesto was submitted for approval to the Mormon congregation. Ever cautious about Mormon intent, non-Mormons were suspicious of the overcareful and, in their view, ambiguous words of President Woodruff. Governor Thomas noted that Woodruff's agreement was to "submit" but not to "obey." "Governor Thomas and the 'Declaration,'" *DN*, October 11, 1890, 8/3. Again the *Tribune* repeated its fundamental concern: "It is the Mormon temporal government that has made all the trouble from the first, and which will continue to keep that trouble alive until it shall be surrendered." "The Manifesto," *SLT*, October 2, 1890, 4/2.

[34]Cannon's message that secrecy of their "concession" was required, that publicity would prevent the LDS Church from to announcing the Manifesto's compromise, casts some question on the claim that it was of divine origin.

[35]Poll, *Utah's History*, 272; "The New Edition," *DN*, December 18, 1908, 4/1.

[36]The demise of the People's Party and the emergence of Republican and Democratic parties in Utah in 1891 are treated in great detail by Lyman, *Political Deliverance*, 150–84.

to meet with the First Presidency, informing them that the Liberals of Ogden had broken up and many were joining national parties. The Ogdenites encouraged the Mormons' three highest leaders to follow suit with the People's Party. After tentative approval was given to Ogden church members, the breakup movement spread to Salt Lake by spring. LDS Church leaders instructed their members to affiliate with either of the national parties, Republican or Democrat. "Let every late People's Party man exercise his own free agency, examine well the question of the hour and be sure that he is right before he goes ahead!" urged the *Deseret News*.[37] The *Tribune*, the old stomping warhorse of the Liberal Party, saw in this another duplicitous move: "The plan of the Saints is to give a certain number of voters to the Republican party and a certain number to the Democratic party, and to await the issue of the Presidential election next year. And if the man elected happens to be a Democrat every mother's son of them will be Democrats. If he happens to be a Republican an overwhelming majority of them will be Republicans."[38] The goal was statehood, said the *Tribune*, and once it was gained, "the Governorship, the Legislature, and the courts [could] be placed in Mormon hands." Baskin agreed with the *Tribune*, and as the featured speaker at a June rally of Liberal Party men, he warned: "It is written on the wall in letters of living light that the theocracy of this Territory is doomed. There is, however, one way in which this dangerous institution can maintain its existence, and that plan lies along the pathway of . . . statehood for Utah. After that the priesthood will fill every office . . . and the old order of things will be restored."[39]

The Liberal success that began in 1889 and moved to further victories in the elections of 1890 was now challenged by Democratic and Republican parties dividing the Liberal voters. At the Liberals' convention in July 1891, Judge Enos D. Hoge nominated Robert N. Baskin for the territorial legislature in a "most eloquent and glowing speech." The convention went wild, cheer after cheer went up, and hats were waved, and the demonstration went on until the delegates were tired, reported the *Tribune*. Judge Charles Goodwin said, "[Baskin] was a Liberal when it required nerve to be a Liberal; he was a Liberal when it required pluck and money, and he supplied them all." One

---

[37] "Don't Be in a Hurry," *DN*, June 13, 1891, 6/1.
[38] "What Shall Be Done?" *SLT*, May 11, 1891, 4/2.
[39] "The 'Liberal' Rally," *DN*, June 13, 1891, 25/1.

Mormon had previously called the Liberals a "bastard" party, so an attendee facetiously remarked that he "desired the convention to meet the assertion by proclaiming R. N. Baskin as its father."[40] Baskin, P. J. Moran, James Glendinning, and Henry W. Lawrence were the four final candidates for the Liberal ticket.[41] In the August statewide elections, Liberal candidates and newly minted Democrats took about a third of the positions.[42] In Salt Lake City and Salt Lake County, Liberals were more successful. Every legislator elected from the city districts was a Liberal.[43] All three seats in the Fourth Council District were taken by Liberal Party men: Baskin, Glendinning, and Moran, each winning by a margin of more than one thousand votes.[44]

In the territorial legislature's Council (as noted, analogous to the Senate at the federal level), Baskin was nominated for president but lost by one vote to William H. King, a prominent Mormon from Provo.[45] Baskin was appointed to several committees: Ways and Means, Penitentiary and Reform School, Railroads, Libraries, Judiciary, and Memorials to Congress. He contributed to the introduction or progress of a number of issues, including a memorial to Congress asking for a constitutional amendment outlawing polygamy; a grant of sixty acres to the University of Utah; the renaming of the University of Deseret; provision for the maintenance of illegitimate children; and $500,000 for the erection of a "public building" in Salt Lake City.

An "act to punish polygamy and other kindred offenses" left the territorial Judiciary Committee with a strong endorsement but received a vigorous minority report by Baskin against the bill. For the territory of Utah to initiate laws punishing polygamy after the passage of the Edmunds and Edmunds-Tucker acts at the federal level was ludicrous. Opening lawbreakers to double prosecution and punishment for the same crime would be patently illegal. Baskin was not confused by this flanking move, attempting to institute a Mormon-controlled territorial

---

[40]E. B. Critchlow was the author of the "bastard" posters that proclaimed, "A Democrat Votes the Democratic Ticket, A Republican Votes the Republican Ticket, What Is He Who Votes a 'Bastard' Ticket?" Lyman, *Political Deliverance*, 158, 184–85 (photo).

[41]"The Liberals: Legislative Conventions," *SLT*, July 15, 1891, 5/3.

[42]"The Election," *SLT*, August 4, 1891, 3/1; "The Legislators Elect—The Liberals Get One-Third of All," *SLT*, August 4, 1891, 2/1.

[43]"Victory! The Liberals Make a Clean Sweep," *SLT*, August 4, 1891, 5/1.

[44]Defeated were Democrats Parley Williams, Le Grand Young, and Wendell Benson, and Republicans Robert Harkness, James Sharp, and George A. Lowe. "The Legislators Elect," *SLT*, August 4, 1891, 2/1.

[45]"The Territorial Legislature," *DN*, January 16, 1892, 17/1.

statute that would prevent prosecution by the United States under its statutes. "I am unalterably opposed to this bill," he growled, weary of recurring attempts to get around the Edmunds and Edmunds-Tucker acts.[46]

A Utah memorial to Congress asked for the repeal of the Poland, Edmunds, and Edmunds-Tucker acts and for the simultaneous passage of the Teller and Faulkner acts that were currently before Congress. The two Liberals on the Committee on Memorials reacted sharply.[47] Baskin, the committee chair, wrote a minority report, to which James Glendinning added his name:

> The memorial aims at the repeal of these measures, and asks for the passage of a law by Congress which will place in the hands of this contumacious majority, powers far greater than any which has ever been extended to those territories which have at all times been true in the execution of their agency. . . . The granting of this request would place the powers of the State in the hands of a church whose history and whose tenets make it both probable and possible that, protected by the safeguards which a State under our system would afford, the priesthood would revive the suspended revelation of polygamy.[48]

Baskin and Glendinning emphasized that "magic changes" had come to Utah from the very laws now under attack by the Mormons. Salt Lake City and Ogden had doubled in population, schools now "would do credit to any community," large amounts of capital had been attracted, and industries and businesses were "never more prosperous or healthy." They warned, "It would be dangerous and disastrous to admit the territory before the Constitution of the United States were amended to prohibit polygamy" and to have a "lapse of sufficient time in which to test the sincerity of the new departure [of the People's Party]."[49]

With the Liberals elected to important positions, with Edmunds-Tucker being enforced, and with the Utah Commission overseeing voting processes, all winds seemed favorable for Baskin. His placement on

---

[46]Utah Legislature, Senate, Records of the 1892 Utah Legislature, 36.

[47]The Teller Bill asked for the immediate, unqualified admission of Utah to statehood. The Faulkner "Home Rule" Bill would afford Utah all the privileges of local self-government. Each had overtones of persuading Utah to enter as a state with a particular party loyalty. "The Faulkner and Teller Bills," *DN*, February 6, 1892, 7/3, 8/1. Governor Arthur L. Thomas, Chief Justice Zane, and Associate Justices Miner and Blackburn all favored Teller Bill passage. "The Utah Statehood Question," *DN*, January 25, 1892, 31/1.

[48]Baskin, *REM*, 179; Records of the 1892 Utah Legislature, 103–104.

[49]Records of the 1892 Utah Legislature, 104–105.

the Education Committee was now his most important role. John D. Peters, chair of the Council's Committee on Education, was a liberal Mormon from Box Elder County and its superintendent of schools. He and Baskin cooperated, smoothly bringing about the passage of legislation refining and improving vital provisions of the 1890 education bill. It was signed into law by Governor Thomas on January 27, 1892.[50] City schools were allowed to select their own textbooks and were freed from "tangling alliances."[51]

Baskin and several other 1892 Council members came under humorous scrutiny by Wil B. Dougall, journalist and telegrapher for the First Presidency of the LDS Church. R. C. Lund, the councilman from St. George, Utah, was acclaimed as *the* upper house orator, said Dougall, but Mayor Baskin would vote "nay" if ever such fanciful resolution were to be made.

> Mr. Baskin may be set in his ways and have opinions on certain subjects that nothing on earth could change, yet he is a good Parliamentarian and his judgment on matters relating to the law and judiciary is generally sound. It is only when he attempts the oratorical style that he is found wanting. His speech against the anti-polygamy bill was a fair specimen of flying machine oratory. It lacked the grandeur and sweep of the eagle's wing, neither was it flimsy enough to catch the current of a gentle breeze and skim the air like a pigeon kite. Baskin is a good speaker when he keeps his legs on the earth, but can turn a somersault on the rhetorical trapeze that would stagger a circus performer.[52]

Near the session's end, Baskin was selected to make the ceremonial presentation thanking and honoring outgoing Council president William H. King. It is clear from his speech that Baskin and King had developed mutual caring and respect. Baskin's casual tribute was simple and touching and revealed his warmth:

> You have watched the proceedings with an eagle eye; you have managed to make us work like galley slaves; . . . and [you have] done a great many very naughty things. In consequence of all this, the members . . . considered . . . that you deserved punishment—and I was delegated to make a speech to you! They delegated . . . other punishment, and it now becomes my duty to announce the sentence. They said you should be

---

[50]The measure was titled "An Act in Relation to the Payment of Interest and Commissions in Aid of the Sale of School Bonds in Cities of the First and Second Classes."

[51]"The School Law for Cities," *SLT*, March 16, 1892, 7/1.

[52]Dougall, "Utah Legislature of 1892," 312–13.

caned! You will, therefore, round up your shoulders and prepare for it. . . . [A]llow me to present you with this cane. You do not need it now, . . . but . . . it will be to you a reminder of the time we spent together, in making laws for this fair territory . . . as an evidence that you have performed your duty here faithfully and well.[53]

On receiving the gold-headed "snakewood cane" inscribed with the names of the Council officers and members, King responded with equal warmth, saying:

> Many of the members of the Council came here strangers to one another, but I believe that they go forth as friends. There is something about Legislative work that draws legislators together. They are criticized on all hands, and this [tends] to make them think more kindly of one another than they otherwise might. . . . I hope also that the generous wishes of [Baskin,] the honored Mayor of this city[,] for me will be realized by him, and every other member.[54]

Baskin's time in the territorial legislature brought contact with two Mormon men for whom he seems to have developed sincere regard. With John D. Peters, he labored to find success in efforts for better education, and with William H. King, respect and admiration began to grow and transcended their long-held positions of Mormon against non-Mormon.

---

[53]Records of the 1892 Utah Legislature, 367–68. In the midst of the session, King's father's died unexpectedly. "Death of William King," *DN*, February 27, 1892, 23/2.

[54]Records of the 1892 Utah Legislature, 368. King's response recognized Baskin as the recently elected mayor.

14

Mayor of Salt Lake City

To work for the common good is the greatest creed.
WOODROW WILSON

BY JANUARY 1892 MANY NON-MORMONS REMAINED DIS-
trustful over the Mormons' division of the People's Party
into Republican or Democratic affiliation. Suspicions were
not eased when Salt Lake City's Democratic chair, Frank H. Dyer,
appeared beside Franklin S. Richards, Joseph L. Rawlins, and John T.
Caine to lobby the Senate Committee on Territories for statehood.
This mid-February effort was to push Utah rapidly to statehood under
the Faulkner Bill, the Teller Bill, or both.[1] Governor Arthur Thomas
vacillated in his opinion of the proposed legislation, first supporting
passage and later speaking against it, saying, "The sympathy of feeling and harmony of purpose does not exist."[2] Chief Justice Charles
Zane was convinced the Mormons spoke truthfully; he openly supported statehood by way of the Teller Act, saying, "The time has
come to abandon the enmities, the contention and prejudice of the
past."[3] However, when the *Tribune* interviewed John Maxcy Zane, the
judge's son, for his opinion on statehood that was sponsored by Utah
Democrats, he answered: "The introduction of their bill was a breach
of faith. . . . The understanding when the party division took place was

---

[1]The Faulkner Bill was also referenced as the Faulkner-Caine Bill. U.S. Congress, Senate,
    Hearings before the Committee on Territories.
[2]"The Utah Statehood Question," *DN*, January 23, 1892, 31/2; "Report of the Governor to the
    Secretary of the Interior," in *Executive Documents of the House of Representatives, 1892–'93*, 443.
[3]"The Utah Statehood Question," *DN*, January 23, 1892, 31/2.

that nothing was to be done immediately toward Statehood[,] . . . that such an act would be looked upon as reflecting upon the honesty of the party division. . . . It was a . . . subterfuge devised by men who do not understand that good politics require honesty of purpose."[4] Confusion was added when the election in Logan, Utah, predicted as an easy Democratic win, was inexplicably won by Republican opposition. Soon it came to light that the LDS First Presidency secretly sent two agents to Logan to influence Mormon voters to switch to the Republican side.[5] Learning of the message sent by the church's highest officials revealing their Republican preference, Liberals immediately saw subterfuge, a violation of the plan to fairly and honestly divide into Democrat and Republican parties. The First Presidency responded with a carefully worded, plausible denial of direct involvement, signed by two of the three men of the presidency.[6]

Liberal Party chair Orlando Powers found that other influential men such as C. Emir Allen, Charles C. Goodwin, and Henry W. Lawrence shared the distrust still held by Robert Baskin.[7] They were "not yet convinced of the good faith or sincerity of the People's party or of the members of the Liberal party who have pretended to divide on party lines."[8] With political allegiances uncertain, Baskin headed the 1892 Liberal ticket as the candidate for mayor, running against the Democrats' H. C. Lett and the Republican nominee, Heber M. Wells, the son of Daniel H. Wells.[9] Liberals took all the city offices, save for three city council seats won by the Democrats. Baskin was the second non-Mormon elected as mayor.[10] Rev. Robert G. McNiece, pastor of the First Presbyterian Church, affirmed that the Liberal Party victory resulted in large part from the distrust of Republicans and Democrats and the unpopularity of the Faulkner and Teller bills.[11]

---

[4]"Mr. Zane on the Situation," *SLT*, January 30, 1892, 8/3.

[5]George F. Gibbs and Robert Campbell were named as the men sent. Lyman, *Political Deliverance*, 178–79.

[6]"Declaration," *DN*, March 26, 1892, 8/1. George Q. Cannon did not sign; he was said to be out of town.

[7]"The Liberals Organizing," *SLT*, January 24, 1892, 5/5.

[8]Lyman details LDS leaders' efforts, continuing through the first year of Baskin's term, to maintain political control while appearing not to do so. Lyman, *Political Deliverance*, 170–79.

[9]"The Provo Liberals," *SLT*, January 29, 1892, 3/2; "City Ticket: Liberals Make Their Nominations," *SLT*, January 29, 1892, 5/1; "The Three Tickets," *DN*, February 6, 1892, 32/2.

[10]The other Liberals in the 1892 legislature from the Salt Lake districts were Henry W. Lawrence, P. J. Moran, James Glendinning, William F. Colton, John A. Marshall, Jacob Moritz, W. H. Irvine, and Franklin Pierce.

[11]Rev. R. G. McNiece, "Questions to Specialists," in Cook, *Our Day*, 307.

Powers, Baskin, and others, suspicious of both parties and concerned that neither adequately represented their views, organized the Tuscarora Society, attracting four to five hundred members. The group was best categorized as "liberally inclined" Democrats; Powers was the executive chairman, and Baskin the chairman of resolutions, with the members including such men as Enos D. Hoge, P. J. Moran, Allen G. Campbell, and longtime Liberals Martin Lannan and Fred J. Kiesel.[12] In 1892 Powers and C. Emir Allen traveled to Washington as representatives of the Tuscarora Society to testify in the House committee meetings against the Faulkner and Teller statehood bills.[13]

The 1892 election for a congressional representative did little to settle doubts of Liberals over the reasons for the division into the two major parties. Democrats nominated Joseph L. Rawlins, an agnostic son of Mormon parents. The Republicans nominated Frank Jenne Cannon, the unconventional and sometimes wayward son of Mormon stalwart George Q. Cannon.[14] According to O. N. Malmquist, the Liberals, fearing a "deal" was afoot between the Mormons and the Democrats, "pig-headedly entered a third candidate," C. Emir Allen.[15] When Rawlins drew 15,000 votes against Cannon's 12,000 and Allen's 7,000, the *Tribune* observed: "They will deny that there is any contract . . . to have a Democratic Delegate elected, but . . . the son of an apostle [Cannon] was defeated by an apostate [Rawlins]. There is not a child 10 years of age in the Territory who does not know that, except for the contract, Mr. Rawlins would have been snowed under so deep that he would not have dug out until late last summer."[16]

In late March 1893, Powers traveled to Washington for a personal interview with President Cleveland, carrying endorsements and requests for a variety of presidential appointments in Utah.[17] Sixty Tuscarora Society members traveled to the National Democratic Convention at Chicago. As Tuscaroras, Powers and Kiesel considered themselves to be Utah's Democratic delegates, but their seating was

---

[12]"The Tuscarora Society," *slt*, March 23, 1893, 2/3.

[13]Allen also presented the committee with a memorial from more than fifty women of the James B. McKean Relief Corps of Salt Lake City, protesting the Faulkner and Teller bills as "throwing the territory into the hands of a people who are worse than traitors to the United States." U.S. Congress, Senate, *Hearings before the Committee on Territories*, 106.

[14]A detailed account of election events is found in Lyman, *Political Deliverance*, 201–204.

[15]Malmquist, *First 100 Years*, 146.

[16]"That Statehood Contract," *slt*, November 5, 1893, 4/2.

[17]"Judge Powers in War Paint," *slt*, March 26, 1893, 5/4; "Tuscaroras on the Way: This Week Utah Warriors Intend to See the Great Father," *slt*, March 28, 1893, 1/7.

contested by Judge Henry Henderson (who by this time had replaced
Powers on the bench) and Congressional representative John T.
Caine.[18] The Tuscarora Society was active for more than a year; when
it disbanded, some of its membership merged with the regular Democrats, and some remained with the Liberal Party.

Progress in Infrastructure

The election victories of 1890 brought the Liberal Party into influence.
Their first two mayors of Salt Lake City, George M. Scott and Robert
Baskin, found that of all the city's needs, an adequate and safe water
system was the first and most important. In 1884 the water system
of Salt Lake City had some closed conduits, with some components
placed underground, but by 1887 public health warnings persisted over
the danger of "typhoid" contamination from well and open stream-
water supplies.[19] Baskin later recalled that "in most of the resident
portions of the city the inhabitants were using water from wells,"
where "in the vicinity human excrement had for years been deposited
in cesspools and privies, which had become a menace to public health
by neglect." Baskin ranked Salt Lake City as the third-worst city "in
mortality in the United States."[20] Water and sewage systems remained
inadequate in 1890, and Baskin did not hesitate to place the blame,
claiming that "the church [People's] party had failed to make such
improvements during the many years of [their] absolute control."[21]

Under Scott and Baskin's guidance, Parley's Canyon water was
brought to the city by a masonry conduit. More than sixteen miles of
buried sewer lines were completed.[22] By spring of 1893, the five-foot-
diameter line extended from Fifth East and Ninth South to Fourth
West and Ninth North.[23] Baskin said that "adequate waterworks and a

---

[18]Whitney, *HOU*, 4:540.

[19]The term "typhoid" was not a precise diagnosis but a catchall for many waterborne infections
    producing diarrhea and illness. Some public works projects of roads and water systems
    began as early as 1852 under Mayor Daniel H. Wells. Holzapfel, *Every Stone a Sermon*, 7.

[20]Baskin, *REM*, 26–27.

[21]Ibid., 26. Baskin does not credit Mayor Feramorz Little for water supply improvements from
    Utah Lake to southern Salt Lake County, or enhancements from Emigration and Parley's
    canyons. Alexander and Allen, *Mormons and Gentiles*, 108–109.

[22]Report of the Municipal Government of Salt Lake City, 1891; annual message of the mayor
    with the annual reports of the city officers of Salt Lake City, Correspondence, 1879–1896,
    ser. 4918, Utah State Archives.

[23]"The new gravity outlet sewer is going to be a magnificent piece of work and a great credit
    to the present administration." Estimated cost at completion was $850,000. "The Gravity
    Sewer Route," *SLT*, April 3, 1893, 8/2–3.

sewer system were constructed." The improved system required special assessments to property owners.[24] However, taxes alone would not have been adequate and would have been "too burdensome for the taxpayers"; therefore, long-term bonds were used for financing, Baskin explained.[25]

Under Mayor Scott, Commercial, Main, and State Streets were paved with "asphaltum" for two blocks, and other streets were surfaced with gravel.[26] Scott pointed out that some streets were not paved because the installation of water and sewage lines needed to precede paving. Water supply was increased by 150 percent, street lighting was bettered and extended, and a Board of Public Works and a Board of Health were organized. The total bond debt stood at slightly over $1 million. Mormons found Scott's contributions worthy of praise: "He has filled the place he now vacates with considerable ability. . . . [H]e has been conciliatory and conservative. . . . [H]e has gained many friends and upheld the dignity of his office and leaves it with the respect of those who have watched closely his career."[27]

When Baskin simultaneously assumed the duties of mayor of Salt Lake City and Board of Education president on February 16, he made a pledge to the people: "The prosperity of the city and the people are placed in our hands, and . . . to the best of my ability. . . we shall be more entitled to the respect and confidence of the people when we go out of office than we have now. If our administration is not a success . . . it will be a mistake of the head and not of the heart."[28] The *News* responded with a warm welcome for the new mayor: "He announces himself and associates as no longer mere party candidates but the officers of the people. It is in this light that he and they should now be viewed."[29]

The major, widespread public improvements in water supply and sewage disposal begun under Scott were continued under Baskin. In March, Baskin committed $25,000, as did several other individuals, as surety on the $300,000 treasurer's bond for Board of Education

---

[24]"More Special Taxes," *DN*, May 14, 1892, 15/3; "The 'Liberal' Boycott," *DN*, June 11, 1892, 11/3.

[25]Baskin, *REM*, 27; "More City Bonds Sold," *DN*, April 23, 1892, 20/1.

[26]"Mayor Scott's Report," *DN*, February 1, 1892, 1/1. Guffaws may have followed the announcement of Scott's choice of the first streets to be paved. For at least nineteen years Commercial Street was widely known as the site of the city's brothels. Nichols, *Prostitution, Polygamy, and Power*, 98. Rumor said wives carefully inspected their husband's trouser legs for telltale signs of dust or mud from the infamous road.

[27]"The City Officers," *DN*, February 27, 1892, 7/3.

[28]"Mayor Baskin's Address," *DN*, February 27, 1892, 28/1. The mayor was also the ex officio head of the Board of Health.

[29]"The City Officers."

funding.[30] More of "the streets in the business portion of the city were paved, and many miles of cement sidewalks were laid."[31] The city "was thoroughly cleansed and made as healthful as any in the Rocky mountains, . . . [as] Salt Lake City was brought up to the standard of a city of the first class," Baskin proudly proclaimed.[32] Improvements were also ordered in the city cemetery. Baskin traveled to Washington in mid-March to testify before the Supreme Court and also to seek, from the secretary of war, legal right-of-way for a boulevard through the Fort Douglas military reservation, giving better public access to Mount Olivet Cemetery.[33] He made another trip in late December to submit a case to the U.S. Supreme Court and to aid the passage of a bill introduced by Joseph Rawlins to increase the city's bonding limits.[34] Included among the other improvements under Baskin's administration were regulations concerning smoke emissions and the incineration of garbage and offal.[35] Further evidence of environmental concern came to light when the wisdom of transporting the city sewage to the Great Salt Lake was debated in the City Council meetings.[36] Fire department response was improved with placement of alarm boxes at numerous corners around the city.[37] For all of the collective accomplishments of two Liberal administrations, Baskin felt that Utahans of every allegiance should be "indebted to the Liberal Party for the new era" that brought "great good to both Mormons and Gentiles."[38]

Not all the changes brought about by the Liberals were considered progressive and praiseworthy. The *News* alleged that transient men were hired for construction projects rather than permanent residents. The earnings of such men went directly into the saloons, according to its editorials.[39] Prostitution, drinking, gambling, and wild theater came under increasingly intense criticism from Mormons and non-Mormons alike. According to a study by Jeffrey Nichols, saloons in

---

[30]"The Treasurer's Bond," *DN*, March 19, 1892, 31/3.

[31]Baskin, *REM*, 27. Disputes over cement sidewalk costs arose despite efforts to give property owners the ability to appeal. "Special Taxes for Sidewalks," *DN*, May 21, 1892, 11/1.

[32]Baskin, *REM*, 27.

[33]"Baskin and the Boulevard," *SLT*, March 16, 1893, 1/2. Rumors in the *News* said Baskin was in Washington seeking support to be nominated as governor of Utah Territory, a claim that he vehemently denied. "Return of Mayor Baskin," *SLT*, March 24, 1893, 5/3.

[34]"Double Reason for Going," CR 100 137, *DEN*, December 11, 1893, 2.

[35]"A City Crematory," *DN*, June 18, 1892, 20/3.

[36]"Disposal of City Sewage" and "Unwarrantable Censure," *DN*, May 7, 1892, 6/1, 38/2.

[37]"Fire Alarm Boxes," *DN*, April 9, 1892, 38/1.

[38]Baskin, *REM*, 27.

[39]"The 'Liberal' Boycott," *DN*, June 11, 1892, 11/3.

the city proliferated from seventy to more than one hundred under the early Liberals' reign.[40] A cacophony of complaints cried that "nearly all of the numerous saloons . . . were run at full blast on Sundays, in open and flagrant violation of law."[41] When councilman E. A. Folland brought the issue to the city council meeting, Mayor Baskin exclaimed his ignorance: "I have no knowledge of any such violation and it seems to me that the matter is over-drawn." To Baskin's question of why the matter had not been reported, Folland answered that frequent complaints to the police had been ignored.[42] Baskin ordered the police to close saloons on Sunday, but the police frequently ignored him as well. Discord in the council from members strongly opposing Baskin's attempts at Sunday closing was evident.[43] A citizens' meeting of "the order-loving elements of the community" at the First Methodist Church protested "the deteriorating moral climate."[44] Judge Charles S. Varian, Henry W. Lawrence, Rev. Robert G. McNiece, and a number of others spoke, exhorting the mayor, the chief of police, and city authorities to enforce existing law, to close saloons on Sunday, and to cease the sale of liquor to minors.[45] According to Nichols, "the Franklin Street Variety Theater was a particular target" because of its "bawdy entertainment and drunken crowds," with no female face to be seen in the audience.[46] With the city police unable or unwilling to act effectively, the U.S. marshal's office attempted, with only modest success, to enforce the laws. A minority saw elements of laxity and corruption in Scott's Liberal administration that kept it from dealing more forcibly with violations, and these concerns, together with the question of premature statehood, likely contributed to Baskin's election as mayor. Baskin's fairness and reforms in his first term impressed even his stern critics.[47] According to historian Wayne Stout, Mayor Baskin's record "of fighting corruption in the city government, in the eyes of the Mormons, atoned for his 30 years of anti-Mormon activities in Utah."[48]

---

[40]Nichols, *Prostitution, Polygamy, and Power*, 99.

[41]"Are Saloon-Keepers above the Law?" *DN*, April 30, 1892, 7/2.

[42]"King Alcohol Conquers," *DN*, April 23, 1892, 30/3. Throughout 1892, city council meetings were extensively reported in the *Deseret News*, often receiving several pages of coverage.

[43]"The Mayor and the Council," *SLT*, July 28, 1892, 5/4.

[44]Nichols, *Prostitution, Polygamy, and Power*, 99.

[45]"Citizens Mass Meeting," *SLT*, December 30, 1890, 5/1.

[46]Nichols, *Prostitution, Polygamy, and Power*, 99–100; "The Variety Theatre," *DN*, January 16, 1892, 2/2.

[47]Magleby and Peterson, *Justices*, 7–8.

[48]Stout, *HOU*, 1:463.

TROUBLE IN THE RANKS

As midsummer approached, Baskin was busy planning for the cornerstone laying of the combined City and County Building, but his attention was required to address a problem that had arisen within the city council's ranks. It was an embarrassing episode of vice and scandal involving councilmen, city police officers, and ladies of the night, particularly Rose Miller and Elsie St. Omar. Nichols reports the happenings in great detail, beginning with city patrolman George Albright's arrest of Miller, charging her with prostitution in the house of St. Omar.[49] As Mayor Baskin looked into the details, he found that several city council members, together with city policemen, had gone to the St. Omar house, allegedly to investigate the charges against the two women, but instead were "having a general good time." The group removed to the bawdy house of Hattie Wilson, then to the Variety Theater, and next to the establishment run by Helen Blazes, where they supposedly continued investigating. After "fifteen or twenty minutes drinking beer and dancing with the women," the group moved to Malvina Beauchamp's "Big V" on Plum Alley for more "investigation."

As mayor, Baskin no longer held direct authority over the city councilmen, for the territorial legislature had very recently divested him of that control.[50] Knowing his authority was limited, but concerned that the men's actions reflected negatively on his administration, he carried out his own inquiry. When questioned by the *Tribune*, Baskin explained that the newspapers had reported the details "before I learned anything about them, when they were clearly matters that should first have been reported to me." He added, "I instigated this investigation for my personal benefit. I want to know what is going on."[51] Baskin asked a number of pointed but brief questions: How much did the men drink, who paid for the drinks, were the women touched, and why had he learned of the investigation only through the articles appearing in the city newspapers?[52] From the tone of his questions, it seemed that the mayor "had no objection to well-regulated brothels but felt 'it is scarcely proper for members of the City Council to participate

---

[49]Nichols, *Prostitution, Polygamy, and Power*, 100–105; "The Elsie St. Omer [*sic*] Case," *SLT*, June 28, 1892, 6/1.

[50]"Due to the Mayor," *DN*, June 11, 1892, 26/2.

[51]"The Police Investigation," *SLT*, June 29, 1892, 5/4; "Dark Lantern Inquisition," *DEN*, June 29, 1892, 4.

[52]"The Testimony," *SLT*, July 7, 1892, 5/1.

in a drunken revelry at a house of ill-fame at 1 and 2 o'clock in the morning.'"[53]

Baskin's action following his investigation risked goodwill among the city administration's non-Mormons: he removed chief of police Edward Janney, police sergeant George Sheets, and police detective Alfred E. Ecklund for unbecoming conduct. At the same city council meeting, Baskin found four of its members and Justice of the Peace Fred A. Kesler guilty of "conduct unbecoming members of the council and of city officials."[54] Baskin admitted that the council, not he, had jurisdiction over its members and recommended that the members take "such actions as you deem necessary."[55] Demonstrating a level of "considerable bitterness," council members reported the majority opinion, exonerating themselves from all blame. A minority report went further, insisting that the investigating visits were conducted on their own responsibility, without authority from the council. Furthermore, the council had no authority to censure itself, they said.[56] Baskin had little time for continued ruminating over the troubling brothel visits of his city officials, for the cornerstone laying of the building project that was one of Baskin's most important and ambitious projects was only days away.

A Monument in Stone for the Non-Mormons

At this moment, glass and metal towers of a still-burgeoning central city continue to sprout in increasing numbers and to greater heights in downtown Salt Lake City. Although they must now compete for recognition among the many newcomers to the dramatic skyline, the sandstone spires of Salt Lake's City and County Building, like the Mormon Temple's granite spires, catch the eye from any vantage point of the valley's surrounding foothills.

---

[53]Nichols, *Prostitution, Polygamy, and Power*, 100–105; "The Police and Council," *SLT*, June 28, 1892, 5/5. Baskin's investigation also revealed that the U.S. marshal was allowing a man convicted of embezzling to live at the St. Omar establishment. "The U.S. Marshal's Shame," *SLT*, July 23, 1892, 5/5.

[54]Baskin's censure of Kesler was undoubtedly awkward, since it was in the home of Kesler's father that Olive L. Gardner Stafford, who became Baskin's wife, was kindly provided with months of solicitous nursing care following her injury in a Wells Fargo crash.

[55]"Janney Fired, Also Officers Sheets and Ecklund: The Mayor's Vigorous Act," *SLT*, July 6, 1892, 5/1.

[56]The council concurred in the replacement of Justice of the Peace Kesler. "It Refuses to Whitewash," *SLT*, July 13, 1892, 5/1.

The Mormons began construction of their first Utah Temple in Salt Lake City in February 1853; it progressed under Brigham Young's direction, albeit more slowly than the other three Utah temples, which were completed before the Salt Lake edifice.[57] While the Mormon building was progressing, the non-Mormons were restive. The question was raised in 1888 of building a new city hall and county courthouse; however, nothing was done during Mayor Francis Armstrong's administration. The next two mayors, Scott and Baskin, worked diligently to bring about a suitable edifice of non-Mormon origin. A combined city-county building might rival the flagship of the Mormons' several temples.

The offices of city government had for some time been housed in the city hall at 120 East First South, and county offices were located in the Salt Lake County Court House at 268 West Second South, but both had been outgrown. When the elections brought in more Liberals whose views were much like those of Scott and Baskin, thoughts of a new structure to house both the city and county offices surfaced. Originally plans called for a joint venture, a single structure not far from the Temple grounds, on First South and Second East. San Francisco architect C. E. Apponyi designed a five-story Romanesque building, 60 feet by 150 feet, with two wings, tile floors, and a cement roof, at an estimated cost of $279,000. Construction from Apponyi's plans was begun, but complications and controversy soon arose.[58] Newly elected mayor Baskin and the city council moved to other plans. They claimed the lot was too small for current needs: "Salt Lake had risen from its slumber of years and put on the attire of a growing, booming city. The plans of the building, after being subjected to a rigid examination, proved to be unsatisfactory in many important particulars, and were finally rejected, the architect discharged, and the fate of the building sealed."[59] Baskin also insisted that a public building of its importance "should be surrounded by a park," which "should be made the most attractive spot in the city, a spot which all the people, rich and poor alike, may enjoy."[60] The county paid the city $41,250 for its share of

---

[57]The first cornerstone was laid April 6, 1853, in Salt Lake City. Temples at St. George, Logan, and Manti were finished before the Salt Lake City Temple.

[58]Geologic conditions for the foundation and safety issues were also cited. *Docent Guide to the City and County Building.*

[59]"Laying the Corner Stone," *SLT*, July 26, 1892, 5/1.

[60]Ibid.

the unused lot, and the city was offered—and accepted—half interest in a more commodious, ten-acre city block in the Eighth Ward, named Washington Square, on State Street between Fourth and Fifth South.[61] For the new site, the non-Mormon firm of Henry Monheim, George W. Bird, and Willis T. Proudfoot designed an opulent building whose original contract was for $377,987.[62]

To no surprise, controversy attended the site's choice. The *News* complained that it was too far from the city center, the Liberals in power were wasting taxpayer money, and the location had been chosen to benefit non-Mormon members of the city council who owned adjacent property.[63] Controversy continued, but the Liberals prevailed. A contract was adopted on May 25, 1891, and construction proceeded. The structure would be a monument whose very presence would wordlessly proclaim the end of Mormon domination.

The Mormon Temple's Capstone

To the cheers of devoted thousands, LDS president Wilford Woodruff conducted the capstone ceremony at the Salt Lake City Temple, laying the topmost stone of the central east spire on April 6, 1892.[64] It was atop this stone that a statue of the angel Moroni would be placed. On the last day of April the stern message went out from the First Presidency—Woodruff, George Q. Cannon, and Joseph F. Smith—that forty years had passed, yet the parent Temple in Salt Lake City remained unfinished. An urgent call went to the Saints that time was

---

[61]Formerly known as Emigration Square, the site had served as the resting place for countless emigrant groups while they refurbished their wagons before continuing on to California or Oregon. Indian treaties were signed here, while carnival and circuses tents, cricket and baseball games, and horse pasture all claimed time on the square.

[62]Alexander and Allen, *Mormons and Gentiles*, 130–31; "Corner Stone of the Joint City and County Building Laid," *DN*, August 6, 1892, 26/1. Since 1870 Monheim had lived in the non-Mormon city of Corinne, where he designed the Corinne Opera House. He moved to Salt Lake City in 1872 and died there before his magnificent building was finished.

[63]It was estimated the base contract costs would rise to "about $500,000." Actual costs rose to nearly $900,000. The building deteriorated over the years, and a three-year restoration was completed in 1989. It became the first retrofitted historic building in the world to have a base-isolation system for cushioning against earthquake movement. Utah Heritage Foundation, *Symbol of the City: The City and County Building Teacher's Guide* (n.d.), www.utah heritagefoundation.com/images/stories/pdf/socs/sc5required1.pdf; John S. McCormick, "Utah's Constitution Was Framed in Salt Lake City and County Building," *Utah History to Go*, http://historytogo.utah.gov/utah_chapters/statehood_and_the_progressive_era/.

[64]"The Capstone Ceremonies," *DN*, April 9, 1892, 18/2; Holzapfel, *Every Stone a Sermon*, 41–50.

up and money was the problem. Mormons were "to furnish as fast as it may be needed, all the money that may be required to complete the Temple . . . so that the dedication may take place on April 6th, 1893."[65] Mormons responded, and the Salt Lake Temple was completed as planned and dedicated in April 1893, amid massive celebrations by the Mormon people, many of whom traveled great distances to attend.[66] The "greatest landmark in all Mormondom," it was "to the Mormons what St. Peter's is to Rome and the Catholic."[67]

In a surprise move, many non-Mormon dignitaries, including supreme court chief justice Charles S. Zane, were allowed a tour of the building before it was closed to the general public. The city mayor at the time, Baskin almost certainly was one of the "outsiders" invited, but his name was not recorded among the names of those included in the tour.[68] Of this event, one Saint recorded in his journal:

> The Governor, Judges, lawyers and principal outsiders were permitted to enter and were shown through the building. This was a great surprise to me and most everyone else I suppose. It seems that great pressure was brought to bear upon the authorities and if they refused the outsiders would have thought or pretended to think there was something there we were afraid for them to see. It won't hurt the temple and will allay a great deal of suspicion.[69]

Another account said: "About 1000 gentiles and apostates were permitted to go through the building before it was dedicated, who were filled with amazement at its beauty, grandeur and magnificence."[70] Even the *Tribune* was lavish in its praise and its coverage of the Temple dedication and opening.[71]

---

[65]"Thanksgiving and Prayer," *DN*, April 30, 1892, 4/1. April 6 was chosen since it corresponded with the Mormons' semiannual conference meetings, and it was on this date in 1830 that the LDS Church was established. "To Complete the Temple," *DN*, April 23, 1892, 10/1.

[66]The Salt Lake City Temple's cost was estimated at slightly less than $3.5 million. There were innumerable, inestimable sacrifices by the Saints, and at least five lives were lost in construction accidents. Holzapfel, *Every Stone a Sermon*, ix, 67–85.

[67]Holzapfel, *Every Stone a Sermon*, 105.

[68]Sillitoe, *History of Salt Lake County*, 114; Hatch, Wightman and Decker, *History of Salt Lake County*.

[69]Joseph Henry Dean Journals, 63.

[70]Godfrey and Martineau-McCarty, *Uncommon Common Pioneer*, 395.

[71]"The Temple Dedication," *SLT*, April 6, 1893, 4–8; April 7, 1893, 2; April 8, 1893, 8.

THE NON-MORMONS' CORNERSTONE

Within weeks of the laying of the Mormon Temple capstone, Baskin noted that the foundation work was nearly finished on the City-County Building, four blocks away. He decided it was time to honor a long-standing—but non-Mormon—tradition and called on his fellow non-Mormons of the Masonic Brotherhood to lay and bless the building's cornerstone. The event was scheduled for July 25, 1892.[72]

The day of July 24, 1892, did the Mormons an imposition: it fell on a Sunday, requiring them to move Pioneer Day celebrations to Monday, the day already selected for the Masonic cornerstone-laying event. It was déjà vu, for simultaneous—but often separate—celebrations of the Fourth and the Twenty-fourth of July holidays, by non-Mormons and Mormons, respectively, had repeatedly happened in Utah. This Monday dawned bright, clear, and very warm. By midday the sun's heat was unmerciful on more than 660 Utah Freemasons who had come for the event. Long lines of parked carriages and horses jammed the streets, with the crowd estimated at 4,000. Four tall steel derricks rose from the building's base, each decorated with the red, white, and blue of the nation's flag, giving the building "the appearance of a gigantic ship swung wide at her moorings."[73] Led by a platoon of policemen and the Denhalter's Band in full uniform, the Utah Commandery No. I, Master Masons, Held's Band—the processional of officers and members of the Grand Lodge of Utah—began their march. With an escort of Knights Templars, they proceeded from the Masonic Hall, at the northeast corner of Second East and First South, to the city hall, where they were joined by city, county, and federal officers in carriages. All were under the leadership of Most Worshipful Brother Samuel Paul (who also served at this time as the Salt Lake City police chief), and they arrived together at the building site on Washington Square.[74] The platform for the dignitaries and speakers, located at the foundation's traditionally correct northeast corner, was decorated with flowers and evergreens and a canopy in the form of a ship's bow.

Worshipful Brother Robert Newton Baskin, Past Worshipful Master of Mount Moriah Lodge No. 2 and now the mayor of Salt Lake City, opened the festivities shortly after three o'clock. Baskin spoke of the

---

[72]"The Corner-Stone Laying," *SLT*, July 24, 1892, 6/1.
[73]"Laying the Corner Stone." See illustration on page 240.
[74]*Proceedings of the Grand Lodge of Ancient, Free and Accepted Masons*, 4.

Cornerstone-laying ceremony for the City-County Building, carried out by Utah's Masonic Lodge in July 1892, during Baskin's tenure as mayor. *Used by permission Utah State Historical Society.*

country's heritage of freedom and praised the pioneers, Mormon and non-Mormon:

> When these pioneers struck the edge of what was formerly called the Great American Desert they thought their work done, but a later band of pioneers penetrated onto those wastes, and in their wake followed green fields, and the valleys became fertile and productive. Then another class of pioneers followed, and schools and manufactories sprung up, and railroads came after them, and today they declare the energy, skill and taste of that people.[75]

Mindful of the day's heat, Baskin's remarks were short; he moved to the business at hand: "From time immemorial it has been the custom to call on the Masonic Fraternity to lay the foundations of such buildings, and to you[,] Most Worshipful Grand Master, I now present the tools of the craft that you may perform this work." With these words the mayor handed the mallet and trowel to Grand Master Newton Watson Shilling, who replied, "I accept the trust and will proceed to lay the stone according to the ancient rites." Grand Chaplain James Lowe offered a prayer; a copper box was placed in the cornerstone, into which were laid a variety of Masonic Lodge historical documents, city and county government records, newspaper issues, vials of grain, police shields and fireman's buttons, photographs, and coins. The box was sealed and the cornerstone slowly lowered into place, as the solemn Masonic ritual was recited: "The square that teaches the squaring of all actions to the rule of virtue, the level that teaches equality, and the plumb, rectitude, were applied to the stone, and it was pronounced square, level and plumb, and that the craftsmen had performed their work well."[76] Grand Master Shilling scattered corn kernels on the stone as a symbol of plenty, poured wine as an emblem of joy and gladness, and finished with oil, symbolic of peace.[77] Tapping the stone with the mallet, Shilling pronounced it sound.

Grand Orator Charles Bruerton Jack, Judge George W. Bartch (representing the county), city council president Charles F. Loofbourow, and Governor Arthur L. Thomas—non-Mormons all—spoke on the

---

[75]Ibid., 5.

[76]"Laying the Corner Stone."

[77]Historical details of Utah's Masonic Lodges, Baskin's Masonic activities, and the correct designation of Masonic titles were generously provided by Aaron E. Saathoff, Past Worshipful Master, Wasatch Lodge No. 1, 33rd Degree Scottish Rite Mason, and Past Potentate of El Kalah Shrine, of Salt Lake City.

history of the building each praising it in different words but agreeing that it was "a symbol of a new era marked by the end of Mormon church domination of political affairs and the triumph of civil government."[78] Neither the *Tribune* nor the *News* commented, but no Mormon leaders participated in the cornerstone celebration. Omitted from the brief *Deseret News* report was mention of the Masons' role in the processional, the ritual of the mallet and trowel, the square, level, and plumb, and the anointing. The single reference to the Craft was in the *News* comment: "The [G]rand [M]aster Masons then made their appearance on the platform."[79]

Baskin's efforts for improvement projects in city infrastructure, such as roads, sewers, and public utilities, as well as the City-County Building's construction, were severely troubled by the nationwide economic depression that struck in the early 1890s. Historian Thomas Alexander cites its impact on Utah, with railroad construction slowing to a halt in 1891–92; in addition, silver production dropped 33 percent, copper production fell 48 percent, and salt plummeted 92 percent. Estimates set city unemployment at 48 percent of the workforce.[80] The City-County Building's completion required that it become a public works project.[81]

To Baskin's great embarrassment, he found that city councilmen had made expenditures unknown to the council at large. Men had been employed and large sums allocated without supervision and approval, leading to further money shortages.[82] Work stoppages, delays, and other financial issues resulted in the dismissal of John H. Bowman, the construction supervisor. In May 1893 the city council took over the responsibility of completing the building.[83] These problems slowed progress, and certain planned features, such as stained-glass windows, were eliminated. Impressed by the gardens he had seen in California on a recent trip there, Mayor Baskin insisted, despite budget constraints,

---

[78]"Corner Stone of the Joint City and County Building Laid," 26–28; McCormick, "Utah's Constitution Was Framed" (quotation).

[79]"Corner Stone of the Joint City and County Building Laid," 26–28.

[80]Alexander and Allen, *Mormons and Gentiles*, 127.

[81]To spread the wages over a larger pool, workers were hired for only a one-week contract, then replaced by other workers with the same limits. For a time, employment was limited to married men.

[82]"The Mayor's Advice," *DN*, August 12, 1893, 5/2.

[83]"Bowman Assigns," *DN*, May 20, 1893, 7/3; "Bowman's Little Dilemma," *DN*, June 3, 1893, 16/2.

Completed City-County Building, December 1894.
Used by permission Utah State Historical Society.

on having more than ten thousand flowers and shrubs planted on the grounds. One historian cites $884,400 as the total cost for the building and its contents, with the land valued at an additional $250,000.[84]

The City-County Building was admired as an extraordinary treasure of Richardson Romanesque architecture; its 256-foot-tall center clock tower was crowned by the impressive female figure of Columbia, standing more than 12 feet tall.[85] Inviting comparison with the twelve foot, five inch, gold-surfaced angel Moroni capping the 222 foot central east spire of the Mormon temple, Columbia holds a torch, the light of knowledge, in one hand, and the dove of peace in the other.

In the understated beauty of the City and County Building halls and rooms, many significant events took place in subsequent years.

---

[84]Fohlin, *Salt Lake City*, 25.
[85]The angel figure on the Salt Lake Temple is twelve feet, five and one half inches tall. "The Statue of Moroni," *DN*, April 9, 1892, 19/3.

Details of the City-County Building clock tower.
Used by permission Utah State Historical Society.

In preparation for Utah statehood, the building was used by the 107 delegates to draw up a state constitution. Offices for state government were located there for twenty years, from 1895 until the Utah State Capitol was completed in 1915. It also housed the first public library in Salt Lake City. In 1914 it saw Joe Hill (Joseph Hillstrom), Industrial Workers of the World radical, tried for murder. During the Great Depression of 1932–33, when Utah's unemployment rate was 30 to 50 percent, thousands of Utahans held protest rallies that covered the building's grounds. Presidents Theodore Roosevelt and William Howard Taft spoke from its steps. It was a scene of celebration when Salt Lake City and Utah's resorts were selected as the site for the 2002 Winter Olympic events. The spires, designated by the builders as "Knowledge," "Peace," "Justice," and "Commerce," remain an attraction for their majestic architectural beauty, but more important, they continue as a symbol and reminder of the separation of church and government that took almost fifty years to achieve.

The photo of Robert Newton Baskin on the cover of *Reminiscences* is taken from the collection of Alta Club charter members. In it he appears as an avuncular, white-haired senior statesman, looking somewhat tired and worn. Quite different is the full-length color portrait, noticed by few in the dimly lit, south wing of his enduring legacy, the City-County Building. Honoring the achievements of his two terms as the city mayor, this portrait is near life size and is flanked by portraits of other former Salt Lake City mayors.[86] His habiliments are those of his office and profession: jacket, trousers, shoes, and tie, all conservatively dark. His eyes are unmistakably crystal-blue; his red hair and sorrel beard have yet to change into the maturity of white. More than six feet tall, he stands erect, without rings or other jewelry. In his left hand is a thick, carved Irish shillalah, easily doubling as, and mistaken for a cane. The image of a serious, imposing man, his portrait suggests the energy, clear vision, and assertive leadership that resulted in diverse contributions to his city and his state.[87]

[86]Only the two non-Mormon mayors, George M. Scott and Robert Newton Baskin, are honored with full-length portraits.

[87]See illustration on page 246. Baskin's portrait was done by John Willard Clawson (1858–1936), whose portraits of eight other mayors also hang in the building. The grandson of Brigham Young through Alice Young, he also painted portraits of four Utah governors that hang in the Utah State Capitol. Clawson studied under European impressionists and at the National Academy of Design in New York. *Docent Tour Book and Biography.*

Mayor Robert Newton Baskin. Full-length portrait by John Willard Clawson, the grandson of Brigham Young. Note the shillelagh in the left hand. *Photo by Michael Roberts of Michael Roberts Photography of Salt Lake City.*

As the City-County Building neared ninety years of age, controversies over its restoration or demolition for a new structure were as intense as those over the original construction. Of ten options explored, restoration was no more expensive than other proposals and was favored by the public, and a multimillion-dollar renovation was completed in 1989.[88] The reopening celebration on April 29, 1989, began with a Masonic processional patterned after the original of 1892, ending at

---

[88]*Docent Guide to the City and County Building.*

Washington Square, where the Masonic ritual of cornerstone laying was reenacted. As before, the Knights Templars formed an honor
guard, and the Grand Lodge of Utah officers took their stations on
scaffolding at the same northeast corner The Masonic acts with mallet and trowel, the sequence of square, level, and plumb, and the triple
anointing were repeated. Mayor Palmer DePaulis spoke appropriately.
LDS Church president Ezra Taft Benson was absent, but the First Presidency's Gordon B. Hinckley quietly attended, without addressing the
audience. As before, *Deseret News* reports were brief and without notation of Masonic involvement.[89] Although no speaker gave honor to
Baskin or referenced his leadership and efforts, the building stands as
an enduring tribute to the man whose accomplishments served Mormons and non-Mormons and helped bridge the harsh divide between
the two.

---

[89]*Proceedings of the One Hundred Eighteenth Annual Communication*, 22–27; "Utah's Movers and
    Shakers Celebrate Reopening of S. L. City-County Building," *DN*, April 29, 1989; Cathy
    Kelly, "Rebirth of City-County Building," *DN*, April 29, 1989; Lisa Riley Roche, "Utahns
    Throng to Admire Restoration," *DN*, April 30, 1989.

15

Epiphany or Transformation: Reelection

You cannot shape the forces of change by resisting them.
WALTER REUTHER

B Y SUMMER 1893, BASKIN AND THE CITY COUNCIL WERE
receiving sharp criticism from the *Deseret News* for the "alarm-
ing condition of the city's finances" arising from the expensive
overhaul of public utilities and the costs of the City-County Building
construction.[1] In the November elections these and other allegations
of financial mismanagement and disharmony would crescendo and
affect the Liberal Party, but not Baskin.

In July and August the *Tribune* returned to making political accusations that had consistently been the Liberal Party line for some time:
the People Party's breakup and the migration to major political parties
were devious attempts to flank non-Mormon opposition and to obtain
statehood by way of promises made to one of the parties.[2] Many Liberals continued to consider Utah statehood premature. As the *Tribune*
argued, "The slate will be made up of . . . Democrats and Republicans.
. . . Then the Democratic string will be pulled . . . and the Republicans
will bring up the tail. . . . It will unite the two wings of the old Church
party, and . . . turn all the offices back into the hands of the [LDS]
faithful."[3]

---

[1]"The City Threatened" and "The Dilemma," *DN*, July 29, 1893, 10/3, 3/2.
[2]"The Mendacious Critics," *SLT*, July 24, 1892, 6/2.
[3]"Shall the People's Party Reunite?" *SLT*, August 4, 1893, 5/4.

Adding to political tensions was the emergence of the Amorines, a secret organization, numbering about six hundred men in Utah, dedicated to fighting the spread and influence of Catholicism. The *Tribune* reported the organization's instructions: "No Catholic must be given employment. . . . No Catholic must be allowed to work side by side . . . with a member, for by his oath [the Amorine] is compelled by fair means or foul to oust him."[4] In bringing the Amorines to public gaze, the *Tribune* aimed to reveal the group's true motive: to have its own members elected to public office. The Amorines' ambition was to dictate nominations on different tickets and thereby elect sufficient numbers of their members to carry out their anti-Catholic goals. They encouraged Jew and Gentile, Liberal and Mormon, Democrat and Republican to unite, to "fraternize on a common footing."[5] In extra-large type, the *Tribune* exclaimed, "The Amorines: A Secret and Oath-Bound Club," and the accompanying article emphasized, "So unprincipled and nefarious a plot . . . against society itself, has not before been exposed." Revealing their existence and naming their leaders would be detrimental if not a death blow, presumed the *Tribune*.[6]

Irish emigrants were few among the Mormons of Utah, but in the business, laboring, and mining population there were sufficient numbers for two Catholic congregations, St. Mary's and St. Patrick's. Notable Catholics among the Liberals included Gen. Patrick E. Connor, a party founder, and Patrick Lannan, a *Tribune* editor and owner and a businessman. Both would rank high on any anti-Catholic list. At least three people whose names appeared as candidates on the November elections lists were known to be Amorines. In his study, Leo Lyman casts suspicion on Liberal Party mayoral candidate J. C. Conklin because of his refusal to take a stand for or against the secret group.[7]

Ever the Liberal Party defender, the *Tribune* expressed concern that Amorines could jeopardize Liberal election hopes.[8] In discussing

[4]"The Amorines: A Secret and Oath-Bound Club," *SLT*, August 27, 1893, 1/5. Known by various names—Patriotic Sons of America, Amorines, Amorine-Amor Club, Amorine Society, and Western Star—they were a National Protestant Association branch. C. M. Jackson and Fred W. Dennis were cited as responsible for its origin in Utah.

[5]Ibid.

[6]"The Amorines: A Secret and Oath-Bound Club," "A Nefarious Organization," and "The Amorines," *SLT*, August 27, 1893, 1/5, 4/1, 8/2.

[7]Lyman, *Political Deliverance*, 212–13.

[8]"For the Amorines," *SLT*, October 25, 1893, 4/1.

Patrick H. Lannan, businessman, Mason, *Salt Lake Tribune* owner, and Liberal Party member. *From the Alta Club Photographic Collection of Special Collections Department of the J. Willard Marriott Library, University of Utah in Salt Lake City.*

potential candidates for office, William H. Dickson identified Fire Chief Charles E. Stanton, a Liberal in Baskin's former administration, as an Amorine; Dickson warned that placing Stanton on any ballot would lose the vote of every Irishman and Catholic in the city.[9]

A MOST PROFOUND CHANGE

Late on the evening of September 27, a *Tribune* editor rushed to the home of Mayor Baskin, eager to verify the rumor of the most profound change in the life of Robert N. Baskin in all his years in Utah. Rampant on the city streets the previous night was the report that Baskin had severed his ties with the Liberal Party and would at once join the independents and tender his resignation as mayor. Visibly shaken by the reporter's sudden exposition, Baskin initially denied the account, but then quietly confirmed its partial truth:

> This is a movement that is independent of party considerations. It is a movement of the people in which they bury party. It is a movement composed of men of all parties. I accepted the nomination [of the Independent-Citizen Party] as I believe it will be the means of vindicating my course. My own self-respect, after what has occurred,

[9] "The Citizens' Committee," *SLT*, September 28, 1893, 5/1. Historians suggest that the anti-Catholic move in Utah was part of a process taking place on a national scale.

prevents me from accepting a nomination from the Liberal party, and my only chance for a vindication was possible through the spontaneous action of the people.[10]

In these lines, Baskin confirmed the words of Judge Elias A. Smith at the Independent Convention, where Baskin was quoted as saying "that he had voted the last Liberal ticket he ever expected to; that he had declined a renomination from the Liberal party, and that the Independent Citizens' movement would receive his hearty support whether he was nominated or not." Baskin corrected the rumors and Smith's report to say that the Liberal Party nomination was "never tendered" to him, and added, "If other citizens can ignore party considerations for the purpose of correcting very grave abuses, I certainly can also afford to do it." The reporter pressed Baskin, presumably to clarify the "abuses" or discuss the allegation that he intended to resign his position as mayor, but Baskin replied testily that he wished not to be further questioned. The *Tribune* reporter ended his column with the sensitive, pensive comment: "The next moment the big door of the lonely house on the hill swung to noiselessly on its hinges, and the Mayor of Salt Lake City was alone with his thoughts."[11]

By his mention of "correcting very grave abuses," Baskin referenced the financial problems and mismanagement issues of city council members. In most of these cases he did not have a primary role, but he held the ultimate responsibility of the public's trust. As mayor under a new party and with men working for the common good, he anticipated the "vindication" he sought by serving the city and the public.[12]

At the open-air meeting at the Cullen Hotel, Liberal Party chair Orlando W. Powers introduced J. C. Conklin as the party's candidate for mayor. While Powers did not name Baskin, there could be no doubt Baskin was the target when Powers said that "a cowardly assault . . . by a self-important public officer will also do much to join the Liberal party closer together."[13] At a later meeting, Powers again turned on Baskin, saying he had been thrust down the Independents' throat, not selected by the people. Baskin was accused of

---

[10]"The Political Situation," *slt*, September 28, 1893, 8/2.

[11]Ibid.

[12]However, Baskin's enemies were quick to publish his June 1892 tributes and thanks to his council. "Political Drift," *slt*, October 30, 1893, 8/3.

[13]"Judge Powers Serenaded," *slt*, September 28, 1893, 8/2; "Liberal Serenade," *dn*, October 7, 1893, 30/2.

currying favor with those he formerly despised and of "using holy water instead of the old-time hell-fire to capture their votes." Another speaker at the meeting asserted, "Orders used to come from the Lion House [Brigham Young's home]; now they come from the Walker House [the non-Mormons' hotel]."[14] In a lengthy article in the *Tribune*, Liberals unearthed a collection of speeches of derision and criticism that Baskin had voiced about Mormons in past years, hoping to refresh Mormon voters' memories of his earlier scathing criticisms of polygamy and theocracy. Not to ignore the opposing views, Liberals also exhumed the Mormon-authored publications that had appeared over the years in the *News* that caustically maligned Baskin, and these were also republished in the *Tribune*.[15] The personal attacks by Mormon historian Orson F. Whitney were added, as the Liberals brought out implements from all quarters against their former party leader.[16]

As the Independent and Citizen group grappled with completing a full ticket of candidates, the questions arose—not easily answered—of whether men under consideration were inclined toward Republican or Democratic party affiliation.[17] By mid-October the various inharmonious political elements reluctantly came together. The Independent Committee of Fifty and the Citizen Committee of Five merged and officially nominated Robert Baskin as their candidate for the forthcoming election. With some reluctance and only a modicum of enthusiasm, the *Deseret News* admitted that Baskin, as its man on the Independent-Citizen ticket, was a lawyer of marked ability and a former Utah upper house legislator. None had ever questioned his integrity or sincerity, and he had been upright, fearless, and independent. "He is a Democrat of the most decided cast, and in support of his political convictions elsewhere has had some trying experiences. He will make a strong run," the *News* observed. The allusion to "trying experiences" elsewhere suggests the editor knew of Baskin's Ohio altercation, incited by political differences, in which Baskin shot Andrew West. It was a veiled and subtle cut inserted in already faint

---

[14]"A Mighty Liberal Meeting," *SLT*, October 29, 1893, 8/2.

[15]"Mormon Papers Malign Him" and "Citations of History," *SLT*, October 30, 1893, 5/3; "What Baskin Said of Them," *SLT*, October 30, 1893, 5/5.

[16]"Powers on Baskin's History," *SLT*, October 30, 1893, 5/3.

[17]The complicated intertwining of issues such as Republican and Democratic party formation, the gold standard, the free silver alignment, and the political preferences of Mormon leaders are described by others, including Lyman, *Political Deliverance*, 150–84.

praise.[18] Joining Baskin on the ticket were Gustave H. Backman, C. S. Burton, Arthur Pratt, and Grant H. Smith, running for the positions of recorder, treasurer, city marshal, and justice of the peace, respectively.[19] Baskin asked that his performance be judged by the departments that he controlled and, if it was found wanting, for the citizens to so express their opinion at the polls. Placards supporting the ticket criticized the Liberal Party with messages such as "The platform of promises of the Liberals are [*sic*] now a list of its past failings" and "We want a government of the people, not of the politicians."[20] Arrayed as opponents were Baskin's friends and former advocates: C. Emir Allen, James Glendinning, Christopher Diehl, and P. J. Moran.

On the Saturday preceding the election, the *Tribune* reported large numbers of Mormons coming to the city from outlying settlements "in obedience to a command issued by the church authorities" to march in a parade, to fire up the electorate. Declaring them to be loyal to the defunct People's Party, the newspaper described them as "hoodlum boys, ex-Danites, and church heelers."[21] Orlando Powers claimed that the imports were more than raucous celebrants; they were people brought to vote illegally, fraudulently using the names of absent or dead citizens.[22] That evening Baskin's Independent-Citizen Party supporters gathered to hear his address. He told them he was "confident that the voters on Tuesday next would rebuke the [Liberal] party that had wrecked the city." In answer to Powers's allegations, Baskin "delivered a very pretty essay on the need of absolute purity of the ballot box, and admonished every citizen to see that no fraud was practiced."[23]

Of all the harsh words printed by the *Tribune*, those that undoubtedly troubled Baskin most severely were not those shouted in vitriol and flame but those fashioned almost as a whisper. In a small, untitled article, sandwiched between an unrelated editorial ironically titled "What Democracy Costs" and small advertisements for candy and prompt delivery of clean coal was this brief note:

---

[18]"The Citizens' Ticket," *DN*, October 7, 1893, 7/2. Rare was public mention of this detail of Baskin's past.

[19]"Municipal Election," *SLT*, October 29, 1893, 5/5.

[20]Stout, *HOU*, 1:464.

[21]"Gathering of the Saints," *SLT*, November 5, 1893, 5/3.

[22]"To the Voters of Salt Lake City," *SLT*, November 5, 1893, 6/2.

[23]"At the Theater," *SLT*, November 5, 1893, 5/3.

Orlando W. Powers. A political force in the Liberal and American parties, Powers was a prominent lawyer and judge. *Used by permission Utah State Historical Society.*

It was a quarter of a century ago that Dr. J. K. Robinson was assassinated in this city. . . . Robert N. Baskin, who was a bosom friend of Dr. Robinson, took a solemn oath over the bier of his dead friend that the remainder of his life should be dedicated to the purpose of bringing his murderers to justice. Last night's procession contained several of Dr. Robinson's assassins, and every one of them, now living, will vote for Baskin next Tuesday.[24]

November's elections gave Republicans a sweep, with Ohio, New York, Massachusetts, and Iowa all taking victories; however, control of Congress remained with the Democrats. Salt Lake City's election results were delayed because of a large number of scratch ballots, but at final count, Mayor Baskin was reelected over Conklin, 4,178 to 3,773. Liberals had polled only half the votes they had gathered the year earlier.[25] Baskin was joined in victory by Backman as recorder, Arthur Pratt as city marshal, and Citizen candidates who won twelve of the eighteen city council seats.[26] According to the *Tribune*, Mayor

---

[24]Untitled article, *SLT*, November 5, 1893, 4/4. Additional evidence that the identity of Robinson's assassins was widely known in the community comes from the report of Rev. Norman McLeod's 1872 memorial: "Emanating from some one at the back of the perpetrators of that crime, was the inspiring cause of that cowardly murder." "Memorial Service," *SLT*, October 23, 1872, 3/3.

[25]Lyman blames the issue of Amorines on the ballot for the diminished Liberal vote. Lyman, *Political Deliverance*, 213.

[26]"Summing Up of the City," *SLT*, November 9, 1893, 8/4.

Baskin's response to the makeup of the remainder of the council was less than enthusiastic, for when congratulated, he replied, "Congratulate me? What for? For being in hell for the next two years?" Said one of the Liberals, "We wanted a Liberal Council, but a Gentile Council is better than an out and out church aggregation."[27]

The control of the *Salt Lake Herald* had been acquired by non-Mormon Democrats, and it paid Baskin a tribute for his accomplishments. Baskin was first elected, it recalled, when the Liberal Party was in its full heyday of power, and there were two courses that he could have followed, one of which was "to fall in with Liberal council programme—to run the city for the benefit of one class, to allow it to be bled by favorites, to see it smothered in extravagance, and to allow its laws to be trampled on." This approach would have guaranteed harmony and goodwill within the Liberal Party, but it was not the course on which Baskin's trenchant analysis took him, for within three months the *Herald* emphasized that Baskin and the practices of Liberal Party politics had been "hopelessly separated." Now Gentiles, Jews, and Mormons were all behind him, said the *Herald*. Baskin had chosen to lift "his voice against the course of the council [and] warn the city of the perils which menaced it." The *Herald* continued:

> This meant . . . denunciation of himself—the probable disruption of the [Liberal] party; but not for a moment did the mayor hesitate. His stern and rugged honesty and business prudence were superior to party considerations. He took his stand on the side of honesty; chopped off the heads of thieving chiefs of departments, even though those heads belonged to pets of the party; vetoed dishonest bills right and left; reformed where he could; warned where he could not, and last night had the satisfaction of seeing his old time party . . . parade his name up the streets [denouncing his approval by the Saints].[28]

On the morning after the election, Baskin was met unexpectedly on the street by an old, ardent Mormon adversary. The *Tribune* described the meeting: "A very touching spectacle was presented to passers-by on First South street yesterday morning. That was the meeting and congratulations between Apostle George Q. Cannon and Mayor Baskin. It looked a little funny to such old-timers as were passing by, but the new generation looked on and smiled." The editor

[27]"After the Election," *slt*, November 9, 1893, 8/3.
[28]"Winning Ticket," *slh*, October 22, 1893, 8/2.

added a sarcastic doubt to the observation: "It would be worth a peck of St. George apples to have the affection which those gentlemen feel toward each other tried by a fire assay, to see how much of the real precious metal is contained in the crucible."[29] However, the *Tribune's* sarcasm and distrust were short-lived, for soon the old engine, the war-horse against Mormon theocracy, was to publish a reconciliation call that many old-time Liberals would never have predicted.

THE LIBERAL PARTY DISBANDS

The *Tribune's* columns acknowledged the dramatic change now exhibited in the attitude of non-Mormons regarding statehood for Utah: "Inasmuch as they have groaned under the oppression . . . by Federal law; inasmuch as they have been afflicted with foreign officers, and have been denied the[ir] rights . . . , we tell them now to renew their appeals for Statehood, and there will be no opposition."[30] The Mormons answered with their own plea for the common good to replace the enmity that for so long had divided Utahns: "Everybody ought to rejoice at this triumph of principle over partisanship. . . . [O]pponents will feel that yesterday's work was well-intended and most excellently done; the soreness of defeat will be relieved, and all parties and classes will join in applauding the uprising that resulted so happily."[31]

Given the unrelenting, insoluble differences over theocracy and polygamy that had prevailed from 1865, when Baskin arrived, to this election in 1893, the rate of change between Mormons and non-Mormons that followed the November voting was, by comparison, instantaneous. From 1870—twenty-three years—the Liberal Party had worked to eliminate the need for its own existence. In little more than twenty-four hours, it came as an epiphany to Orlando Powers and other Liberal stalwarts that their goals had been achieved, their organization was no longer needed. Meeting in the Salt Lake Theater, Liberals first took up the questions of "postponement of all political functions" and raising subscriptions in order to liquidate the party's indebtedness. In deliberations lasting hours, the members heard from Judge Powers, Charles C. Goodwin, C. Emir Allen, Enos D. Hoge,

---

[29]Untitled, *slt*, November 9, 1893, 4/1.
[30]"Proceed, Gentlemen," *slt*, November 11, 1893, 4/2.
[31]"Election After-Thoughts," *dn*, November 11, 1893, 9/1.

and many others. A Liberal Party resolution absolved legislators of any allegiance to the party. Discussion progressed until a resolution affirming the permanent dissolution of the Liberal Party was entered. It passed with only two dissenting votes.[32] The only remaining task, according to Powers's solemn admission, was to make the party's end official: "I have become so strongly attached to the Liberal party that I hate to see it go down. Nevertheless, it . . . accomplished its purpose, and . . . can now, in all honor, disband."[33] The *Tribune* rushed to the gray beards of the city, posing the question, should the disbanding of the Liberals have come earlier? Attorney, politician, and educator Parley L. Williams said yes, as did Chief Justice Zane, Charles S. Varian, Supreme Court justice Samuel Merritt, Governor Caleb West, Masonic leader and businessman Christopher Diehl, and city official Charles F. Loofbourow.[34] Suddenly Baskin was further vindicated. His preelection recognition that the "movement of the people" would "bury" the continuing need for the Liberal Party had been correct. He was not a traitor but a prescient.

With two of its goals achieved, statehood for Utah remained the only unfulfilled Liberal Party purpose. On the afternoon of December 13, the Democrat-controlled House of Representatives, with only two dissenting votes, passed the Rawlins Bill, an enabling act preparatory to Utah's admission to statehood.[35]

The Liberal Party finale took place on December 18, 1893, by disbanding at its last formal meeting. "It has been decided by the party itself that its usefulness as a political organization is ended," the *Tribune* noted, commenting that the organization had now "become a part of the history of our country."[36] *Tribune* editor Goodwin penned the benedictory lines: "The men who began the work certainly cannot be charged with any selfish ambition to further their own ends." Rather they were faced with "unmeasured opposition, possibly violence," and "all their property interests in this Territory" had been "put in jeopardy." When any "one brave torch-bearer fell out of the ranks,

---

[32]Untitled article, *DN*, December 23, 1893, 16/2.

[33]"Shall the Liberals Quit?" *SLT*, November 11, 1893, 8/4.

[34]"Discussing the Situation: Opinions as to Liberal Party Disbandment," *SLT*, November 12, 1893, 8/2.

[35]Ohio's Michael D. Harter was the bill's strongest opponent, saying Utah's admission would add two "free silver" senators to the divide on monetary policy. "PASSED," *SLT*, December 14, 1893, 1/5.

[36]"The Liberal Party Quits," *SLT*, December 19, 1893, 8/2.

overborne by the world's attritions, there was another to take his place, and so the work went on, often as bitter as death, always at a disadvantage. . . . More than once it seemed a hopeless task." Goodwin's final words were another acknowledgment that Baskin's assessment had been correct, for "their final triumph would at the same time be the death of the party," as citizens would now work together "to build up here one of the most beautiful and prosperous States in the Republic, and . . . to add to its splendor, its prosperity and its power."[37]

The end of the People's Party appeared to mark the end of Mormon theocratic government as well. The words of LDS Church president Wilford Woodruff in his Manifesto appeared to end the practice of polygamy. With an enabling act passed in the House of Representatives, statehood for Utah Territory was seemingly assured. The goals of Robert Newton Baskin, Patrick Edward Connor, George R. Maxwell, James Bedell McKean, Jacob Smith Boreman, Frederic Lockley, and the scores of unheralded non-Mormon men who worked to end theocracy and polygamy, to provide true republican government and its freedoms for all people in a *State* of Utah, appeared to be finally achieved.

Yet, appearances can be deceiving.

---

[37]"Vale, Liberal Party," *SLT*, December 19, 1893, 4/2. Not all were ready to work together. Former Liberal party leader Henry W. Lawrence and others formed the Populist Party in November. McCormick and Sillito, "Henry W. Lawrence," 220–40.

16

Mayors, Industrial Armies, and City Crises

Hunger makes a thief of any man.
PEARL S. BUCK

T HE FINANCIAL DEPRESSION THAT BEGAN IN THE EARLY 1890s as silver, lead, and wool prices fell may have been the most severe ever experienced by America.[1] By 1894, unemployment rates were as high as 20 percent across the nation. The formation of destitute workers into an "army" had its origin in Ohio when Jacob S. Coxey proposed the novel idea that the federal government build roads using workers for whom no other employment existed. That failing, Coxey urged the unemployed to organize and march on Washington to make their demands before Congress.[2] It followed that "industrial armies" of unemployed workers, almost all of them men, formed in dozens of cities across the United States, particularly in its western half. Oregon, California, Washington, and the Rocky Mountain states of Montana and Idaho all bred their own legions of out-of-work laborers.

Utah and its cities were not spared from the depression. Thomas Alexander's history cites more than 4,000 unemployed in a workforce estimated at 9,000.[3] In mid-February, 300 unemployed men

---

[1] A *Tribune* article cited the depression as beginning as early as 1873. "The Cause of It All," *SLT*, April 9, 1894, 4/2; "Utah," *SLT*, January 1, 1894, 4/4.
[2] R. H. Roberts and Sadler, "Riding the Rails," 208.
[3] Alexander and Allen, *Mormons and Gentiles*, 127; Arrington, "Utah and the Depression of the 1890s," 6.

demonstrated in downtown Salt Lake City, and on the following
day the numbers swelled to 1,500 people, all gathered to plead with
city and county leaders for work on the roads to be expanded and for
construction of the planned state capitol to be started. Utah's mining
industry was particularly hard hit. "By the closing of the mints in
India and by the repeal of the Sherman law without offering any substitute, such a decline has come to silver as to practically close silver
mining," the *Tribune* reported.[4] "Silver King mine in Park City . . . is
simply a wonder, . . . yet there is . . . very little profit in sending the
ore to market. . . . [its former] benefits would nearly equal the profits
of any one agricultural State in the Union."[5]

The 1893–94 crescendo of widespread economic woes was particularly inopportune for Mayor Baskin and the city council, for it coincided with the City-County Building construction and the extensive
public works under way, and further intensified the financial stress
already afflicting the city and county. As the national calamity worsened, Governor Caleb West, Mayor Baskin, and Ogden mayor C. M.
Brough were brought into the vortex of the workers' dilemma when
the territory, and Salt Lake City and Ogden in particular, became the
targets of an army of desperate, unemployed, near-starving men coming primarily from northern California.

Coinciding with the semiannual conference of the LDS Church in
Salt Lake City in the first week of April, a telegram warned Governor
West of the imminent arrival in Utah of 1,250 to 1,500 men from the
environs of San Francisco, Oakland, and Sacramento.[6] Immediately he
communicated with Box Elder and Weber county officials, instructing them to enforce the territorial statute prohibiting common carriers
from allowing paupers to land. Entry of the train into the territory
was to be prevented, even "if the tracks have to be torn up."[7] West's
notice to three Southern Pacific officials—attorney Thomas Marshall,
Ogden superintendent S. W. Knapp, and general superintendent J. A.
Fillmore in San Francisco—forbidding the disembarking of the passengers was ignored, and the train passed, unimpeded, across Nevada.[8]

[4]"Utah," *SLT*, January 1, 1894, 4/4.
[5]"Park City for the Week," *SLT*, May 16, 1894, 3/1.
[6]The coverage of the industrial army by the *Deseret News*, its pages occupied with LDS conference reports, was slight in comparison with reporting in the *Tribune* and the *Ogden Standard*.
[7]"Special Train with Troops," *SLT*, April 8, 1894, 8/2.
[8]"The Army's Hot Reception," *SLT*, April 8, 1894, 8/2.

The group had originated in San Francisco, where that city's mayor arranged their transportation by train to Oakland. There the police, the fire department, and military authorities drove the men out, and Oakland's citizens allegedly ponied up the group's train fare to Sacramento. The source of the $600 fare (50 cents each) for the one-way trip from Sacramento to Ogden was unknown.[9] Governor West activated the territorial militia, recently commissioned as the Utah National Guard, with Salt Lake City units providing two companies of infantry. Ogden mustered an infantry and a cavalry company. At the request of Ogden's mayor, Baskin also formed a special unit of thirty "chosen men" of Salt Lake City, commanded by that city's chief of police, Arthur Pratt, with instructions to maintain order. A bizarre combination of two thousand loaves of bread, a Gatling gun, and a battery of artillerymen—the latter two from Fort Douglas—accompanied the policemen on a special railroad flatbed ordered by the governor. West was sympathetic with the army of destitute men but was also mindful of similar problems among Utah's people. He assured his men, "We will . . . see that the lives and property and interests of the people are protected, and that . . . the men of the army must obey the laws."[10] On April 7, the Salt Lake County Court issued an order forbidding the Rio Grande Western Railway and the Utah Northern and Oregon Short Line from transporting men into Salt Lake City, and it was served by the sheriff.[11] Organized in a military-like command with "General" Charles T. Kelly of San Francisco as their leader, they arrived in Ogden on April 8. Armed only with meager donations of food, the men traveled in twenty-seven unheated cattle cars without a roof, seats, bedding, or water.[12] Their goal was Washington, D.C., where they hoped to join Coxey's Ohio group and others to petition Congress for "legislation tending to furnishing of labor . . . for the benefit of the unemployed."[13]

On the Kelly industrials' arrival in Utah, the train's crewmen reported that the passengers were not vicious criminals but harmless men, having no weapons and seemingly inclined to peaceful means. Among them was a contingent of seventy-five elderly men, all GAR

---

[9]One leader said that no part of the fare was paid by the men composing the army. "Industrial Army Must Go," *SLT*, April 10, 1894, 1/1.

[10]"Army's Hot Reception."

[11]"The County Court Objects," *SLT*, April 8, 1894, 8/3.

[12]Ibid.

[13]"Commonweal Army Arrives," *SLT*, April 9, 1894, 1/1.

veterans, also seeking redress from Washington. "It was an exceedingly pitiful sight," said the *Tribune*, with "men, pale, cold, without covering or blankets, and wan, with hollow, sunken eyes, hunger and destitution pictured in their faces."[14] Police chief Pratt's survey found that fully half of the men were foreign born, largely Catholic and Irish. Many had been attracted to California from homes in the East by misleading advertisements picturing the state as the working man's paradise.

Robert Baskin and Franklin S. Richards obtained a court injunction confining the transients to the Ogden stockyards and denying them access to the city. West convened the Southern Pacific's Knapp and the Union Pacific's W. H. Bancroft to reach a solution, but was upset when the destitute passengers were denied further transportation by officials of the Denver and Rio Grande Western Railroad, who cited Colorado law requiring $200 for each pauper entering its borders. The Union Pacific refused to carry the army eastward at less than full fare. West was infuriated at the Southern Pacific, which demanded $40,000 to $45,000 ($35 a head) to return the men to California.

Baskin lashed out at the Southern Pacific, saying it had done "a brutal, wicked thing in shipping the men . . . like cattle, and subjecting them to hardship and suffering." He added that the company "ought to be made to repair the wrong as far as possible and to return these people to the community which ought to take care of them."[15] The *Tribune* described the army as "a living petition, a helpless protest against intolerable wrongs."[16] The *News* agreed that the Southern Pacific's action showed a "heartlessness that is almost without a parallel in railway history." The newspaper suggested, "Let the Southern Pacific railway be remembered for the service it has done us; and since we shall want to continue to do legitimate business with the golden Pacific coast, let us not lose too much time in getting another railroad through that will have a little regard for the people at its Utah end."[17]

Laboring men from Ogden were critical of West for the reception given the unemployed. A parade of several thousand Ogden workers formed in the streets, many carrying the Stars and Stripes. Others had banners with slogans such as "All those who sympathize, fall in

---

[14]Ibid.

[15]"Industrial Army Must Go."

[16]"What to Do," *slt*, April 11, 1894, 4/1.

[17]"Remember the Southern Pacific," *dn*, April 14, 1984, 11/2; "The Industrial Army," *dn*, April 14, 1894, 18/3–20.

line," "Gold at a premium and humanity at a discount," "Spike the Gatling gun," and "Governor, take your kids [soldiers] back to Salt Lake." The *Tribune* editorials alternately supported and criticized the actions of West and Baskin, announcing first that "this Territory cannot support the thousands of idle, lawless, demoralized and disheartened men."[18] Next was an assertion that "the governor ought to have . . . extended to them everything in his power to relieve their present distress."[19] Baskin reaffirmed the decisions he and West had made, saying no other course of action was open but to protect the people and property of the territory from an influx of paupers. This was especially applicable when the industrial army's plans were constantly in flux, and their actions unpredictable. Baskin added that had Utah's response not been one of opposition, another ten to fifteen thousand men in California might shortly have followed Kelly's path.[20]

Secret negotiations between Kelly, Ogden mayor Brough, and the Union Pacific were not shared until later with Governor West and Mayor Baskin. The negotiated plan was that the industrials, marching as a body and supervised by the Utah National Guard troops, would walk out of Ogden into Weber Canyon, along the tracks of the Union Pacific line, and make camp. The impression would be that they were commencing a long foot march. If it happened by *chance* that they were met by a train *incidentally* carrying empty boxcars capable of transporting 1,400 men and supplies, the train's crew would be unable to prevent boarding. The men would then be transported as far east as possible. Events played out as planned. Kelly's men were well-behaved, followed orders without fail, and carried patriotic flags and banners, with their blankets strapped on their backs. Twenty-Fourth Street and Washington Avenue were lined with townspeople; cavalry units headed the march and brought up the rear. Early next morning a Union Pacific train of thirty empty boxcars and six cars fully loaded with coal, serendipitously headed east, stopping at the Kelly army campsite, seven and one-half miles from Ogden. More than 1,400 industrials, with sixty-one new recruits among them, calmly "took possession of the train, just as though it had been sent by Providence for their especial use."[21] Ogden's city council donated seven wagon-

---

[18]"What To Do," *SLT*, April 11, 1894, 4/1.
[19]"All Right at Last," *SLT*, April 12, 1894, 4/1.
[20]"The Army Will Go East," *SLT*, April 11, 1894, 1/1.
[21]"The Industrial Army War," *SLT*, April 13, 1894, 5/1.

loads of provisions, including blankets, hats, and shoes. "The men were overcome by the generosity," the *Tribune* reported, "and . . . gave three hearty cheers for Ogden."[22]

Celebrations and congratulations followed the bloodless, nontraumatic resolution of the presence of Kelly's army in Utah. Governor West addressed his troops, saying, "You deserve the thanks and gratitude of the people of the Territory. I now dismiss you to your peaceful homes."[23] The episode was handled "without loss of life or destruction of property," at an expense of only $10,000.[24]

To the criticisms in Ogden newspapers that Baskin had come to Ogden needlessly, he responded by likening the emergency to a fierce fire, when one city's fire department should respond to the mayor's call from its sister city. When Mayor Brough informed Mayor Baskin that he needed food, Baskin sent food. When Brough said his police force was too small to manage the army's ingress, Baskin was quick to offer the help of Chief Arthur Pratt and his men. "Under these circumstances, the snarl of the Ogden press is both ungracious and small-minded," said Baskin with emphasis. The *Ogden Sun* apologized for any words of disparagement and complimented the troops highly.[25]

Utah's Own "Army" and Other Rumbles

If Baskin thought that, after the departure of Kelly's army, he would see no more destitute workers, he was overoptimistic. On April 15 another contingent from the west reached Ogden, also bound for Washington, D.C. Numbering only fifty-four, the men in this group were met by Mayor Brough and told they might march unimpeded out of the city. After being fed, the men walked to the Uintah area, stopping near the same spot where the Kelly army had camped and presumably where they would jump eastbound trains, undetected or unacknowledged.[26]

Utah's unemployed were themselves emboldened by the California commonwealers. H. E. Carter, from a Salt Lake City group called the Workingmen's Association, formed a "Utah Industrial Army" and was

[22]"The Army Moves Eastward," *SLT*, April 12, 8/2.
[23]"Industrial Army War."
[24]"Army Moves Eastward."
[25]"Industrial Army War."
[26]"Another Industrial Army Arrives," *SLT*, April 16, 1894, 4/5.

elected as its commanding "general." Patterned after Kelly's group, they proposed to abide by the same rules of proper conduct. They had no funds but hoped to find transportation for as many as 1,000 men, to join with other groups.[27] The *Tribune* predicted that an appeal to Mayor Baskin would be answered, like that of the Ogden group, with the city contingency fund donating $200 and two thousand loaves of bread.[28] Carter's army was estimated at 700 men. On April 30 the Utah army of poverty, giving speeches laced with disturbing words like "war," "on the eve of a revolution," and "spring to arms," paraded out of Salt Lake City. Sympathetic crowds estimated at four thousand lined the streets, as the men marched from the city and camped near Murray, Utah.[29] Despite entreaties by Henry W. Lawrence, Governor West, Mayor Baskin, Selectman Herman Bamberger, and several other prominent citizens, the Rio Grande Western repeatedly refused transportation. The men faced quagmire at Murray, their enthusiasm draining. Carter's daily speeches, rallies, entreaties, and meetings produced little progress; the opposition of the rail carriers was seemingly set.[30]

By May 10 the army was restless and moved south to a Lehi, Utah, campsite one mile from the Rio Grande Western tracks and near the Union Pacific tracks.[31] Utah's contingent complained they would have been with Coxey and Kelly "but for the combine that existed against them" in which "Grover is the head, Baskin the tail and Governor West the center of gravity."[32] Among the men at Lehi were about 250 from another California contingent, and on May 11 this group started northward toward Provo, contributing to rumors that the "army" was breaking up.[33] In the early hours of May 12, about forty men boarded and captured a westbound Union Pacific train, switching it from the Union Pacific tracks to those of the Rio Grande Western. As the men drove the train into the Provo station, the rail employees threw a switch, derailing the engine and the coal tender.

---

[27]"Utah's Industrial Army," *SLT*, April 18, 1894, 5/6; "Industrial Army Organized," *SLT*, April 19, 1894, 8/4.

[28]"The Industrial Army," *SLT*, April 20, 1894, 8/3.

[29]"Industrials March Out," *SLT*, May 1, 1894, 8/2; "The Industrials Lose a Day," *SLT*, April 27, 1894, 8/6.

[30]"The Parades and Meetings," *SLT*, May 5, 1894, 5/3; "No Transportation Likely," *SLT*, May 6, 1894, 5/3.

[31]"The Industrials March," *SLT*, May 10, 1894, 5/2.

[32]"The Industrials at Lehi," *SLT*, May 11, 1894, 8/3.

[33]"The Divided Industrials," *SLT*, May 12, 1894, 5/5.

The rebels were within minutes of restoring the two massive vehicles on the tracks when they were arrested by forty deputy U.S. marshals, in full view of about 500 Provo citizens, many of whom were sympathetic to the men's cause. Tinder was added to an already unstable mix when the Denhalter Rifles of the Utah National Guard arrived on the scene, prominently displaying the now notorious Gatling gun that had caused resentment in Ogden.[34] The Union Pacific's workmen reclaimed their train, and about 400 of Carter's army were arrested and placed on a train to the Utah Penitentiary.[35]

Increasingly, bands of the unemployed across the nation resorted to lawlessness and violence. In Ogden a new group commandeered another train; in Boise, Idaho, 600 men were massing; in Green River, Wyoming, more than 400 were threatening train seizures; in Vacaville, California, bands terrorized Chinese and Japanese settlements. In Nampa, Idaho, 80 men stole a Union Pacific train, and 2,000 men were threatening to do the same in Denver.[36] As another 1,500 were being transported on the Southern Pacific to be left in Ogden, the *Tribune* expressed further concern and frustration: "For the Southern Pacific to dump its hundreds . . . into Utah is such a dastardly act . . . that the Governor would be justified in calling the Legislature in extra session to enact penalties."[37]

Mayor Baskin was no less concerned as he wrote to Governor West that Chief Pratt had been informed by the California men of a tacit agreement between the "Industrials of California" and the Southern Pacific Railroad that freight trains would stop at various stations to permit industrials to board for transport to Ogden. Pratt had information that an additional 1,500 to 1,800 were already in transit, with 15,000 more expected to arrive within months. "As my jurisdiction of Mayor is limited to the corporate limits of the city, I am powerless in the premises," Baskin wrote to the governor. There must be "some legal remedy to redress the wrong and prevent its continuance," Baskin implored, for the men would otherwise "scatter and become a charge

---

[34]"The Industrials Capture a Train," *SLT*, May 13, 1894, 5/1.

[35]Federal marshals were sent by court authority on the request of railroad officials. "The Court Interferes," *SLT*, May 13, 1894, 5/1. Utah County sheriff John A. Brown sent National Guardsmen at Governor West's request. "The Militia Called Out," *SLT*, May 13, 1894, 5/3.

[36]"Train Seized at Ogden," *SLT*, May 17, 1894, 5/3; "War Declared in Idaho," *SLT*, May 18, 1894, 1/5; "Industrial Army Rioters," *SLT*, May 18, 1894, 1/6; "Herding the Industrials," *SLT*, May 21, 1894, 1/3; "An Industrial Rendezvous," *SLT*, May 23, 1894, 1/5.

[37]"The Industrial Menace," *SLT*, May 21, 1894, 4/2.

and menace to several counties."[38] A Third District Court's injunction prevented the indigents from entering Davis County, where they had been troubling the residents: "For weeks [people] have been terrorized, their gardens pillaged and their larders emptied. Farmers dared not leave their families to work in the fields lest a band of these industrialists should come along with insolent demands and wreak vengeance if their needs could not be supplied."[39] Baskin, together with Salt Lake City's Police and Fire Board, gave permission for Chief Pratt, with a force of patrolmen, to proceed to Davis County to enforce the injunction. Twenty-two officers from Salt Lake City joined a force of thirty Davis County sheriff's deputies and a number of county residents in sympathy with efforts to stem the tide.[40]

Meanwhile, 375 men of a third "army," this one commanded by "Lt. Col." Dr. F. Deming Smith, arrived in Ogden and promptly denied the allegations of any secret pact with the Southern Pacific. Smith added that his was the last of any known army, and he denied that 15,000 more were awaiting transport. Not unlike Kelly and Carter, he wished to pass through Utah peacefully, breaking no laws.

Anonymous postcards delivered to Governor West, Chief Justice Merritt, and Mayor Baskin carried threats against their lives.[41] "The messages on the cards are couched in the most disgusting language, and state that unless the officials named leave [Salt Lake] city within four days they will be killed, if dynamite has to be resorted to effect the purpose," reported the *Deseret Evening News*.[42]

In the dark, early morning hours, Pratt's forces, some on horseback, all heavily armed with Winchester rifles and pistols, met face-to-face with Smith's industrial army at the county line. With the opposing lines separated by only a few feet and illuminated only by lantern light, Pratt read the injunction aloud to Smith and his men. Very tense moments followed, when bloodshed might have erupted except for the cool judgment of Pratt and Dr. Smith. Although a number of Ogdenites, including the city attorney, urged Smith to force the issue and cross the line, he backed down and encamped his men on the

---

[38]"Mayor to the Governor," *SLT*, May 24, 1894, 3/3.

[39]"Davis County's Injunction," *SLT*, May 25, 1894, 5/1; "The Industrials in Camp," *SLT*, May 27, 1894, 5/1 (quotation).

[40]"The Officers Start," *SLT*, May 26, 1894, 8/2.

[41]"Keeping Out the Commonwealers, *NYT*, May 28, 1894.

[42]"Threatening Letters," *DEN*, May 26, 1894, 4.

Weber side of the Weber-Davis county line.[43] Several days of stand-
off followed, until Ogden officials found a solution. They persuaded
Chief Justice Merritt to dissolve the previous injunction, allowing the
men to pass through Salt Lake City and go south, where they, like
Carter's men, could divide into small groups and surreptitiously jump
trains headed east.[44] When asked his opinion about lifting the injunction, Baskin said: "We are law abiding citizens, and I bow to the decision of the Court. . . . [T]here is [now] no way to keep them out of
the city. . . . If any of these contractors who are doing city work give
them employment when our own home people need it so badly, I shall
be very mad."[45]

A violent and startling explosion in the jail yard at the rear of the
city hall, directly under Mayor Baskin's office window, took place on
May 29. According to the *Deseret Evening News*, a bomb, charged
with gunpowder was "thrown . . . from the fire station and exploded
by means of a fuse or cap." It fell into unoccupied space, however,
and apart from minor injury to the janitor, no serious damage was
done. Whether the bomb was thrown by the disaffected of the industrial armies or it originated with the fire brigade personnel, Baskin
"sat quietly in his chair and paid only passing attention to the disturbance." He remarked, "I am not so easily frightened as some fellows
might think. Dynamite talk does not scare me."[46]

Baskin must have sighed deeply as he was faced, at the end of May
and early June, with still another group of unemployed workers, this one
named Sutter's army, on its way from Ogden to Salt Lake City.[47] The
conflicting issues of serving the security of Utah's people and respecting the legal rights of large numbers of men from California—however desperate—to enter and remain in the territory, while providing
humanely for them until they could move on, posed immense practical, legal, and ethical challenges for Baskin and other Utah leaders.

---

[43]"Halted at the Line" and "Stopped at the Davis Line," *slt*, May 26, 1894, 8/2; "Another
    Account of It," *slt*, May 27, 1894, 5/3.
[44]"The Injunction Dissolved," *slt*, May 30, 1894, 8/2.
[45]"Mayor Baskin Discusses It," *slt*, May 30, 1894, 8/4.
[46]"Violent Explosion," *den*, May 29, 1894, 1.
[47]"The Coming of Armies," *slt*, May 31, 1894, 8/4.

17

Unrelenting Problems but Statehood Arrives

Accept the challenges so that you may feel the exhilaration of victory.
GEN. GEORGE S. PATTON

H AD ROBERT BASKIN'S LIFE BEEN SO UNCOMPLICATED that he could have focused his energy and attention to the problems of mass immigration of desperate men seeking work, he would have been, by this alone, stressfully tested. However, he was simultaneously dealing with strongly opinionated city council members, the depression's financial constraints on the construction projects related to the City-County Building, and the efforts toward completing the city's water, sewer, and roadway improvements.

Not unlike the circumstances facing men in the industrial armies, Baskin's problems centered around money—the lack of it. In his annual mayor's report to the city council on February 6, he listed debt amounting to $975,779, with city assets at $300,666. Emphasizing the obvious, he cautioned that it would be a difficult year financially.[1] On April 2, Baskin signed a public offering of eight hundred bonds at $1,000 each, on a twenty-year term, bearing interest at 5 percent per annum. A deadline of May 7, 1894, was given for the bidding.[2] Brisk discussion brewed among bond agents on what figure the bonds would bring. "The prospects are that there will be smart competition

---

[1]"The Mayor's Message," *SLT*, February 7, 1894, 3/5.
[2]"Notice of Sale of Salt Lake City Bonds," *SLT*, April 12, 1894, 7/7.

for the bonds," the *Tribune* reported, "and the general impression is
that they will realize slightly over par."[3] The newspaper published
a revised account of the city's indebtedness to $816,150, against esti-
mated receipts of $235,000.[4] A "ring" of buyers bid only low figures,
but at the last moment, the bonds were taken by the New York Life
Insurance Company by its intermediary, Heber J. Grant and Company of Salt Lake. Those who had intentionally underbid were furious
when Baskin would not allow them to rebid, because their tactics had
"humiliated the city and the Council." "The Mayor and the Finance
Committee are congratulating themselves on the sale made and on
having outwitted the ring," said the *Tribune*. The sale yielded $801,550
to the city, less $1,000 commission to the intermediary.[5]

Problems crescendoed. In mid-April, Baskin vetoed franchises
granted to city railroads and a sprinkling company.[6] A shortage of
iron pipes for the City-County Building was the problem on April
20, with a delay of weeks anticipated to obtain them from eastern
suppliers. Plain glass windows were to be substituted for stained glass
in a cost-saving measure, and lighting for the grounds surrounding
the building was debated.[7] In early May, financial issues prompted
consideration of a temporary construction cessation, but a newspaper
subhead read, "It Is Not Likely That the Members Will Favor the
Abandonment of Work—Mr. Daly Objects to $10,000 Clocks—Mr.
Clawson Wants to Stop Short—Mr. McCormick Wants to Figure—
Mr. Young Opposed to Useless Expenditures—Mr. Cohn Wants to
Keep On—Federated Trades Protest."[8] City taxes rose dramatically,
to the dismay of both Mormons and non-Mormons.[9] A long, contentious city council meeting on May 8 concluded that the city would
continue with both the sewer project and the City-County Building.[10] Still, the problems facing Baskin hammered on: fifty saloons
threatened to go out of business because they could not survive the
requirement of Sunday closing; boilers for the joint building would

[3]"Discussing the City Bonds," *SLT*, April 24, 1894, 6/1; April 29, 1894, 6/1.
[4]"City's Financial Condition," *SLT*, May 13, 1894, 8/2.
[5]"City Bonds Finally Sold," *SLT*, May 17, 1894, 8/2.
[6]"Three Vetoes by the Mayor," *SLT*, April 18, 1894, 8/2.
[7]"Joint City and County Building," *SLT*, April 21, 1894, 8/5.
[8]"Work on the Building," *SLT*, May 3, 1894, 8/2 (quotation); "Joint Building Question," *SLT*,
    May 4, 1894, 6/1; "Shall the Building Stop?" *SLT*, May 5, 1894, 8/4.
[9]Alexander, *Mormons and Gentiles*, 100.
[10]"Work on the Joint Building," *SLT*, May 9, 1894, 2/6.

cost an extra $5,000; and defective wiring already installed in the City-County structure needed replacement.[11]

Constructing the city's gravity sewer was no less vexatious. A closed meeting of the Sewer Committee was held on April 30 to discuss problems hindering completion, and the manner of settling with contractors. The city had failed to meet one of its scheduled payments, resulting in damages of $25,000 due the contractor. Baskin favored paying the damages and moving on, in which he was supported by the union tradesmen, who feared unemployment. Resolution was reached by paying the damages and including a clause that only Salt Lake City workmen, and none of the hordes of unemployed outsiders from California continuing to haunt the territory, would be hired.[12]

Political matters were also added to the boiling pot of problems Baskin was stirring. An invitation, signed by Henry P. Henderson, circulated through the city, saying that, to maintain the perfect organization of the Democratic Party, a meeting on April 7 would present "matters of grave importance."[13] This was also the time of the LDS Church's semiannual spring conference, when Mormon leaders and members from throughout the territory would gather. The issue behind the invitation appears to have been changes looming in the Democratic Party of which Mormons should be aware. In fact, on June 25, Orlando W. Powers resigned his positions as Grand Sachem of the Tuscarora Society and chair of the Salt Lake County Democratic Committee.[14] June also found Utah's Republicans—led by Charles C. Goodwin, C. Emir Allen, and Frank J. Cannon—meeting in Denver to select candidates for their national convention.[15]

Near this time, Baskin traveled to Washington "to procure a special act authorizing the issuance of a million dollars of extra bonds" for Salt Lake City's construction projects. He later recalled, "While there I met, in the lobby of the Arlington hotel, Geo. Q. Cannon, . . . Bishop [Hiram B.] Clawson and Isaac K. Trumbo, who were in Washington to aid in procuring the passage of the Enabling Act

---

[11]"Saloons to Be Less Numerous," *SLT*, May 12, 1894, 6/1; "Joint Building Payrolls," *SLT*, May 12, 1894, 6/1; "The Joint Building," *SLT*, May 19, 1894, 8/4.

[12]"Mayor Baskin's Act Endorsed," *SLT*, May 9, 1894, 5/2; "The Gravity Sewer," *SLT*, May 1, 8/5; May 17, 8/3, 8/5; May 23, 5/3; and May 25, 1894, 6/1.

[13]"Conference Democratic Meeting," *SLT*, April 8, 1894, 6/2.

[14]"The Democracy Startled," *SLT*, June 26, 1894, 8/4.

[15]"Slogan of Utah Delegates," *SLT*, June 26, 1894, 1/5.

which was then pending." Trumbo asked Baskin if he had come to oppose Utah's admission. On Baskin's reply that he had not, Trumbo asked for Baskin's support in its passage, to which he answered, "The president of the Mormon church has the power in Utah to defeat or elect any party ticket or candidate for office whenever he desires to do so, and while that power exists, I cannot favor statehood for the Territory." Baskin went further, allowing that he would not actively oppose the proposed legislation, given that most of the influential members of the former Liberal Party now favored statehood.[16]

Through the remainder of 1894 the mayor of the territory's largest city labored with a myriad of difficulties: the continued flow of unemployed men from California, the byzantine twists and turns of completing the City-County Building, and the headaches of the street paving and gravity sewer construction.[17] Even the signing of the Utah Enabling Act by President Grover Cleveland on July 16, the celebration of this event on August 1, the naming of 107 delegates to formulate a state constitution, and the campaign salvoes of Democrat Joseph Rawlins and Republican Frank J. Cannon all came and went with Baskin apparently having little time or energy to devote to them.[18] Baskin left no comment about the LDS First Presidency's sitting prominently on the Republicans' stage and applauding Frank J. Cannon's speech on October 19. Neither did he comment on the implications regarding the separation of church and state when LDS president Wilford Woodruff was seen by all to ceremoniously return the Democratic ballot and accept instead the blue-and-white Republican voting papers he was offered.[19]

DEDICATION FOR DEDICATION

The crowning event of the year for Baskin came on December 28. With hundreds of people present, the dedication of the joint City-County Building took place. All city and county business was temporarily

---

[16]Baskin, *REM*, 192.

[17]Examples taken at random: monthly expenses to be controlled ("The Municipal Expense," *SLT*, June 5, 1894, 8/4); road materials not meeting specifications ("Asphaltum in the Paving," *SLT*, June 8, 1894, 8/5); untreated Fort Douglas sewage ("A Fort Douglas Nuisance," *SLT*, June 16, 1894, 8/2); accusations of bribery ("Attempted Bribery Charged," *SLT*, June 20, 1894, 5/3); smoke pollution not enforced ("Relief Assured at Last," *SLT*, August 3, 1894, 8/2).

[18]"Signed by the President," *SLT*, July 18, 1894, 1/7; "Starter for Statehood" and "Statehood Was the Theme," *SLT*, August 2, 1894, 5/1, 5/3.

[19]"A Monster Demonstration," *SLT*, October 20, 1894, 5/1; "President Woodruff Votes," *SLT*, November 7, 1894, 3/1.

suspended, and the rooms were made available for visitors. As master of ceremonies, city councilman E. P. Newell opened the program by asking LDS Church president Wilford Woodruff to offer a prayer. Woodruff gave an "eloquent invocation for divine approval," with thanks for the gifts lavished upon the valley from which the structure they were about to dedicate had arisen. Mayor Baskin was honored as the first speaker, and he pointed out the period of severe financial depression that had existed for much of the construction period. For three years, he said, his desire was to see the work well and economically done, so that the incoming generations would reap the benefits of the building. There followed appropriate words of praise by ex-mayor George M. Scott and others. Shortly after the tower clock rang four o'clock, the wraps covering the figure of Columbia on the central spire were removed. Governor West spoke words of congratulations and praise, and city councilman LeGrande Young reminded the listeners of the myriad uses to which the land now occupied by the building had been put since 1847.

As Newell prepared to close, his eyes swept over the audience and stopped on the nattily dressed, impeccably groomed First Presidency member George Q. Cannon. Having given him no prior warning, Newell impulsively called on Cannon for closing remarks. Well qualified in improvisational speaking, Cannon was brief, articulate, and appropriate. He affirmed that the differences of opinion between Mormons and non-Mormons about investing in the project had vanished with its consummation. The building was ennobling and elevating and would inspire the creation of a better class of dwellings that other Utah cities should emulate, he added.[20] The ceremony ended, but on the upper floors, which had been promised for the upcoming Constitutional Convention, music and celebration carried on until almost midnight. Salt Lake City, Salt Lake County, and the non-Mormons of Utah now had an edifice whose beauty and size rivaled those of the Mormons' Temple. Baskin could take immense satisfaction from the opening of the building that had required joint efforts rarely achieved in partisan-divided, religiously divided Utah. The magnificent structure would shortly be put to good use in the next step toward statehood.[21]

---

[20]"With Music and Oratory, Dedication of the City and County Building," *SLT*, December 29, 1894, 5/1; "Brilliant Illumination" and "Splendid Music," *SLT*, December 29, 1894, 5/4. The untitled account in the *News* was brief, laudatory, and buried in the business section. *DN*, January 5, 1895, 16–17.

[21]"With Music and Oration," *SLT*, December 29, 1894, 5/1.

THE MAYOR RETIRES

The final year of Robert Baskin's mayoral term, 1895, was marked by the frustration that accompanies responsibility not commensurate with authority. He held the overall responsibility of both the city and county councils, as well as various boards made up of men whose ability, political allegiance, and moral fiber encompassed a wide spectrum. His power to control the complex tasks and ensure effective communication among such a group was more in theory than in effect.

In January's report, Baskin specified that city receipts totaled $1,237,661 and expenditures $1,019,170, but he received criticism from Councilman Clawson, who said that "the Mayor had likely put a little too much coloring upon the financial feature of the report in order to improve the administration exhibit."[22] Baskin addressed the unsolved problems of maintaining clear water supplies, even referring to the fanciful possibility of raising the level of Utah Lake four feet or drilling drain sites in the deepest part. He targeted the need for cheaper, more effective, and more encompassing city lighting and noted the much decreased incidence of water-borne contagious disease.[23]

In the first week of March the new City-County Building hosted the opening events of the Republican-dominated Constitutional Convention. George Q. Cannon offered a prayer to initiate the meeting. The Republican caucus met in secret; the Democratic caucus, seemingly impotent in the face of Republican force, held only a "mournful session."[24] The task of composing the constitution document was completed in mid-May, and Mayor Baskin—without guest or partner—was among the gala crowd celebrating in Christensen's Hall.[25]

In July, Baskin dealt with a situation in the Fire Department after the chief fireman summarily fired Assistant Chief M. M. Donovan and Capt. P. J. Sullivan.[26] A scandal of major proportions erupted in September when a pile of dusty papers was found in a storage closet at the new City-County Building. These receipts gave evidence that furnishings had been purchased without a competitive bid, at prices at least double those of the prevailing market. The city attorney indicted

[22]"The Mayor's Report," *SLT*, February 6, 1895, 8/4.
[23]"Only Half a Million," *SLT*, February 6, 1895, 5/1.
[24]"In Session," "Convention Gossip," "Republican Programme," and "Democratic Caucus," *SLT*, March 5, 1895, 1/1, 3/4, 3/3, 3/3.
[25]"Great Task Is Finished," *SLT*, May 17, 1895, 1/1.
[26]"Fire Officials Suspended" and "The Fire Chief and Commission," *SLT*, July 13, 1895, 8/3, 12/3.

Martin Hayken, the representative of Chicago's Andrews Furniture Company, for offering bribes to former city and county officials.[27] Charges, denials, and investigations stretched over weeks, and Mayor Baskin was called to explain. The city contracts for fixtures were separate and submitted differently from county contracts for the building's needs. Both were often done without his knowledge or council approval, he reported. He explained that the delineation of authority between city and county for expenses beyond the building's construction was unclear. He knew nothing of the Andrews Furniture contract until long after the agreement had been made, he insisted.[28] At the investigation's conclusion, former officials Herman Bamberger and Joseph R. Morris were among those charged with bribery.[29]

REPUBLICAN SWEEP AND LONG-DELAYED STATEHOOD

The Republicans remained dominant as election time approached in the fall. The small voice of Salt Lake City's black-owned and -edited newspaper, the *Broad Ax*, had the temerity to say, "The Democrats have plenty of first class material from which to select a mayor. First the true and well tried R. N. Baskin."[30] However, Baskin received no warm reception when he addressed a predominantly Republican crowd who had come to hear him speak at Democratic headquarters on October 31. Baskin's topic was "municipal politics." Once or twice he was interrupted by hand-clapping from two spectators occupying the front bench, but "otherwise was received in silence." Sensing his unreceptive audience, Baskin spoke instead of problems of his mayor-ship, and the many vetoes he had applied against W. P. O'Meara and Louis Cohn's plan to take $325,000 from the city treasury to support a copper plant.[31]

"We consider the State ticket as good as elected," proclaimed the *Tribune*, referring to the Republican slate of Heber M. Wells for governor, C. Emir Allen for congressman, Charles S. Zane for Supreme Court justice, and James Glendinning for mayor.[32] A huge crowd at

---

[27]"Hayken's Job," September 17, 1895, 1/1; "Hayken Indicted," "Let No Guilty Man Escape," "Hayken and Morris," "Hearing Demanded," "Bamberger's Denial," and "Discussed the Jail Bids," September 18, 1895, 1/1, 4/2, 5/2, 5/3, 5/2, 7/3.

[28]"Mayor Baskin's Query," *SLT*, September 19, 1895, 2/2.

[29]"Old Selectman Indicted," *SLT*, September 24, 1895, 8/4.

[30]Untitled article, *Broad Ax*, September 14, 1895, 4/2.

[31]"Baskin's Philippic," *SLT*, November 1, 1895, 8/3.

[32]"See to the Local Ticket" and "The Republican Ticket," *SLT*, November 1, 1895, 4/1, 6/3.

the Salt Lake Theater saw LDS president Lorenzo Snow sitting prominently with Orson F. Whitney, Isaac Trumbo, and Trumbo's wife. The
candidates criticized the preceding Democratic policies and praised
the gains of the Republicans.[33] In an odd twist, the *Tribune* reported
that Democratic campaign manager Trumbo approached Baskin for
his endorsement: "The Colonel is a game man, evidently, and obtained
that indorsement [*sic*] just to show the people here how safe he considered his campaign—safe enough to risk even an indorsement by the
[Democratic] Mayor."[34] Indeed, Trumbo was correct. Republicans
garnered every major office: Wells, Allen, Zane, and Glendinning
were all victorious.[35] There was much to suggest that LDS Church
influence played an important role in the outcome; Democratic governor Caleb West asserted that without church interference, the election would have gone to Democrats.[36]

The gravity sewer, begun in December 1892, was finally completed in December 1895, at a cost of $420,000. Baskin's report gave
the capacity as 15 to 41 million cubic gallons per day and detailed the
complex connections of the new sewer line with the smaller existing lines in the city. Baskin gave credit for the project to the efforts
of A. F. Doremus, chairman of the Board of Public Works, and his
board members.[37] In December, Baskin, as the supervising authority
of the sewer construction, was charged by a grand jury with keeping
an open sewer pit. Represented by William H. Dickson and Joseph L.
Rawlins, Baskin demanded an immediate appearance before U.S. district attorney John Judd and Judge George Bartch. The two promptly
responded; the charge was instantly dismissed.[38]

With the Utah State Constitution adopted by a popular vote of
31,305 to 7,687 and its approval in Washington, a proclamation of
statehood was promised for January 4, 1896. At precisely 10:03 eastern
time, President Cleveland placed his signature on the bill, and at 9:13
mountain time a "flash" telegram was received in the Western Union

[33]"Trumbo Draws a Crowd," *SLT*, November 1, 1895, 5/3.

[34]Untitled article, *SLT*, November 4, 1895, 4/4.

[35]"Wells Wins" and "The City," *SLT*, November 6, 1895, 1/1, 15/2.

[36]Cited in Lyman, *Political Deliverance*, 275.

[37]"Cost of the Gravity Sewer," *SLT*, January 1, 1896, 6/1.

[38]"Dismiss Baskin Indictment," *SLT*, December 19, 1895, 3/1; "Local and Other Matters," *DN*,
    December 28, 1895, 16/2. Several years later, Board of Health officials alleged code violations
    in Mayor Baskin's failure to require use of dry earth closets along the sewer lines in 1892.
    "To Forever Exterminate Typhoid in Salt Lake," *SLH*, September 6, 1903, 1/1.

office, announcing the signing and Utah's place in the Union. The telegraph manager stepped outside and fired two shots skyward. The city erupted in celebration.[39] Steam whistles at the George M. Scott's hardware store and the Eagle Foundry screamed, flags and banners were hoisted, bells were rung, "public and private buildings were appropriately decorated, business was generally suspended, and the people contented themselves with general and heartfelt rejoicing."[40] The *Tribune* optimistically predicted: "There shall never be anything done in Utah to make [the people] or their children regret the coming of Statehood to Utah. . . . [W]hatever clouds may obscure the other stars in the august galaxy, ours shall always shine on with no mist or cloud or eclipse to dim its perfect splendor."[41]

Statehood, without theocracy and without polygamy, had been the goal Robert Baskin and scores of non-Mormons long held for the people of Utah. For a time this goal was thought to have become a reality, but in less than a decade the seating of another Utah senator would trigger investigations revealing that LDS president Joseph F. Smith had lied before Congress, that LDS Church theocracy continued, that plural marriages in secret were still a fact.[42] The vision and hope for "perfect splendor" was too soon dimmed, too soon eclipsed.

---

[39]A flash telegram was a confirmation of a previously established message. "Utah State" and "Great Day," *SLT*, January 5, 1896, 1/1, 1/7.

[40]"Report of the Governor of the Territory of Utah," in U.S. Department of the Interior, *Annual Report of the Secretary of the Interior, 1896*, 3:4.

[41]"The Forty-Fifth Star," *SLT*, January 5, 1896, 12/2.

[42]Flake, *Politics of American Religious Identity*, 75–76; Hardy, *Solemn Covenant*, 389–426. Cannon reveals that the "First Presidency and at least seven members of . . . the Twelve strongly supported . . . new plural marriages on a limited, secretive basis." K. L. Cannon II, "Wives and Other Women," 101.

18

Into the Judicial Arena

Four things belong to a judge: to hear courteously,
to answer wisely, to consider soberly, and to decide impartially.
SOCRATES

FTER THE CHALLENGES OF THE MAYOR'S OFFICE WERE handed off, after the celebration of "Statehood Achieved!" subsided, the remainder of 1896 and the following year were relatively quiet for Baskin. In January 1897 the *Broad Ax* overoptimistically placed Baskin's name among those it considered as proper candidates for Utah's Senate seat, but his name was not brought before the Democratic Committee.[1] In September, Baskin was considered for another run as the city mayor, but he lost the nomination to W. H. Dale.[2] The next month, Baskin, now sixty years old, entered a law practice partnership with sixty-six-year-old Enos Dougherty Hoge; the two advertised their services in the *Tribune*.[3]

The death of LDS Church president Wilford Woodruff in San Francisco and the ordination of Lorenzo Snow as its fifth president made the fall of 1898 a stressful time for the church. The state Democratic convention nominated faithful Mormon and avowed polygamist Brigham

---

[1] Democrats Moses Thatcher, Joseph L. Rawlins, Henry Henderson, and John T. Caine were among others suggested by the *Broad Ax*. "The Senatorial Candidates," *Broad Ax*, January 9, 1897, 1/1. Rawlins narrowly defeated Mormon apostle Thatcher in a long and bitter internecine battle in the legislature, requiring fifty-three ballots. This was a marathon that Baskin was likely pleased to have avoided. "Rawlins," *SLT*, February 4, 1897, 1/1.
[2] "The Democratic City Convention," *Broad Ax*, September 25, 1897, 1/3.
[3] "The Winning Ticket," *Broad Ax*, October 2, 1897, 1/2.

Henry Roberts as its candidate for Congress. Since the new state constitution called for popular election of Utah Supreme Court judges,
Robert Baskin, despite his legacy as the territory's foremost pugilist
against polygamy and theocracy, was one of several nominated for the
post. At the nomination convention, Baskin defeated Ogden judge
and prominent Mormon businessman Henry H. Rolapp.[4] Details of
Baskin's win appeared in the *Tribune*. "The Baskin men . . . began to
jollify" after the results were announced: Baskin, 242; Rolapp, 233;
Charles Baldwin, 1; and Samuel Thurman, 4. The report continued
that Chairman [Joseph] Rawlins appointed two attendees to escort
the nominee to the stage. "Mr. Baskin was in seclusion somewhere,
however, for after a diligent search the committee failed to find him,
and so reported."[5] It is uncertain whether any significance should be
attached to Baskin's nonappearance for a curtain call, but the *Tribune*
entered a cryptic comment after Baskin's selection: "Judge Baskin is
. . . [an] honest man, and good lawyer, and if elected he would make
a righteous Judge as God might give him to see the right. But it was
a cruel thing to put such a man up to be knocked down. He was a
very brave and true man here when it required a great stock of man-
hood to carry his burden. It is a shame that he should be punished for
that record in his old age."[6] The *Tribune*'s implication may have been
that Baskin had little chance to succeed against the strong Republican
incumbent, Charles Zane, and was being punished by being placed in
a race against his old friend. Another interpretation did not become
apparent until 1902, when the Utah bar association met to complain
about the qualifications of the Utah Supreme Court judges and their
record from 1896 to 1902. "The majority of the judges in the Supreme
Court do not come up to the standard we seek to attain," charged
lawyers Parley L. Williams. Charles S. Varian and James H. Moyle,
a member of the bar and prominent Mormon figure, joined Williams
and others of the bar in requesting a standing committee for endorsements of supreme court candidates. Thus the *Tribune* may have consid-

---

[4]"Roberts Beats the Field—Baskin Named by Democrats for the Supreme Judgeship," *slt*,
September 15, 1898, 1/1. Rolapp practiced law in Ogden; he held a number of offices in
Weber County, was a State Board of Corrections member, and in 1895 served in the ter-
ritorial Supreme Court. Prominent in LDS affairs, he became the president of the Eastern
States Mission in 1928.

[5]"Baskin for Judge," *slt*, September 15, 1898, 5/7, 7/4; "Democratic State Convention," *Broad
Ax*, September 17, 1898, 1/4.

[6]"The Democratic Nominees," *slt*, September 15, 1898, 4/2; "Penrose and Baskin," *slt*, October 28, 1898, 5/4.

ered it punishment to place Baskin in a setting with judges of alleged marginal competence.[7] In one of Baskin's later court proceedings, he interrupted arguments to chastise the lawyers present, for their briefs contained overt criticism of certain judges. Baskin did not identify the judges named but considered material alluding to either district court or supreme court judges to be inappropriate within the briefs. Baskin warned, "Hereafter [I] will resort to extreme measures upon the recurrence of such practice by the attorneys."[8]

The 1898 Democratic ticket was illogical. Despite the traumatic experiences stemming from George Q. Cannon as a polygamist representing Utah in Congress, the Mormons now presented another known polygamist, paired alongside a widowed, non-Mormon judge noted over many years for his hard line against Mormon polygamy. On the *Tribune's* front page were handsome line-drawn portraits of the candidates, but the accompanying article did not address the polarity of the two men's backgrounds. The *Tribune* would later charge that Baskin had a hidden agenda for supporting Roberts despite his polygamy, for Baskin worked against the anti-Roberts elements of his party by delivering vigorous speeches in which he "declared it was the duty of the party" to stand for Roberts. A quid pro quo was implied— that Democrats would later support Baskin's candidacy for the U.S. Senate—for it was claimed Baskin had said that a Senate post would "round out his career in Utah."[9]

Roberts was widely popular despite his polygamy and despite his stance against female suffrage, and he and Baskin achieved clear-cut victories.[10] Postelection pundits impugned the Republican Party's failure to activate its members, particularly the non-Mormon element; yet Republicans gained seventeen legislative seats over those they held in 1897. The *Tribune* observed, "It was the . . . most placid election in years, was the verdict universally delivered last evening by the various campaign chairmen in the city."[11] Roberts triumphed—5,902 to 4,181, with a majority in seventeen of twenty-six counties—over opponent

---

[7]"Meeting of Bar Association," *DN*, January 21, 1902, 5/3. In 1897–98 the court seated Zane, Bartch, and Miner. Zane left the court in 1899; Bartch and Miner seem to have been the targets of the criticism.

[8]"New Ruling for Attorneys," *DN*, October 15, 1902, 2/5.

[9]"Baskin for Senator," *SLT*, May 24, 1900, 8/4.

[10]"Roberts Is Elected," *SLT*, November 9, 1898, 1/1–5. Roberts married his third wife in April 1900.

[11]"Was a Quiet Election," *SLT*, November 9, 1898, 15/2.

Alma Eldredge, a Republican who had many times been mayor of Coalville, Utah. Although in the past Baskin had named Alma Eldredge, his brothers Edmund and Hyrum, and six others as guilty "beyond reasonable doubt" of the 1867 murders of Isaac Potter and Charles Wilson in Coalville, one searches in vain for evidence that Baskin told or reminded Roberts during the campaign about Alma Eldredge's alleged role in the crimes.[12] Roberts's victory was short-lived, for a six-week contest in Congress made it clear that no more would a Utah polygamist be accepted in the halls in Washington. Roberts was sent home on a House vote of 268 to 50.[13]

At the time Charles Zane and Baskin vied for election to the Supreme Court position, Zane occupied the chair as the chief justice, by virtue of a unique event associated with Utah's statehood. When statehood came in January 1896, the territorial chairs of the three sitting judges—Zane, James A. Miner, and George W. Bartch—no longer existed. The law called for a luck-of-the-draw chance for staggered terms of three, five, and seven years for the state offices. The judge drawing the three-year term (Zane) immediately became the chief justice, and the two longer-term judges (Bartch drawing the five-year term, and Miner the seven-year) would each move up as his predecessor cycled out of the chief justice position.[14]

Baskin tallied 5,670 votes against 4,824 for his long-admired friend, Zane, the non-Mormon who remained highly respected for fairness despite having sent hundreds of Mormon men to prison for polygamy. Baskin took a majority in eighteen counties, giving little support to the notion that he was simply riding Roberts's Mormon coattails.[15] Baskin carried Davis County, including the Wood's Cross precinct, where some voters may have been Baskin's former neighbors.[16]

On January 1, 1899, Judge Zane's end of term took effect, with Bartch becoming chief justice, Miner the senior associate justice, and Baskin the junior associate justice. Over three years, Baskin ascended, and his two years as chief justice began on January 5, 1903, and ended January 2, 1905.[17]

---

[12]Baskin, *REM*, 9–13.
[13]"Roberts Excluded from House," *SLH*, January 26, 1900, 1/1.
[14]"Zane Is Chief Justice," *SLT*, January 5, 1896, 8/2.
[15]"Salt Lake Democratic," *SLT*, November 9, 1898, 6/1.
[16]"Election Returns of Davis County," *DAVCC*, November 11, 1898, 3/1.
[17]"List of Justices of the Utah Supreme Court," http://en.wikipedia.org/wiki/List_of_Justices _of_the_Utah_Supreme_Court.

Race Matters

It is difficult to understand an individuals' stance on race-related issues after the passage of more than one hundred years, but the evidence indicates Baskin to be supportive of African Americans in Salt Lake City. Near election time the weekly *Broad Ax*, a black-owned newspaper, published several reports that Baskin was well thought of by the city's black community. The paper cited several reasons why Salt Lake City's "colored" citizens should vote for the Democratic and not the Republican ticket. For example, Mayor Glendinning had "openly demonstrated by word and deed that the negro was not worthy of the least consideration," and in the preceding "two years of Republican rule (misrule) we have not even had a colored juryman sit on any kind of a jury." In contrast, the newspaper noted, Mayor Baskin had appointed William H. DeYoung (presumably a well-known black man) to the police force.[18] Another *Broad Ax* article lauded Baskin and his law partner, Enos D. Hoge, as well as other city Democratic leaders, for their refusal to sign a petition to keep the all-black Twenty-Fourth U.S. Infantry unit from stationing at Fort Douglas.[19] A third article told of G. H. Ganaway, also presumed to be black, who had employed John Maxcy Zane, the son of Baskin's opponent, to represent him in a legal matter. On becoming aware that Ganaway was campaigning for Baskin, his father's opponent, the younger Zane, indignantly informed Ganaway he would no longer continue as his attorney. Ganaway replied that "no influence which he [Zane] could exert would prevent him from working and voting for ex-Mayor R. N. Baskin, who had appointed more colored men to office in this city than all the Republicans combined."[20]

Baskin's motive in treating black people as he did could not have been self-interest, for the number of African Americans in Salt Lake City was far too small to influence election outcomes. To the contrary, support of blacks likely cost him Mormon Democratic votes, given the well-known position of the LDS Church priesthood of not proselytizing among black populations and of denying blacks full fellowship in the church.[21]

---

[18]"Let the G. O. P. Leaders Crack the Following Nuts," *Broad Ax*, October 30, 1897, 1/4.

[19]"United States Senator Frank J. Cannon's Personal Organ," *Broad Ax*, April 9, 1898, 1/3.

[20]"The Hon. John M. Zane and G. H. Ganaway," *Broad Ax*, November 12, 1898, 1/4.

[21]It was not until 1978 that African American men were allowed entry into the higher levels of the LDS lay priesthood.

A One-Hundred-Year
Anniversary Celebration

Supreme Court justice Robert Baskin did not go to his office on the spring morning of Saturday, June 1, 1901. He had another important obligation for the day. As the sun cleared the Wasatch Mountains, Saints and non-Mormons alike were roused by cannon fire from the rusty throat of "Old Sow," the veteran gun of the Nauvoo legion, and two other cannons, fired from the state capitol grounds, high above the city's north side.[22] For two hours, the cannons barked, precisely one hundred times, once for each year from Brigham Young's birth date.[23] Until early afternoon, flower displays, music, and banner hanging took place by the life-size bronze of Young at Main and South Temple Streets. A special thirteen-car railroad caravan, packed to its limit, conveyed thousands to the pavilion at Saltair, a resort on the western shore of the Great Salt Lake. Canticles and speeches were offered by the Mormon faithful, including Governor Heber Manning Wells, who eulogized Young as "God's chief representative here on earth."[24] LDS Church president Lorenzo Snow was present but took no speaking part in the exercises. A tribute to Young as pioneer, educator, commercial leader, apostle, and prophet was given by Dr. James E. Talmage. Then Baskin, who, the *Salt Lake Herald* pointed out, was "considered by some the originator of the liberal movement in the old days," took the stage.[25] He was greeted with "uproarious applause" and proceeded diplomatically by saying that an invitation for him to speak "was the best evidence that conditions in Utah ha[d] changed," noting that "twenty-five years ago we find wormwood in the mouths of both sides . . . but now we meet each other as brothers." There were a few present who remembered that Baskin had "differed with Brigham Young's policies in many particulars," but he "believed the Mormon leader to be a great man, . . . possessed of some *characteristics not equaled by any man* of modern times" and that "it was his *power over men* and his great common sense" that were commendable.

---

[22]"Many People Attend Brigham Young's Birthday Celebration at Salt Lake," *Idaho Falls Times*, June 6, 1901, 4/2.

[23]Bagley, "History Matters: A Lone Feisty Lawyer Helped the 'Americanization' of Utah," *slt*, July 4, 2004.

[24]"Many Attend the Centennial Celebration, Tribute by Judge Baskin," *slt*, June 2, 1901, 5/1. Wells had unsuccessfully challenged incumbent Baskin in the 1892 city mayoral election.

[25]"Judge Baskin Speaks," *slh*, June 2, 1901, 2/3.

Celebration of the one hundredth anniversary of
Brigham Young's birthday. Illustration from the *Salt Lake Tribune*
report, June, 2, 1901. Baskin was a featured speaker, giving guarded praise
to Young's memory. Three of Young's seven surviving wives
were among the attendees.

With the aplomb of a veteran speaking before a court, Baskin chose
his words carefully, describing Young as "not only a great leader but
a judge of men, and [one who] *never made a mistake in selecting those
who would carry out his will.*" Baskin continued, "If Mormonism has
the elements of perpetuity in it, it will survive all opposition and . . .
will come out brighter. . . . I hope the bitterness of the past is gone. . . .
There is a great future ahead for Utah."[26]

---

[26]"Many Attend the Centennial Celebration"; "In Memory of Pioneer Leader," *DN*, June 3,
1901, 1/4–5 (italics added); "Many People Attend Brigham Young's Birthday Celebration at
Salt Lake," *DAVCC*, June 7, 1901, 2/5.

Brigham Young, a sculpture by Kraig Varner (1947–),
was completed in 1994 and resides in the Utah State Capitol.
In Young's massive frame, Varner has captured a sense of power
and determination, portraying Young as a man of action, directness,
and raw energy rarely seen in other depictions of him. Photograph by
Scott Streadbeck, 2009. *Published by permission of Scott Streadbeck
and Main Street Art, Inc., Alpine, Utah.*

Several of Baskin's compliments are subject to dual interpretation. Baskin wished to recognize that many men were responsible for implementing Young's ambitions and visions. In the high spirits of celebration any negative connotations of his "power over men," of "*some* characteristics not equaled," of vengeance and violence associated with the words "those who would carry out his will," all sailed over the audience without apparent recognition. Baskin was not so heedless as to resurrect the accounts of murder and blood atonement done at the Prophet's command or the specters of the dead at Mountain Meadows or those at Kingston Fort near the Weber River and Ogden, where the apostate Joseph Morris and several of his followers were killed at their campsite, after three days of siege. He passed over any mention of the disasters of the 1856 handcart companies when hundreds died in early winter snow, the embarrassing episode of building a lockless canal where the water refused to flow uphill to allow boats to carry temple stones from the Big Cottonwood quarry, the failed enterprises of silk and iron production, or of the abortive experiment of communal ownership called the Order of Enoch. Perhaps his most important omission was his past description of Young's speeches as the "ravings of a vicious lunatic" such as "no Christian would deliver." Thus the day ended well, with a tranquil sunset. By skillful, diplomatic use of double entendres and selective omission, Baskin said nothing that he did not believe and nothing that was false. With his beau geste, a courteous, nonconfrontational relationship that had formed over difficult decades of softening between former bitter adversaries was continued undisturbed.[27]

A DIFFERENT BASKIN

During the debate in Washington over the seating of B. H. Roberts, Baskin wrote a letter to Congress in support of Roberts by citing President William McKinley's appointment of two known Utah polygamists to postmaster positions as evidence that no judicial or

---

[27]The city's newspapers did not meet Baskin's challenge to forgo insults over past issues. Both papers criticized Baskin's eulogizing the man he and Judge James B. McKean had charged with cohabitation and murder in 1871. Contrasting the "many sneers" against McKean recently published by the *News* with the favorable treatment now afforded Baskin, the *Tribune* expressed its disdain: "The *News* scores the dead jurist and praises the living Judge. It is a queer world: some go up and some go down—very low." Untitled article, *SLT*, June 3, 1901, 4/1.

political requirement existed that plural wives be repudiated as a qualification of holding office.[28] That Roberts was overwhelmingly rejected by the House proved that Baskin's assessment of the tone in Washington's halls was incorrect. Baskin now supported—or at least did not oppose—the candidacy of another Mormon, this time not a polygamist. Reed Smoot, a young businessman from Provo, had two encumbrances that in previous years would have precluded any Baskin endorsement: Smoot was an aspiring Republican, and more significantly, he was an LDS apostle.[29]

Early January 1903 saw Utah's junior senator, Thomas Kearns, returned from Washington and bearing a message allegedly from President Theodore Roosevelt. The president did not mention or disparage Smoot by name but wrote strongly against the ecclesiastical position he held: "The election to the United States senate of an apostle would work great harm to the state. . . . It would certainly lead to contentions and strife and bitterness here."[30] Mormons insisted that the message was spurious.[31] Authentic or not, Roosevelt's words were prophetic, for the investigation of the dark corners of LDS leadership in the ensuing several years proved that the promises of the 1890 Manifesto abandoning polygamy had been violated, as had LDS Church promises to relinquish control of political, economic, and familial matters in Utah.[32] The facts unearthed by the Smoot investigation prompted Shelby Cullom, still Illinois's senator and the sponsor of several severe anti-Mormon legislative acts, to observe, "Mormonism is the same menace to this country as it was from the beginning."[33]

The extensive record that would be unearthed of Mormon duplicities following the People's Party disbandment and the Woodruff Manifesto was not then known to Baskin, who had, against odds, defended LDS sincerity through those traumatic events. He took time from his first days as chief justice to speak to state lawmakers as they opened the joint legislative session on January 20. Their purpose was

---

[28]"The Roberts Case," *SLH*, January 14, 1900, 12/6.

[29]It is unknown if Baskin ever made public that Reed Smoot's wife, Alpha May Eldredge, was the first cousin of the several Eldredge men of Coalville whom Baskin accused of the Summit County murders of 1867.

[30]"Kearns Don't Want Smoot," *DN*, January 9, 1903, 1/1.

[31]"President's Secretary Makes Denial," *DN*, January 9, 1903, 1/1.

[32]Flake, *Politics of American Religious Identity*.

[33]Curry, *First Freedoms*, 177. Details of the Smoot hearings are found in Flake, *Politics of American Religious Identity*.

to endorse Smoot, elected in November to represent Utah as a U.S. senator. Five men were seated on an elevated platform before the assembly: Governor Heber M. Wells was in the center, Republican candidate Smoot on his right, and Chief Justice Baskin on his left. At the peripheries were House Speaker Thomas Hull and Senate president Edward M. Allison, Jr.[34] Smoot spoke first, pledging, "Every vote of mine . . . shall be free and untrammeled and conscientiously cast for the best need of our government as I see it." Next came Governor Wells, who cautiously avoided words inappropriate with his role as the state's chief executive officer. He indicated he would gladly sign a letter of election for Smoot, but that he must represent the people and not "foist" his personal opinions and convictions on them. In his experience with Smoot, he said, the man had been "honest, high-minded, conscientious and able."[35]

Senate president Allison then admitted, "It is not often that we get an opportunity to make a politician out of a Justice of the Supreme Court," and the audience responded warmly to Baskin's presence. Perhaps to relieve any tension in the situation, Baskin evoked laughter by making his first sentence a reminder that he was not a Republican but a full-fledged Democrat, "since I cast my first vote." Smiling and drawing more laughter, he said he wished to be a Democrat of "the Lincoln variety," that government should be "of the people, by the people, and for the people." Like Wells, Baskin was careful not to cross the propriety of his office and said that under the Constitution "the only duty devolving upon the people . . . in selecting their representative . . . should be [to] select a man that has the constitutional qualifications prescribed, and [to] exercise their own judgment honestly and select the man who is competent . . . to fill the office." Baskin was emphatic in saying, "In the movement against Mr. Smoot . . . I don't have any sympathy. If he has the constitutional qualifications, I say it would be a sad commentary on republican institutions if he was not allowed to carry out the agency with which you have invested in him."[36] In the case of B. H. Roberts, Baskin was supporting the man and the Democratic Party. In his remarks to the legislature concerning Smoot, Baskin was critical of President Roosevelt's interference

---

[34]"Tales of the Town," *SLT*, January 24, 1903, 4/6.
[35]"Smoot Launched," *SLT*, January 22, 1903, 2/2.
[36]Ibid.

and stressed—more than Smoot's qualifications—the legal principle that the citizens of Utah now carried a constitutional right and privilege to make their choice.[37] Notable for its absence was any judgment on Baskin's part that Smoot's status as an active apostle was—or was not—a violation of the separation of church and state.

Judge Baskin was among the guests transported in style on the Oregon Short Line Railway to Provo for a gala for Senator-Elect and Mrs. Smoot. While at Brigham Young Academy, Baskin spoke briefly as a representative of the state supreme court. Ever the defender of education, he departed from the praise-to-Smoot theme and urged the legislators "not to economize in educational appropriations, but to do the trimming somewhere else."[38]

On February 9, U.S. senator Julius Caesar Burrows of Michigan, chair of the Committee on Privileges and Elections, received a sixty-two-page pamphlet originating from Rev. W. M. Paden, pastor of the First Presbyterian Church of Salt Lake City; attorneys Parley L. William and E. B. Critchlow; and sixteen other Utah men. They conveyed their objections to Smoot's seating, on the grounds that plural marriages had continued after the 1890 Manifesto and after statehood in 1896, that the intertwined status of church and state remained a conspiracy in Utah, and that the First Presidency and the Twelve Apostles were still the supreme authority in all things.[39]

These and other complaints over Smoot's background set in motion four years of intensive U.S. Senate investigation. As with the investigations and first trial of John D. Lee, it was obvious that the subject of the inquiry was not the person, Reed Smoot, but the LDS theocracy. Through the efforts of Senator Burrows, Idaho senator Fred T. Dubois, and Senate doyen George Frisbie Hoar, all the same shadow areas that had troubled Robert Baskin, George R. Maxwell, and the parade of Utah's Liberal Party men over the years, were again probed: plural marriages in Utah, Canada, Mexico, and elsewhere; the allegiance of the LDS leaders to the United States; the contents and meaning of the Temple oath; whether the church Prophet—in this case, President Joseph F. Smith—received revelation that superseded federal and state law. From his testimony given before Congress and before the Mormon people, Smith was judged at one extreme

---

[37]"Election of Reed Smoot Is Formally Completed," *SLH*, January 22, 1903, 1/1.
[38]"Legislators Made Welcome," *SLH*, February 7, 1903, 1/6.
[39]Alter, *Utah, the Storied Domain*, 484.

as "God's Own Liar" by the *Tribune*'s Frank J. Cannon. A *Tribune* article said that "in the Tabernacle . . . in the presence of 4,000 people, including nearly all the apostles and prominent men of the Mormon Church," Smith had admitted having "purposely prevaricated in his testimony at Washington."[40] The other extreme was expressed in the charitable opinion later offered by historian Kathleen Flake, that by very careful wording Smith had "engaged in sophistry" but did not lie. In 1905 the *Tribune*'s judgment was harsh: "More sacrifice of the things which they esteemed as the high idealities of their religion and its priesthood, and more sorrow for the shameful attitude in which men were compelled to stand before the world, have come to the Mormon people through the Smoot case than has come through any other situation in their history."[41] As the behavior of the LDS leaders was exposed, Baskin surely experienced a sense of betrayal of the trust he had placed in their promises. Although it may not have been appropriate during his supreme court tenure to make public comment, the opinion he preserved in *Reminiscences* is very clear but remarkably subdued:

> It is indeed regrettable, and even humiliating, to all who have endeavored to advance the good name of Utah and to place her in a position of equality in the sisterhood of states, to record that the solemn pledges made to the federal government by the Mormon priesthood for the purpose of procuring general amnesty, the restorations of escheated church property, and the advancement of the Territory as a State, have not been fulfilled.[42]

The lying and deceit of the LDS priesthood leaders during the Smoot hearings rekindled smoldering embers of distrust and suspicion among former Liberal Party men. Together with factions of the Democratic Party, remnants of the disbanded Liberals were transmuted in the fall of 1904 into the American Party.[43] The political consequences from the disingenuous testimony of the Smoot hearings were major and long-term.[44] With Frank J. Cannon as its frequent

---

[40]"By Command of God the Prophet Lied," *SLT*, March 20, 1905, 1/6–7. Notwithstanding the *Tribune* report, Smith's defenders would be quick to point out that Frank J. Cannon and Smith were engaged in a long-running personal vendetta.

[41]"Smoot and the Conference," *SLT*, April 1, 1905, 4/2.

[42]Baskin, *REM*, 236.

[43]"American Party Petition Filed," *SLH*, October 9, 1904, 27/2.

[44]The political complexities of the American Party, Kearns, and the *Salt Lake Tribune* are beyond the scope of this work.

orator, the American Party mustered a full field of candidates for the November election, but they were unsuccessful.[45] Gathering adherents, the American Party swept the city posts in 1905, taking six of ten city council seats, with non-Mormon Ezra Thompson elected for his third term as mayor of Salt Lake City. In 1911 Baskin had one minor election encounter with the fading American Party when he was one of five candidates for Salt Lake City mayor on the Good Government Ticket, composed of Republicans and some men with American Party affiliations. Baskin was eliminated in the October primary, and Samuel C. Park, a prominent jeweler in the city, was elected. While the American Party never won a position in Salt Lake County government and never was a serious threat at the state level, it maintained close control of the city government from 1905 to 1912 with a "coalition of anti-Mormon ministers, businessmen, and professional people."[46]

Baskin's Record in the Court

The cynic's reminder that not everything that counts can be counted applies here. Rating any lawyer or judge poses a difficult challenge, including the Utah Supreme Court career of Robert Baskin. Certainly, professional credentials are important, and Baskin was well credentialed with his private school and Harvard Law School background. Candid assessments by former clients were probably circulated but are not recorded. Examples of past work and feedback from peers, already cited, enter in the process. Three years after his term ended, the state Democratic committee said he "achieved a great reputation for judicial fairness and learning."[47] Today commercial vendors offer services that comprehensively evaluate lawyer performance, but no such tools can apply to Baskin.[48] Nonetheless, searching begins where the light is best, and examination of the basic statistical data of his court provides insight on Baskin's ethical standards, his knowledge of the law, and his capability to apply the law to the satisfaction of the judicial community of his peers. Peer evaluation in this context, done at arm's

---

[45]"Plain Talk by Frank Cannon," *slh*, November 3, 1904, 5/4.

[46]Snow, "American Party in Utah," 257; Alexander and Allen, *Mormons and Gentiles*, 140, 147.

[47]"Committee Meets Today," *slh*, October 2, 1908, 3/1.

[48]Examples are Martindale-Hubbell Ratings, FindLaw, and Lawdragon. Other criteria include acceptance of pro bono commitments, social behavior, and overall acceptance within the community, and regarding each of these criteria, Baskin would be highly rated.

length by learned, trusted men of the U.S. Supreme Court, may be the most objective and trustworthy measuring tool available in rating Baskin's fairness and judicial decision-making skill.

In his six years as a Utah Supreme Court justice, Baskin wrote the majority opinion in at least 141 cases, covering a broad spectrum of mining claims, personal injury claims, property ownership cases, divorces, tax issues, and estate disputes. He wrote 28 majority opinions in his first year, and 51 in his final two years as chief justice, averaging more than two opinions written each month. Some are brief, but many are lengthy, comprehensive, and filled with citations of prior Utah and U.S. Supreme Court cases whose thorough analysis resulted in his final decision. Only 3 of his 141 opinions were submitted to the U.S. Supreme Court, and none of the three was reversed.[49] Nothing stronger can be cited as evidence that Baskin was an exemplary Utah Supreme Court justice. Proof is lacking, but reason says that Baskin, after the stinging criticism of the other state supreme court judges by Parley Williams and the Utah bar association, also mentored and carefully monitored Justices Bartch and Miner to ensure that their written opinions met his standards.

JUDGING COLLEAGUES

One of the most challenging decisions Baskin faced was the case of *Utah v. Evans et al.* The challenge came not only from the correct application of law but also from the costs extracted in the personal relations within the Utah legal community. Salt Lake City attorney and former territorial legislator Parley L. Williams brought charges against Ogden attorneys David Evans and Lindsay R. Rogers for disbarment, asking that "their names be stricken from the roll."[50] The charge had its origins in a Southern Pacific Railway incident in January 1892 in which Charles A. Nelson was killed; his widow engaged Alfred H. Nelson, a lawyer and the brother of the deceased, to sue

---

[49]The three cases were *Harkness v. Guthrie*, 27 Utah 248, 199 U.S. 148, concerning the right of stockholders in a national bank to inspect the bank's financial records; *Lavagnino v. Uhlig*, 26 Utah 1, 198 U.S. 443, concerning a mine inspector who influenced others to enter suit while concealing his interest in the mine involved; and *Silver City Gold and Silver Min. Co. v. Lowry*, 19 Utah 334, 179 U.S. 196, concerning ownership and lessee rights to mining property and ore from that property.

[50]"Rogers and Evans on Trial," *os*, June 12, 1900, 7/2; "Disbarment Proceedings," *os*, June 29, 1900, 5/2; *22 Utah 366*, September 15, 1900.

for damages. Alfred Nelson proceeded to employ Evans and Rogers as counsel, agreeing to split the 50 percent contingency fee, with two-thirds to go to Evans and Rogers. However, Nelson secretly arranged to give his portion of the fee to his heavily indebted brother, Thomas, allegedly for services rendered during the trial. When the court awarded $10,000 for damages, Evans and Rogers refused to allow payment to Thomas Nelson, on the grounds that he had not performed services stipulated in his agreement with Alfred Nelson. In his majority opinion, Baskin was scathing in criticism of Evans and Rogers, yet he was empathetic to them. Baskin ruled that neither Alfred Nelson's contract with Evans and Rogers nor the verbal agreement between the two Nelson brothers had been revealed to the widow Nelson or her children. Baskin cited the Evans contract as "champertous," because the law firm had illegally prepaid court costs and trial expenses for its client.[51] The contract was also "obnoxious" because it was against the interests of the widow and her children, and the attorney's first obligation was to guard the clients' interests with strict fidelity.[52] Baskin softened in his summation, saying that, in a disbarment action, more than the preponderance of evidence must be established, since the outcome would "often be to decree poverty . . . and destitution" to the lawyer's family. Since Evans and Rogers had "for a long time maintained good standing before the courts " Baskin wrote, "we do not think they should be absolutely disbarred."[53] Baskin suspended both lawyers until a fine of $1,793.33, an amount considered due the widow, and all court costs were paid. Justice Miner concurred, but Bartch thought a more severe punishment was appropriate, since "punishment ought to be commensurate with . . . wrongdoing."[54] The stress of the Evans case may have prompted Baskin to take leave, for

[51]"Such agreements directly tend to promote litigation, to disturb the peace of individuals, and are directed to subverting the settled policy of this state . . . (sections 73 and 74 of the Code)," wrote Baskin (22 Utah 366).

[52]Champerty, the prepayment of the client's expenses, was illegal under English common law but is now legal and commonplace, often a part of the contingency fee agreement.

[53]Baskin and Evans had shared experience in the Utah legislature when the two were in agitated opposition regarding the Mormons' passage of state anti-polygamy legislation that would have nullified recent federal action.

[54]Utah State Supreme Court, 22 *Utah* 366. The dispute was carried to the streets of the city, where Evans and Williams came to blows. Evans struck Williams as they were passing in opposite directions, attesting, "He can't make his sneers at me in public." Williams reported, "The d——d coward struck me in the back of the head. I had passed him without saying a word to him." "Former Ogdenite in a Fight," *os*, June 5, 1900, 7/1.

in August he traveled to Portland, Oregon, then to San Francisco, Catalina Island, and Pasadena, returning to Salt Lake much rested.[55]

Also in Baskin's workload during his years in the court were scores of concurring and dissenting opinions that were written but not published. In addition, he wrote seventeen major dissents from his fellow justices, nine of them against decisions by Miner, and six against Bartch's decisions. A notable dissent against one of Miner's rulings was written in May 1899, early in Baskin's court tenure. Joseph Potter of Payson had entered into a contract with Juab County lawyer J. E. Page and Salt Lake City lawyers Orlando W. Powers, Daniel N. Straup, and Joseph Lippman to bring suit against the Ajax Mining Company for injury. The contract was for the lawyers to receive 50 percent of any settlement and to advance the necessary fees and expenses. As in the Evans and Rogers case, common law of the time deemed advance payment by the attorneys as champertous.[56] Before the case came to court, another Salt Lake City lawyer, Thomas Marioneaux, made Potter an offer, without the knowledge or consent of the other lawyers, to settle and release Ajax from all claims by payment of $1,190 for damages and $1,000 in lost wages. Potter accepted Marioneaux's offer but did not pay the lawyers with whom he had a contract. This made Marioneaux party to Potter's attempt to defraud his lawyers. In his dissent to the majority opinion, Baskin again emphasized the issue of champerty and strongly criticized the ethics of all the lawyers involved, whose conduct, he said, was "reprehensible" for failing to meet professional standards.[57]

Analysis of Baskin's cases gives evidence not only of his stellar professional ability but also of his ethical standards. He elevated himself and his profession through his insistence that those who administer the law must also assiduously obey it and that moral dedication to the public good is essential in all those engaged in the law.

Revealing Vignettes

Two events during the 1903 Utah Supreme Court's summer break tell something of Baskin's social interests and his character outside the courtroom. In June he was one of fifteen guests invited for a dinner

---

[55]"Personal," *DN*, August 6, 1900, 8/3; "Judge Baskin Home Again," *DN*, August 22, 1900, 8/6.

[56]*Potter v. Ajax Mining Co.*, 19 Utah 421, May 3, 1899.

[57]Marioneaux was later a district judge, and at least eight of his cases were sent to the Utah Supreme Court.

at the Knutsford Hotel to celebrate the Salt Lake Theater's opening presentation of *The Art of Friendship*, starring Nat C. Goodwin. Also among the guests were some of Baskin's friends from his days as in the Utah legislature, Judge and Mrs. William H. King and Senator and Mrs. Edward M. Allison, Jr.[58]

In August, Baskin was leaving a Ringling Brothers Circus performance, when he crossed paths with a man in a great hurry, threatening to drive his open carriage through a packed group of women and children exiting the tent. Experienced with horses, Baskin grasped the reins and halted further passage of the rig. When the driver yelled at Baskin to release his horse, raising "his whip to strike the aged barrister," District Attorney Dennis C. Eichnor and Internal Revenue collector Ed Callister, who were nearby, reacted quickly and warned the man that they would deliver him a severe beating should he strike the judge. Baskin continued to hold the reins until the crowd thinned and the carriage passage was no longer a threat to the passersby. The impatient man drove off, saying nothing.[59]

A Puzzling Withdrawal

Electors' enthusiasm was high in September 1904 when the Democratic state convention nominated James H. Moyle for governor and Orlando W. Powers for congressional representative.[60] As the position of supreme court justice was reached in the agenda, Judge Charles C. Dey rose and made an unusual, if not bizarre, nomination speech, proposing the name of Judge Charles S. Varian of Salt Lake City. Varian, he said, was now available and willing to run for the office, since the state legislature had, "in its wisdom and for the object of placing upon the bench the best that we had in the profession, substantially raised the salary." He continued, "Now we can get Mr. Varian, let us do it."[61]

Judge J. W. Burton then stood and placed in nomination the name of incumbent justice R. N. Baskin, saying the office required one "learned in the law, fair and impartial, with a temperate mind and thought, just, patient as to arguments, a good man, a just man, as well as a fair man." Burton described Baskin as having "Democracy older

[58]"Society," *SLH*, June 14, 1903, 10/1.
[59]"Chief Justice Baskin Saves People from Being Injured at Circus," *SLH*, August 7, 1903, 3/3–4.
[60]"Powers and Moyle Head Democratic Ticket," *SLH*, September 9, 1904, 1/1.
[61]"Immense Enthusiasm in State Convention," *SLH*, September 9, 1904, 2/6.

than the state," with "every qualification that a judge should have for the office." B. T. Lloyd of Salt Lake County seconded the nomination and challenged the delegates to provide any reason why Baskin should not receive their vote. Pointing out that Baskin was one of the few Democrats consistently able to win in Utah, Lloyd observed, "Now for six years [*sic*] he has filled his office with distinction, to the satisfaction of all, to the satisfaction of the entire bar and people. . . . Every man and woman in this town knows him." As the chairman moved toward the vote, Baskin's friend and partner, Enos Hoge, raised a point of order. Hoge and Baskin had been acquainted since 1875, when Hoge served on the defense team—opposite Baskin—in the first Mountain Meadows murders trial of John D. Lee, and they had been law partners for several years. Baskin was apparently not present, for Hoge said, "I feel that I have the authority—I know I have—to withdraw his name from before this convention, and I move to make the nomination of C. S. Varian by acclamation." The chair ruled that withdrawal of Baskin's name was out of order, and Varian was elected with 401 votes to Baskin's 119.[62]

Explanation is wanting for Dey's undiplomatic, ill-phrased speech saying his candidate, Varian, was available only if well paid and for his faux pas of publicly suggesting that Baskin, the accomplished and lauded supreme court incumbent, was less capable than Varian. Also puzzling is Baskin's reason for having Hoge request his name withdrawn from the field. Baskin may have foreseen the coming sweep in which, behind Theodore Roosevelt, Republicans would defeat most Democratic opponents in Utah and across the nation. Another tenable motive for Baskin's withdrawal is that he may have desired to be available should he be nominated as the Democratic candidate for U.S. senator from Utah.

---

[62]Ibid., 2/6–3/1.

19

Evanescence of
Financial Success

*I have the consolation, too, of having added nothing to my private fortune,
. . . and of retiring with hands as clean and they are empty.*
THOMAS JEFFERSON, 1807

IT WAS NOT THE "DIRT UNDER THE FINGERNAILS," "SLAP ON
the back," and "pint of suds" mining crowd that formed a men's
club in Salt Lake City in October 1881. Money talking to money,
collars starched and white, Havana cigars, and a restrained acquaintance with "Bacchus and his pards" were the entrepreneurs' indulgences
when they sent this invitation, which began "Dear Sir": "It is proposed
to organize a social club combining the best features of the Union Club
of San Francisco and the larger clubs in the East . . . with the comforts
and luxuries of a home together with the attraction . . . of meeting each
other in a social way."[1] Thirteen men, all non-Mormons, all directly or
indirectly tied to the territory's mining industry, affixed their signa-
tures to the invitation. No provisions in the club's bylaws or organizing documents excluded Mormons from membership; however, none
were invited. No Mormon in good standing would publicly associate
with a non-Mormon club whose major features were to "include a card
room, a bar stocked with the finest liquors and wines available in the
territory, [and] a tobacco stand with the best cigars."[2] Imbibing in such

[1]Malmquist, *Alta Club*, 2.
[2]Ibid.

pleasures would endanger any Saint's standing.[3] True also was that a non-Mormon associating on social terms with Mormons would be labeled a "Jack Mormon" and viewed as collaborating with the enemy. The club founders wished to avoid the conflict between non-Mormons and Mormons that pervaded the territory. Neutral ground, for Republican or Democrat, for Christian or Jew, for agnostic or devout, all to intermingle—to network, in today's parlance—was the vision. The membership fee for the first one hundred men accepted into the Alta Club would be "only $100," with monthly dues of $5.00.[4]

The leading man among the thirteen initiating members was William S. McCornick, wealthy from banking and mining business. He was the first Club President, and the City Council President in 1894, during Robert Baskin's second term as mayor. The two worked together—and against each other—for the City and County building's completion.[5] James R. Walker, spokesman for a family dynasty of bankers, Jewish businessmen Fred Auerbach and A. Hanauer, the Utah Territorial Gov. Eli H. Murray, the Utah Supreme Court Judge Samuel A. Merritt, and U.S. deputy marshal Michael Shaughnessy, were among the motley assembly of organizers. Some were distinctly anti-Mormon rather than merely non-Mormon. It was Murray, for example, who refused to grant an election certificate to George Q. Cannon, even though the vote tally over the Liberal Party's Allen G. Campbell was overwhelming. Marshal Shaughnessy and Judge Merritt handled polygamy arrests and trials whose numbers escalated drastically following the 1882 Edmunds Act.

Despite its allure, there was no stampede to become Alta Club charter members. Sixteen months after sending invitations, the club was not yet incorporated, because they were nineteen members short of their goal. Robert Baskin was one of eighty-one charter members the *Tribune* labeled as high-toned: "It gives dignity . . . by furnishing a place where gentlemen from abroad can be entertained, . . . where important news and information are dropped in social talk. . . . [I]t

---

[3]Mormon leaders were critical of saloons, but the LDS Church restriction on alcohol in its Word of Wisdom received less emphasis in this era than it did later.

[4]Signing the invitation were W. S. McCornick, James R. Walker, Eli H. Murray, T. R. Jones, A. Hanauer, R. C. Chambers, J. E. Dooly, George A. Lowe, F. H. Auerbach, Joab Lawrence, Samuel A. Merritt, R. Mackintosh, and M. Shaughnessy.

[5]In 1887, McCornick was the first president of the Salt Lake City Chamber of Commerce, a joint non-Mormon and Mormon effort to attract business, while leaving religious differences aside.

Enos Dougherty Hoge. He defended John D. Lee against Baskin in Lee's first trial and was later Baskin's law partner in Salt Lake City. *From the Alta Club Photographic Collection of Special Collections Department of the J. Willard Marriott Library, University of Utah in Salt Lake City.*

combines the schoolhouse, the newspaper and the ledger. . . . [It is] a high toned gentlemen's club."[6]

Among the first club members were William S. Godbe and one of his many sons, Anthony, whose interests were in mining and retailing and previously in publishing and retail pharmacy; Charles C. Goodwin, articulate *Salt Lake Tribune* editor; Enos D. Hoge, Baskin's law partner; Edwin A. Ireland, the U.S. marshal whose overenthusiastic deputies, searching for "co-habs," violated Mormons' civil rights to be secure in their homes; and Patrick J. Lannan, rotund Irish saloon-keeper, butcher, and *Tribune* owner and business manager.[7] Many were also bound in varying degrees by their fellowship in the Masonic brotherhood.[8] By January 1885, Alta Club membership had climbed to more than one hundred, and the wives and lady friends of members joined in the celebration marking the achievement, just as they had done for the club's opening festivities.[9]

The first Mormon to be admitted was William Jennings, a wealthy merchant who had two wives and had assisted Brigham Young in establishing Zion's Cooperative Mercantile Institution, the enterprise that non-Mormons, such as Godbe, claimed was intended to put them out

[6]"The Alta Club," *slt*, November 18, 1883, 2/5.
[7]Malmquist, *Alta Club*, 2–7, 129–40.
[8]From 1885 to 1887, Parley L. Williams was the Grand Master of the Grand Lodge of Free and Accepted Masons of Utah, and in 1912 was the Alta Club president.
[9]"The Alta Club," *slt*, January 20, 1885, 4/6.

Robert N. Baskin, member of Salt Lake City's Alta Club.
*From the Alta Club Photographic Collection of Special Collections Department
of the J. Willard Marriott Library, University of Utah in Salt Lake City.*

of business. Jennings was the mayor of Salt Lake City in 1882 and joined the Alta Club in February 1885. By the century's turn, about a dozen Mormons were members, and by 1973 the prominent Mormon surname "Cannon" was the most common in the membership roster.[10] With its gray oolite limestone exteriors, its understated ambience of brass and finished oak, its deep, leather armchairs, its reading rooms and dining areas, the Alta Club retains its dignity in service to the present.[11]

At times Robert Baskin was a member and resident at the University Club; he attended the Harvard Club meetings, and he likely spent many pleasant evenings and luncheons among his intellectual peers at the Alta Club.[12] Unfortunately the evening he was never able to forget was the one in 1890 when, celebrating the election outcomes at the Alta Club, he received an emergency telephone call telling of his wife's collapse. Possibly wanting to avoid this memory, or wishing to avoid contact with his critics in the mayor's office, or responding to a dip in his roller-coaster financial career, or merely lacking time, Baskin resigned his Alta Club membership in May 1895.

Dr. Robinson's Hot Springs Resurrected

Throughout his professional life as an attorney in Utah, Baskin was active in a variety of financial endeavors. A charitable description would be "balanced," for his investments were mostly risky ventures in land development, thoroughbred racehorse breeding, mining and mineral claims, and railroads. At times Baskin appeared inept in business acumen. For example, on March 31, 1885, one day before the expiration of his right of first refusal to John William Snell to purchase a parcel of land from him, Baskin realized he had set the price low. Baskin offered Snell $1,000 to annul the contract. The land being offered had significant historical importance in Utah, particularly for Baskin. The seventeen acres, near the foothill's point northwest of the city, encompassed a natural warm spring and a small lake, called the Hot Springs. Filing for ownership of it had cost the life of Baskin's

---

[10]Malmquist, *Alta Club*, 16–18.

[11]By 1898 the Alta Club was located where it remains today, on the historically illustrious intersection of South Temple and State Streets. The Emery-Holmes Apartments (owned by "Silver Queen" Susanna Bransford Emery Holmes), later called the Eagle Gate Apartments, were on the northeast corner; Brigham Young's Beehive House was on the northwest; and the famous Gardo House (demolished in 1921) was on the southwest.

[12]The University Club was located on South Temple Street and 200 East, not far from the Alta Club. It was demolished in 1963.

friend and client Dr. John King Robinson in 1866.[13] Snell refused Baskin's offer and immediately sold the entire Hot Springs package to John Beck of Tintic, Juab County, for $12,000.[14] Beck, in turn, was immediately offered $15,000 by a third unidentified buyer but refused that offer. Beck announced he planned to invest $25,000 in the site to establish a sanatorium with plunge baths and to bottle and ship the springwater for its alleged medicinal properties, with a further goal, not unlike Dr. Robinson's, of creating a popular health and pleasure resort. Served with two railroad lines and situated not far from downtown Salt Lake City, it would be heavily patronized, the *Deseret News* predicted.[15] The *Tribune* advised that its waters were "beneficial for rheumatism, diabetes, skin and kidney diseases and dyspepsia."[16] Neither newspaper account mentioned that the land Baskin sold was the property whose title had led to the murder of Dr. Robinson.

Breeding Thoroughbreds

Robert Baskin's activities with thoroughbred racehorses began in 1886, the same year that found him busy lobbying for the Edmunds-Tucker Bill. This interest in horses was sustained, perhaps even stimulated, when he overcame severe depression after his wife's death in February 1890. With his children and his wife gone, Baskin openly spoke of selling his ranch in Wood's Cross and his stable of horses and returning to Ohio. He was able to rise from his depression, however, and retained a portion of the ranch and some livestock. His accomplishments in this esoteric field were described in the *Tribune* in 1891:

> Judge Baskin first engaged in the breeding of fine stock about five years ago. His farm and stables were at Wood's Cross, in Davis County. His summer range consisted of a tract of nearly 5000 acres just north and east of Beck's Hot Springs, extending east as far as City Creek.
>
> Inca was his first stallion, and he is the best Mambrino stallion in the country. . . . A little more than a year ago the Judge sold . . . all

---

[13]A city council letter to Dr. Jeter Clinton in October 1876 recorded that the property, variously called Warm Springs or Hot Springs, was leased to Dr. George Monroe from March 1, 1876, for a period of five years. BYLC, CR 1234 1, box 10, vol. 14, 564–66. In the 1880 Utah census, George Monroe is listed as an apostate Mormon and a farrier, living in Scipio, Millard County.

[14]Beck was part owner of the Tintic District's well-known Bullion Beck Mine.

[15]"The Hot Springs," *DN*, April 15, 1885, 1/3. Beck's Hot Springs resort was a popular Salt Lake City attraction for many years.

[16]"Beck's Hot Springs," *SLT*, August 6, 1886, 4/3.

his horses excepting Inca and four of his fillies, to Mr. A. G. Bast, intending to permanently retire from the business. However, a visit to Kentucky tempted him to re-enter the ranks of breeders of fine stock, and he brought back with him to Utah ten brood mares, the richest in Hambletonian blood to be found in Kentucky, with the purpose of combining the richest Mambrino blood of Inca with this rich Hambletonian blood, thus uniting the best trotting blood on both sides. . . . [Baskin] has twenty-five head in all, six stallions and nineteen mares.

The sale made to A. G. Bast . . . included 52 horses, one . . . being Incas [sired by Inca].[17] The Judge says that, as horses . . . are rated, he is worth $50,000, a sum about twice as large as Bast paid for the farm of 173 acres and all the horses.[18]

The *Tribune*'s prediction that "Utah will prove herself superior to any other place on earth as the breeding-place of thoroughbred horses," rivaling those produced among the white-fenced, blue-green grasslands of Kentucky, was overoptimistic. The precise duration of Baskin's commitment to fine horse breeding is now lost in the historical record.

LAND, MINERALS, AND MINING

In his books, Baskin suggests that potential success from mining influenced him to remain in Utah. As early as 1871 he, along with William S. Godbe, Henry W. Lawrence, J. N. Kimball, and several others, made claim on the 213 acres of the San Joaquin Lode in the Ophir Mining District of Tooele County. [19] Ten years later Baskin filed another claim on 317 acres of the Struck It Lode, in the same location.[20]

"The mining industry of Utah is yet only in its infancy," the *Salt Lake Mining Review* observed. "This is one of the richest mineral states in the Union . . . but [only] a very small part of the state has been prospected. . . . [T]here has not been sufficient advertising to bring to the notice of the world the unexcelled opportunities which this state affords."[21] To meet this need for promotion, several prominent citizens opened the Salt Lake Stock and Mining Exchange in December

---

[17]In October 1890, Baskin entered his horses in the Territorial Fair, with Incas winning a gold medal and $25; Nellie, a diploma and $10; and Cooley, a gold medal. Untitled article, *DN*, October 25, 1890, 28/3.

[18]"Judge Baskin's Horses," *SLT*, September 13, 1891, 3/5.

[19]"Legal Notice," *SLT*, November 27, 1871, 3/6. This area had been opened to mining by Patrick Connor in 1870.

[20]"Utah," *SLT*, September 7, 1881, 4/5.

[21]"The Salt Lake Stock and Mining Exchange," *SLMinR*, December 30, 1902, 3/1.

1895. John W. Donnellan was its first president, and Mayor Robert Baskin was joined by Charles C. Goodwin and Judge E. F. Colborn as "the brilliant speakers" who addressed the group at its opening night banquet.

During the summer break of 1897, free from mayoral duties, Baskin devoted time to explore and investigate land and mining ventures. He and several other Salt Lake businessmen purchased 640 acres containing a substantial deposit of natural coke, located about 140 miles south of Salt Lake City. Exploration revealed that the site, not far from the railroad line, held a promising quantity of clean-burning material.

Among Baskin's land purchases was a five-acre plot in Block 20 of the Salt Lake City's "Big Field" in 1872, and his "home on the hill," mentioned in news reports, was likely his home on First North Street, obtained before 1890. In June 1899, Baskin offered a sizeable area of land for purchase by the city's Committee on Public Grounds. The committee considered offers from both W. E. Taylor and Baskin to sell land in Parley's and City Creek Canyons. "Taylor has ninety acres . . . for which he wants $5000," the *Tribune* reported, "while Judge Baskin has 640 acres. . . . [T]he City Engineer was directed to look over the Baskin tract."[22] The fate of the land offered by Baskin is uncertain.

Apparently Baskin's law practice helped fuel his forays into real estate and minerals.[23] The *Tribune* and the *News* carried many reports of Baskin representing either the plaintiff or the defendant in various civil and criminal cases. One example was an October 1900 suit in which Baskin and Hoge successfully sued for the recovery of professional fees. The amounts sought suggest the prevailing compensation level: "The suit was brought . . . against Driver & company to recover the sum of $1,975[,] . . . the balance of $2,500 due plaintiff and his former partner, Judge Hoge, for professional services rendered between November 10, 1896, and January 1, 1899."[24]

As Baskin approached the completion of his supreme court duties, he increasingly devoted his efforts to mineral exploration and mining investments. His most intense interest was focused on American Fork Canyon in Utah County, which had begun to be mined as early as the

---

[22]"Offers of Real Estate," *slt*, June 30, 1899, 6/3.

[23]Baskin's supreme court salary was set by the state constitution at $3,000 per year, plus an allotment for travel expenses.

[24]"Wants Driver to Pay Fees," *dn*, October 25, 1900, 2/2. In 1906 Baskin sued Goodell Mining and Smelting to collect $3,078.15 on a promissory note. "Baskin Begins Suit," *slt*, February 16, 1906, 4/2.

1890s.[25] Baskin, along with Col. J. A. Aspenwall and his son, joined with the Miller Mining and Smelting Company, "in the early days of Utah's mining industry" to develop what became known as the Miller Hill, "the mother of the district."[26] In 1904 the *Tribune* announced that Baskin had reentered the "field that had once enriched him":

> Judge Baskin is at present working a force of men at the Hot Stuff, which is located just below the Miller Hill. . . . For many years Judge Baskin has held onto his interests on Miller Hill, which at one time responded so freely to his needs, and few, perhaps, are more intelligently advised concerning its resources. Indeed, he has rejected numerous propositions, preferring to develop his interests unaided, and the wisdom of that policy promises to be demonstrated the present season.[27]

In 1905 George Tying of New York participated with Baskin, Aspenwall, and F. P. Foster in reorganizing the Miller Company.[28] Within two years Baskin was "personally supervising the Mountain Dell Mining and Milling Company's property in American Fork Canyon." The *Salt Lake Herald* reported, "The property was in fine condition with a five-foot vein of carbonate and galena ore. . . . The force of the miners will be increased as soon as the new whim has been installed."[29] The *Herald* also commented that this development had "attracted more attention than probably any other property in the district" and that the property was "owned almost entirely by Judge R. N. Baskin of Salt Lake City."[30]

In May 1906, Baskin, together with speculators Andrew Campbell, A. W. Raybould, Benjamin B. Hall, and H. H. Twinning, invested $9,300 to form the Imperial Mining and Smelting Company to support the ventures in the American Fork District.[31] They combined

---

[25]Not as productive or well known as the Alta and Park City mines, Utah County's American Fork Canyon had many digs, including Hot Stuff, Mineral Flats, Bluerock, Wyoming, Whirlwind, Pittsburg, Silver Dipper, Surprise, Live Yankee, Mountain Dell, Shamrock, Bog, Pacific, Miller, Wild Dutchman, and Imperial.

[26]Higgins, "The Mines of American Fork Canyon, Utah," *slMinR*, October 15, 1907, 1/3.

[27]"On Miller Hill," *slt*, February 13, 1904, 6/2; "American Fork Mining Notes," *slMinR*, November 14, 1904, 12/3.

[28]"Around the State," *slMinR*, May 15, 1905, 34/3.

[29]"Mass Meeting of Citizens," *slh*, September 24, 1906, 7/4. A whim is a form of capstan, often utilizing horses, to raise materials from the mine shaft to the surface. "Increases Force," *imr*, May 12, 1906, 6/3.

[30]"American Fork Canyon Takes Place as Producer of Ore," *slh*, December 30, 1906, 38/1.

[31]Untitled article, *slMinR*, May 30, 1906, 16/3. Benjamin Brown Hall—the son of Mary Edna Brown Hall, with whom Baskin boarded—was the secretary of Imperial. "New Incorporations," *slMinR*, May 15, 1906, 16/2–3. For many years Hall remained active in mining interests apart from those he shared with Baskin.

several properties into the Mountain Dell Mine, and Baskin remained
optimistic, saying that "the American Fork canyon is to be made one
of the most productive portions of the state."[32] At this time Baskin
also became involved in another nearby enterprise, the Surprise Mining Company.[33]

Litigation accompanied mining throughout its history in Utah, and
Baskin also found himself drawn into that aspect of Utah's mining
ventures, as appellant, defendant, and litigator. The Stockton District's mine, the Shamrock and Katherine, owned by Baskin, Senator Joseph L. Rawlins, Senator Arthur Brown, and E. B. Critchlow,
brought suit against the Honerine Mining Company to recover damages in the sum of $600,000 for ores alleged to have been taken by
Honerine.[34] In 1907 Baskin, along with Charles S. Zane, John M.
Zane, and H. F. Edwards, represented the Mammoth Mining Company in the Utah Supreme Court in a claim against the Grand Central Mining Company regarding a dispute over underground property
lines. Baskin remained as one of those representing Mammoth in the
subsequent Utah Supreme Court action, but the decision was made in
Grand Central's favor.[35]

Through most of 1907, prospects and results appeared bright for
Baskin's mining efforts.[36] By fall he claimed that very high-grade ore
was being extracted from the Mountain Dell, with at least $30,000
worth in sight.[37] Charles Earl and the two Wooten men of the earlier
partnership of the Surprise Company filed on other property in the
American Fork Mining District, and in 1908 Baskin ended a prolonged legal wrangle by paying them $20,000 for a quitclaim deed to

---

[32]"American Fork Is Looking Up," *IMR*, August 17, 1906, 6/3.

[33]His partners were Charles W. Earl, John H. and Joseph A. Wooten, John J. Jones, and H. E.
Boley. Untitled article, *SLMinR*, December 15, 1906, 13/2.

[34]"Stockton Miners to Unite for Warfare," *IMR*, December 2, 1906, 24/2. The Honerine was the
largest mine in the district. Garcia, *Brief History of Stockton, Utah*, 32.

[35]"Grand Central Apex Suit," *IMR*, January 9, 1907, 10/5; "Grand Central Mammoth Case,"
IMR, February 5, 1907, 14/1. The U.S. Supreme Court confirmed the verdict. "Grand Central
Mining Co. Given $151,030.34 Damages," *IMR*, September 14, 1909, 1/2–3; *Mammoth Mining
Co. v. Grand Central Mining Co.*, 213 U.S. 72 (1909).

[36]"Much Activity in American Fork Camp," *IMR*, April 5, 1907, 6/3; "Another Ore Body in
Surprise Ground," *IMR*, May 7, 1907, 6/6; "American Fork Notes," *SLH*, May 9, 1907, 8/5;
"American Fork," June 16, 1907, 18/1.

[37]"Surprise Suit to Be Compromised," *IMR*, July 9, 1907, 6/4; "New Shippers Being Made,"
SLH, September 3, 1907, 6/3; "American Fork a Lively Camp," *SLH*, September 10, 1907, 6/3;
"American Fork Mines," *SLH*, September 24, 1907, 7/3; "Get Ore at 10 Feet in American
Fork," *IMR*, September 20, 1907, 6/4.

the Surprise and Shamrock lode claims.[38] In the fall of 1909, Baskin added the Mineral Flat to his list of productive mines in American Fork Canyon, and a new three-foot vein of lead-silver carbonate was simultaneously discovered at the Mountain Dell.

Baskin continued buying and selling mining properties, but ultimately the American Fork mines, like most of his others, failed his plans for sustained profit. In 1915 he finally sold his holdings to the Miller Hill Mining Company's remnants.[39] His recurring, ever-optimistic prediction that "there is every reason to believe that the *next season* will be the most productive one the district has seen" was never fulfilled.[40]

Mining historian Corydon W. Higgins offered one explanation, saying that "Col. Aspenwall's son was sent out . . . to take active charge of affairs and immediately began operations upon a large and somewhat costly scale . . . [including] the building of a railroad as far as Deer Creek, and the erection of a smelter. . . . [T]his lavish first expenditure [was] the cause of the company's final failure."[41] Additional explanations were given by the *Inter-Mountain Republican*:

> The early history of the Miller mine is . . . a long story of poor management. . . . Judge R. N. Baskin . . . was one of the incorporators . . . but unfortunately the company did not avail itself of his sound knowledge of mining matters. The first great run of the mine was about 1890. . . . A fault cut off the ore body and discouraged the company. . . . This fault . . . would be as easy for us to solve at the present day as it would be to pick up the broken ends of a telegraph wire between two poles.[42]

Pressure and encroachment by aggressive competitors also contributed to the ultimate failure of Baskin's mining business: "In June 1901 an experienced mining man was sent . . . to examine the mine. This man [George Tying] was . . . impressed with the simplicity of the mining problems presented . . . and the great reward to be reaped. . . . [H]e immediately began acquiring adjoining ground."[43]

With land speculation, "succeed or bust" mining ventures, and raising, breeding, and selling thoroughbred horses all part of Baskin's

---

[38]"Baskin Obtains Patents," *DN*, February 22, 1908, 6/2.

[39]"Around the State," *SLMinR*, April 30, 1915, 28/1.

[40]"Says Mineral Flat Will Soon Be Shipper," *SLH*, October 19, 1909, 12/4; italics added.

[41]Higgins, *SLMinR*, October 15, 1907, 2/1; "Mine and Smelter Building," *SLMinR*, March 15, 1906, 18/3.

[42]"Miller Mine Likely to Rival Old Record," *IMR*, November 20, 1908, 6/3.

[43]Ibid.

portfolio, what of railroads? Others were making fortunes in them, but only one instance is known of Baskin's investing in railroad ventures. He and the apostate Walker brothers, Joseph R. and David F. (Fred), were among the prominent non-Mormons who, in 1873, participated in a $300,000 investment in the Bingham Canyon and Camp Floyd Railroad Company, linking Alta on the north and Bingham mines on the south to the Utah Southern Railroad in Sandy, and extending the line south to Camp Floyd Company. According to Leonard Arrington, this railroad investment was unlike most others in Utah, as it was done without LDS Church participation.[44]

Baskin owned at least 3,200 acres of land in Davis County, near present-day Wood's Cross.[45] In summer months he leased land use from other property owners, making up to 5,000 acres available for grazing. He owed Davis County back property taxes for 1895 through 1898.[46] In 1900 his five sections of 640 acres each were advertised for sale by W. O. Lee and Company for $8,000, or $2.50 per acre.[47] In midsummer of 1903, Baskin, well into his supreme court duties, listed for sale 173 acres of Baskin Ranch, in West Bountiful, Davis County—the property on which Baskin raised horses. The asking price was not given.[48] For many years after his death the Wood's Cross property continued to be called the Baskin Ranch. Portions of it were later sold to duck hunters for the Centerville Gun Club and an access road for hunters. For a time, the property became productive sugar beet farmland; then the Bonneville Ranch Company took some of it for the placement of a seventy-foot tunnel whose purpose and fate are now uncertain.[49]

At his death, the *Deseret News* sharply noted, "Judge Baskin made quite a fortune during his career in this state but is said to have lost

[44]Sillitoe, *History of Salt Lake County*, 3, 83; Arrington, *Great Basin Kingdom*, 279.

[45]Baskin's property adjoined that of Carlos Sessions, one of many children of Mormon polygamist Perrigrine Sessions, commonly named as the founder of Bountiful, Utah. DAVCC, August 23, 1894, 4/3.

[46]"Delinquent Taxes," DAVCC, November 29, 1895, 4/4; December 17, 1896, 4/4; and December 16, 1898, 2/2.

[47]"W. O. Lee & Co.'s Column," DAVCC, July 27, 1900, 4/6.

[48]"For Sale—Real Estate," SLH, June 2, 1903, 9/4. Baskin listed with the real estate firm of Tibbals and Nettleton.

[49]"Hunters Take Notice," DAVCC, January 1, 1909, 8/2. Portions were home to the Herman Wagner family, Mr. M. O. Parrish, the Walter Keeler family, and a Bloomfield family. "Woods Cross," May 29, 1914, 1/3; "Woods Cross," September 3, 1915, 1/3; "Woods Cross," May 6, 1921, 5/3; "Bountiful Briefs," July 22, 1921, 8/2; "Former Woods Cross Man Drowned in Ore.," May 14, 1926, 1/6, all in DAVCC.

most of it through unfortunate investments."[50] The *Tribune*'s acknowledgment of his interests in mining and his financial fortunes and misfortunes was appropriate, more empathetic, and much softer:

> With great confidence in the mineral resources . . . [he] did much for the development of Utah. He gave both money and influence to opening up the hidden riches and during his career he is said to have made and lost many fortunes. At one time he was interested to a considerable extent in the Miller mine in the American Fork canyon. He refused an offer of $150,000 by the Vanderbilts of New York for his one-quarter interest in the property.[51]

Baskin's speculative holdings, formerly diverse and numerous, ultimately shrunk to ownership of three relatively minor mining properties, all acquired during the time of his earliest mining investments. At his death the Christopolis Lode, the Christopolis Easterly Lode, and the Struck It Lode, all in Tooele County, constituted his entire estate. The probate court set their combined value at $2,000. Following his wife's death, Baskin either lived at the University Club or boarded, and when he died, he did not own a home or a homesite in Salt Lake City.

Federal officers sent to Utah Territory during Brigham Young's reign were repeatedly labeled by the Mormons as carpetbaggers and blacklegs, whose true purpose in Utah was alleged to enrich themselves at the expense of its people. While not a federal appointee, Baskin was classed among the top three in the "Federal Enemies of the Saints" list: James B. McKean, Robert Newton Baskin, and George R. Maxwell all died in Utah in various degrees of poverty.[52] McKean's non-Mormon admirers provided him with a burial monument. Maxwell's burial plot was donated by Reuben Howard Robertson, and his only burial stone, a modest one furnished by the GAR, includes no information regarding his wife and three children. At his death, Robert Baskin had no funds for purchase of his burial site marker or a marker for Olive, his wife, or for any of their three children. Wealth, even prosperity, eluded these men who had devoted their lives to government and civil service, and they died with hands as clean as they were empty.

---

[50]"Former Mayor Baskin Dies at Age of 81," *DN*, August 27, 1918, 1/4.

[51]"Judge R. N. Baskin Dies in Salt Lake," *SLT*, August 27, 1918, 14/6.

[52]The *Cincinnati Gazette*'s George Alfred Townsend awarded the three men their rankings in his 1871 list of enemies of the Saints. Townsend, *Mormon Trials*, 16–18.

20

Obey the Law

We believe in being subject to kings, presidents, rulers,
and magistrates, in obeying, honoring, and sustaining the law.
TWELFTH ARTICLE OF FAITH OF THE LDS CHURCH

T HE MOTIVATION DRIVING MOST OF THE DESPISED FED-
eral officials serving in Utah Territory was not religious bigotry
or intolerance, fame, or profit, but the goal of bringing Mormon leadership into obedience to the law. Said Utah Supreme Court
justice Robert N. Baskin, "I desire the establishment of the supremacy
of law."[1] Said another Utah Supreme Court justice, Charles S. Zane,
"Come within the law and all this trouble will cease."[2] Said U.S. marshal George R. Maxwell, "[My] prime, only, and everlasting instruction [was to] compel obedience to the laws."[3] Said Judge Jacob Smith
Boreman, "The only way to peaceably settle . . . the Mormon problem
is simply to enforce the laws."[4] Said U.S. attorney Charles S. Varian,
"Come within the law and advise your people to likewise."[5]

Thirteen articles stating certain of the fundamental beliefs of the
Church of Jesus Christ of Latter-day Saints originated from Joseph
Smith in March 1841. The Articles of Faith were revised in 1878 and
became doctrine when canonized in 1880.[6] If obedience to law is

---

[1]Baskin, *REM*, 25.
[2]Whitney, *HOU*, 3:748.
[3]"Brigham Young's Janissary," *New York World*, November 25, 1871.
[4]Arrington, "Crusade against Theocracy," 45.
[5]Baskin, *REM*, 215.
[6]Perry, "Articles of Faith," 23.

doctrine, as stated in the twelfth article of faith, what explains the paradox of Mormons' sustaining the longest period of organized civil disobedience against federal law in the history of the United States and its territories? The paradox rests on *whose law* would be obeyed.

Federal officers, almost uniformly non-Mormons, considered the residents of Utah Territory to be subject to federal laws, just as were inhabitants of other states and territories. These officials, together with businessmen, journalists, and independent attorneys, including Robert Baskin, were intent on achieving compliance.

Mormons were focused on living the laws of the Kingdom of God and saw in non-Mormon efforts a conspiracy, formed out of malicious purpose. The Kingdom of God was a theocracy, wherein Utah was governed by God's immediate directive, through divinely appointed leaders. As had happened in several counties in Missouri and Illinois, whenever officers in Utah Territory attempted to enforce laws related to civil actions, land ownership, voting rights, or court jurisdiction, Mormon leaders denounced the effort as an attack on their religious freedoms and painted it with the broad brush of persecution.

Six U.S. presidents had their say on the Latter-day Saints and obedience to the laws of their country. President James Buchanan said, "With the religious opinions of the Mormons, as long as they remained mere opinions, . . . I had no right to interfere. Actions alone, when in violation of the Constitution and laws of the United States, become the legitimate subjects for the jurisdiction of the civil magistrate."[7] On another occasion, Buchanan said, "If you obey the laws, . . . you . . . may live on in your present faith."[8] President Ulysses S. Grant, the controversial Civil War hero, spoke of the Mormons: "They will be protected in the worship of God according to the dictates of their consciences, but they will not be permitted to violate the laws under the cloak of religion."[9]

In his 1880 message to Congress, President Rutherford B. Hayes said, "Polygamy will not be abolished if the enforcement of the law depends on those who practice and uphold the crime. It can only be suppressed by taking away the political power of the sect which encourages and sustains it."[10] And in his inaugural address, President James A. Garfield said sternly, "The Mormon Church . . . prevents the administra-

---

[7]Richardson, "First Annual Message," 31.
[8]Buchanan, "A Proclamation" (April 6, 1858), in B. H. Roberts, *Comprehensive History of the Church*, 4:425–28.
[9]Poore and Tiffany, *Life of U. S. Grant*, 169.
[10]Van Wagoner, *Mormon Polygamy*, 116.

tion of justice. . . . [I]t is the duty of Congress . . . to prohibit within its jurisdiction all criminal practices, especially of that class which destroy the family relations and endanger social order."[11] President Chester Arthur, in a message to Congress, asserted that "the stoutest weapons which constitutional legislation can fashion" were necessary to counter polygamy, because "the existing statute . . . has been persistently and contemptuously violated."[12] And President Grover Cleveland described polygamy, as practiced in the Mormon theocracy, as "a principle and belief which set at naught that obligation of absolute obedience to the law of the land which lies at the foundation of republican institutions."[13]

The same opinions came from other tiers of government. Utah governor Eli H. Murray's 1880 annual report to the Secretary of the Interior was filled with injunction against Mormon behavior.[14] In 1882 Murray wrote for a national audience, "The exercise of temporal power by ecclesiastical authority . . . will no longer be tolerated."[15] In 1884 he added, "May we . . . lift Utah . . . and place her in accord with . . . every particular demanded by lofty patriotism, and unfaltering obedience to law."[16]

By 1890 the out-of-state luminaries appointed to the Utah Commission, whose existence in Utah resulted from provisions of the Edmunds Act, included the following in its annual report: "The Commission has acted on . . . the intention of Congress to impress upon the Mormon people that it has a fixed purpose to compel obedience to the laws enacted by it."[17]

PERSECUTION WAS REAL

Mormon history is replete with heinous and horrific crimes perpetrated on the innocent Saints, who were guilty of having peculiar beliefs while innocent of any wrongdoing. For mass tragedy and gross violation of basic human rights, the 1838 massacre of seventeen Mormons, including women and children, at Haun's Mill by elements of the Missouri militia, and the expulsion of the Latter-day Saints from

---

[11]Ibid.; Richardson, *Messages and Papers*, 7:11.

[12]Richardson, *Messages and Papers*, 7:208–10, 606.

[13]Ibid., 8:11, 184, 361.

[14]"Report of the Governor of Utah," in U.S. Department of the Interior, *Annual Report of the Secretary of the Interior, 1880*, 2:523.

[15]Murray, "The Crisis in Utah," 346.

[16]Murray, *Message of His Excellency*, 9.

[17]Godfrey et al., *Report of the Utah Commission*, 7.

Missouri that year, stand as strong evidence. D. Michael Quinn tells of a personal example in the "persecution-caused death" of his "ancestral Mormon mother of twenty children." After being "burned out of her farmhouse," she and her "surviving husband and their adult children shepherded five minor siblings from their temporary recovery at Nauvoo—to cross the frozen Mississippi in 1846."[18] It was persecution when southern farmers murdered missionary Joseph Standing at Varnell's Station, Georgia, on July 21, 1879; when Elders John H. Gibbs and William S. Berry were brutally murdered in Tennessee in 1884; and when bigots abused and killed other missionaries in the South, often on the mere rumor that the LDS Church marriage doctrine promulgated sexual deviance.[19] Mormons in Arizona settlements in 1886 were "robbed, attacked, hounded," and "their leaders were threatened with castration and lynching." They were "desperately impoverished" and "bobbed up and down in a sea of animus."[20]

Persecution was the faith-promoting explanation for the diaspora of LDS faithful to Illinois and ultimately to the Great Basin. Mormons invoked religious intolerance, bigotry, and Satan's operatives to explain the opposition to God's restored church. Even in 1890 after the Edmunds and Edmunds-Tucker acts, and with the Woodruff Manifesto imminent, the Utah Commission reported, "in all the teachings in the Tabernacle . . . every effort of the Government to suppress this crime is still denominated as a persecution, and those charged with ferreting out and prosecuting the guilty are denominated persecutors of the saints."[21] Whether undeserved persecution or deserved prosecution, it unified the Mormon people through tragically difficult times. Persecution became the Mormons' defense.

A substantial historical record also suggests that Mormon provocation did much to merit their mistreatment. Historians point to financial frauds, counterfeiting, vote trading and bloc voting, land seizure, violence wreaked by secret societies, and disturbing marriage practices as sources of repeated trouble.[22] Nevertheless, the faith-driven illusion of persecuted innocence, without acknowledgment of accountability for any number of Mormon crimes, persisted. The myth continued

---

[18]Quinn, "Us-Them Tribalism," 103–104.

[19]W. W. Hatch, *There Is No Law*, 1968; Wingfield, "Myth, Mormonism, and Murder," 212–25; Rolph, *"To Shoot, Burn, and Hang"*; "Attempt to Mob Mormons," *os*, June 19, 1900, 1/4.

[20]Herman, *Hell on the Range*, 199.

[21]Godfrey et al., *Report of the Utah Commission*, 20.

[22]LeSueur, *1838 Mormon War in Missouri*; Quinn, *Mormon Hierarchy*.

that the Saints had been driven from New York to Ohio and then Missouri, although in both cases the moves were voluntary. The real persecution the faithful endured in Missouri and Illinois was indeed horrific, as was the murder of their founding Prophet while in the custody of the State of Illinois. Federal excesses in the government's long struggle to persuade the LDS Church to obey the law led to more than a thousand prosecutions for polygamy, in which there was undoubtedly elements of blatant persecution. Test oath requirements, violations of the sanctity of their homes and bedrooms by marshals searching for husbands hiding in the homes of their plural wives, and the denial of voting privileges all took place. Whether all the actions stemming from federal laws were court-upheld examples of religious persecution, as Texas legal scholar Douglas Laycock argued in 1993 in support of the Religious Freedom Restoration Act, is questionable.[23] Speaking about the same act, Apostle Dallin Oaks supported Laycock when he insisted, "I know of no other major religious group in America that has endured anything comparable to the officially sanctioned persecution imposed upon members of my church by Federal, State, and local government officials."[24] In a 1999 publication, law professor Frederick Mark Gedicks adds as strongly that "no other Christian denomination in the United States, not even Roman Catholics, can lay claim to such a recent and violent legacy of persecution at the hands of American government authorities."[25] And lawyer Elijah L. Milne wrote in 2006, "Nineteenth-century anti-polygamy laws . . . were motivated primarily by religious prejudice and intolerance."[26]

Evidence suggests a contrary interpretation. For centuries English common law prohibited taking more than one wife, and by 1833 a number of states, notably Illinois as one, had passed laws explicitly prohibiting bigamy.[27] Supreme Court justice Joseph P. Bradley ruled in 1890 that "whatever persecutions they may have suffered in the early part of their history in Missouri and Illinois, they [Mormons] have no excuse for their persistent defiance of law under the government of the

---

[23]Laycock, "Religious Freedom Restoration Act," 222–24. The act was declared unconstitutional; *City of Boerne v. Flores*, 117 U.S. 2157.

[24]Oaks, *Testimony before the Senate Judiciary Committee*, 35:30, cited in Gedicks, "'No Man's Land,'" 5. Oaks overlooks the religious persecution of seventy-six members of the Branch Davidians, who were shot and incinerated at Waco, Texas, by state and federal forces in the spring of 1993.

[25]Gedicks, "'No Man's Land,'" 4.

[26]Milne, "Blaine Amendments," 292.

[27]Homer, "Judiciary and the Common Law," 98.

United States."[28] Marriage, while from its very nature a sacred obligation, was also the subject of a civil contract, wherein the rights of wife and husband were regulated by law in most states and territories, but not in Utah.[29] Brigham Young's correspondence is replete with letters instructing the local bishop to intervene in instances where women—often the first wife—were unfairly treated or unsupported by their polygamous husbands. Not until the Edmunds-Tucker Act of 1887 were marriages in Utah Territory protected by being placed in the civil record.[30]

Polygamy was very useful outside Utah as a basis for criticizing Mormonism. Its sexual overtones captured public attention and evoked salacious and prurient images in the mind's eye of most Americans. After the Civil War the practice of polygamy became the convenient handle Mormonism's critics grasped to demand change in the matter of theocracy. The practice of polygamy, with its sexual innuendoes, was far more effective in stimulating congressional legislation than were the prosaic problems of an inextricable fusion of church and state.[31] In 1885 the *Tribune* asserted that "the essential principle of Mormonism is not polygamy at all, but the ambition of an ecclesiastical hierarchy to . . . rule the souls and lives of its subjects with absolute authority, unrestrained by any civil power."[32] Idaho's Frederick Dubois, who worked with Baskin on legislation in Washington, also understood the pragmatic importance of opposing polygamy: "There was a universal detestation of polygamy, and inasmuch as the Mormons openly defended it we were given a very effective weapon."[33]

The defense of the unwavering Mormons against following the law was that their opponents were agents of Satan, that Baskin and those who came after the Civil War were evil men with evil purposes. Speaking of the Cullom Bill, Judge Elias Smith said it contained the "most damnable in its provisions of anything that the wicked have devised for the overthrow of the people of God."[34] Looking back

---

[28]*Mormon Church v. United States*, 136 U.S. 1 (1890), 135.

[29]Justice Waite, in *Reynolds v. United States*, 98 U. S. 146 (1879).

[30]Firmage and Mangrum, *Zion in the Courts*, 149.

[31]C. A. Cannon, "Awesome Power of Sex," 61–82.

[32]"The Mormon Church," *SLT*, February 15, 1885, 5/5.

[33]Dubois, *Autobiography of Frederick T. Dubois*, cited in Hansen, *Quest for Empire*, 179. Research in 2007 validated the preeminence of theocracy. An meticulous analysis of the *Salt Lake Tribune*'s opposition to Utah statehood, showed convincing evidence that theocratic control was the non-Mormons' target far more commonly than was polygamy. Mills, "Pushing the Car of Progress Forward," 84.

[34]Thomas, *Elias Smith's Journal*, vol. 2, March 28, 1870.

on his long career, Judge Smith, added, "I have fought . . . [,] often against the advice of friends [to remain silent] who feared the consequence of opposing what I deemed, and they acknowledged, to be evil." He could not understand Governor Murray's actions, except that "the Devil is not dead and agents [in the form of Murray] are on the alert."[35] Brigham Young said, "The opposition which we have to meet is not because we believe in polygamy. That principle is not the real bone of contention, but it is the power of Satan against the power of Jesus Christ here upon this earth. . . . There is a constant warfare between the good and the evil. . . . [I]t is a war which has always existed, and will always continue to exist, between the good and the bad, between the power of God and the power of the devil."[36] Historian Wayne Durham Stout repeated this point, saying that the history of Mormon and anti-Mormon "has been a record of the conflict between the forces of evil and good, between right and wrong, between Satan and the spirit of Christ—in all ages."[37] Describing Col. Albert S. Johnston's 1857 progress westward toward Utah Territory with the troops of the Utah Expedition, Stout observed, "The legions of Satan moved ever closer to Utah."[38] History would be better served if "the fight of good against evil" argument no longer had proponents among modern historians, and if such implications and undertones were absent from contemporary history publications.

Accomplished modern historians of Utah and the West continue either to ignore or despise Robert Baskin or to see him as "the Other . . . what I myself am not," in the words of social philosopher Emmanuel Levinas.[39] Baskin is widely remembered for his role in forming the first non-Mormon political party, the Liberal Party in Utah, but is forgotten and unacknowledged for his wisdom in ending the party's existence when its objectives had been achieved. Baskin is not cited in Andrew Love Neff's *History of Utah 1847 to 1869*, Dean L. May's *Utah: A People's History*; Charles S. Peterson's *Utah: A Bicentennial History*; Wain Sutton's *Utah, a Centennial History*; *Portrait, Genealogical, and Biographical Record of the State of Utah, Containing Biographies of Many Well Known Citizens of the Past and Present*; Leonard J. Arrington's

---

[35]Ibid., vol. 3, April 8, 1884, and March 11, 1882.

[36]Brigham Young in the Tabernacle, *JOD* 11 (1866): 234, 236.

[37]Stout, *A War on the Saints* (New Era Press), 193. Of Governor Murray's appointment, Stout added, "The forces of evil won a victory when Governor Murray was appointed to a second term." Stout, *HOU*, 1:219.

[38]Stout, *War on the Saints* (New Era Press), 155.

[39]Cited by Quinn, "Us-Them Tribalism," 95.

Great Basin Kingdom; or Allan Kent Powell's massive *Utah History Encyclopedia*. He is not mentioned in Samuel George Ellsworth's account of Utah historians, *Utah History: Retrospect and Prospect*. His name does not appear in the recent compilation by Paul Reeve and Ardis E. Parshall, *Mormonism, A Historical Encyclopedia*. In Richard D. Poll's *Utah's History*, he is merely "a young lawyer from Ohio who was sent to Washington to lobby for additional legislation."[40] Edward Brown Firmage and Richard Collin Mangrum, in their *Zion in the Courts*, mention Baskin only very briefly in regard to his attempt to implicate Brigham Young and LDS leaders in John D. Lee's first trial.[41] Sarah Barringer Gordon does not cite Baskin in her important work *The Mormon Question*. In his history of Salt Lake City, Thomas Alexander is one of the few to deal in some depth with Baskin, praising his role as mayor and his fairness in balancing Mormon and non-Mormon demands.[42]

By the time Baskin had achieved a remarkably fine judicial record in Utah's Supreme Court, thirty years separated him from the courtroom of Judge James B. McKean, the judicial figure most hated by the Mormons. Yet Clifford L. Ashton, in his monograph on the federal judges of Utah, allotted Baskin no praise, but only three short, derogatory lines, describing him as "[a] rabid anti-Mormon who had vigorously and ably urged and supported Judge McKean," "an outspoken anti-Mormon and friend of Judge McKean," and "Mormondom's greatest enemy."[43] When Baskin lobbied for the Cullom-Struble Bill, LDS Church historian and apostle Joseph Fielding Smith described him as being "as bitter against the Saints as it was possible for him to be."[44]

As an instigator of unwanted change in the Kingdom of God, Baskin is still seen by Mormons as a man of sinister intent. More than ninety years after his death, he remains a maligned figure for his efforts to bring Mormon theocracy in line with the laws of the United States.

---

[40] Poll, *Utah's History*, 248.

[41] Firmage and Mangrum, *Zion in the Courts*, 247–48.

[42] Alexander, *Mormons and Gentiles*, 91, 100, 125–27. In *Utah, the Right Place* (174–75), Alexander treats Baskin's run against George Q. Cannon and his role in the indictment of Brigham Young, Daniel H. Wells, and Hosea Stout for the murder of Richard Yates.

[43] Ashton, *Federal Judiciary in Utah*, 33, 38, 43. Baskin was not a charter member of the 1894 Utah State Bar Association but delayed joining until January 1896. *Report of the Fourth Annual Meeting of the State Bar Association of Utah*, 119.

[44] J. F. Smith, *Essentials of Church History*, 605–606.

21

Gently They Go

Gently they go, the beautiful, the tender, the kind;
Quietly they go, the intelligent, the witty, the brave.
EDNA ST. VINCENT MILLAY

R OBERT BASKIN'S FINAL OFFICIAL SUPREME COURT DUTY
was administering the oaths of office for incoming Utah state
officers on January 3, 1905. The senate chamber within the
joint City-County Building, whose existence was due, in large part,
to Baskin's efforts while mayor, was decorated with American flags
and bunting, and a life-size painting of Brigham Young. The festivities began at noon, when the Christensen Orchestra struck up "The
Star-Spangled Banner." A large group of dignitaries, led by departing governor Heber M. Wells, the governor-elect John C. Cutler,
the secretaries of state and the treasury, and supreme court justice–
elect Daniel N. Straup, entered and were seated. Noteworthy guests
included Mrs. Emmeline B. Wells, Mayor Richard P. Morris, former
congressman John T. Caine, legislator Edward M. Allison, Jr., District Attorney Joseph Lippman, and several local probate and district
court judges. After Cutler completed his brief inaugural address, Chief
Justice Baskin administered the oath of office, making him Utah's
second state governor. Baskin also administered an oath to Straup, as
the newest member of Utah's supreme court.[1] In its editorial review
of those leaving and coming into office, the *Deseret News* remarked:

---

[1] Judges Bartch and McCarty administered the other oaths. "New Officers Are Sworn In," *SLH*,
January 3, 1905, 8/1–2. Cutler and Straup came in with the 1904 Republican sweep.

Chief Justice R. N. Baskin must not be omitted from the list of dignitaries who deserve special mention on retiring from public office. We
believe he is regarded by both the great political parties, as we view
him, as a sound lawyer, a wise judge, an upright and honest man, and
a public spirited citizen who is devoted to the welfare of this State and
Nation and true to his convictions of right. He bears with him into
private practice the good will and esteem of a host of friends.[2]

Retirement did not result in inactivity for Baskin, for he remained
in law practice with his partner, Enos D. Hoge. Baskin more actively
explored for promising sites for mineral acquisition. American Fork
Canyon mining ventures, in which he held great hopes, received a
major commitment of his time and consumed his money. Interrupt-
ing his activities in 1906 was the death, in Saline County, Missouri, of
Thomas H. Baskin, one of his two surviving older brothers. Thomas
Baskin's obituary could have been written for Robert: "He would have
honored any public position. . . . He had fine brain power—a lively
imagination—good command of language, and a remarkably reten-
tive memory. . . . He was a thorough and staunch Democrat. . . . [H]e
had the zeal of a martyr and the valor of a patriot."[3] Death also interrupted Robert Baskin's usual activities in April 1908 when Luacine
Hoge Peery, the thirty-five-year-old daughter of Baskin's law partner,
died in Salt Lake City after a long period of poor health.[4]

In 1906 the *Inter-Mountain Republican* noted that only five of the
men who had met in Corinne in 1869 to found Utah's Liberal Party
remained alive. Fred J. Kiesel of Ogden, Robert N. Baskin, and Simon
Bamberger of Salt Lake City, all Democrats, were named, as well as
Republicans Christopher Diehl and Aaron Greenewald, also of Salt
Lake.[5]

In February 1907, Baskin traveled to Washington with mining capitalist David Keith and his wife, Mary.[6] Keith, born in Nova Scotia,
had emigrated to the United States about 1867 and had been involved

[2]"Entrances and Exits," *DN*, January 3, 1905, 4/1.

[3]"Death of T. H. Baskin," *Missouri Progress*, reprinted in *SLH*, November 20, 1906, 3/3. Thomas
   Baskin was an Independent Order of Odd Fellows member. Records do not state whether
   Robert Baskin traveled to the funeral.

[4]U.S. Federal Census Collection, Utah State Burials, Ogden City Cemetery sexton records.

[5]"Only Five Are Left," *IMR*, October 29, 1906, 8/1. Christopher Diehl died on September 17,
   1912, in Salt Lake City; Frederick John Kiesel died on April 22, 1919, in Ogden; Aaron
   Greenewald died in Salt Lake City on January 8, 1921; and Simon Bamberger died in Salt
   Lake City on October 6, 1926.

[6]"Washington Visitors," *SLH*, February 5, 1907, 1/7.

in mining in Nevada and California before coming to Utah. He had
been named *Salt Lake Tribune* editor after the paper was purchased by
Thomas Kearns, and both Keith and Kearns aligned with the American Party when it was formed in 1904.

CONSIDERED BUT NOT SELECTED

In 1908 the Democrat Party in Utah was struggling when Baskin's
name was raised by Joshua H. Paul, a devoted Mormon and a professor
of nature study at the University of Utah, as the most appropriate candidate for election as governor of the state. "The judge is an unswerving
Democrat of the Jeffersonian type . . . , dealing fairly and humanely
with every person, without regard to wealth, social position or political affiliation," Paul observed. With "no blemish on his successful
record," there was no man more likely to swing the Democratic vote,
insisted Paul, adding, "He represents no church[,] . . . is independent
financially and politically . . . [and] is in robust health. . . . Baskin is
the man to lead the party upwards."[7] When the name of "Uncle Jesse"
Knight, a Mormon and a wealthy and successful lead and silver mining magnate of Provo, was raised in a Logan meeting as a potential
gubernatorial candidate, the *Box Elder News* pointed out that several
important facts were being overlooked. Knight was seventy-two years
of age, had no interest in public life and no ambition to serve, and had
been advised by friends, family, and his church not to run. The *Box
Elder News* suggested several far better possibilities; among them were
Joseph L. Rawlins, William H. King, Simon Bamberger, William
Roylance, James H. Moyle, and Robert N. Baskin.[8] Roylance was the
personal friend and choice of Jesse Knight, and a man with many
friends among the railroad interests. The *Salt Lake Herald* considered
Roylance and Baskin to be the two best choices. "Mr. Baskin is a
Gentile and is probably equally well known all over Utah," the *Herald*
noted. "As chief justice of the supreme court of Utah he achieved a
great reputation of judicial fairness and learning."[9] Knight declined
nomination, and ignoring the individuals previously suggested, the
Democratic Party selected his son, Jesse William Knight, heir to his

[7]"Declares for Baskin," *SLH*, September 13, 1908, 13/4. Professor Paul was later the president of
Brigham Young College and of Utah State Agricultural College in Logan, Utah.
[8]"Politics and Things," *Box Elder News*, October 1, 1908, 1/6.
[9]"Committee Meets Today," *SLH*, October 2, 1908, 3/1.

father's business interests, as its champion.[10] Knight was defeated for the governorship by the Republican candidate, William Spry.

DEMISE OF FRIENDS AND PEERS

The Independent Order of Odd Fellows (IOOF) gathered at the Lincoln Avenue home of Enos Dougherty Hoge on the last day of July 1912 to honor their brother, who had died the previous day at age eighty-one. Hoge was born in 1831 in Virginia; by 1860 he was living in Perry County, Illinois, and married to the former Luacine Williams. He volunteered in the Civil War and served as a lieutenant in the 110th Illinois Infantry, rising to the rank of captain before the war's end. He was appointed as associate justice to Utah Territory's supreme court in July 1868, then entered law practice, and in 1876 was hired as part of the legal team defending John D. Lee in his first trial, while sitting on the opposite side of the table from Robert Baskin. Hoge was one of five Joint Legislative Committee members responsible for preparing and compiling the laws of Utah in June 1888.[11] The *Salt Lake Herald* report described a "large concourse of Odd Fellows and Rebokahs" attending the IOOF funeral service, with Grand Warden W. I. Snyder officiating. While it is almost certain that Baskin attended, the only men identified in the *Herald* were Odd Fellows members. Hoge was survived by his wife and his married son, Enos D. Hoge, Jr.[12]

In July 1914 the *Tribune* announced the publication of an "interesting volume of reminiscences" by Judge R. N. Baskin, giving it a positive review: "A volume of intense interest to the student of conditions during the troublous days before statehood, Judge Baskin's book is well written . . . and worthy of perusal by those interested in the early history of the territory. . . . Manifest care has been taken to keep the record within the facts of which he has written." Quoting from Baskin's book, the review continued: "The priesthood, not the Liberal Party, is responsible for any hardships which its adherents may have suffered. The Gentiles . . . would have shown themselves unworthy of American citizenship had they failed to organize and make a united effort to Americanize Utah."[13]

---

[10]"Jesse William Knight Named for Governor," *SLH*, October 3, 1908, 1/6–7.

[11]The other members of the Joint Legislative Committee were Samuel R. Thurman, Charles C. Richards, Luther T. Tuttle, and John R. Carlisle. *Compiled Laws of Utah, 1888.*

[12]"Odd Fellows Hold Rites for Judge Hoge," *SLH*, July 30, 1912, 8/4.

[13]"Early Life in Utah Is Subject of Book," *SLT*, July 19, 1914, 24/1.

Baskin had been confined to his home for three months with severe rheumatism when a *Salt Lake Telegram* reporter rushed to his residence at 214 Colfax Avenue in the midmorning hours of March 29, 1915, to inform Baskin of the death his dear friend and longtime colleague, Charles S. Zane. Judge Zane had died after experiencing a massive stroke at the home of his daughter, Mrs. Margaret Cherndon.[14] Baskin responded to the reporter: "I am shocked, deeply shocked. I was probably as close to Judge Zane as any man in Utah. We were long, warm personal friends. His death, coming so suddenly, is a shock."[15] Baskin took a moment for reflection and went on:

> I have not at my command language to express the high estimate I hold of Judge Zane's character. He was every inch a man. He had the courage of honest conviction. It was indeed a happy day for Utah when, at the recommendation of Senator Shelby M. Cullom of Illinois, the president of the United States appointed Judge Zane chief justice of the supreme court of the Territory of Utah. He arrived here on August 24, 1884. . . . A more conscientious, impartial and humane judge than he never sat upon the bench.[16]

The morning was cool, for the reporter describes Baskin settling in his big chair before the fireplace: "One could imagine his mind and his heart traveling back to the old days when he and his associates, among whom Judge Zane numbered, were the leaders of their parties and principles here in Utah." Baskin continued his reflection on becoming chief justice of the supreme court by defeating Zane. "I was the Democratic candidate, and he was my political opponent. . . . And I went to Judge Zane after I was elected and told him I considered it a great honor to defeat him. And further, I said, I would have considered it a greater honor to have been defeated by him than by any other man. . . . We were very close personal friends, the judge and I."[17] "As the reporter prepared to leave," the *Telegram* noted, "Judge Baskin drew himself up to his full six feet—strong and able even in his eighty-first year [*sic*]," and finished his response.

> "Not only does the death of Judge Zane come as a shock because it means another friend is gone," he said. "It also reminds me again that I myself may go any day now—almost any day." And then, raising his

---

[14]"Former Chief Justice of State is Called by Death," *SLTel*, March 29, 1915, 9/1.
[15]"Judge Baskin Pays Tribute to Friend," *SLTel*, March 29, 1915, 9/1–3.
[16]Ibid.
[17]Ibid.

arm and pointing his finger as one might well believe he did in his days on the bench when he wished particularly to emphasize a point, the judge said: "Judge Zane did much for Utah. Utah should erect a monument to his memory." With that he parted the curtains and stepped from the room, still grieving over the loss of his friend.[18]

Two days later, the supreme court named a Utah bar association committee to draft a resolution of regret and honor for Charles S. Zane. Atop an impressive list of names in the legal community was that of Robert N. Baskin. Also listed were George W. Bartch, Waldemar Van Cott (who had served Reed Smoot in his appearances before Congress), William H. King, Franklin S. Richards, Charles S. Varian, and William H. Dickson, all of Salt Lake City, together with judges J. E. Booth of Provo and Henry Rolapp of Ogden. Following the funeral at the First Congregational Church, Zane's body was removed to Springfield, Illinois, for burial near another longtime friend and mentor, Abraham Lincoln.[19]

Baskin's mental and physical health were sufficient for him to complete another history-writing endeavor. He published *Reply to Certain Statements by O. F. Whitney in His History of Utah* in 1916. Whitney's book of Utah history, published earlier in the same year, attacked Baskin's Mountain Meadows massacre account, which charged that the LDS hierarchy was complicit in the massacre, if not the orchestrator of it. In *Reply*, Baskin answered Whitney's charges and went on to correct what he considered another of Whitney's intentional falsifications: the Mormon Battalion's history. Whitney contended that forming the battalion to march to California was forced upon the Mormons by a hostile federal government. Baskin countered with what subsequent historians have confirmed: that the battalion's march to California was highly beneficial to the destitute Saints and was done at their request. The battalion men were given pay and benefits matching those of regular army participants, thereby bringing desperately needed cash to the church. At the end of the march, the men were given their arms and accouterments, which were put to use in helping the body of Saints westward into the Great Basin's valleys. Baskin wrote, "In my Reminiscences and in my review, I have asserted that certain atrocious statements by Whitney are 'as dishonest as they

---

[18]Ibid. His age is incorrect in the report; he was seventy-eight years old.
[19]"Loved Jurist's Death Will Be Regretted in Resolutions," *slTel*, March 31, 1915, 9/1.

are despicable.'" He added, "My Reminiscences contain many historical facts which are very unpleasant to Whitney and his class, 'but happen they did' and no record of the times of their occurrence 'would be complete if they were omitted.'"[20]

The Democratic ticket for 1916 included William H. King for senator, Simon Bamberger for governor, and four distinguished elderly men for the largely honorary positions of presidential electors: Robert N. Baskin of Salt Lake County, Jesse Knight of Utah County, A. Anderson of Cache County, and John Seaman of Weber County.[21] Democrats King and Bamberger were both winners, and with Utah's Republicans outvoted four to three by Democrats, the state's four electoral votes were to go for Woodrow Wilson.[22] It was a fitting end to Baskin's lifelong allegiance to the Democratic Party that his last political act was to register Utah's electoral vote for a successful Democratic candidate as the president of the United States.

BOARDING OR COHABITATION?

When Olive Lavinia Baskin died on February 11, 1890, she and Robert were living at 17 East on First North in Salt Lake City. Twelve days later, Erasmus Foote Hall, living only a few doors away at 35 East First North, also died. His widow, Mary Edna Brown Hall, twenty-one years younger than her husband, was pregnant with her second child at the time.[23] The deaths of their respective spouses within days of each other, and their being near neighbors, were a coincidence that became significant in the remaining lives of Robert Baskin and Mary Hall.

Baskin lived on First North until at least August 1893.[24] From that date to 1898, Baskin's living arrangements are uncertain, but at the time of his abdication from the Liberal Party the *Tribune* commented that its reporter had gone to the "house on the hill," which might yet have been the First North location. The *Salt Lake City Directory* for 1898 lists him as bedding at the Cullen Hotel, 33 West Second South. However,

---

[20]Baskin, *RCSW*, 25.

[21]"Bourbons Name State Ticket," *Box Elder News*, August 22, 1916, 1/3; *DavCC*, November 3, 1916, 4/3–4.

[22]"Majorities of Bourbons Climbing Up," *SLH*, November 10, 1916, 14/1.

[23]Both First North properties disappeared in 2000 when the LDS Church Conference Center was built.

[24]Baskin was surprised by night intruders at the First North address, and rising late, he surprised two men, who ran and escaped. "Live Burglars at the Mayor's," *DEN*, August 22, 1893, 7.

Mary Edna Brown Hall, daughter of polygamist Homer Brown of Manti, Utah, thought to have been involved in the Aiken party murders in 1857. Baskin boarded in the widow Hall's home for many years. Undated. *From, and by permission of Steven Leathem Malia, of Salt Lake City, a descendant of Mary Hall.*

in the years 1899, 1900, and 1901 Baskin was designated as residing in the home of Mary E. Hall ("widow of Erasmus F. Hall") at 25 S Street. In 1902 Baskin was "bedding" at 816 East Seventh South, again in the home of Mary E. Hall. The five years of 1903 through 1907, during and after his time in the Utah Supreme Court, Baskin resided with Mary Hall at 135 B Street; and from 1908 to 1910 he lived with the widow Hall at 187 F Street. When the 1910 federal census was taken, he lived at the University Club, 136 East South Temple, while Mary E. Hall lived alone at 624 South Main Street. For the next five years Baskin lived with Mary Hall at 214 Colfax Avenue, within walking distance of the City-County Building (if his arthritis allowed), and from 1916 to his death, they lived at 435 East Fourth Avenue.[25]

Thus, for at least nineteen of twenty-eight years following the deaths of their respective spouses, Robert Newton Baskin and Mary Edna Brown Hall resided under the same roof in Salt Lake City. The 1900 census record shows Mary Hall's son Benjamin, age sixteen, in the home, but no boarders other than Baskin were noted. In the years before his wife's death, Baskin had a great deal to say in criticism of Mormon cohabitation with several women and worked assiduously for federal legislation against it. However, he left no comment or explanation

---

[25] *Salt Lake City Directory* (Salt Lake City: R. L. Polk Co., 1893, 1898, 1899–1919).

about his nineteen or more years of boarding with the widow Hall. At his death, the *Salt Lake Herald* graciously omitted any comment on the arrangement, saying only that for thirty-five years Judge Baskin had been a widower, "living part of that time at the University club."[26]

Mary Edna Brown was born in Nephi, Utah, one of twenty-nine children of the four wives of Mormon bishop Homer Brown, recently identified as one of the men from Nephi who murdered four of the six Aiken party members in November 1857.[27] If anyone of the Homer Brown family supplied Mary Edna with details about the massacre, it did not come to light in Baskin's writings.

Did Baskin's living with Mary Hall constitute a common-law marriage? The answer from applicable Utah statutes is unclear; it would have made an unsettling, however interesting, case in a Salt Lake court.[28] The same question can be posed over cohabitation. Baskin knew of the 1885 Utah Third District Court ruling that defined the minimal elements of conviction for cohabitation. It was Baskin's friend and professional associate Judge Zane who had ruled on the charge of cohabitation brought against polygamist and Mormon dignitary Angus M. Cannon, noting several behaviors *not* required to meet the criteria for conviction: "It is not necessary that the evidence should show that the defendant and these women . . . occupied the same bed . . . or slept in the same room. Neither is it necessary that the evidence should show that . . . he had sexual intercourse with either of them."[29] The separation of cohabitation from sexual intercourse was upheld by the U.S. Supreme Court, which proclaimed: "The offense of cohabiting with *more than one woman* . . . is committed by a man

---

[26]"Former Mayor Baskin Is Dead," *slh*, August 27, 1918, 10/6.

[27]Horace Bucklin was killed by William A. Hickman in Davis County, and the sixth man, "Big John" Chapman, escaped to California, where he was later killed in a dispute over a woman. Bigler and Bagley, *Mormon Rebellion*, 234–35. Mary Edna Brown's mother was Sarah Ann Wolff (also spelled "Woolf"), the first of Homer Brown's four wives and the younger sister of Absolom (named by Bigler as "Abraham" Woolf, also "Wolff"), one of the perpetrators. Bigler, "Aiken Party Executions," 457.

[28]"In this territory there is no law regulating marriage. No form or ceremony is required, and no record of marriage is kept." Furthermore: "Under our law a marriage depends solely upon the mutual consent of the contracting parties. They may enter into the marriage relation secretly, and the fact may be unknown to all save the man and woman." *The United States, Respondent, v. Thomas Simpson, Appellant*, 4 Utah 227, 228–29; 7 P. 257, 258 (1885).

[29]John Irvine, reporter, *The Edmunds Law: Unlawful Cohabitation, as Defined by Chief Justice Chas. S. Zane of the Territory of Utah, in the Trial of Angus M. Cannon, Esq., in the Third District Court, Salt Lake City* (Salt Lake City: Juvenile Instructor Office, 1885), April 27, 28, and 29, 1885, 7, 96, 105.

who . . . holds them out to the world, by his language or conduct, or both, as his wives, and it is not necessary to the commission of the offense that he and the two women, or either of them, should occupy the same bed or sleep in the same room or that he should have sexual intercourse with either of them."[30] There is no evidence that another woman was ever present in the household or that Baskin ever held Mary Edna Brown Hall before society as his wife or intimate companion. The depth of their relationship remains uncertain, but nonetheless Baskin's will, drawn in 1915, named Mary E. Hall the sole recipient of his estate. After expenses were paid from the $2,000 sale of the three mining claims in Tooele County, Mary Hall received the remainder, $1,712, and more than one hundred unsold copies of Baskin's *Reminiscences of Early Utah*.[31] Following his death, she lived for a time at the Fairmont Apartments in Salt Lake City. She died on February 16, 1939, in Salt Lake City, where she had been living with her son, Benjamin Brown Hall, his family, and her descendants.

Gently He Is Gone

The newspapers and society sections and the mining reports are silent about the life events of Robert Baskin after 1916 until his death. Without gathered family or fanfare, other than the presence of Mary Edna Brown Hall, he expired on August 25, 1918, in the home where he boarded, at 435 East Fourth Avenue. His death certificate, signed by Dr. Howard P. Kirtley, gave as the cause an unspecific, catchall diagnosis of "generalized arteriosclerosis."[32] One of the first to note Baskin's death was the *Salt Lake Telegram*, which said the man had been "for more than a score of years a prominent and powerful figure in the public life of Salt Lake and Utah."[33] The *Ogden Standard* printed a brief synopsis of Baskin's life, describing him as a "veteran jurist, and social and political reformer of territorial days," and adding, "Judge Baskin was one of the strongest opponents of polygamy . . . and it was due to his efforts largely that laws were passed by congress forbidding the practice."[34]

---

[30]*Cannon v. United States*, 116 U.S. 55 (1885), 115. The ruling applied to the circumstance where one man was living with more than one woman; applicability to Baskin's circumstance is doubtful. Italics added.

[31]Utah Third District Court Probate Cases, ser. 1621, reel 737, case no. 9469.

[32]Kirtley, a general practitioner, kept an office in the Boston Building.

[33]"Former Mayor Baskin Dies at Home," *slTel*, August 26, 1918, 1/3.

[34]"Judge R. N. Baskin, Noted Jurist, Dies in Salt Lake," *os*, August 27, 1918, 6/5.

Mary Edna Brown Hall, older.
Baskin named her the sole recipient of his
estate. Undated. *From, and by permission of
Steven Leathem Malia, of Salt Lake City.*

The *Tribune* followed with an appropriate message and a summary of Baskin's life and accomplishments, but the most revealing comments came from the *Deseret News*, whose Mormon editor said that Baskin's life in Utah had encompassed "some of the stormiest and unhappiest years in the commonwealth's history."[35] The editor admitted:

> It would be futile to say that the part played by so strong, positive, and aggressive a personality was always such as to meet the support and win the approbation of everybody. . . . [T]here will be no compunctions in admitting the *Deseret News* often found it necessary to oppose his operations and criticize his methods with all the force it could command. At such times he paid us the compliment to strike back as vigorously—not to say violently—as he knew how. . . . [I]f we were sometimes constrained to charge him with bitterness, he was doubtless equally convinced in his own mind of the correctness of his own position.

The editor went on to emphasize a mellowing on both sides, with praise for both: "The *News* and the Judge . . . learned something from experience—this paper found itself able conscientiously to support him for high public office and to commend his official acts and policies. . . . He lived to see wonderful changes in the isolated country to which he came as a young man, and none will dispute the influential role he performed in effecting these changes." The notice ended with a short admiration of Baskin's personal traits: "He was not of the

---

[35]"Judge Baskin," *DN*, August 27, 1918, 4/2.

amiable, social temperament that makes friends everywhere; but he had the qualities that grappled to him with hoops of steel those with whom he entered into the bonds of real intimacy."[36]

The *Salt Lake Tribune* recapped Baskin's life in Utah, ending with this accolade: "Having brought about those reforms for which he and his associates fought, Judge Baskin became one of the most generally esteemed men in the state. He was admired by Mormon and Gentile alike."[37] In September the Utah Supreme Court impaneled a select group of men, similar to that assembled to memorialize Judge Zane, to formulate a commemoration of recognition and honor for Judge Baskin.[38]

The location of Baskin's funeral report, relegated to the lesser pages of the *Salt Lake Herald*, was insultingly inconsistent with the respect due him for his public service that spanned more than fifty years. Nestled among items titled "Gas in the Stomach Is Dangerous," "Patriotic Pageant at Liberty Park," and "Mrs. Dooley's Advice to Working Girls" was a short report: "Utmost simplicity marked the services held yesterday afternoon in the Masonic temple for Judge Robert N. Baskin, who died Monday. The funeral was conducted by Mt. Moriah Lodge No. 2, with Dr. H. P. Kirtley presiding." Regarding the funeral service program, it was reported that Rev. Elmer I. Goshen had reviewed "the remarkable career of the accomplished jurist, dwelling upon the accomplishments of Salt Lake the inspiration for which came from Judge Baskin, such as the erection of the city and county building." Parley Williams, an intimate friend of Judge Baskin for many years, delivered a panegyric, "dwelling at length upon the sterling character of his friend, as revealed through the many years of intimate acquaintanceship which he enjoyed."[39] There was no music, but a profusion of flowers attested the esteem of many friends.[40]

---

[36]Ibid.

[37]"Judge R. N. Baskin Dies in Salt Lake," *SLT*, August 27, 1918, 14/6.

[38]Those named to the committee were Judge Bartch, Parley L. Williams, Charles C. Dey, Franklin S. Richards, William H. Dickson, Charles Baldwin, and E. B. Critchlow. "Baskin Remembered," *SLTel*, September 25, 1918, 8/7.

[39]"Final Rites for Judge R. N. Baskin," *SLH*, August 30, 1918, 12/3. Parley L. Williams came to Utah in 1871, became a Mount Mariah Lodge member, and followed Baskin as Worshipful Master in 1882 and 1883. A founding member of the Alta Club, Williams had been a Mormon but became an opponent and critic. "Most Worshipful Brother Parley Lycurgus Williams," Grand Lodge of Utah website, www.utahgrandlodge.org/pgm/pgm-parley-lycurgus-williams.html.

[40]"Masons Conduct Baskin Funeral," *SLT*, August 30, 1918, 9/5. Pallbearers were Charles F. Jennings, William G. Churches, A. W. Christensen, Samuel Paul, William H. Branel, and C. J. Higson. "Baskin Funeral at Masonic Temple," *DN*, August 30, 1918, 8/6.

At Baskin's death, he was survived by three sisters, one sister-in-law, and at least eight nieces and nephews. None were named in his will, none cared for him in his final days. and except for one nephew, none were present at his funeral. Newspapers reports indicate that the funeral was delayed until instructions could be received from nephew William Craig McBride, a railroad employee in Portland, Oregon. He was the son of Baskin's sister Martha J. Baskin McBride.[41] McBride arrived in the city, apparently not accompanied by his wife, on August 28 and attended the funeral.[42]

Baskin's family burial site at Mount Olivet Cemetery is without any headstone or identifying marker. Other than two brief notations of "R. N. Baskin" and "M. Baskin," no dates, no names, gender, or indication of relationship are to be found in the sexton's records. Daughter Katherine C. Baskin Peyton's remains, allegedly moved from their initial interment in the Salt Lake City Cemetery to Mount Olivet, are not documented in the latter's existing records. The twelve-grave Baskin plot lies directly west and adjacent to the twenty-foot-high obelisk on Judge James Bedell McKean's plot, donated by the community in memory of their much maligned contemporary.[43]

A Serious Man, A Loner

It is consistent with his personality that Robert Newton Baskin was devastated by the death of his wife of twenty-three years, for he was a reserved individual who did not share his emotions or deeply personal matters with others but Olive Lavinia. With their three children prematurely deceased, their relationship as husband and wife was the only family constant. Even so, Baskin had spent long periods in Washington, away from Olive, seeking through personal contacts to bring legislation to Utah.

Despite sharing several very significant events of Utah's battles over polygamy and theocracy, such as the arrest of Brigham Young, the

---

[41]"Nephew Will Come to Baskin Funeral," *SLTel*, August 27, 1918, 6/3.

[42]"W. C. McBride Here for Baskin Funeral," *SLH*, August 29, 1918, 5/6. William Craig McBride, age thirty-two, and Clara H. Ruffner, age twenty-eight, both of Salt Lake, were issued a marriage license on August 18, 1896, in Salt Lake City. "City and Neighborhood," *SLT*, August 19, 1896, 8/1. Clara had been previously married and had a son, Ralph R. Ruffner, born in 1886 in Colorado.

[43]Recent exploration by the sexton of plot O-124 found no evidence of sunken gravestones, excluding the possibility that stones were gradually covered by ninety-two years of turf buildup.

trial of John D. Lee, and the contest of George Q. Cannon's congressional seat by fellow Liberal Party stalwart George R. Maxwell, there is bare mention by Baskin of Maxwell or of Patrick Connor or other founders the Liberal Party. Baskin gave modest praise to U.S. attorney William Carey for having been incorruptible and having faithfully discharged the duties of his office. However, Baskin confided before the trial to *Tribune* editor Frederic Lockley that he judged Carey incapable of conducting the prosecution of John D. Lee for the Mountain Meadows murders.[44] Baskin had for many years wanted the opportunity to charge Brigham Young as responsible for the deaths at Mountain Meadows and his ability led to his upstage of Carey in this matter.

Infrequently, Baskin's short temper led him to physical violence—for example, when he came to battle with fellow Mason and judge Cyrus Myron Hawley and with former U.S. prosecuting attorney Sumner Howard. He nearly came to blows with Judge Orlando Powers, who had made remarks critical of Judge Charles S. Zane, the person for whom Baskin held highest admiration.

With the exception of Enos D. Hoge, little is known of conviviality between Baskin and former military officers who came to Utah after the Civil War. Baskin had no seat at a Grant campfire or with Lee's enduring admirers, for he lacked the shared experiences that transformed enemies during the war into respected comrades afterward. The commander of Camp Douglas, Gen. Andrew Morrow, and the California Volunteers' Gen. Patrick Connor were not likely candidates with whom Baskin would spend an evening imbibing a few alcoholic beverages, even if he had been so inclined. No instances of overindulgence in, or even an inclination toward, alcohol consumption is found in any contemporary accounts. Quiet time among colleagues at the Alta Club or the University Club was a better fit. Unlike Gen. George R. Maxwell, who was loved in spite of his faults, or perhaps because of them, Baskin showed no soft underside of vulnerability that would have been endearing to imperfect friends. He was certainly capable of humor, but the record is scant for occasions when he indulged in a hearty belly laugh or made himself the target of a humorous episode. When Baskin—persistent in pursuing what he judged correct, essentially good-hearted and self-denying—formed bonds of friendship, they were not readily broken.

---

[44]Lockley to his wife, Beaver, Utah Territory, July 26, 1875, "Lockley Manuscript," 87.

Judging by the sparsity of his estate and by the reports at his death, Baskin outlived his funds, and in his longevity he also outlasted admiring contemporaries who might have provided for him. However, his pride would likely have prevented his accepting such a gift.

It is tempting to speculate that Baskin's 1863 fatal confrontation with Andrew West permanently affected his ties to his family, since no record has been found that he visited them in the Midwest or that they ever visited him in Utah. If his surviving blood relations in Oregon, California, Ohio, or Missouri provided for a memorial gravestone, it is no longer present.

In the last pages of his final published work, Robert Baskin gently affirmed his many friends, saying, "I have . . . , at the present time, the friendship and respect of a host of 'Mormons.' I am now, and ever have been, a friend of the masses of the people of the Territory."[45]

---

[45]Baskin, *RCSW*, 27.

22

The Father of Modern Utah

It is in our lives, and not from our words, that our religion must be read.
THOMAS JEFFERSON, 1816

T HE CORE ISSUE WHOSE RESOLUTION EARNS ROBERT
Newton Baskin recognition as the intrepid father of modern
Utah is well articulated by distinguished historians David L.
Bigler and Will Bagley:

> A theocracy, ruled by God from the heavens above, cannot live within a
> democratic republic, governed by its people from earth below, without
> civil warfare. By nature, the two governing systems are incompatible
> and cannot exist side by side, or one within the other, without conflict.
> As long as both live under the same roof, there will be a struggle for
> supremacy that can end only when one compels the other to either
> bend or be gone.[1]

Baskin's life in Utah was a pertinacious forty-year struggle. From
organizing the Liberal Party to serving on Utah's supreme court,
he conducted indefatigable "civil warfare" to eliminate theocracy, to
compel the Mormons' law of God to bend to the laws of the nation.
His quarrel was not with the Mormon rank and file. His was primarily an engagement with the elite of Mormon leadership, who, from
1850 to 1890, would—and could—see no theologically acceptable way
to compromise their religious practices. The Mormon people were
told—and within their ken, many sincerely believed—that they were

---

[1]Bigler and Bagley, *Mormon Rebellion*, 8–9.

loyal American citizens whose federal government, under the influence of a Protestant-based establishment, had denied their right to free and full exercise of their religion, as provided by the Unites States' divinely inspired constitution. In their "Kingdom of God on earth," Saints insisted that God's law—as revealed to them alone—was primary, and they righteously disagreed that federal law was preeminent, as the non-Mormons living in Utah and elsewhere insisted.

A title of special recognition would embarrass Baskin, who would say only that he sought to bring to all the territory's people the same benefits and freedoms of U.S. citizenship that other Americans enjoyed. Validation of the title might come if, by some miracle, Brigham Young, Sr., George Q. Cannon, John Taylor, and others who had been the strongest proponents of theocracy were to be resurrected to visit Salt Lake City during a spring or fall semiannual conference. Such visitors would find, not a body of Saints espousing polygamy, but a populace who had approved a state constitutional amendment defining the only acceptable marriage as that between "a man and a woman." By this action, Mormons placed on themselves a legal limitation of marriage that they had vehemently opposed for nearly 160 years when others, outside the faith, tried to place it on them by legislation and by constitutional amendment. It is ironic that opposition in the contemporary issue of same-gender marriage, not in the matter of plural wives, brought Utah's Constitutional Amendment 3 of 2004. Touring Salt Lake City now, the formerly revered, now long-gone Mormon brethren would find that church and state are no longer one, ruled by the powerful few. In Utah, society is not structured to the ends they dedicated their lives and energies to achieve but is more precisely aligned with the goals and freedoms that Robert Baskin foresaw as the bright future of Utah: supremacy of civil law; freedom of thought, speech, and action; acceptance of open dissent; and honest elections without fear of ecclesiastical punishment. He worked for a society in which all citizens could exercise their individuality, could freely choose their own goals, political leaders, and business relations. Each could have an equal chance, by personal worth and dint of honest effort, to attain the highest social, political, and economic advancement. Each could manage his own affairs, hold secure title to his property, and "run the course of life without weight upon his shoulders."[2]

---

[2]Baskin, *RCSW*, 27–28.

A Life of Contributions to Utah

Robert Baskin's decision to stop in Salt Lake City after killing a farm-hand bully in self-defense in Ohio was probably preplanned. Speculation in mining seemed unlikely as the primary motivation for a Harvard-educated and seasoned lawyer. Baskin likely reasoned that vengeance-seeking men from Ohio were far more inclined to search the booming lands farther west than to seek him among the weird Mormons in their mountain stronghold. Whatever drove his decision to live in Salt Lake City, he left a lifelong record of service and accomplishment that should have earned him commemoration, recognition, and the gratitude of the people of Utah Territory.

On first reading Utah statutes, Baskin was surprised that the Utah legislature had excluded the principles of common law and legal precedent from judicial use in the territory and accepted only laws that the Mormons themselves had written. Shock followed surprise as Baskin reacted to the violence transpiring in the territory. The opening chapter of *Reminiscences* tells of a number of audacious murders, including that of his friend and client Dr. John King Robinson. Baskin's enduring desire for justice for Robinson's murder was never realized.

Mormon marriages were not made a public record, so Baskin recognized early that proving the existence of plural marriage was almost impossible. Thus, he took some pride for achieving the first conviction for behavior that arose from a second marriage, without the need for documenting the marriage. Thomas Hawkins was found guilty of violating a territorial law against adultery, based on the testimony of his first wife's description of the sexual union of her husband and his new, second wife. While Baskin placed substantial importance on this first conviction, it seems relatively inconsequential in comparison with the later changes for which he was responsible.[3]

Early in Baskin's Utah career, his courage and desire for justice, together with those of Judge James B. McKean and U.S. marshal George R. Maxwell, surpassed good judgment as the three fearlessly accused Brigham Young of "lewd and lascivious cohabitation" and of complicity in the 1857 murder of munitions seller Richard Yates. The general public held a measure of sympathy for the Mormon leader, and some among the non-Mormons were relieved that violence would be avoided when all charges against Young, along with 130 other unrelated

---

[3]Baskin, *REM*, 39–41.

district court actions, were dismissed based on the U.S. Supreme Court's *Clinton v. Englebrecht* decision.[4]

Baskin devoted more space in *Reminiscences* to the Mountain Meadows mass murders than to any other issue. As the chief prosecutor in the trial of John D. Lee, he was convinced that Mormon leaders much higher in rank than Lee had at least been complicit in the killings, if not ordered them. Baskin saw confirmation of their guilt in the failure of the Mormon Militia's officers at the highest levels who had the authority and obligation to convene an immediate drumhead court-martial to try, convict, and punish the perpetrators forthwith. Further proof was evident when the LDS Church made no provisions for the welfare of the orphans created by the murders. With a predominantly Mormon jury, Baskin recognized the unlikelihood of a verdict against Lee; therefore he used the trial as a bully pulpit to broadcast his convictions about the responsibility of Mormon leaders. Appearing in newspapers across the nation, his trial remarks were important in Young's conviction in the much larger court of public opinion following Lee's trials and his execution. Though he held no doubt of Lee's guilt, Baskin decried the conviction obtained via a packed jury and evidence that was substantially concocted. He harbored no uncertainty that secret agreements had been made between prosecutor Sumner Howard and Brigham Young to avoid placing responsibility on anyone but Lee.

Baskin saw the origins of the Mountain Meadows atrocity in the Mormon Reformation that preceded his arrival. A culture of violence characterized this period and involved, in numbers not documentable, blood atonement for the remission of sins. Historian Michael Quinn has extensively documented that "themes of violence and vengeance became both normal and pervasive in LDS sermons, hymns, newspaper editorials and patriarchal blessings for decades" and that such themes were "officially approved and published by the LDS Church in pioneer Utah."[5] Baskin did not use the term "dictator" or "totalitarian state," but he lived through a time when Utah possessed a monarch with tenure for life, and most of the ingredients of a totalitarian state, including a single political party; a private army; scrutiny of the mail; a secret police force; commonplace euphemisms, even from the pulpit,

---

[4]Maxwell, *GGSL*, 160–62.
[5]Quinn, "Culture of Violence," 28.

for sanctioned murder; election slates chosen by religious leaders, and elections that were virtually unanimous; a controlled economy; a refashioning of written history; isolation from outside influence; and a high degree of control of entry and departure from the territory—especially on Mormon apostates and critics of the Mormon leadership—often enforced by violence or its threat.

With pathetically small numbers to challenge the overwhelming majority enrolled by the Mormons' People's Party, Liberals repeatedly brought attention to matters in Utah by contesting the qualifications of Mormons elected to Congress. William H. McGroarty, an early Liberal Party man, did so after his loss to William Hooper in 1867. Baskin also aided George R. Maxwell in challenging the seating of George Q. Cannon. When these efforts failed, Baskin himself twice challenged Cannon but failed to unseat the Mormons' luminary. Baskin proved that Cannon's citizenship had been obtained by fraud, and in 1880 this issue, together with Cannon's multiple marriages, effectively ended the apostle's career in national politics. Another Baskin effort at election to Congress resulted in another defeat, this time by his frequent adversary John T. Caine.

Senator Shelby Cullom of Illinois introduced an 1870 bill drafted by Baskin and several of his Salt Lake City lawyer friends. Its provisions would have ended theocracy in Utah much earlier, and the later Edmunds Acts would not have been needed, Baskin insisted. The Cullom Bill did not pass, and joined the bone pile that would eventually include at least twenty-five failed attempts at federal legislation.[6] All were defeated or derailed by making the abolition of polygamy analogous to that of slavery, through the cooperation and mutual benefit of a complex network of influential businessmen and politicians cultivated by Young and George Q. Cannon, and through the judicious use of well-placed cash disbursements.

Baskin spent much of 1886 in Washington, where he was responsible—more than any other individual—for the enactment of the draconian Edmunds-Tucker Act, which confiscated LDS Church properties

---

[6]Bills that were entered in the House or Senate but died in committee or failed passage include Logan, 1860; Nelson, 1860; Browning, 1863; Richardson, 1863; Julian, 1863; Wade, 1866; Cragin, 1867; Ashley, 1869; Cullom, 1870; Stewart, 1870; Clagett, 1872; Voorhees, 1872, 1886; Merritt, 1873; Frelinghuysen, 1873; Logan, 1874; McKee, 1874; Luttrell, 1876; Christiancy, 1876, 1877; Woodburn, 1886; McAdoo, 1886; Van Eaton, 1886; Hailey, 1887; and Cullom and Struble, 1889.

and dissolved the Perpetual Emigrating Fund. These two acts—the Edmunds and the Edmunds-Tucker—were pivotal in finally reducing Mormon theocracy. Following his efforts to bring in the verdict by Judge Thomas J. Anderson that Mormons were unfit for citizenship, Baskin returned to Washington in April 1890, having written another bill. Had it passed, it might have been the coup de grâce to the LDS Church, which was struggling under the two Edmunds bills. Introduced in the Senate as the Cullom Bill and in the House as the Struble Bill, the proposed legislation would have denied the privileges of voting, serving on juries, and holding public office to those who lived in, believed in, taught, or supported polygamous marriage. A test oath would have required each elector to swear that he or she was not a bigamist or polygamist and was not a member of any organization that taught or supported polygamous marriage. Passage of the Cullom and Struble bills was avoided only after Mormon leaders and emissaries personally appealed to Shelby Cullom and Isaac Struble, who agreed to temporary stay of action, pending a move by Mormons to end polygamy. President Wilford Woodruff's Manifesto against the practice was thought to be the sincere implementation of that promise, but later events proved its insincerity. Repeatedly the promise was broken by Woodruff and other LDS leaders, with plural marriages continuing in secret until 1910.

Although leaving little in his records regarding the Senate investigations that followed the 1902 election of Reed Smoot, Baskin believed that Smoot met the requirements, had been duly elected, and should have been seated. When the actions of LDS president Joseph F. Smith and other ranking leaders were revealed, Baskin was uncharacteristically muted in his criticism, saying that it was regrettable and humiliating to all that the solemn pledges made by these senior holders of the Mormon priesthood had been violated and dishonored.[7]

Despite the early effectiveness of the Edmunds Acts, the fusion of government and religion continues to a degree in present-day Utah. Mormons still control the state legislature and most elected public offices; for many years political leaders met with the First Presidency prior to state legislative sessions. In 1966, Brigham Young University president Ernest Wilkinson told students, "We are under the same moral obligation to follow [the Prophet's] advice on political as on

[7]Baskin, *REM*, 236.

religious matters."[8] This remains an unspoken or unexamined tenant for many church members. In April 1999 the all-Mormon Salt Lake City Council sold a portion of a downtown block of Main Street to the LDS Church to unify the Temple block space with that of the church's administrative offices; at great expense to the church, the plaza was completed in 2000. The LDS Church's First Presidency published its support of the redefinition of marriage, as proposed in Utah's Constitutional Amendment 3, in a statement released on October 20, 2004, timed to be only days prior to the November election.[9] In 2005 the LDS Church purchased an easement from the city, granting it legal control of entry and behavior on its Main Street property. In 2008 the church leaders worked through an obscuring coalition to raise an estimated $25 million from faithful members and others to promote passage of California's Proposition 8, which—like Utah's Constitutional Amendment 3—limited marriage to a man and a woman.[10] And with LDS Church backing and some level of church participation, a multibillion-dollar City Creek Center revitalization of commercial properties and new business ventures on Main Street and beyond was begun in 2006 when LDS Presiding Bishop H. David Burton presented the conceptual design to the Salt Lake City Council. Henry B. Eyring, First Counselor in the LDS Church First Presidency, was the prominent speaker at the official ribbon-cutting ceremony on March 22, 2012.

As a legislator in 1891, Baskin was influential in the passage of the first territorial act to provide for free public education in Utah, which Mormons had opposed for forty years. The exclusive Mormon control of education was finally overcome only by Baskin's political connection to Senator George Edmunds, who introduced federal legislation written by Utah's non-Mormons that would have been more demanding and costly for Utah than the bill then pending before the territorial lawmakers. The LDS Church continues to be significantly involved with Utah public schools, with Mormon "seminary" school buildings situated adjacent to almost all public high schools and public universities in the state. Before school and during free periods, students may leave school property to attend classes in Mormon history, theology,

---

[8]Bergera, "1966 BYU Student Spy Ring," 170.

[9]LDS Church, "First Presidency Statement on Same-Gender Marriage," www.mormonnewsroom .org/article/first-presidency-statement-on-same-gender-marriage.

[10]Californians Against Hate, www.californiansagainsthate.com.

and doctrine, and in past years students received academic credit for seminary classes.[11]

It is difficult to say whether the mellowing of the conflict between Mormons and non-Mormons led to Baskin's election as Salt Lake City's mayor, or whether the praiseworthy changes brought by his responsible actions in his two terms as mayor initiated moderation and better relations. Evidence supports the latter, as Baskin set into place many much-needed and long-delayed upgrades to the city's infrastructure. Water supply, sewage lines, paved roads, sidewalks, and lighting, all financed by a combination of long-term bonds and special taxes, brought modernity to the city and vastly improved the community's health. Remarkably, these improvements were accomplished as Baskin herded the fractious elements of the city and county councils and avoided the self-serving resistance among council members.

During his time as mayor, Baskin was also responsible for construction of the City-County Building on Washington Square that housed city, county, and state offices until the Utah State Capitol was completed in 1915. Non-Mormons could take pride in a structure that rivaled, in size and splendor, the Salt Lake Mormon Temple. The 1989 multimillion-dollar restoration of the City-County Building was both a tribute to and a confirmation of Baskin's vision and that of his colleagues who also supported the project.

With the Woodruff Manifesto ending plural marriages, with the People Party's disbandment, and with Utah statehood seemingly assured, the purposes of the Liberal Party had been achieved. Baskin was the first to recognize and admit that the organization to which many non-Mormon men had devoted much of their lives was now without purpose. Or so it seemed. Baskin shifted his allegiance to the Independent and Citizens movement, a fluid group composed of former Democrats and former Republicans, and under this new banner he was reelected as mayor. After the passage of the Utah Enabling Act by Congress, the Liberal Party meekly followed Baskin's lead and officially disbanded, leaving, for a time at least, the political landscape to the nation's two major parties. Baskin aligned briefly with

---

[11]The 1948 U.S. Supreme Court held that religious instruction in public schools was unconstitutional, but allowed "released time" to attend private religious classes off campus, subject to certain restrictions. *McCollum v. Board of Education*, 333 U.S. 203. In Utah, the criteria are defined in the Utah Administrative Code, Rule R277-610.

the liberal Democrats of the Tuscarora Society, and even more briefly with the American Party, formed in 1904 when the Mormon priesthood's deceit was exposed by the findings in the Smoot hearings.

In Baskin's final year as mayor, he dealt fairly with the invasion of Utah by thousands of unemployed workers from California, on their way to Washington to plead for government-sponsored employment. Baskin and Ogden officials initially tried to take a hard line against the migrants. But when the Southern Pacific continued to transport them to Utah, and the Union Pacific refused to take them eastward, it soon became apparent to Baskin that food and aid to the migrants were a better solution than forceful removal.

Three years after statehood became official, Baskin began his term as a judge in the Utah Supreme Court, having defeated his close personal friend Charles S. Zane, the Utah judicial figure he most admired. Through Baskin's years on the court, including two as the chief justice, he compiled a judicial record uniformly praised by his peers.

For more than a decade after concluding this supreme court service, Baskin vigorously sought action and wealth by exploration for silver, lead, and other Great Basin mineral treasures. Most of this enthusiasm was focused on the ventures in American Fork Canyon, but successes battled with failures, with failures finally winning. He died financially depleted, his wealth disappearing in mining, thoroughbred horse breeding, land speculation, and other investments. His mind was still facile at age seventy-seven when he wrote his corrections of Utah history, *Reminiscences of Early Utah*, and it remained so at age seventy-nine, for writing his last book, *Reply to Certain Statements of O. F. Whitney*.

SILENCES

Mormon historian and analyst Michael Quinn has observed, "In the writing of Mormon history there have been many silences. Although one person's definition of a significant topic in human experience is another's irrelevance, most silences in Mormon history writing are the results of public relations and defensive censorship."[12] It is understandable, even expected, that the Saints contemporary with Baskin

---

[12]Quinn, *Same-Sex Dynamics*, ix.

would not, could not, look dispassionately at efforts that they saw as destructive to what they firmly believed was God-ordained, and find any reason for recognition or praise. Yet contemporary historians have also remained mute on any positive effect of non-Mormon opposition in Utah's pre-statehood era.

An opinion frequently voiced in the nineteenth century's latter half was that Utah would never gain statehood until polygamy was forsaken and some measurable separation of church and state achieved. Polygamy, not theocracy, was more often named as the chief obstacle, as it was more effectively opposed. Mormon-authored publications have not suggested the possibility that well-intentioned stalwarts who repeatedly delayed or derailed numerous congressional acts made costly mistakes of judgment. Utah could have been brought sooner into statehood, and the Church of Jesus Christ of Latter-day Saints sooner into more general acceptance, had these leaders been flexible in living what they considered to be God's command, and had they not invoked a cry of persecution against each effort made for change. This qualifies as one of the silences of which Quinn speaks—the failure to acknowledge that the Mormon Church and its people benefitted from the laws forced on them, that statehood benefits and acceptance closer to the religious mainstream resulted when the Saints were required to relinquish theocracy and plural marriage practices. A recent study reported that 68 percent of Mormons believe they are not yet viewed as part of mainstream American society, but 63 percent believe that Mormonism will become so.[13]

"Ultimately, Mormonism was forced from its sectarian character and into the mainstream of American life by the revocation of its charter and the escheatment of its property, rather than by the free competition of ideas," says Robert Kent Fielding.[14] Historian Lawrence Foster did not specifically credit non-Mormon opposition for bringing about change, but that conclusion is implicit in his observation: "If, indeed, the Mormon Church had not begun to give up the practice of polygamy in 1890, Mormonism could never have achieved

---

[13]Pew Forum on Religion and Public Life, "New Poll: Pew Forum on Religion and Public Life Surveys Mormons in America," January 12, 2012, www.pewforum.org/Press-Room/Press-Releases/New-Poll--Pew-Forum-on-Religion---Public-Life-Surveys-Mormons-in-America.aspx.

[14]Fielding, *Unsolicited Chronicler*, v.

any degree of acceptance in America. Instead, the group would have remained at best a deviant and despised subculture, rather than the world-embracing church which it aspires to become."[15] From a broad perspective of social change, historian and sociologist Armand Mauss offers another interpretation, that Mormonism may have disappeared entirely: "The unpopular Mormon movement, having failed in a desperate nineteenth-century struggle for religious and political autonomy, finally achieved success and respectability in North America by abandoning its most offensive practices and deliberately pursuing a policy of assimilation with the surrounding American culture."[16] Disappearance by full assimilation into the religious mainstream was the risk on one side. On the other was the movement's elimination for remaining too extreme. In negotiating that narrow middle path, Mormonism has been one of the very few "peculiar" religious movements to survive and grow, Mauss said in his 1994 work.[17] In his reassessment in 2011, Mauss weighs the balance between Mormon "assimilation"—that is, movement toward liberal social positions— and "retrenchment," retaining conservative and distinctive features that marked the past. He notes assimilation in matters such as gender roles, sexual orientation, openness to criticism, transparency, and outreach, but retrenchment on matters of "the only *one* true church," the primacy of priesthood authority, recruitment through missionary proselytizing, and the salvation of the dead. Overall, he concludes, "The actual pattern seems to be two steps toward assimilation and only one back toward retrenchment. The end result is . . . a well-assimilated religious community in the long term."[18] Historians Edwin Brown Firmage and Richard Collin Mangrum hold that, "after the 1890s, the church remained a dominant force, but it became more nearly like one among many churches in a rapidly pluralizing society."[19] Other authors, like Terryl Givens, more recently assert that Mormons remain "schizophrenic," desiring both mainstream acceptance and simultaneous recognition for their distinctive and unique theology. Mormons now take great pride in their acceptance, in counting their

---

[15]Foster, *Religion and Sexuality*, 245.
[16]Mauss, *Angel and the Beehive*, ix.
[17]Ibid., 5.
[18]Mauss, "Rethinking Retrenchment," 21.
[19]Firmage and Mangrum, *Zion in the Courts*, 259.

increasing worldwide membership, and in the prominent role Mormons are taking in national affairs.[20] Today the Saints are viewed by many as "a model of civil order and a pillar of American values," say Bigler and Bagley.[21]

Utah history and much of Great Basin history have been predominantly the history of the Church of Jesus Christ of Latter-day Saints. For many years, the Saints' majority in numbers helped make it so. Immense accomplishment by the Mormons, a record-keeping people who wrote their history as it was occurring, made it so. Even to the present, the sheer volume of testimony-strengthening, faith-promoting bromides, while not qualifying as documented, researched history, contributes to the imbalance of Mormon over non-Mormon accounts.[22] Non-Mormon presence and accomplishment in pre-statehood Utah has often been treated as an element that was, at best, negative, nefarious, and irrelevant to the Mormon record. Early non-Mormons, particularly federal appointees, were described as incompetents, carpetbaggers, and agents of Satan who must be overcome when pitted against the Kingdom of God. The presence of such men gave proof to the Mormon catechism "There must be opposition in all things," and victory validated that God stood with the Saints.

This biography of Robert Newton Baskin, especially when added to those of several Mormon dissenters and of other non-Mormon voices, aims to be "more deeply instructive than a single history" of Utah. It becomes a new historiography to correct the near exclusion of such voices by placing in the record the contributions made by non-Mormons to societal progress and to the attainment of statehood,

---

[20]In 2012 two Mormons, Willard Mitt Romney and Jon Meade Huntsman, Jr., were among those vying for selection as the Republican candidate for the U.S. presidency. Although the LDS Church claims first rank in growth among Christian faiths, the methodology of calculation and the definition of membership cloud the claim. Evangelists and much of the general public continue to class it as a non-Christian cult. In *People of Paradox*, Givens cites a 2007 survey that ranks Mormons among the least-liked faiths, along with Buddhists and Muslims. See also "Prof: LDS Seek and Shun Mainstream Acceptance, Which Hinders Them," *SLT*, November 12, 2010, B5.

[21]Bigler and Bagley, *Mormon Rebellion*, 6.

[22]One historical novelist, Gerald N. Lund, has published eleven books, amounting to nearly seven thousand pages of faith-promoting Mormon stories, with sales of nearly three million copies. Thurston, review of Lund, *The Undaunted: The Miracle of the Hole-in-the-Rock Pioneers*, 220. In June 2011, Deseret Book, the publishing organ of the LDS Church, announced that more than 1,400 books in several genres were available for download to mobile electronic devices.

purposefully denied territorial Utah for forty-six years. As one of Utah's adopted sons, Baskin appreciated the undeniably admirable traits of the Mormons: their industry, their creativity, their devotion to family, and "their suffering, endurance, discipline, faith, brotherly and sisterly charity."[23] Baskin was not an overtly religious man. It is in his beliefs as a Mason, and in his many years of service, that we must read his religion. The father of modern Utah left his message: "I assure the Mormon people I am not their enemy, but their friend. I claim no rights or privileges for myself, as an American citizen, which I do not [wish to] accord to my fellow citizens. . . . In that long contest [between the Liberals and the Mormons], I openly, and above board honestly and untiringly strove to Americanize theocratic Utah."[24] When Robert Newton Baskin left his last words of how he wished— and deserved—to be remembered, he intentionally paraphrased the admission made years before by Brigham Young:[25]

> Though not a prophet, I have been profitable
> to the masses of the Mormon people.

---

[23]Bagley, "'Except as a Friend,'" 114.
[24]Baskin, *RCSW*, 27, 29.
[25]Ibid., 29.

Chronology

December 20, 1837	Born in Jackson, near Hillsboro, Highland County, Ohio.
1853	Attends private school in Ohio.
1856–57	Attends Harvard Law School.
September 1857	Baker-Fancher party is massacred at Mountain Meadows.
March 31, 1863	Shoots Andrew West in self-defense. West dies the following day.
May 1864	Released from all charges in the shooting of West.
August 1865	Arrives in Salt Lake City.
1866	Dr. John King Robinson is murdered.
1867	Enters partnership with Stephen DeWolfe.
1869–70	Writes Cullom Bill, which fails to pass in Senate.
October 1871	Convicts Thomas Hawkins for adultery; charges LDS president Brigham Young with sexual misconduct and murder.
1872	*Ferris v. Higley* goes to U.S. Supreme Court.
October 1874	*Ferris v. Higley* decision affirms restriction of probate courts in Utah.
1874	Challenges George Q. Cannon seating in Congress.
January 1875	Hearing in Salt Lake City to investigate citizenship of George Q. Cannon.
July 1875	Prosecutes first trial of John D. Lee.

January 7, 1876	Death of daughter Della Stella Baskin.
1876	Again challenges George Q. Cannon seating.
August 1877	Death of Brigham Young.
1878	Liberal Party boycotts elections.
1886–87	Has major role in passage of Edmunds-Tucker Act.
February 17, 1888	Death of daughter Katherine C. "Kitty" Baskin Peyton.
November 1888	Defeated for Congress by John T. Caine.
November 1889	Is prosecutor in Third District Court when Mormons declared unfit for citizenship.
1889–90	Major role in formation and near passage of Cullom-Struble Act.
February 1890	Liberals sweep Salt Lake City elections.
February 11, 1890	Wife, Olive Lavinia Gardner Stafford Baskin, dies suddenly.
October 4, 1890	With passage of Cullom-Struble pending, Wilford Woodruff's Manifesto of September 24 published in *Deseret News*.
1891	Mormons' People's Party disbands.
1891	Elected to Utah Territorial Legislature.
1892	Influential in passage of Edmunds Act.
July 1892	Cornerstone laid for City-County Building.
November 1892	Elected mayor of Salt Lake City (the city's second non-Mormon mayor).
September 1893	Severs ties to Liberal Party.
November 1893	Reelected for second term as mayor.
December 1893	Liberal Party disbands.
April 1894	As mayor, faced with "armies" of starving, unemployed workers flowing into Utah.
December 1894	Dedication of completed City-County Building.
January 1896	Utah statehood achieved.
October 1897	Enters partnership with Enos Dougherty Hoge.
November 1898	Elected to Utah State Supreme Court.
June 1901	Gives tribute to Brigham Young at one hundredth anniversary celebration of Young's birthday.
January 1903	Becomes chief justice of Utah Supreme Court.

1905–14	Pursues mineral exploration and mining ventures.
1914	Publishes *Reminiscences of Early Utah*.
1916	Publishes *Reply to Certain Statements by O. F. Whitney*.
November 1916	Elected as Utah's presidential elector; casts a Utah vote for Woodrow Wilson
August 25, 1918	Death and burial at Mount Olivet cemetery in Salt Lake City.

Bibliography

Archival Collections and Public Documents

Buchanan, James. *The Utah Expedition: Message Transmitting Reports from the Secretaries of War, of the Interior, and of the Attorney General, Relative to the Military Expedition Ordered into the Territory of Utah.* 35th Cong., 1st sess., 1857–58. H. Ex. Doc. 71, Serial Set 956.

Buerger, David John. Papers. Special Collections, Marriott Library, University of Utah, Salt Lake City.

Cannon, John Q. Diary, 1857–1931. MS A 155-1. Utah State Archives, Research Center, Salt Lake City.

Collins, William Oliver, and Family. Papers. WH73. Western History Collection, Denver Public Library, Denver, Colo.

Dean, Joseph Henry. Journals, 1876–1944. MS 1530. LDS Church History Library, Salt Lake City.

Godfrey, G. L., A. B. Williams, Alvin Saunders, and R. S. Robertson. *Report of the Utah Commission to the Secretary of the Interior, 1890.* Washington, D.C.: Government Printing Office, 1890.

Harvard Law School. *A Catalogue of the Law School in Harvard University, for the Academical Year 1856–1857.* Cambridge [Mass.]: Charles Folsom, Printer to the University, 1856.

——. *Quinquennial Catalogue of the Law School of Harvard University, 1817–1924.* Cambridge [Mass.], 1925.

Jonas, Frank Herman. Papers. Special Collections, Marriott Library, University of Utah, Salt Lake City.

LDS Church. FamilySearch. International genealogical index. www.familysearch.org.

Lockley, Frederic E. "The Lockley Manuscript." Herbert S. Auerbach Collection on Mormons and Indians, 1808–1935, box 2, folder 6. Department of Rare Books and Special Collections, Princeton University Library, Princeton, N.J.

————. Papers. Henry E. Huntington Library, San Marino, Calif.

Morgan, Dale Lowell. Papers. Bancroft Library, University of California, Berkeley; and microfilm copy, Special Collections, J. Willard Marriott Library, University of Utah, Salt Lake City.

Murray, Eli H. *Message of His Excellency Gov. Eli H. G. Murray, to the Twenty-Sixth Session of the Legislative Assembly of Utah Territory, 1884.* [Salt Lake City]: T. E. Taylor, 1884.

Proceedings of the Grand Lodge of Ancient, Free and Accepted Masons of Utah: Twenty-second Annual Communication. Salt Lake City: Tribune Printing, 1893.

Proceedings of the One Hundred Eighteenth Annual Communication of the Most Worshipful Grand Lodge of Utah. Salt Lake City: Tribune Printing, 1990.

Report of the Fourth Annual Meeting of the State Bar Association of Utah. Salt Lake City: Review Publishing Co., 1897.

Thomas, Sarah C. Castle. Elias Smith's Journal. Vol. 1, 1836–1862; vol. 2, 1863–1874; vol. 3, 1875–1888. Special Collections, Marriott Library, University of Utah, Salt Lake City.

Transcript of the First Trial of John D. Lee, 1875. MS 8191. LDS Church History Library, Salt Lake City.

U.S. Federal Census Collection, 1790–1930. www.ancestry.com.

U.S. Congress. House. *Arguments against the New Edmunds Bill, before the Committee of the Judiciary of the U.S. House of Representatives, First Session, Forty-Ninth Congress.* Washington, D.C.: Government Printing Office, 1886.

————. *Cannon vs. Campbell: Testimony and Papers in the Contested Election of George Q. vs. Allen G. Campbell.* 47th Cong., 1st sess., January 13, 1882. H.R. Mis. Doc. 25.

————. *The Executive Documents of the House of Representatives for the Second Session of the Fifty-Second Congress, 1892–'93.* Washington, D.C.: Government Printing Office, 1893.

————. *The Executive Documents of the House of Representatives for the Third Session of the Fifty-Third Congress, 1894–95.* Washington, D.C.: Government Printing Office, 1895.

————. *George R. Maxwell vs. George Q. Cannon: Papers in the Case of Maxwell vs. Cannon, for a Seat as Delegate from Utah Territory in the 43rd Congress.* 43rd Cong., 1st sess., 1873. H.R. Mis. Doc. 49.

————. *Papers in the Case of Baskin vs. Cannon.* 44th Cong., 1st sess., 1876. H.R. Mis. Doc. 166.

U.S. Congress. House. Committee on Elections. *Cannon vs. Campbell: Contested-Election Case from the Territory of Utah, February 28, 1882.* 47th Cong., 1st sess., H.R. Report 559. Washington, D.C.: Government Printing Office, 1882.

U.S. Congress. Senate. *The Admission of Utah: Arguments in Favor of the Admission of Utah as a State, Made before the Committee on Territories of the United States Senate, First Session, Fiftieth Congress, February 18, 1888.* Washington, D.C.: Government Printing Office, 1888. (USHS, PAM 1928.)

———. *Hearings before the Committee on Territories of the U.S. Senate in Relation to S. 1306, 1892.* Washington, D.C.: Government Printing Office, 1892.

U.S. Department of Justice. Files relating to Utah, 1855–1912, MS 18871, box 1, folder 7, item 20. Utah State Archives, Salt Lake City.

U.S. Department of the Interior. *Annual Report of the Secretary of the Interior, 1880.* Washington, D.C.: Government Printing Office, 1880.

———. *Annual Report of the Secretary of the Interior, 1896.* Vol. 3. Washington, D.C.: Government Printing Office, 1897.

Utah Commission. *Minority Report of the Utah Commission: Existing Laws Declared Sufficient.* [Salt Lake City?] 1887.

———. *Report of the Utah Commission.* Washington, D.C.: Government Printing Office, 1877.

———. *Report of the Utah Commission to the Secretary of the Interior.* Washington, D.C.: Government Printing Office, 1887.

———. *Utah Statehood: Reasons Why It Should Not Be Granted.* Salt Lake City: Tribune Printing, 1887.

Utah Legislative Assembly. House. *House Journal of the Twenty-Eighth Session of the Legislative Assembly of the Territory of Utah, 1888.* Salt Lake City: Tribune Printing and Publishing Co., 1888. (Utah State Archives, ser. 00456, reel 2.)

Utah Legislature. Senate. Records of the 1892 Utah Legislature. Council (Senate) ser. 00499, reel 2. Utah State Archives, Salt Lake City.

The War of the Rebellion: A Compilation of the Official Records of the Union and Confederate Armies. Washington, D.C.: Government Printing Office, 1880–1901.

Welch, Rev. Josiah (1871–1877). Scrapbook. First Presbyterian Church Records. Special Collections, J. Willard Marriott Library, University of Utah, Salt Lake City.

Young, Brigham. Letterpress Copybooks. LDS Church History Library, Salt Lake City. Available at http://churchhistorycatalog.lds.org/primo_library/libweb/pages/dvds/dvd21/contents.jsp.

PUBLISHED WORKS

Aird, Polly. *Mormon Convert, Mormon Defector.* Norman, Okla.: Arthur H. Clark, 2009.

———. Review of *Innocent Blood,* ed. David L. Bigler and Will Bagley. *Journal of Mormon History* 36, no. 2 (Spring 2010): 250–62.

———. "'You Nasty Apostates, Clear Out': Reasons for Disaffection in the Late 1850's." *Journal of Mormon History* 30 (Fall 2004): 129–207.

Aird, Polly, Jeffery A. Nichols, and Will Bagley, eds. *Playing with Shadows: Voices of Dissent in the Mormon West.* Norman, Okla.: Arthur H. Clark, 2011.

Alexander, Thomas G. *Brigham Young, The Quorum of the Twelve, and the Latter-day Saint Investigation of the Mountain Meadows Massacre.* Leonard J. Arrington Mormon History Lecture Series, no. 12. Logan: Utah State University Press, 2007.

———. "Charles S. Zane, Apostle of the New Era." *Utah Historical Quarterly* 34 (Fall 1966): 302.

———. "Faithful Historian Responds." *Dialogue: A Journal of Mormon Thought* 41 (Winter 2008): v–vii.

———. "Federal Authority versus Polygamic Theocracy: James B. McKean and the Mormons." *Dialogue: A Journal of Mormon Thought* 1 (Autumn 1966): 85–100.

———. "Historiography and the New Mormon History: A Historian's Perspective." *Dialogue: A Journal of Mormon Thought* 19 (Fall 1986): 25–49.

———. *Utah, the Right Place: The Official Centennial History.* Salt Lake City: Gibbs Smith, 1995.

Alexander, Thomas G., and James B. Allen. *Mormons and Gentiles: A History of Salt Lake City.* Boulder, Colo.: Pruett Publishing Co., 1984.

Alford, Kenneth L. "Utah and the Civil War Press." *Utah Historical Quarterly* 80 (Winter 2012): 75–92.

Allen, James B. "The Unusual Jurisdiction of County Probate Courts in the Territory of Utah." *Utah Historical Quarterly* 36 (1968): 132–42.

Alter, J. Cecil. *Utah, the Storied Domain: A Documentary History.* 3 vols. Chicago and New York: American Historical Society, 1932.

Amherst College Biographical Record, Centennial Edition, 1821–1921. Edited by Robert S. Fletcher and Malcolm O. Young. Amherst, Mass.: The College, 1927.

Anderson, Bernice Gibbs. "The Gentile City of Corinne." *Utah Historical Quarterly* 9 (July–October 1941): 141–54.

Appletons' Annual Cyclopaedia and Register of Important Events, 1888. N.s., vol. 13. New York: D. Appleton and Co., 1889.

Arrington, Leonard J., ed. "Crusade against Theocracy: The Reminiscences of Judge Jacob Smith Boreman of Utah, 1872–1877." *Huntington Library Quarterly* 24 (November 1960): 1–45.

———. *From Quaker to Latter-day Saint: Bishop Edwin D. Wooley.* Salt Lake City: Deseret Book Co., 1976.

———. *Great Basin Kingdom: An Economic History of the Latter-Day Saints, 1830–1900.* Cambridge, Mass.: Harvard University Press, 1958.

————. "Utah and the Depression of the 1890s." *Utah Historical Quarterly* 29 (January 1961): 3–21.

Ashton, Clifford L. *The Federal Judiciary in Utah*. Salt Lake City: Utah Bar Foundation, 1988.

Bagley, Will. *Blood of the Prophets: Brigham Young and the Massacre at Mountain Meadows*. Norman: University of Oklahoma Press, 2002.

————. "Conan Doyle Was Right: Danites, Avenging Angels and Holy Murder in the Mormon West." In *A Tangled Skein*, edited by Leslie S. Klinger, 3–29. New York: Baker Street Irregulars, 2008.

————. " 'Except as a Friend': Wallace Stegner among the Mormons." *Utah Historical Quarterly* 78, no. 2 (Spring 2010): 100–117.

————. *So Rugged and Mountainous: Blazing the Trails to Oregon and California, 1812–1848*. Vol. 1 of *Overland West: The Story of the Oregon and California Trails*. Norman: University of Oklahoma Press, 2010.

Bagley, Will, and David L. Bigler, eds. *Innocent Blood: Essential Narratives of the Mountain Meadows Massacre*. Norman: University of Oklahoma Press / Arthur H. Clark, 2010.

Bakken, Gordon M. "The English Common Law in the Rocky Mountain West." *Arizona and the West* 11 (Summer 1969): 109–28.

Bancroft, Hubert Howe. *History of Utah*. San Francisco: History Co., 1890.

Barney, Ronald O. *One Side by Himself: The Life and Times of Lewis Barney*. Logan: University of Utah Press, 2001.

Baskin, Robert N. *Reminiscences of Early Utah*. Salt Lake City: Tribune-Reporter Printing Co., 1914, reprinted Salt Lake City: Signature Books, 2006.

————. *Reply to Certain Statements by O. F. Whitney in His History of Utah*. Salt Lake City: Lakeside Printing Co., 1916. Reprint, Salt Lake City: Signature Books, 2006.

Beadle, John Hanson. *Life in Utah; or, the Mysteries and Crimes of Mormonism*. Philadelphia: National Publishing Co., 1870.

Bean, Edwin F., ed. *The Destroying Angels of Mormondom; or, a Sketch of the Life of Orrin Porter Rockwell, the Late Danite Chief*. San Francisco: Alta California Printing House, 1878.

Bennett, Richard E., Susan Easton Black, and Donald Q. Cannon. *The Nauvoo Legion in Illinois: A History of the Mormon Militia, 1841–1846*. Norman: Arthur H. Clark, 2010.

Bergera, Gary James. *Conflict in the Quorum: Orson Pratt, Brigham Young, Joseph Smith*. Salt Lake City: Signature Books, 2002.

————. "The 1966 BYU Student Spy Ring." *Utah Historical Quarterly* 79 (Spring 2011): 164–88.

Bigler, David L. "The Aiken Party Executions and the Utah War, 1857–1858." *Western Historical Quarterly* 38 (Winter 2007): 457–76.

————. *Forgotten Kingdom: The Mormon Theocracy in the American West, 1847–1896*. Logan: Utah State University Press, 1998.

————. *Fort Limhi: The Mormon Adventure in Oregon Territory*. Spokane, Wash.: Arthur H. Clark, 2003.

————. "Garland Hurt, the American Friend of the Utahs." *Utah Historical Quarterly* 62 (Spring 1994): 149–70.

————. Review of *Reminiscences*, by Robert N. Baskin. *Journal of Mormon History* 33 (Fall 2007): 191.

————. "Terror on the Trail." Paper presented at the twenty-third National Convention of the Oregon-California Trails Association, Salt Lake City, August 19, 2005.

————, ed. *A Winter with the Mormons: The 1852 Letters of Jotham Goodell*. Salt Lake City: Tanner Trust Fund, J. Willard Marriott Library, University of Utah, 2001.

Bigler, David L., and Will Bagley. *The Mormon Rebellion: America's First Civil War, 1857–1858*. Norman: University of Oklahoma Press, 2011.

Bitton, Davis. *George Q. Cannon: A Biography*. Salt Lake City: Deseret Book Co., 1999.

Blight, David W. *Beyond the Battlefield: Race, Memory and the American Civil War*. Amherst: University of Massachusetts Press, 2002.

Bolton, Matthew. Review of *Mormon Convert, Mormon Defector*, by Polly Aird. *John Whitmer Historical Association Journal* 30 (2010): 268–71.

Boone, David F. "The Church and the Civil War." In *Nineteenth-Century Saints at War*, edited by Robert C. Freeman, 113–39. Provo, Utah: BYU Religious Study Center, 2006.

Brooks, Juanita, ed. *On the Mormon Frontier: The Diary of Hosea Stout*. Salt Lake City: University of Utah Press, 1964.

Bunker, Gary L., and Davis Bitton. "The Death of Brigham Young: Occasion for Satire." *Utah Historical Quarterly* 54 (Fall 1986): 358–70.

Bushman, Richard Lyman. *Joseph Smith: Rough Stone Rolling*. New York: Vintage Books of Random House, 2007.

Campbell, Eugene E. *Establishing Zion: The Mormon Church in the American West, 1847–1869*. Salt Lake City: Signature Books, 1988.

Cannon, Charles A. "The Awesome Power of Sex: The Polemical Campaign against Mormon Polygamy." *Pacific Historical Review* 43 (1974): 61–82.

Cannon, Frank J., and George L. Knapp. *Brigham Young and His Mormon Empire*. New York: Fleming H. Revell Co., 1913.

Cannon, Kenneth L., II. "Wives and Other Women: Love, Sex, and Marriage in the Lives of John Q. Cannon, Frank J. Cannon, and Abraham H. Cannon." *Dialogue: A Journal of Mormon Thought* 43 (Winter 2010): 71–130.

Clark, James R., comp. *Messages of the First Presidency of the Church of Jesus Christ of Latter-day Saints, 1833–1964*. 6 vols. Salt Lake City: Bookcraft, 1965–75.

Clark, John Elliott, and Frederick William Hanson, eds. *History of Wasatch Lodge Number One, Free and Accepted Masons of Utah, 1866–1966*. Salt Lake City: Centennial Commission, 1996.

Cleland, Robert Glass, and Juanita Brooks. *A Mormon Chronicle: The Diaries of John D. Lee, 1848–1876*. 2 vols. San Marino, Calif.: Huntington Library, 1955.

Colton, Ray Charles. *The Civil War in the Western Territories, Arizona, Colorado, New Mexico, and Utah*. Norman: University of Oklahoma Press, 1959.

Compiled Laws of the Territory of Utah, Containing All the General Statutes Now in Force. Salt Lake City: Deseret News Steam Printing Establishment, 1876. (S. J. Quinney College of Law, University of Utah, Salt Lake City.)

Compiled Laws of Utah, 1887, 1888. Salt Lake City: Herbert Pembroke, 1887, 1888. (Special Collections, J. Willard Marriott Library, University of Utah, Salt Lake City.)

Cook, Joseph, ed. *Our Day: A Record of Review of Current Reform*. Vol. 9 (January–June 1892). Women's Temperance Publishing Co., Boston and Chicago.

Cooley, Everett L., ed. *Diary of Brigham Young, 1857*. Salt Lake City: Tanner Trust Fund, 1980.

Council and House Journals of the Thirtieth Session of the Legislative Assembly of the Territory of Utah, 1892. Salt Lake City: Irrigation Age Press, 1892.

Cresswell, Stephen. *Mormons and Cowboys, Moonshiners and Klansmen*. Tuscaloosa: University of Alabama Press, 1991.

Curry, Thomas J. *The First Freedoms: Church and State in America to the Passage of the First Amendment*. New York: Oxford Press, 1986.

Davies, George K. "A History of the Presbyterian Church in Utah." *Journal of the Presbyterian Historical Society* 23 (December 1945): 237.

Day-Holmer, Kimberly Maren. "The Importance of Frederick Kesler to the Early Economic History of Utah, 1851–1865." Master's thesis, University of Utah, 1980.

DePillis, Mario S. "Bearding Leone and Others in the Heartland of Mormon Historiography." *Journal of Mormon History* 8 (1981): 79–97.

Dern, George H. *Proceedings of the Grand Lodge of Utah, 1925*. Salt Lake City, 1925.

Dixon, William Hepworth. *New America*. Vol. 1. London: Hurst and Blackett, 1867.

Docent Guide to the City and County Building. Salt Lake City: Utah Heritage Foundation, 2009.

Docent Tour Book and Biography of Springville, Utah's Museum of Art. Springville: Utah Heritage Foundation, n.d.

Dougall, Wil. B. "Utah Legislature of 1892." *Young Woman's Journal* 7, no. 1 (April 1892): 311–14.

Du Bois, John Van Deusen. *Campaigns in the West, 1856–1861: The Journal and Letters of Col. John Van Deusen Du Bois*. Tucson: Arizona Historical Society, 2003.

Duffy, John-Charles. "Can Deconstruction Save the Day? 'Faithful Scholarship' and the Uses of the Postmodernism." *Dialogue: A Journal of Mormon Thought* 41 (Spring 2008): 11–43.

Dwyer, Robert Joseph. *The Gentile Comes to Utah*. Salt Lake City: Western Epics, 1971.

Dyer, Frederick H. *A Compendium of the War of the Rebellion*. Des Moines, Iowa: Dyer Publishing Co., 1908.

Edgerton, Clyde. *Redeye: A Western*. Chapel Hill, N.C.: Algonquin Books, 1995.

Edwards, Paul M. "The Irony of Mormon History." *Utah Historical Quarterly* 41 (Fall 1973): 393–409.

Ekins, Roger Robin. *Defending Zion: George Q. Cannon and the California Newspaper Wars of 1856–1857*. Spokane, Wash.: Arthur H. Clark, 2002.

Ellsworth, Samuel George. *Utah History: Retrospect and Prospect*. Salt Lake City: Utah Historical Society, 1973.

Fielding, Robert Kent. *The Unsolicited Chronicler: An Account of the Gunnison Massacre*. Brookline, Mass.: Paradigm Publications, 1993.

Fielding, Robert Kent, and Dorothy S. Fielding, eds. *The Tribune Reports of the Trials of John D. Lee for the Massacre at Mountain Meadows, November 1874–April 1877*. Higganum, Conn.: Kent's Books, 2000.

Firmage, Edwin Brown, and Richard Collin Mangrum. *Zion in the Courts*. Urbana and Chicago: University of Illinois Press, 1988.

Flake, Kathleen. *The Politics of American Religious Identity*. Chapel Hill: University of North Carolina Press, 2004.

Fogelson, Robert M., and Richard E. Rubenstein. *Mass Violence in America*. New York: Arno Press and New York Times, 1969.

Fohlin, E. V. *Salt Lake City, Past and Present*. Salt Lake City: E. V. Fohlin, 1908.

Ford, Thomas Quaife, and Milo Milton, eds. *A History of Illinois from Its Commencement as a State in 1818 to 1847*. Chicago: S. C. Griggs and Co., 1854. Reprint, Lakeside Classics ed., 2 vols., Chicago: Lakeside Press, 1954.

Foster, Lawrence. *Religion and Sexuality: Three American Communal Experiments of the Nineteenth Century*. New York: Oxford University Press, 1981.

Frank, Michael B., and Harriet Elinor Smith, eds. *Mark Twain's Letters*. Vol. 6. Berkeley: University of California Press, 2002.

Fry, Eleanor. *Peter K. Dotson, Federal Marshal, Rancher, 1823–1898*. Pueblo, Colo.: Pueblo County Historical Society, 2004.

Garcia, Zettie Painter, ed. *Brief History of Stockton, Utah*. Tooele, Utah: Stockton Bicentennial History Committee, 1976.

Gedicks, Frederick Mark. "'No Man's Land': The Place of Latter-day Saints in the Culture War." Bloomington: Poynter Center, Indiana University, 1999. Available at http://ssrn.com/abstract=1085443.

Gee, Elizabeth D. "Justice for All or for the 'Elect'? The Utah County Probate Court, 1855–72." *Utah Historical Quarterly* 48 (1980): 129–47.

Givens, Terryl L. *People of Paradox: A History of Mormon Culture.* New York: Oxford University Press, 2007.

Godfrey, Donald G., and Rebecca S. Martineau-McCarty, eds. *An Uncommon Common Pioneer: The Journals of James Henry Martineau, 1828–1928.* Provo, Utah: Religious Studies Center, Brigham Young University, 2008.

Gooding, Gustin O. *First 100 Years of Freemasonry in Utah, 1872–1972, with a Prologue, 1847–1872.* Salt Lake City: Grand Lodge, Free and Accepted Masons of Utah, 1983.

Goodwin, C. C. [Charles Carroll]. *As I Remember Them.* Salt Lake City: Special Committee of the Commercial Club, 1913.

———. *History of the Bench and the Bar of Utah.* Salt Lake City: Interstate Press Association, 1913.

———. "The Mormon Situation." *Harper's Monthly Magazine*, October 1881, 756–63.

Goodwin, Samuel Henry. *Educational Bulletin Issued by the Committee on Masonic Education and Instruction.* N.p.: Grand Lodge of Utah, September 1924.

———. *Freemasonry in Utah: Thirty Years of Mt. Moriah Lodge No. 2, F. & A.M., 1866–1896.* Salt Lake City, 1930.

Goolrick, William K., and Editors of Time-Life Books. *Rebels Resurgent: Fredericksburg to Chancellorsville.* Alexandria, Va.: Time-Life Books, 1985.

Gordon, Sarah Barringer. *The Mormon Question: Polygamy and Constitutional Conflict in Nineteenth Century America.* Chapel Hill: University of North Carolina Press, 2002.

Green, Nelson Winch. *Fifteen Years among the Mormons: Being the Narrative of Mrs. Mary Ettie V. Smith.* New York: Charles Scribner, 1858.

Grow, Matthew J. *"Liberty to the Downtrodden": Thomas L. Kane, Romantic Reformer.* New Haven, Conn.: Yale University Press, 2009.

Hacker, J. [James] David. "A Census-Based Count of the Civil War Dead." *Civil War History* 57, no. 4 (December 2011): 307–48.

Hansen, Klause J. *Quest for Empire: The Political Kingdom of God and the Council of Fifty in Mormon History.* Lincoln: University of Nebraska Press, 1967.

Hardy, B. Carmon. *Doing the Works of Abraham.* Norman, Okla.: Arthur H. Clark, 2007.

———. *Solemn Covenant: The Mormon Polygamous Passage.* Urbana: University of Illinois Press, 1992.

Hatch, Jeff, James B. Wightman, and Larry Decker. *History of Salt Lake County, 1852–2004*. Salt Lake City: Auditor's Office, Internal Audit Division, 2005.

Hatch, Nathan O. "Mormon and Methodist: Popular Religion in the Crucible of the Free Market." In *The Mormon History Association's Tanner Lecture Series: The First Twenty Years*, edited by Dean L. May and Reid L. Neilson, 65–80. Urbana and Chicago: University of Illinois Press, 2006.

Hatch, William W. *There is No Law: A History of Mormon Civil Relations in the Southern States, 1865–1905*. New York: Vantage Press, 1968.

Hauptman, Lawrence M. "Utah Anti-Imperialist: Senator William H. King and Haiti, 1921–34." *Utah Historical Quarterly* 41 (Spring 1973): 116–27.

Herman, Daniel Justin. *Hell on the Range: A Story of Honor, Conscience and the American West*. New Haven, Conn.: Yale University Press, 2010.

Hewett, Janet B., ed. "Utah Territory." In *The Roster of Union Soldiers, 1861–1865*, 1:43. Wilmington, N.C.: Broadfoot Publishing, 2000.

Hickman, William Adams, with explanatory notes by John Hanson Beadle. *Brigham's Destroying Angel*. Salt Lake City: Sheppard Publishing Co., 1904.

Hilton, Hope A. *"Wild Bill" Hickman and the Mormon Frontier*. Salt Lake City: Signature Books, 1988.

Hoffer, Eric. *The True Believer: Thoughts on the Nature of Mass Movements*. New York: Harper and Row, 1951.

Hogan, Mervin B. "Mormonism and the Founding of the Grand Lodge, F. & A.M., of Arizona," *Transactions of the American Lodge of Research, Free and Accepted Masons* 10, no. 2 (January–December 1970): 287–98.

Holley, Robert P., ed. *Utah's Newspapers—Traces of Her Past*. Salt Lake City: Marriott Library, University of Utah, 1984.

Holzapfel, Richard Neitzel. *Every Stone a Sermon*. Salt Lake City: Bookcraft, 1992.

Holzapfel, Richard Neitzel, and R. Q. Shupe. *Brigham Young: Images of a Mormon Prophet*. Salt Lake City: Eagle Gate; and Provo, Utah: Religious Studies Center, Brigham Young University, 2000.

Homer, Michael W. "The Judiciary and the Common Law in Utah Territory." *Dialogue: A Journal of Mormon Thought* 21 (Spring 1988): 99–110.

———. "Masonry and Mormons in Utah." *Journal of Mormon History* 13, no. 2 (Fall 1992): 57–96.

———. "'Similarity of Priesthood in Masonry'; The Relationship between Freemasonry and Mormonism." *Dialogue: A Journal of Mormon Thought* 27 (Fall 1994): 1–116.

Hough, C. Merrill. "Two School Systems in Conflict: 1867–1890." *Utah Historical Quarterly* 28 (1960): 113–36.

Howard, G. M. "Men, Motives, and Misunderstandings: A New Look at the Morrisite War of 1862." *Utah Historical Quarterly* 44 (1976): 112–32.

Hunt, Gaillard. "The President's Defense, His Side of the Case, as Told by His Correspondence." In "The Impeachment of Andrew Johnson," edited by Josiah Gilbert Holland and Richard Watson Gilde, *Century Magazine* 85, ser. 63 (1912): 429–30.

Iverson, Joan Smyth. *The Anti-polygamy Controversy in U.S. Women's Movements, 1880–1925.* New York: Garland Publishing, 1997.

Ivins, Stanley S. "Free Schools Come to Utah." *Utah Historical Quarterly* 22 (1954): 341.

Jack, Ronald Collett. "Utah Territorial Politics: 1847–1876." PhD diss., University of Utah, 1970.

Jenson, Andrew, ed. *The Historical Record.* Vol. 9. Salt Lake City: Deseret Historical Association, 1890.

Johnson, Elsie Ayers. *Highland Pioneer Sketches and Family Genealogies.* Springfield, Ohio: H. K. Skinner and Son, 1971.

Jones, Robert Huhn. *Guarding the Overland Trails: The Eleventh Ohio Cavalry in the Civil War.* Spokane, Wash.: Arthur H. Clark, 2005.

Kelly, Charles, and Hoffman Birney. *Holy Murder—the Story of Porter Rockwell.* New York: Minton, Batch, 1934.

Klise, Rev. J. W. *The County of Highland.* Hillsboro: Southern Ohio Genealogical Society, 2002.

Lamar, Howard Roberts. *The Far Southwest, 1846–1912.* Albuquerque: University of New Mexico Press, 2000.

Larson, Gustive O. *The Americanization of Utah for Statehood.* San Marino, Calif.: Huntington Library, 1971.

Laycock, Douglas. "The Religious Freedom Restoration Act." BYU *Law Review* 221 (1993): 221–58.

Lee, John D. *Mormonism Unveiled; or, The Life and Confessions of John D. Lee.* Albuquerque: Fierra Blanca Publications, 2001.

Lee, John D., and William W. Bishop. *Mormonism Unveiled; or, The Life and Confessions of John D. Lee.* New York: W. H. Stelle and Co., 1877.

LeSueur, Stephen C. *The 1838 Mormon War in Missouri.* Columbia: University of Missouri Press, 1987.

Linford, Orma. "The Mormons and the Law: The Polygamy Cases." *Utah Law Review* 9 (Summer 1965): 543–91.

Lockley, Frederic E. *The Lee Trial! An Expose of the Mountain Meadows Massacre.* Salt Lake City: Tribune Printing, 1875.

London, Jack. *The Star Rover.* New York: Macmillan; London: Collier-Macmillan, 1963.

Long, E. B. *The Saints and the Union: Utah Territory during the Civil War.* Chicago: University of Illinois Press, 1981.

Lyman, Edward Leo. *Amasa Mason Lyman, Mormon Apostle and Apostate: A Study in Dedication.* Salt Lake City: University of Utah Press, 2009.

————. *Political Deliverance: The Mormon Quest for Utah Statehood.* Urbana and Chicago: University of Illinois Press, 1986.

MacKinnon, William P. *At Sword's Point, Part I: A Documented History of the Utah War to 1858.* Norman, Okla.: Arthur H. Clark, 2008.

Madsen, Brigham D. *Corinne: The Gentile Capital of Utah.* Salt Lake City: Utah State Historical Society, 1980.

————. *Glory Hunter: A Biography of Patrick Edward Conner.* Salt Lake City: University of Utah Press, 1990.

Magleby, James E., and John M. Peterson. *Justices of the Utah Supreme Court, 1896–1996.* Salt Lake City: Quality Press, 1997.

Malmquist, O. N. [Orvin Nebeker]. *The Alta Club, 1883–1974.* Salt Lake City: Utah State Historical Society, 1999.

————. *The First 100 Years: A History of the Salt Lake Tribune, 1871–1971.* Salt Lake City: Utah State Historical Society, 1971.

Marquardt, H. Michael. *The Coming Storm: The Murder of Jesse Thompson Hartley.* Collector's Edition Keepsake for vol. 13 of the Kingdom in the West series. Norman: Arthur H. Clark, 2011.

Marquis, Kathy. "Diamond Cut Diamond: The Mormon Wife vs. the True Woman, 1840–1890." In *Women in Spiritual and Communitarian Societies in the United States,* edited by Wendy E. Chmielewski, Louis J. Kern, and Marlyn Klee-Hartzell, 169–73. Syracuse, N.Y.: Syracuse University Press, 1993.

Mason, Patrick Q. *The Mormon Menace: Violence and Anti-Mormonism in the Postbellum South.* New York: Oxford University Press, 2011.

Mauss, Armand L. *The Angel and the Beehive: The Mormon Struggle with Assimilation.* Urbana and Chicago: University of Illinois Press, 1994.

————. "Rethinking Retrenchment: Course Corrections in the Ongoing Campaign for Respectability." *Dialogue* 44, no. 4 (Winter 2011): 1–42.

Maxwell, John Gary. *Gettysburg to Great Salt Lake: George R. Maxwell, Civil War Hero and Federal Marshal among the Mormons.* Norman, Okla.: Arthur H. Clark, 2010.

May, Dean L. *Utah: A People's History.* Salt Lake City: University of Utah Press, 1987.

McCormick, John S., and John R. Sillito. "Henry W. Lawrence: A Life in Dissent." In *Differing Visions: Dissenters in Mormon History,* edited by Roger D. Launis and Linda Thatcher, 220–40. Urbana and Chicago: University of Illinois Press, 1994.

McMillan, Henry G., ed. *The Inside of Mormonism: A Judicial Examination of the Endowment Oaths Administered in All the Mormon Temples, by the United States District Court for the Third Official District of Utah, to Determine Whether Membership in the Mormon Church Is Consistent with Citizenship in the United States.* Salt Lake City: Utah Americans, 1903.

Mills, Robert Patrick. "Pushing the Car of Progress Forward: The Salt Lake Tribune's Quest to Change Utah for Statehood, 1871–1896." Master's thesis, Utah State University, 2007. http://digitalcommons.usu.edu/etd/101.

Milne, Elijah L. "Blaine Amendments and Polygamy Laws: The Constitutionality of Anti-polygamy Law Targeting Religion." *Western New England Law Review* 28, no. 2 (2006): 256–92. Berkeley Electronic Press.

Moffitt, John Clifton. *The History of Public Education in Utah.* Salt Lake City: Deseret News Press, 1946.

Monks, Leander John, ed. *Courts and Lawyers of Indiana.* Vol. 2. Indianapolis: Federal Publishing Co., 1916.

Moody, Ralph. *Stagecoach West.* Lincoln: University of Nebraska Press, 1967.

Mortensen, A. R., ed. "Elias Smith: Journal of a Pioneer Editor." *Utah Historical Quarterly* 21 (January 1953): 1–24; (April 1953): 137–68; (July 1953): 237–66; (October 1953): 331–60.

Mowery, David L. "Copperheadism in Butler County, Ohio: The 1858 Morgan Township House; Ohio Historical Marker Dedicated on June 16, 2007." Cincinnati Civil War Round Table, June 28, 2007, www.cincinnaticwrt.org.

Munro, Wilfred H. "Among the Mormons in the Days of Brigham Young." *Proceedings of the American Antiquarian Society* 36, no. 2 (October 1926): 214–30.

Murray, Eli H. "The Crisis in Utah." *North American Review* 134, no. 305 (April 1882): 327–46.

Neff, Andrew Love. *History of Utah 1847 to 1869.* Salt Lake City: Deseret News Press, 1940.

Neilson, Reid L., ed. *In the Whirlpool: The Pre-Manifesto Letters of President Wilford Woodruff to the William Atkin Family, 1885–1890.* Norman, Okla.: Arthur H. Clark, 2011.

Nichols, Jeffrey. *Prostitution, Polygamy, and Power: Salt Lake City, 1847–1918.* Urbana and Chicago: University of Illinois Press, 2002.

Noall, Clair Wilcox. "Utah's Pioneer Women Doctors." *Improvement Era* 42 (1939): 16–17.

Novak, Shannon A. *House of Mourning: A Biocultural History of the Mountain Meadows Massacre.* Salt Lake City: University of Utah Press, 2008.

Ogden, Annegret S., ed. *Frontier Reminiscences of Eveline Brooks Auerbach.* Berkeley, Calif.: Friends of the Bancroft Library, 1994.

O'Higgins, Harvey Jerrold, and Frank Jenne Cannon. *Under the Prophet in Utah: The National Menace of a Political Priestcraft.* Boston: C. M. Clark, 1911.

Orwell, George. *1984: A Novel.* New York: Harcourt, Brace, 1949.

———. "The Prevention of Literature. *Polemic,* no. 2 (January 1946): 4–13.

Owens, G., comp. *Salt Lake City Directory: Including a Business Directory of Provo, Springville, and Ogden.* 8 vols. N.p.: G. Owens, 1867.

Perry, L. Tom. "The Articles of Faith." *Ensign*, May 1998, 23–24.

Parshall, Ardis E. "'Pursue, Retake and Punish': The 1857 Santa Clara Ambush." *Utah Historical Quarterly* 73 (Winter 2005): 64–86.

Peterson, Charles S. "A New Community: Mormon Teacher and the Separation of Church and State in Utah's Territorial Schools." *Utah Historical Quarterly* 48 (Summer 1980): 293–312.

———. *Utah: A Bicentennial History*. New York: Norton, 1977.

Peterson, John Alton. *Utah's Black Hawk War*. Salt Lake City: University of Utah Press, 1998.

Poll, Richard D. "The Political Reconstruction of Utah Territory, 1866–1890." *Pacific Historical Review* 27, no. 2 (May 1958): 111–26.

———. *Utah's History*. Logan: Utah State University Press, 1989.

Poore, Benjamin Perley, and O. H. Tiffany. *Life of U. S. Grant*. Edgewood Publishing Co., 1885.

Portrait, Genealogical and Biographical Record of the State of Utah, Containing Biographies of Many Well Known Citizens of the Past and Present. Chicago: National Historical Record Co., 1902.

Powell, Allan Kent. *Utah History Encyclopedia*. Salt Lake City: University of Utah Press, 1994.

Prior, David. "Civilization, Republic, Nation: Contested Keywords, Northern Republicans, and the Forgotten Reconstruction of Mormon Utah." *Civil War History* 56, no. 3 (September 2010): 283–310.

Proceedings of the Grand Lodge of Utah, 1877. Salt Lake City: Tribune Printing and Publishing Co., 1877.

Quinn, D. Michael. "The Culture of Violence in Joseph Smith's Mormonism." *Sunstone* 164 (October 2011): 16–28.

———. "LDS 'Headquarters Culture' and the Rest of Mormonism, Past and Present." *Dialogue: A Journal of Mormon Thought* 34, no. 3–4 (Fall–Winter 2001): 135–64.

———. "A Marketplace of Ideas, A House of Faith, A Prison of Conformity." *Sunstone* 64 (March 1988): 6–7.

———. *The Mormon Hierarchy: Extensions of Power*. Salt Lake City: Signature Books, in association with Smith Research Associates, 1997.

———. *Same-Sex Dynamics among Nineteenth-Century Americans: A Mormon Example*. Urbana: University of Illinois Press, 1996.

———. "Us-Them Tribalism and Early Mormonism." *John Whitmer Historical Association Journal* 29 (2009): 94–114.

Rable, George C. *God's Almost Chosen Peoples: A Religious History of the American Civil War*. Chapel Hill: University of North Carolina Press, 2010.

Reeve, W. Paul, and Ardis E. Parshall, eds. *Mormonism: A Historical Encyclopedia*. Santa Barbara, Calif.: ABC-CLIO, LLC, 2010.

Rich, Christopher B., Jr. "The True Policy for Utah: Servitude, Slavery, and

'An Act in Relation to Service.'" *Utah Historical Quarterly* 80 (Winter 2012): 54–74.

Richards, Mary Stovall. Review of *God's Almost Chosen Peoples*, by George C. Rable. *Utah Historical Quarterly* 79 (Summer 2011): 283–84.

Richardson, James D. *A Compilation of the Messages and Papers of the Presidents.* Vols. 1–19. Washington, D.C.: Bureau of National Literature and Art, 1916.

———. "First Annual Message." In *James Buchanan: A Compilation of the Papers and Messages of the Presidents*, 10–40. Whitefish, Mont.: Kessinger Publishing, 2004.

Ricks, Stephen D., and Daniel C. Peterson. "The Mormon as Magus." Review of *Early Mormonism and the Magic World View*, by D. Michael Quinn. *Sunstone* 12 (January 1988): 38–39.

Roberts, B. H. *Comprehensive History of the Church of Jesus Christ of Latter-day Saints.* Salt Lake City: Deseret News Press, 1930.

Roberts, Richard H., and Richard W. Sadler. "Riding the Rails into the Twentieth Century, 1889–1920." Chapter 5, *A History of Weber County.* Utah Centennial County Series. Utah State Historical Society, 1997.

Rogers, Fred B. *Soldiers of the Overland.* San Francisco: Grabhorn Press, 1938.

Rolph, Daniel N. *"To Shoot, Burn, and Hang": Folk-History from a Kentucky Mountain Family and Community.* Knoxville: University of Tennessee Press, 1994.

Schindler, Harold. *Orrin Porter Rockwell: Man of God, Son of Thunder.* Salt Lake City: University of Utah Press, 1966.

Scott, Patricia Lyn. "The Widow and the Lion of the Lord: Sarah Ann Cooke vs. Brigham Young." *Journal of Mormon History* 30 (Spring 2004): 189–212.

Seifrit, William C. "The Prison Experience of Abraham H. Cannon." *Utah Historical Quarterly* 53 (Summer 1985): 223–36.

Sillitoe, Linda. *A History of Salt Lake County.* Salt Lake City: Utah State Historical Society, 1996.

Smith, George D. *Nauvoo Polygamy: "But We Call It Celestial Marriage."* Salt Lake City: Signature Books, 2008.

Smith, Joseph. "The Globe." *Times and Seasons*, April 15, 1844, 508–10.

Smith, Joseph Fielding. *Essentials of Church History.* Salt Lake City: Deseret News Press, 1922.

Snow, Reuben Joseph. "The American Party in Utah: A Study of Political Party Struggles during the Early Years of Statehood." MA thesis, University of Utah, 1964.

Stegner, Page, ed. *The Selected Letters of Wallace Stegner.* Washington, D.C.: Shoemaker and Hoard, 2007.

Stegner, Wallace. *The Gathering of Zion: The Story of the Mormon Trail.* Lincoln: University of Nebraska Press, 1992.

Stegner, Wallace, and Richard W. Etulain. *Conversations with Wallace Stegner on Western History and Literature*. Salt Lake City: University of Utah
Press, 1983.

Stenhouse, Mrs. T. B. H. *Tell It All: The Story of a Life's Experience in Mormonism*. Hartford, Conn.: A. D. Worthington and Co., 1875.

Stenhouse, Thomas B. H. [Brown Holmes]. *The Rocky Mountain Saints: A
Full and Complete History of the Mormons*. New York: D. Appleton and
Co., 1873.

Stewart, Robert Laird. "Pioneer Work in the Territory of Utah." In *Sheldon
Jackson: Pathfinder and Prospector of the Missionary Vanguard in the Rocky
Mountains and Alaska*, 193–218. New York: Fleming H. Revell Co., 1908.

Stout, Wayne. *History of Utah*. Vol. 1, *1870–1896*. Salt Lake City: Wayne
Stout, 1967.

———. *History of Utah*. Vol. 2, *1896–1929*. Salt Lake City: Wayne Stout,
1968.

———. *A War on the Saints*. Salt Lake City: Wayne Stout, 1974.

Stout, Wayne Durham. *A War on the Saints*. Salt Lake City: New Era Press,
1974.

Sutton, Wain. *Utah: A Centennial History*. New York: Lewis Historical Publication Co., 1949.

Tamez, Jared. Review of *House of Mourning: A Biocultural History of the
Mountain Meadows Massacre*, by Shannon A. Novak. *Journal of Mormon
History* 36 (Spring 2010): 215–19.

Taniguchi, Nancy J. *Necessary Fraud: Progressive Reform and Utah Coal*. Norman: University of Oklahoma Press, 1996.

Thurston, Morris A. Review of *The Undaunted: The Miracle of the Hole-in-the-
Rock Pioneers*, by Gerald N. Lund. *Journal of Mormon History* 37 (Spring
2011): 220–29.

Tolton, John F. "History of Beaver." Cited in J. Cecil Alter, *Early Utah Journalism* (Westport, Conn.: Greenwood Press, 1938).

Townsend, George Alfred. *The Mormon Trials at Salt Lake City*. New York:
American News Co., 1871.

Tuttle, Daniel S. *Reminiscences of a Missionary Bishop*. New York: Thomas
Whittaker, 1906.

Twain, Mark. *Roughing It*. New York: Harper and Brothers Publishers, 1871.

Unrau, William E. *Tending the Talking Wire: A Buck Soldier's View of Indian
Country, 1863–1866*. Salt Lake City: University of Utah Press, 1979.

Utah Statehood: Reasons Why It Should Not Be Granted. Salt Lake City: Tribune Printing, 1887. (USHS, PAM 17947.)

Van Wagoner, Richard S., ed. *The Complete Discourses of Brigham Young*. 4
vols. Salt Lake City: Smith-Petit Foundation, 2009.

———. *Mormon Polygamy: A History*. Salt Lake City: Signature Books, 1989.

Van Wagoner, Richard S., and Steven C. Walker. *A Book of Mormons.* Salt Lake City: Signature Books, 1982.

Varley, James V. *Brigham and the Brigadier: General Patrick Conner and His California Volunteers in Utah and along the Overland Trail.* Tucson, Ariz.: Westernlore Press, 1989.

Vaughn, Stephen, ed. *The Vital Past: Writings on the Uses of History.* Athens: University of Georgia Press, 1985.

Wagner, David E. *Patrick Conner's War: The 1865 Powder River Indian Expedition.* Norman, Okla.: Arthur H. Clark, 2010.

Walker, Charles Lowell. *Diary of Charles Lowell Walker.* Edited by A. Karl Larson and Katherine Miles Larson. 2 vols. Logan: Utah State University Press, 1980.

Walker, Ronald W., Richard E. Turley, and Glen M. Leonard. *Massacre at Mountain Meadows: An American Tragedy.* Oxford and New York: Oxford University Press, 2008.

Ward, Austin N. *Male Life among the Mormons; or, The Husband in Utah, Detailing the Sights and Sounds among the Mormons, with Remarks on Their Moral and Social Economy.* Edited by Maria Ward. Philadelphia: John Edwin Potter and Co., 1863.

Waters, William Elkanah. *Life among the Mormons, and a March to Their Zion.* New York: Agathynian Press, 1868.

Watt, Ronald G. *The Mormon Passage of George D. Watt, First British Convert, Scribe for Zion.* Logan: Utah State University Press, 2009.

Werner, M. R. *Brigham Young.* New York: Harcourt, Brace and Co., 1925.

White, Jean Bickmore. "Prelude to Statehood: Coming Together in the 1890s." *Utah Historical Quarterly* 62 (Fall 1994): 300–315.

Whitney, Orson F[erguson]. *History of Utah.* 4 vols. Salt Lake City: George Q. Cannon and Sons, 1904.

———. *Popular History of Utah.* Salt Lake City: Deseret News, 1916.

Wiley, Peter, and Robert Gottlieb. "Salt Lake City: Zion at the Crossroads." In *A World We Thought We Knew: Readings in Utah History,* edited by John S. McCormick and John Sillito. Salt Lake City: University of Utah Press, 1995.

Williams, John Edward. *Stoner.* Fayetteville: University of Arkansas Press, 1988.

Wingfield, Marshall. "Myth, Mormonism, and Murder in the South." *South Atlantic Quarterly* 75 (Spring 1975): 212–25.

Young, Brigham. "The Government of God." *Times and Seasons,* July 15, 1842, 855–58.

Young, Richard W. "The Morrisite War." *Contributor* 11 (1889–90): 470–71.

Zane, John Maxcy. "A Rare Judicial Service of Charles S. Zane: A Paper Read Before a Joint Meeting of the Illinois State Historical Society and the Mississippi Valley Historical Society, at Springfield, Illinois, May 7, 1926." *Illinois State Historical Society Journal* 19 (April 1927): 91–96.

Index

References to illustrations appear in italic type.

Abuses of Liberal Party members of city council, 252

Adair, Jr., George Washington, charged in murders at Mountain Meadows, 129n21

Aiken party murders, 95–96, 96n55, 125, 330, 331, 331n27

Aird, Polly, 13, 82, 88, 105, 131n32

Ajax Mining Company, 297

Albright, George, city patrolman, 234

Alexander, Thomas, 13, 118n54, 242, 261, 322, 322n42

Allen, Clarence Emir, 205, 209, 213; at disbanding of Liberal Party, 257; brief life history, 204n10; candidate for congress, 229, 277; Democratic convention, 273; distrusts People's Party division, 228; father of free schools in Utah, 210; introduces education bill in Utah legislature, 207; joins Tuscarora Society, 229; Master Mason, 59n27; opponent of Independent-Citizen party, 254; role in public education, 204; testifies against Faulkner and Teller Bills, 229

Allison, Edward M., Jr., 298, 323; at joint legislative meeting to support Smoot, 291

Alta, Utah, 23, 29

Alta Club, 214, 245, 336; brief history, 301–302, 305n11; formation, 301; invitation to join, 301; membership fee and dues, 302

Ambrose, John G., release from prison, 87

American Fork Canyon mines, 309; names of mines, 309n25

American Party: controls Salt Lake City government for seven years, 294; forms after findings of Smoot hearings, 293; successful in 1905 elections, 294

Amorines: anti-Catholic nature, 250, 251n9; history in Utah, 250; jeopardize Liberal votes, 250; objectives, 250; other names for, 250n4

Anderson, A., candidate for presidential elector, 329

Anderson, Judge Thomas J., rules Mormons not fit for citizenship, 199

Anderson, Kirk, editor, owner of
  Valley Tan, 55
Appleby, William Ivins, 170, 173, 176;
  brief history of, 170n8; collusion in
  citizenship fraud, 177; court entry
  on Cannon citizenship, 170n8;
  friend of Jedediah M. Grant, 170n8;
  inquest on Judge Shaver's death,
  175; letter to Judge Drummond,
  170n8; procures war munitions
  in Utah War, 170n8; works with
  Thomas Kane, 170n8
Apponyi, C. E., architect at first
  attempt at City and County
  Building, 236
Arizona settlements, Mormons
  persecuted, 318
Arkansas emigrants at Mountain
  Meadows, 125; well stocked, well
  armed, carried gold and cash,
  131n32
Arnold, Josiah, murder of, 89
Arthur, Pres. Chester, on the
  Mormons, 317
Ashley, James, of Ohio, 109
Ashley Bill, 109, 109n8, 177, 343n6
Aspenwall, J. A., 311; joins with
  Baskin on Miller Company mine,
  309
Atherton, Gibson, and Cannon
  citizenship, 176n33
Atwood, R. W., a Josephite, letter to
  Connor over violence in territory, 91
Auerbach, Eveline Brooks: account
  of Robinson murder, 93; lived in
  fear, 75
Auerbach, Fred, businessman,
  founding member Alta Club, 302,
  302n4
Axtell, Samuel: as governor of
  N.Mex. Terr., 166n68, 167;
  cooperates with Cannon, 166n68;
  governor of Utah, 160; issues
  certificate of election, 160, 167

Babbitt, Almon W., and inquest on
  Judge Shaver's death, 175
Backman, Gustave H.: on
  Independent-Citizen ticket, 254;
  wins city recorder seat, 255
Bagley, Will, 15, 19, 53, 68, 112, 127,
  144, 339, 350
Bamberger, Herman: and Carter's
  unemployed, 267; charged with
  bribery, 277
Bamberger, Simon: candidate for
  Utah governorship, 325; elected as
  governor of Utah, 329; last survivor
  of Liberal Party members, 324,
  324n5
Bancroft, W. H., of Union Pacific
  Railroad, 264
Banks, John, 125n2, 167n72; killed
  during apostate rebellion, 143
Barney, Lewis, 13, 15
Barney, Ronald O., 12, 13
Bartch, Judge George W., 241, 278,
  328; cornerstone laying, 323n1;
  supreme court judge, 283n7; term in
  supreme court, 284
Barton, Sarah E.: against Mormon
  recalcitrance, 188; National
  Women's Relief Corps, 188
Baskin, Andrew (father), 31
Baskin, Della Stella (daughter), burial
  at Mount Olivet cemetery, 65,
  65n55; dies from scarlet fever, 65
Baskin, James (brother), farmer, 31;
  secures bail, 38n28
Baskin, John (brother), farmer, 31
Baskin, John (uncle), 31; possible role
  in jury packing, 39n31
Baskin, Katherine "Kitty" (daughter):
  death of, 194n78; marriage to Frank
  Peyton, 188
Baskin, Martha J. (sister of Robert
  Newton), 335
Baskin, Olive Lavinia (wife), 329;
  sudden death of, 214; eulogy and

tributes, 214–15; funeral and burial, 215

Baskin, Robert Newton, 259, 265; actions in legislature, 223; administers oath of office to Cutler, 323; administers oath of office to Straup, 323; advises seizure of LDS financial base, 185; affected by invasion of Calif. unemployed, 262; anticipated Lee trial unwinnable, 132; appointed to territorial legislative committees, 223; appointed U.S. attorney, 113, 113n33; argues against LDS Church corporation, 184–85; arrest for shooting West, 37–38; arrival in Utah, 23, 53; as potential candidate for Utah governorship, 325; asks for new LDS revelation rescinding polygamy, 186; at joint legislative meeting to support Smoot, 291; at BYU gala for Smoot, 292; attempts to unseat George Q. Cannon, 343; attends Salt Lake Theater performance, 298; authors Cullom Bill, 343; authors Cullom-Struble Bill, 217–19; believed LDS leaders responsible for massacre of Ark. emigrants, 342; believed secret agreements made with Sumner Howard by Mormon leaders, 342; birth, 31; Board of Education, 231; Board of Public Works and Board of Health, 231; boarding arrangements after death of wife, 329–30; boards with Mary Edna Brown Hall, 329; bomb explodes beneath office window, 270; brings free public education, 345; building City and County Building, 235–37, 346; burial at Mount Olivet Cemetery, 335, 335n43; campaigns against delegate Cannon, 157–58; campaigns with B. H. Roberts,

283; candidate for presidential elector, 329; Carter's unemployed army, 266–69; cause of death, 332; ceremonial honoring of William King, 225–26; challenges election of George Q. Cannon, 153; chance street meeting with George Q. Cannon, 256–57; charged with violation in sewer construction, 278; charges Dyer with fraud, 206; charges Sumner Howard with secret pact with Brigham Young, 137; charter member of Alta Club, 302; chief justice, 28; cites fifty-two men as perpetrators of Mountain Meadows killings, 129, 129n20; cites Mormons' misuse of word polygamy, 194; cites relationship with Zane, 327; cites theocracy worse than polygamy, 194–95; city sewer line, obtains bonds for city improvements, 231; city improvements, 28; cohabitation only legal provision effective against plural marriage, 194; contends insincerity in polygamy, 186; cornerstone of City and County Building, 234; counsel for case on citizenship for Mormon temple oaths, 199; counsel for Jerome Stillson inquiry, 100; court injunction confining Kelly's army, 264; credits Doremus with sewer project, 278; credits Liberal Party for city improvements, 232; critical of champertous conduct of lawyers, 296; criticism of lawyers Evans, Rogers, 295–96; criticism over expenses of public utilities and City-County building, 249; criticized for leaving Liberal Party, 252–53; dates of supreme court judgeship, 284; Davis County ranch land for sale, 312; Davis County

Baskin, Robert Newton (*continued*),
     ranch at Wood's Cross, 312;
     deals with misconduct of brothel
     investigation, 234, 235n53; death
     of, 332; dedication of City
     and County Building, 274–75;
     defeated for congress by John T.
     Caine, 199, 207; defeats Zane for
     judgeship, 284; defeats Henry
     H. Rolapp for supreme court
     Democratic candidate, 282;
     depression following wife's death,
     215–17; description of personality,
     333–34, 335–36; disputes Cannon
     citizenship, 159–60; distrusts
     People's Party division, 228; does
     not oppose congressional seating of
     Reed Smoot, 290; drafts legislation
     for benefits of children surviving
     massacre, 127n7; drafts resolution
     of regret on Zane's death, 328;
     early schooling, 31; Edmunds,
     and Edmunds-Tucker acts, 224;
     efforts to close saloons on Sunday,
     233; elected mayor while serving
     in legislature, 226; elected second
     non-Mormon mayor of Salt Lake
     City, 228; elected to legislature, 28;
     elected to territorial legislature,
     222; encounter with Sumner
     Howard, 161–62, 161n39; 162n44;
     energized during Lee trial, 129;
     enters partnership with Hoge,
     281; environment protection, fire
     department improvements, 232;
     explains scandal over building
     furnishings, 277; father of modern
     Utah, 339; fighting Carlton's oath
     fashioned for Edmunds-Tucker,
     190–91; fighting corruption in city
     government, 233; fights memorial to
     congress for repeal of Poland, 224;
     fights territorial legislation attempt
     to override Edmunds-Tucker

Act, 224; financial stress of City
     and County Building, 271; first
     leader to break with Liberal
     Party, 251; founding member,
     Utah State Historical Society, 29;
     freed by Highland County court,
     39–40; friend of the people, 337;
     friendships long and enduring,
     336; full-length portrait in City
     and County Building, 245; funeral
     service by Masonic brotherhood,
     334; gives others credit for public
     education progress, 204; heads
     Liberal ticket for mayor, 228; held
     lifelong guilt over Robinsons'
     death, 95; improvement in city
     infrastructure, 346; in conviction
     of George Reynolds, 62–63;
     Independent-Citizen ticket, 253;
     interests in mining in American
     Fork Canyon, 308–309; invokes
     English laws of mortmain, 185;
     kills Andrew West in street, 37;
     lack of drumhead court martial
     proved guilt of Mormon Militia,
     131; leaves Highland County,
     Ohio, 40–41; lenient in sentencing
     of David Evans, 296; letter
     contesting Cannon seating, 166;
     life threatened at arrest of Young,
     114; life threatened during invasion
     of unemployed, 269; light-hearted
     description of his orations, 225;
     loses mayoral nomination to
     W. H. Dale, 281; majority opinions
     written, 294–95; marriage to Olive
     Gardner, 61; Mason titles and
     offices, 28, 239; Masonic funeral,
     59; meets with Gov. West, 184;
     member of Harvard Club and
     University Club, 305; mining
     exploits after supreme court duty,
     324; names Brigham Young as
     ordering or accessory to meadows

murders, 131; newspaper articles of support after wife's death, 217; no burial markers, 313; no Civil War service, 34; no deep friendship with Civil War veterans, 336; no immediate family members attend funeral, 335; nominated as president of territorial legislature, 223; not remembered at City and County building restoration ceremony, 247; not a prophet, but profitable to the people, 351; notes benefits following Edmunds-Tucker enactment, 205; obtains bonds for city financing, 271–72; obtains Washington Square for City and County Building, 237; offices in Freemasonry held, 59; officiates at ceremony for incoming Utah state officers, 323; one of last surviving Liberal Party members, 324; organizes Tuscarora Society, 229; organizing Liberal Party, 339; partners with DeWolfe, 55; photograph of, *246, 304*; place in history of Utah ignored, 321–22; plans to leave Utah, 216; possible common law marriage to Mary Edna Brown Hall, 89, 331, 331n28, 332n30; praised by *Broad Ax* for appointment of blacks to city offices, 285; praise from *Broad Ax* for position on Twenty-Fourth Infantry at Fort Douglas, 285; praise of Brigham Young had double meaning, 286–89; praise of Zane as jurist and man, 327–28; prevents carriage from injuring crowd at circus event, 298; problems in completing sewer construction, 272–73; prolonged trial for West's death, 37–40; prosecutor in first trial of John D. Lee, 126–29; proves Cannon citizenship as fraud, 343; public education, 205; public education bill passes territorial legislature, 209; purchases city property from Daniel H. Wells, 62; pushes for passage of Luttrell Bill, 164; question of jury packing, 39, 39n31, 40; railroad ventures, 312; raises and breeding horses, 306–307; reasons for acquittal in case of Andrew West, 40; record in Utah Supreme Court unrecognized, 322; record in Utah Supreme Court, 294–95; re-elected mayor, 255; residences during life in Salt Lake City, 329–30; resigns from Alta Club, 305; response to invasion of Utah by armies of unemployed, 347; response to unemployed people in Davis County via police and sheriff's deputies, 269; runs against Zane in election for supreme court, 282–83; runs for mayor on Good Government ticket, 294; second election against Cannon, 161; secures right of way for road to Mount Olivet Cemetery, 232; sees Mormon guilt in not compensating orphans of Ark. emigrants, 131; sells Miller Hill Mining Co., 311; separates from Liberal Party policies, 256; service as mayor, 28; short temper, 336; southern sympathies, 26, 37; speaker at opening of mining exchange, 308; speaks at Brigham Young birthday celebration, 286–89; stress of city improvements, 271; speaks for Christiancy Bill, 160; stresses atmosphere of violence that preceded Mountain Meadows murders, 139–40; studies territorial laws, 53; subdued in response to promises broken by Mormon leaders, 293; summation at Edmunds-Tucker hearing, 186–87;

Baskin, Robert Newton (*continued*),
supportive of black citizens in Salt
Lake City, 285; supreme court
duties end, 323; supreme court
salary, 308n23; supreme court work
praised by *Deseret News*, 324–25;
suspicious theocracy not ended by
statehood, 222; temper outburst
against Judge Hawley, fined
and jailed, 61–62; testimony for
Edmunds-Tucker, 184–85; testimony
on Edmunds-Tucker praised,
187; three opinions sent to U.S.
Supreme Court, none reversed,
294–95; to lobby for Edmunds-
Tucker, 180; to carry Murray
resignation to Washington, 181; to
sell horses, 216; tributes at death,
332–34; trustee to Salt Lake City
schools, 206; unprintable response
at lenient sentence for Cannon,
199; value of estate at death, 313;
visits John Randolph Tucker, 183;
visits President Cleveland, 184;
warns counsel regarding criticism
of judges, 283; warns of move
to remove Judge Zane and U.S.
attorney William H. Dickson, 187;
will not lobby against enabling act,
274; Wood's Cross ranch, 216; work
on Edmunds Act, 179; work on
Poland Act, 179; works for election
of Roberts, 283; works with Peters
for public education legislation,
209; Worshipful Master Mount
Moriah Lodge, 57; writes memorial
to congress for constitutional
amendment against polygamy,
223; writes scant discussion of
contemporaries, 335–36
Baskin, Thomas H. (brother), 31;
death of, 324, 324n3; lawyer,
31; secures bail, 38n28; state
representative, 31

Bast, A. G., and race horses, 307
Bates, George Caesar: admits guilt
of George A. Smith, 135; aligned
with Mormons, 134; appointed U.S.
attorney, 134; avoids prosecution of
W. A. Hickman, 134; bogus divorce
practice, 135; charges McKean
with corruption, 113n33; counsel
defending Lee, 127; counsel for
Haight, Higbee, Lee, and Stewart
in meadows murders, 135; defense
of John D. Lee, 127; engages Baskin
and DeWolfe to collect fees due
from Mormons, 135; leaves Utah
for Leadville, Colorado, 136; legal
career, 133–34; office destroyed by
Chicago fire, 134
Baugh, Maud, mother of Karl Quayle
Cannon, 154n5
Baum, John J., immunity under
mountain law, 86
Beadle, John Hanson, on non-
Mormons in Utah, 84
Bean, Curtin Coe, works for Utah
statehood, 194
Beauchamp, Malvina, owner of
brothel "Big V," 234
Beaver, Utah, 169; crowded for trial,
128
Beck, John, purchases property from
John W. Snell, 305
Beck's hot springs, 306, 306n13
Beheading, punishment for sexual
sins, 104n141
Bennett, Charles Washington,
190, 191; berated by alliteration,
189; goes with Baskin to support
Edmunds-Tucker, 189; Liberal
Party member, 189; Loyal League,
Republican leaning, 189; works for
Edmunds-Tucker oath, 190–91
Benson, Ezra Taft, 247
Benson, Wendell, 223n44
Bernhard, Andrew, murder of, 89

Bernhisel, John M., 74; election
of unanimous, 78–79; in Shaver
funeral procession, 175
Berry, William S., murder of, 318
Betts, Thomas: ambush failed, 87;
release from prison, 87
Bigler, David L., 19, 53, 67, 96, 115,
339, 350; opinion of Baskin, 27, 29
Bingham and Camp Floyd Railroad
Co., 312
Bird, George W., architect, 237
Bishop, William W.: counsel
defending Lee, 127; second Lee
trial, 136
Blackburn, Judge, favors Teller Bill,
224n47
Black Hawk War, 90, 90n29
Blaine, James G., and Cullom-
Struble legislation, 220n31
Blair, Seth, at Robinson inquest, 94
Blazes, Helen, brothel owner, 234
Blood atonement, for apostates, 71–72,
97–98, 104n141, 139, 160, 289, 342
Board of Health, formed by Baskin, 231
Board of Public Works, formed by
Baskin, 231
Bockholt, Dirk, court clerk for Judge
Elias Smith, 151
Boley, H. E., and Surprise Mining
Co., 310, 310n33
Bomb explodes at Baskin's office, 270
Bonneville Ranch Co., 312
Booth, J. E., Provo judge, 328
Boreman, Judge Jacob Smith, 29,
205, 259; corroborates opinion
of Howard's pact with Young,
137–38; denies admission of ex parte
depositions of Young and Smith,
130; judge in trials of John D. Lee,
126, 126n4, 136; on compliance to
law, 315; on control in Utah, 83;
on Judge McKean's dismissal,
118n54; report as territorial school
commissioner, 207–208, 208n26

Boutwell, George S.: against
Edmunds-Tucker Bill, 182;
appearance called window dressing,
186; positions held, 182n18
Bowman, Bella, 167n72; killed during
Morris apostate rebellion, 143
Bowman, John H., construction
supervisor dismissed, 242
Bradly, Supreme Court justice
Joseph P., on LDS persecution, 319
Branch Davidians, 319n24
Brassfield, Squire Newton, murder
of, 86–87
Brewer, Myron, 98
Brigham Young University, 344
Broad Ax: black-owned newspaper,
277; considers Baskin for Senate,
281; mentions Moses Thatcher for
Senate, 281n1; mentions John T.
Caine for Senate, 281n1; mentions
Joseph Rawlins for Senate, 281n1;
praises Baskin for position on
black troops, 285; praises Hoge
for position on black troops, 285;
suggests Baskin for mayor, 277
Brocchus, Perry C., 70
Brothel "investigation" by city police,
234–35
Brough, C. M., 265; asks Baskin for
additional police, 263; invasion
of unemployed from Calif., 262;
mayor of Ogden, 262; requests to
Baskin for aid, 266
Brown, Arthur, 170n7; with Baskin
on Shamrock and Katherine mine,
310
Brown, Homer, perpetrator of Aiken
party murders, 96n55, 330
Brown, John A., Utah County sheriff
and industrial army, 268n35
Brown, Mary Edna (wife of Erasmus
Foote Hall), 329, 331
Browning Bill, 177, 343n6
Bruner, James P., 23, 23n1

Buchanan, Pres. James, 25;
declaration of rebellion in Utah,
47; on the Mormons, 316; pre-war
policies, 34

Bucklin, "Buck" Horace, killed by
William A. Hickman, 95–96,
331n27

Bullion Beck mine, 306n14

Burdett, Gen. S. S., against Mormon
theocracy, 188

Burnside, Gen. Ambrose E.: Battle of
Fredericksburg, 36, 36n19; General
Order 38, 36

Burr, David H.: attests to Judge
Shaver's poisoning, 176; criticism of
Mormon land claims, leaves Utah,
71; mail not secure, 74; surveyor
general, 44

Burrows, Sen. Julius Caesar, of
Mich., and Smoot senate hearings,
292

Burt, Andrew: as city policeman
at Robinson murder, 95n49;
demolition of Flint's bordello, 123;
Force Act riot, 159

Burton, C. S., on Independent-
Citizen ticket, 254

Burton, David, presiding bishop, 345

Burton, Judge J. W., nominates
Baskin for supreme court, 298

Burton, Robert T.: absolved by Judge
Schaeffer, 167n72; court entry of
subpoena, 172; in Shaver funeral
procession, 175; inquest on Judge
Shaver's death, 175

Cahoon, Mahonri, cited for Coalville
murders, 86n6

Caine, John T., 28, 170, 176, 177, 187,
323; contests Tuscaroran seating
of Powers and Kiesel, 230; denies
union of church and state in
Utah, 195; efforts for statehood
constitution, 192; fights Edmunds

education bill, 209; for removal of
William Nelson from Associated
Press, 211n37; leads statehood
effort, 193–94, 227; opposes
Cullom-Struble, 219; speaks
against Edmunds-Tucker Bill, 182;
suggested for Senate by *Broad Ax*,
281n1

Cain, Joseph, 171, 174, 176; collusion in
citizenship fraud, 177

Calder, David O., 55; copy of
DeWolf's mail sent to B. Young
and W. Clayton, 75

Caledonian Club, 55

California Proposition 8, passage
backed by LDS Church, 345

Calkins, William H., and Cannon
citizenship, 176n33

Call, Asa Cyrus, on Brigham Young's
power, 70

Callister, Ed, aids Baskin at
encounter at circus, 298

Campbell, Allen Green, 207, 302;
awarded certificate of election,
169; brief history, 169n1; challenges
election of George Q. Cannon,
153; contests Cannon citizenship,
169; defeated by Cannon, 169; joins
Tuscarora Society, 229; not awarded
seat in Congress, 177; owner of
Horn Silver Mine, 169; run against
Cannon, 169, 169n1

Campbell, Andrew, joins Baskin in
Imperial Mining and Smelter, 309

Campbell, Robert, Mormon sent to
influence Mormon voters, 228n5

Camp Cameron, 95, 133

Camp Crittenden, 49

Camp Douglas, 61, 62, 86, 91, 96, 100,
113n32, 117, 336. *See also* Fort Douglas

Camp Floyd, 312; sale of stores to
Mormons, 49; soldiers brought
lawlessness, 99–100

Cannon, Abraham Hoagland:

prison sentence, 198n105; son of George Q., 181; speech before Judge Zane, 182; speech taken to congress by Baskin, 182

Cannon, Angus Munn, 198n103, 331

Cannon, Anne Y., 198n104

Cannon, Elizabeth Hoagland, wife of George Q. Cannon, 170n4

Cannon, Frank Jenne, 154n5, 204n10, 274; alleges ecclesiastical control, 105; American Party, 293–94; candidate for congress, 229; cites Pres. Joseph F. Smith as liar, 293; Citizen Party, 221; Democratic convention, 273; works to oppose Cullom-Struble, 220, 220n31, 221n34

Cannon, George Q., 112, 190n57, 283, 336; against Cullom-Struble, 220n31; appointed to First Presidency, 169; arrest, 197; arrival in Salt Lake valley, 154; assists Parley P. Pratt with autobiography, 156; bail forfeited, 182n15, 197, 197n96; born Liverpool, 154; brief history, 154–55, 154n5; citizenship questioned, 153; citizenship by fraud, 173, 173n23; confidant of Brigham Young, 154; death as punishment for sexual sins, 99; defeats Maxwell for congress, 157; disqualified from congress, personal appeal to Edmunds, 177, 177n35; election challenged four times, 153; epithets for, widely known, 154, 154n2; hiding from arrest, 193n76; husband of six wives, 154; labors in Calif. gold fields, 156; lobbies for enabling act, 273; marriage to Elizabeth Hoaglund, 156; mission to Sandwich Islands, 156; opinion of Baskin, 27; plan to colonize territories with Mormons, 165–66;

powerful in Washington, 154; preaches for continued polygamy, 219; preaches to Saints to defy law, 219; principal accomplishment in congress was fighting legislation, 178n36; proponent of theocracy, 340; purchase of land in Mexico, 197n97; record as LDS leader, 153–54; reports John W. Young's secret work against Edmund-Tucker, 189; returns from Islands mission, 156; reward posters for capture, 196; secret plan for political control western territories by Mormon influx, 166; selected to congress, 157; sentence for bigamy by Judge Sandford, 197; speaker at City and County Building dedication, 275; U.S. House votes to expel, 160; wants AP dispatches by William Nelson, stopped, 211n37; wants cash for congressmen for defeat of Voorhees Bill, 119

Cannon, John Q.: extramarital affair, embezzling funds of LDS Church, 190n57; father's citizenship records, 170, 170n5; son of George, 190n57

Cannon, Karl Quayle, son of Franklin Jenne Cannon, adopted by George Q. Cannon, 154n5

Capstone, of Salt Lake temple, laying ceremony, 237–38

Carey, William, 134, 336; alignment with Brigham Young questioned, 128, 128n15; capability questioned in Lee prosecution, 128; lobbies against Cannon seating, 157; prosecutor in first trial of John D. Lee, 126–29; Reynolds trial, 64

Carlisle, John G., facilitates Baskin testimony on Edmunds-Tucker Bill, 184

Carlisle, John R., on Joint Legislative committee, 326n11

Carlton, Ambrose Bolivar: brief
history of, 190n59; constructs
oath for Edmunds-Tucker, 190;
hired by LDS Church to fight
Cullom-Struble, 192n69; Utah
Commissioner, 190

Carrington, Albert: glosses over Dr.
Robinson murder, 93; witness in
Cannon citizenship hearing, 159

Carter, H. E.: forms "army" in Salt
Lake City, 267; commandeers
Union Pacific train, 267; similar to
Kelly army, 267; Utah unemployed,
266–67

Cash disbursements to defeat anti-
Mormon legislation, 119

Cass, Lewis, Secretary of State, 71

Castration, punishment for sexual
sins, 90, 104n141

Centerville Gun Club, 312

Chandler, Jeff: against Edmunds-
Tucker Bill, 182; argues against
government controlling church,
185–86

Chapman, "Big John," of Aiken
group, 95–96, 331n27; escapes from
Hickman, 96n54

Cherndon, Mrs. Margaret (daughter
of Charles S. Zane), 327

Christiancy, Sen. Isaac, 143; bill of
1876 against Mormons on Utah
juries, 160, 177, 343n6

Christianson, N. L., charged with
murder of Andrew Bernhard, 89,
89n22

Christopolis Easterly Lode, in
Baskin's estate, 313

Church of Jesus Christ of Latter-day
Saints, 18, 24, 58, 77, 105, 140, 184,
315; positioning into mainstream,
348–50; retrenchment vs.
assimilation, 349, survival, 348. *See
also* LDS Church

Citizen Committee of Five, and
Baskin, 253

Citizen Party, 221, 251, 254

Citizenship, requirements, oath
required, 155

City and County Building, 28,
235–37, 323; begun by Baskin,
236, construction impacted by
economic depression, 242, 242n81,
245; controversy over, 236–37;
cornerstone ceremony, 239–40;
cornerstone of restoration, 246; costs
of, 237n63, 243; dedication, 274–75;
Denhalter's Band, 239; difficulties
completing, 242–43; history of,
236–37; host to Utah constitutional
convention, 275–76; Masonic ritual
repeated at restoration, 246–47;
original contract price, 237, 237n63;
parade at restoration, 246–47;
parade to Washington Square, 239;
photograph of, *240, 243*; photograph
of clock tower of, *244*; reopening
celebration, 246–47; restoration of,
237n63; retrofitting of base isolation
for earthquake protection, 237n63;
role of Utah Freemasons, 239–40;
scandal over furnishings fraud,
276–77; uses of building, 245

City Creek Center, in Salt Lake City
revitalization, 345

City water contamination, 230

Civil War: Brigham Young puts
damnation on both sides, 50, 50n24;
federal ammunition, destroyed by
troops leaving Utah, 50; financial
windfall for Mormons, 49;
prediction by Mormon founder,
Joseph Smith, 50; providential
interpretation, 48; revised counts
of dead and wounded, 50; unique
Mormon view of, 48–49; Utah
cotton exported during, 49

Clagett, William Horace, of Mont.:
Clagett Bill, 177, 343n6; support of
Poland Act, 122

Clawson, Hiram B., 128;

Cullom-Struble, 220n31; lobbies for enabling act, 273–74

Clawson, John Willard, portrait painter, 245n87, 246

Clawson, Moroni, killing of, 99

Clawson, Spencer, defeated by George Scott, 214

Clay County, Mo., 24

Cleveland, Pres. Grover, 184; on the Mormons, 317

Clinton, Dr. Jeter: absolved by Judge Schaeffer, 167n72; charged with murder of John Banks, 123; death for prostitution, 71–72; destroys Kate Flint's bordello, 123; Force Act riot, 159; implicated in death of apostate John Banks, 125n2; leaders meet at his farm after Young charged with crimes, 116; threatens DeWolfe over newspaper articles, 125; Warm Springs property, 306n13

Clinton, William Jefferson, inaugural address, 68

Clinton v. Englebrecht, 342; charges voided for many, 117; jury selection ruled improper, 117; shocking to non-Mormons, 118

Cohabitation: definition of, 331–32; respecting sexual intercourse, 331–32

Cohn, Louis, plans vetoed by Baskin, 277

Colborn, Judge E. F., speaker at opening of mining exchange, 308

Coleman, Thomas, murder of, 95

Colfax, Schuyler, 166; supports Cullom Bill, 110–11

Collett, Joseph, teamster of William Dame Company named in murder, 90n26

Collett, Sylvanus, Aiken party murders, 96n55, 374n55

Collett, William G., 209

Collett Bill: on public education, 209, provisions of, 209

Collins, Caspar W. (son), 34; Casper, Wyo., named for, 34, 34n16; killed by Indians, 34

Collins, William Oliver: Civil War Service, 34; forms Hillsboro Female College, 33; Fort Collins, Colo., named for, 34n16; legal background, 32–33; takes Baskin in practice, 32; organizes Eleventh Ohio Cavalry, 34

Colton, William F., 228n10

Commercial Street, first street paved, known for brothels, 231n26

Committee of Forty-Five, 158, 158n23

Communal experiments, 80–81

Conditt, Lilace W., also known as Asa W. Cinditt, 98n65; killed by John Gheen, 97

Conditt, Martha (daughter of Lilace), wife of Merritt Rockwell, 98

Conklin, J. C.: candidate for mayor, 252; Utah Amorine, 250

Connor, Gen. Patrick Edward, 13, 15, 84, 107, 113n32, 216, 259, 336; known as Irish Catholic, 250; organizes Liberal Party campaign, 213; seeks position as U.S. marshal, 199n110; suggested as replacement for Cannon, 165n64; transferred out of Utah, 90; indignation at lenient sentence for Cannon, 199

Connor, Gen. Selden, against Mormon theocracy, 188

Conscription Act, 36, 36n21

Context, useful to historian, 105

Conway, Cora, partner of Kate Flint, 123

Cooke, Sarah Ann, 158, 158n22

Copperheadism, 26, 33

Copperheads, 26

Cornerstone, and Masonic ritual, 239–41

Council of Fifty, 67, 77, 77n56

Cowan, Benjamin Rush: asst. sec. of int., 64; at Reynolds trial, 64

Coxey, Jacob S.: and destitute workers, 261; forms "army" of unemployed, 261

Cradlebaugh, Judge John, 126; investigates Parrish murder, 88; investigates Utah murders, 55

Cragin, Sen. Aaron Harrison, of N.H., 109

Cragin Bill, 109, 109n11, 177, 343n6

Craig, Brig. Gen. James, 26n7

Critchlow, E. B.: author of "bastard" posters, 223n40; raises objections to Smoot seating, 292; with Baskin on Shamrock and Katherine mine, 310

Crouch, G. W., apostate asks for protection after Lee trial, 133, 133n43

Crow, Charley, demolition of Flint's bordello, 123

Croxall, Caroline P. Young, 154n5

Cullom, Shelby Moore, 109, 344; claims Mormons remain menace after statehood, 290

Cullom Bill, 27, 57, 177, 179, 343n6; Cullom, "means war," newspapers oppose, 111–12; passes House, dies in Senate, 112; provisions, 109–10; written by Baskin, 109

Cullom-Struble, 27, 177, 199, 322, 344; authored by Baskin, 199, 218; opposed by Chamber of Commerce, 220; passage deferred, 220; provisions of, 218–19; prominent Mormons ask for delay, 220

Culture of violence, 13, 67, 71, 73, 85–86, 90–93, 96, 99, 102, 104n141, 107, 113, 139–40, 342–43

Cutler, John C., governor elect, 323

Dalton, Edward M., 202n7

Dalton, Simon, charged with murder of Horace Bucklin, 114

Dame, William Horne, 127n11; advises Saints to ignore murder of family members, 105; charged in murders at Mountain Meadows, 129n21; had authority to convene court-martial, 131

Danites, in Nauvoo, 68

Daviess County, Mo., 24

Davis, Jefferson, and letter of Hartley, 96–97

Davis County, residents alarmed at unemployed army, 269

Davis v. Beason, 218n22

Dawson, John W., territorial governor, 71, 99

Dee, Thomas D., and Citizen Party, 221

Deer Creek mine, 311

Democratic Party, 325, 345; divides Liberal vote, 222

Democratic ticket of 1898 illogical, 283; for 1916, 329

Denhalter Rifles: and Carter army, 268; of Utah National Guard, 268

Denney, Presley, assists Howard in second Lee trial, 136

Dennis, Fred W., and Utah Amorines, 250n4

DePaulis, Palmer, Salt Lake City mayor, 247

Devens, Charles (U.S. attorney general): argues in *Reynolds v. United States*, 162n42; on Cannon citizenship, 162; praises Sumner Howard, 162n44; U.S. attorney general Charles, and divorce mills, 152n49

DeWolfe, Stephen, 55n11, 73; as secretary of territory, 55; editor of *Valley Tan*, 55, 55n11, 73; founds Wasatch Lodge, 57; life threatened, 125; mail opened, 75; Master Mason, 55; partners with Baskin, 55; represents Olive Gardner, 60

Dey, Charles C., 298; makes bizarre supreme court nomination, 298

DeYoung, William H. (black policeman appointed by Baskin), 285

Dickson, William H., 191, 250–51, 328; counsel for case on citizenship and Mormon oaths, 199; Mormons work to remove, 187; opposes Carlton oath, 191; represents Baskin, 278

Dictatorship, 67–69

Diehl, Christopher: one of last surviving Liberal Party members, 324, 324n5; opponent of Independent-Citizen party, 254; restriction of Mormons from Freemasonry, 57–58; validates Baskin departure from Liberal Party, 258

Divorce mills, 152

Dixon, William Hepworth (Presbyterian leader), 76

Dodson, Thomas, cited for Coalville murders, 86n6

Donnellan, John W. (president Salt Lake Stock and Mining Exchange), 308

Donovan, M. M. (assistant fire chief), 276

Dooley, John E., 190; Edmund-Tucker oath, 190–91; founding member Alta Club, 302n4

Doremus, A. F., Board of Public Works, credited with completion of sewer, 278

Dotson, Peter K. (U.S. marshal), 92n34

Dougall, Wil B., on Baskin orations, 225

Drown, C. M., murder of, 89

Drumhead court-martial, 132, 342; used by British for trial and punishment for killing women and children, 132n34

Drummond, William, 71, 74n36, 170n8; asserts Judge Shaver poisoned, 176n31

Dubois, Frederick T., 219; on polygamy and theocracy, 320; opposes statehood, 195; reelected in Idaho, 199; report on polygamy, 218; Smoot senate hearings, 292; works with Baskin to oppose Utah statehood, 194

Dyer, Frank H., 204; accused of conspiring with Mormons, 205–206; conducts George Q. Cannon to prison, 198; contributor to Liberal Party, 215n15; disputes over LDS Church assets, 199; lobbies for statehood, 227; marshal, receiver of LDS Church property, 181n11; receiver of LDS property and funds, 205; runs afoul of Baskin, 181n11; Salt Lake Gas Co., 206n21; with Baskin to Washington, 181

Earl, Charles W., and Surprise Mining Co., 310, 310n33

Eckels, Judge Delana R., 71, 92n34

Ecklund, Alfred E. (police detective), 235

Eden, John R., 183

Edmunds, Sen. George: Baskin's federal education bill for Utah, 345; provisions of, 208–209

Edmunds Act, 177, 197, 223, 317, 318, 344; and Baskin, 28

Edmunds-Tucker Act, 204, 170n5, 223, 318; Baskin the author of, 28; became law March 1887, 190; LDS Church property, 190; passes House, 190; Perpetual Emigrating Fund, 190; provisions of, 190; requires marriages made public record, 320

Edwards, H. F. (counsel for Mammoth Mining Co.), 310

Egan, Howard, killer of James Monroe, 85

Eichnor, Dennis C., 298

Eldredge, Alma: cited for Coalville
murders, 86n6; defeated by
Roberts, 283–84; mayor of
Coalville, Utah, 284; named by
Baskin in murders of Isaac Potter
and Charles Wilson, 284
Eldredge, Alpha May: cousin to
Eldredge men accused by Baskin
of murder, 290n29; wife of Reed
Smoot, 290n29
Eldredge, Edmund, cited for
Coalville murders, 86n6
Eldredge, Hyrum, cited for Coalville
murders, 86n6
Election ballots, numbered, not
secure, 157n19
Elections, of February 1890, 213–14
Elections, unanimous, 78, 79, 165–67
Eleventh Ohio Cavalry, 34
Emery, Gov. George W.: apostates ask
him for cavalry protection after Lee
trial in Beaver, 133; awards election
certificate to Cannon, 143, 162–63,
165; labeled "Elder," 164; irrational
choice of William Hickman to
guard John D. Lee, 129n24; plans
with Cannon, 165–66; removal
asked, 166; secret agreements,
165–66; signs restrictive bill on non-
Mormon voting, 163; starts butcher
shop, 164n50; starts newspaper,
Whistle, 164n50
Emigration Square, 237n61. *See also*
Washington Square
Emma mine, 23
Emrie, John R., 31n2, 33; forms
Hillsboro Female College, 33
Endowment house, 63, 139, 163
Endowments, 58n25, 132, 185
Englebrecht, Paul, 17n49, 123
Englebrecht v. Clinton, 65, 116n42, 117,
117n49
Etulain, Richard, on Utah as police
state, 80–81

Euphemisms for sanctioned murder,
102–104
Evans, David: disbarment case heard
by Baskin, 295–96; shared time in
legislature with Baskin, 296n53;
street altercation with P. Williams,
296n54
Evans, John (gov. of Colo.), 41
Eyring, Henry B., 345

Failed federal legislation against
polygamy and theocracy, 343;
chronological list of, 343n6; total of
at least twenty-five bills, 343
Faulkner Bill, 227–29, 227n1, 228;
home rule for local government, 224
Faulkner-Caine Bill. *See* Faulkner Bill
Federal appointments, to Utah Terr.,
108
"Federal Enemies of the Saints," 313,
313n52
Federal officials, motivation for
service in Utah, 315
Ferris v. Higley: entered by Baskin
as route for changing jurisdiction
of courts, 120–21; relationship to
Poland Act, implications seen by
Baskin, 120–22
Ferry, Edward Payson (brother of
Thomas and William): engaged
in mining, 181; lived in Park City,
Utah, 181
Ferry, Elisha P., opposes Utah
statehood, 194
Ferry, Thomas White (Mich. senator),
181; brother of Edward and
William Ferry, 181
Ferry, William (brother of Thomas),
181; engaged in mining, 181; lived in
Park City, Utah, 181
Field, Kate: lecturer, 183; pseudonym
for Mary Katherine Keemle,
183n22; support of Edmunds-
Tucker Act, 183

Field, Stephen J., 118n54

Fillmore, J. A. (Southern Pacific RR official), 262

Financial depression of 1890s, 261

First Presidency. *See* LDS First Presidency

Fish, Hamilton (secretary of state), 111

Fitch, Thomas, opposes Cullom, 112, 112n27, 116, 117

Flint, Kate: house of prostitution, 123; represented by Baskin, 123; sues for damage to business, 123; write in votes, 165

Folland, E. A., 233

Forbes, Henry, murder of, 88

Force Act riot, 159

Ford, Thomas (gov. of Ill.), 68

Fort Bridger, 26, 49

Fort Douglas, 197, 232, 263, 274n17, 285. *See also* Camp Douglas

Fort Laramie, 170n8

Fort Leavenworth, 170n8

Foster, F. P., 309

Foster, J. C., 136

France, Dr. William, and inquest on Judge Shaver's death, 174–75

Franklin, Benjamin Joseph, 166

Franklin Street Variety Theater, 233

Fraternal organizations, in Utah Terr., 55

Free and Accepted Masons: history in Nauvoo, 55–56, 56n14; history in Utah, 55n13, 56

Freemasonry, Mormons excluded from until 1984, 58. *See also* Free and Accepted Masons

Frelinghuysen Bill, 177, 343n6

Fulton, Nancy (mother), 31

Ganaway, G. H., black man campaigning for Baskin, 285

GAR: meeting in Washington, 187–88; members, among Kelly's unemployed, 263–64; Salt Lake City meeting for support against theocracy, 188

Garfield, Pres. James A., on the Mormons, 316–17

Gatling gun, 265, 268; sent to Ogden by Gov. West, 263

Gedicks, Fred Mark, 319

George, Lt. Col. Milo, 91

Gheen, John: killed Lilace W. Conditt, 97; murdered, 97–98

Gibbs, George F., 228n5

Gibbs, Isaac L. (U.S. marshal in arrest of Brigham Young), 109n10

Gibbs, John H., murder of, 318

Gilson, Samuel H., 196n94

Givens, Terryl, 349, 350n20

Glendinning, James, 228n10; candidate for mayor, 277; Liberal ticket candidate, elected to legislature, 223; notes benefits following Edmunds-Tucker enactment, 224; opponent of Independent-Citizen party, 254

Godbe, Anthony (son of William), early member of Alta Club, 303

Godbe, William S., 82, 210; disputes with Brigham Young, 100–101; early member of Alta Club, 303; excommunication from LDS Church, 101; financial ruin attempted after excommunication, 101; fortifies house against retribution for apostasy, 101; joins Baskin in mining ventures, 307; on control in Utah, 79; opposes Cullom, 110

Godbeites, ask for Cullom modifications, 112–13

Godrey, George L. (Utah commissioner), 196, 219

Goodell, Jotham: writes of winter with Mormons, 13; tells mail violated, 74

Goodrich, George Aaron, 57

Goodwin, Charles, C., 169n1; at disbanding of Liberal Party, 257; Democratic convention, 273; distrusts People's Party division, 228; early member of Alta Club, 303; goes with Baskin to lobby, 181; lauds Baskin, 222; photograph of, *180, 216*; speaker at opening of mining exchange, 308

Goodwin, Nat C., and theater production, 298

Goodwin, Samuel H., account of Robinson murder, 94

Goshen, Rev. Elmer I., at Baskin funeral, 334

Grand Central Mining Company, 310

Grand jury, to investigate divorce mills, 150–51

Grant, George D., charged with murder of Horace Bucklin, 114

Grant, Heber J., 204; assists in obtaining bonds for Salt Lake City improvements, 272

Grant, Jedediah M., 27; death for those bringing prostitutes to Utah, 71; mayor arranges for Judge Shaver's funeral and burial, 175; mayor of Salt Lake City, and inquest of Judge Shaver's death, 175

Grant, Pres. Ulysses S., 108, 113n32, 118; on the Mormons, 316

Greenewald, Aaron, 324, 324n5

Grover, Gen. Cuvier: apostates ask for cavalry after Lee trial in Beaver, 133; brief history, 133n42

Haight, Isaac Chauncey, 87; authority to convene court martial, 131; charged in murders at Mountain Meadows, 129n21

Hailey, John, 189

Hailey Bill, 177, 189, 343n6

Hall, Benjamin Brown, 309n31, 330; joins Baskin in Imperial Mining and Smelter, 309; secretary of Imperial Mine, 309n31

Hall, Erasmus Foote: death, 329; husband of Mary Edna Brown, 329

Hall, James, 86

Hall, Mary Edna Brown (daughter of bishop Homer Brown), 28, 309n31, 329, 330; death of, 332; depth of relationship with Baskin unknown, 332; never held before public as Baskin's wife, 332; photograph of, *330, 331*; sole recipient of Baskin estate, 332, 333; survivors of, 332

Halliday, Wilford H., 86

Hambleton, Madison, killer of Dr. Vaughn, 85

Hamblin, Jacob, 137

Hamilton, Dr. John F., 214; indignation at lenient sentence for Cannon, 199

Hampton, Brigham Y.: demolition of Flint's bordello, 123; Force Act riot, 159

Hanauer, A., founding member Alta Club, 302

Hancock, George W., and murder of Hannah and Henry Jones, 89n19

Harkness, Robert, 223n44

Harney, Gen. William Selby, 45, 170n8

Harrison, Elias Lacy Thomas: questions authority of Young, 79; threatened after excommunication, 101–102

Harrison, Pres. Benjamin, 206n19; dismisses Judge Sandford, restores Judge Zane, 206, 206n19

Harter, Michael, 258n35

Hartley, Jesse Thompson: his mail intercepted, 97; letter to Jefferson Davis, 96–97; murder of, 97; singled out by Brigham Young to be killed, 97

Harvard Law School, 11, 23, 43;

Baskin attends, 32; entrance requirements, 32

Haslam, James: letter carried to Young requested by Jerome Stillson, 143; witness in second Lee trial, 137n61

Haun's Mill, murders at, 317

Hawkins, Harriet (first wife of Thomas), 114

Hawkins, Thomas: conviction, 341; tried for adultery, 114–15

Hawley, Judge Cyrus Myron, 61, 108, 336; lobbies against Cannon seating, 157; Mason, 59n27; scheme to cede land to Idaho called "harebrained idea" by Baskin, 62

Hayes, Pres. Rutherford B., 166; on the Mormons, 316

Hayken, Martin, 277

Heath, Henry (city policeman), 95n49

Hemingray, Judge J. C.: lobbyist for Luttrell Bill, 164; searches with Baskin for letter contesting Cannon seating, 166

Hempstead, Judge Charles H.: editor of *Union Vedette*, 113n32; resigns as U.S. attorney, 113; Robinson inquest, 94

Henderson, Judge Henry Parry, 205; contests seating of Tuscarorans' Powers and Kiesel, 230; Democratic party organizer, 273; mentioned by *Broad Ax* for Senate seat, 281n1

Hickman, William Adams: beating of surveyor, 74; bizarre assignment to guard Lee, 129n24; charged with murder of Horace Bucklin, 114; Lee trial, 129, 129n24, 134; murder of Drown, 89; murder of Richard Yates, confessions of, 96; tells Baskin details of murders, 115

Higbee, John Mount, charged in murders at Mountain Meadows, 129n21

Highland County, Ohio, 11, 31;

newspapers, 43; reports of Utah War, 45

Hill, Joe, trial for murder, 245

Hillsboro, Ohio, 23

Hillsboro Female College, formed by Baskin family, 33

Hillstrom, Joseph. *See* Joe Hill

Hinckley, Pres. Gordon B., 247

Hinkley, Arza, cited for Coalville murders, 86n6

Hirst, William Lucas, Jr., and mining, 23n1

Hirst, William Lucas, Sr., and mining, 23n1

Hoar, George Frisbie, 292

Hobbs, William, 86

Hoge, Enos D., 204, 207, 308, 324, 326, 336; assists Howard in second Lee trial, 136; associate supreme court justice, at second Lee trial, 136; brief history, 326; *Broad Ax* praises for position on Twenty-Fourth Infantry at Fort Douglas, 285; compiler of the laws of Utah in 1888, 326; death of, 326; defense of John D. Lee, 127, 127n11; disbanding of Liberal Party, 257; early member of Alta Club, 303; funeral, 326; nominates Baskin for territorial legislature, 222; joins Tuscarora Society, 229; partner of Baskin, 127n11, 137, 204n12, 281; photograph of, *303*; trial of John D. Lee, 326; withdraws Baskin's name for supreme court position, 299

Holeman, Jacob, 74

Hollister, Ovando J.: brief history of, 191n62; indignation at lenient sentence for Cannon, 198; opposes Carlton oath, 191; part owner of Salt Lake Tribune, 191n62

Homer, Michael W., 17; Masons and Mormons, 57, 59n28; temple ceremonies published, 58

Honerine Mining Company, 310

Hooper, William H., 28, 343

Horn Silver Mine, 169

Horrocks, James, 63

Howard, Sumner: elusive career, 137n63; failure to investigate Cannon citizenship, 161–62, 162n42; investigates divorce mills, 150–51; investigates Morrisite deaths, 162; leads prosecution in second Lee trial, 136; letters to attorney general Devens regarding Cannon citizenship, 161–62; packs jury with Mormons, 136; rumors of evidence tampering, 143

Howath, John, murder of, 95

Howe, Timothy O., 118n54

Hughes, William, 86

Hull, David, murder of, 96

Hull, Thomas, 291

Hunter, Chief Justice John A., 174, 177; investigation of Cannon citizenship, 170–74 , 170n7; ruling on Cannon citizenship, 173–74

Huntington, Dimick B., record of appointment as interpreter to the Indians, 177

Huntington, Lot, killed by Orrin Porter Rockwell, 99

Huntsman, Jon Meade, Jr., prospective U.S. presidential candidate, 350n20

Hurt, Dr. Garland: Indian agent, 44, inquest on Judge Shaver's death, 174–75

Hyde, William "Bill": city policeman at time of Robinson murder, 95n49; demolition of Kate Flint's bordello, 123

Improved Order of Red Men, 55

Independent and Citizens parties, 346

Independent-Citizen Party, 251

Independent Committee of Fifty, and Baskin, 253

Independent Order of Odd Fellows (IOOF), 55; funeral of Enos Hoge, 326

Industrial army, 263

Industrial Workers of the World, 245

Ireland, Edwin A. (U.S. marshal), 303

Irish-American Society, 55

Irish shillalah, 11, 245

Iron County Brigade of Utah's Territorial (Mormon) militia, 131

Irvine, W. H., 228n10

Jack, Charles Bruerton (Grand Orator), 241

Jackson, C. M., and Utah Amorines, 250n4

Jackson County, Mo., 24

Jacobs, Ferris, 176

James, William F. (Republican Party chair), 193

Janney, Edward (city police chief), 235

Jennings, William: first Mormon member of Alta Club, 303; mayor of Salt Lake City, 305; ZCMI, 303

Jewkes, Samuel, charged in murders at Mountain Meadows, 129n21

Jocelyn, Capt. Stephen E.: at death of Dr. Robinson, 92, 93n39, 93n41; predicted violence, 92

Johnson, Nephi, 137n61

Johnson, Robert Keith "Joachim," killed with Myron Brewer, 98

Johnston, Col. Albert S., 45, 47, 133n42; said to command "legions of Satan," 321

Jones, Hannah Gailey murder of, 89

Jones, Henry, murder of, 88–89

Jones, John J., and Surprise Mining Co., 310, 310n33

Jones, Lila (daughter of Olive L. Gardner), 214

Judd, John (U.S. district attorney), 278

Judges named to write Baskin's commemoration, 334, 334n38
Julian Bill, 177, 343n6

Kane, Thomas L., 170n8; claims can kill Cullom Bill, 112; possible role in Judge McKean dismissal, 118n54; promised election to Congress by Brigham Young, 78
Kay, John, 92, 92n34
Kearns, Thomas, 290, 324–25
Keith, David (mining capitalist), 324–25
Kelly, Charles T., 265; "general" of the industrial army of unemployed, 263; his army exits Ogden peacefully, 265; plans to join Coxey's unemployed, 263
Kelsey, Eli B., on control in Utah, 82–83
Kesler, Fred A. (son of Frederick): brothel "investigation," 235; censured by Baskin, 235, 235n54; justice of peace, 235
Kesler, Frederick: long serving bishop, 59; ranch near Great Salt Lake, 59; wife cares for Olive L. Gardner Stafford, 59
Kiesel, Fred J.: attends Democratic Convention as Tuscaroran, 229; joins Tuscarora Society, 229; one of last surviving Liberal Party members, 324, 324n5
Kimball, James Nathan (notary public), 159
Kimball, J. N., 307
Kimball, William H., charged with murder of Richard Yates, Horace Bucklin, 114
King, William H., 225, 298, 328; elected president of territorial legislature, 223; elected senator from Utah, 329; potential candidate for Utah governorship, 325; response to honor, 226

Kingdom of God, 13, 24, 25, 26, 69, 70, 76, 90, 139, 190, 193n76, 195, 204, 211, 316, 322, 340, 350
Kinney, Judge John F., 78
Kirtland, Ohio, 24
Kirtley, Dr. Howard P.: attends Baskin, 332, 332n32; conducts Baskin funeral, 334; gives Baskin's cause of death, 332
Klingensmith, Philip: charged in murders at Mountain Meadows, 129n21; not called in second Lee trial, 136; witness in first Lee trial, 82, 129
Knapp, S. W., 264; Southern Pacific RR official, 262
Knight, Jesse William (son of Jesse), Democratic candidate for governor, 325–26
Knight, Samuel: participant in Mountain Meadows murders, 82; witness in second Lee trial, 137n61
Knight, "Uncle Jesse": as potential candidate for Utah governorship, 325; candidate for presidential elector, 329
Knights of Honor, 55
Knights of Pythias, 55
Knights Templars, and cornerstone laying, 239, 247
Knott, J. Proctor, 166

Lamar, L. Q. C. (secretary of interior): asks for Governor Murray resignation, 180–81; considers Murray a bitter foe, 181n9; influenced by Cannon, 181n8
Lance, Jacob, murder of, 88
Land purchases, by Baskin, 308
Lannan, Martin, 229
Lannan, Patrick, 59n27, 163; early member of Alta Club, 303; photograph of, 251; well known as Irish Catholic, 250
Law of Retribution, 58n25; and Joseph Smith, 58n25

Lawrence, Henry W., 163, 207; Carter's unemployed army, 267; distrusts People's Party division, 228; efforts to close saloons on Sunday, 233; forms Populist Party, 259n37; indignation at lenient sentence for Cannon, 199; in legislature, 228n10; joins Baskin in mining ventures, 307; Liberal Party leader, 210; Liberal ticket candidate, 223; receiver of LDS assets, 199n109

Lawrence, Joab, founding member Alta Club, 302n4

Laws of Mortmain, 185

Laycock, Douglas, 319

LDS Articles of Faith, 315–16

LDS Church, wealth and property confiscated by Edmunds-Tucker, 190

LDS First Presidency, 134, 137, 154, 169, 193n76, 219, 222, 225, 237, 247, 274, 275, 344; secretly support plural marriage, 279n42; secretly urge Logan members to vote Republican, 228; supports City Creek Center, 345; supports redefinition of marriage, 345, 345n9; supreme authority in all things, 292

Lee, John Doyle, 12, 15, 336; arrested, 122; bail withdrawn, 136n56; charged in murders at Mountain Meadows, 129n21; convicted of first-degree murder, 139; deadlocked jury gives a mistrial, 132; execution, 139; jury tampering, 139; newspaper reactions to second trial, 138–39; predicts Young's death, 144; second trial, 136–39

Liberal Party, 28, 84, 157, 163, 167, 181, 189n52; Baskin leads in it disbanding, 346; boycotts 1878 elections, 164; chooses Baskin for run against Cannon, 157; critical of Independent-Citizen ticket, 254; disbands, 257–58; final meeting, tributes to accomplishments, 258–59; members work against Baskin, 253; Ogden members disband, 221; opposes 1872 statehood, 117; some members consider statehood premature, 249; support of public education, 209; sweep of 1890 election, 213–14

Lincoln, Abraham, and Emancipation Proclamation, 36

Lippman, Joseph, 323

Little, Feramorz: early city improvements, 230n21; mayor of Salt Lake City, 123; pays damages to Kate Flint, 123; relationship with Mormon families, 123

Little, Jesse C., 175

Little Cottonwood canyon, 23

Livingston, Grant (city policeman), 95n49

Livingstone, J., and Force Act riot, 159

Lloyd, B. T., 299

Lockley, Frederic, 29, 166, 259, 336; editor *Salt Lake Tribune*, reports Lee trial, 128; frustrated with non-Mormon defeats, 167; letters to wife on Lee trial, 128; praises Baskin's role in Lee trial, 130; predicts no conviction of Lee, 129; sees Lee mistrial as leading to stronger legislation, 132

Logan Bill, 177, 343n6

Loofbourow, Charles F.: cornerstone ceremony, 241; validates Baskin departure from Liberal Party, 258

Lott, John, and Aiken party murders, 96n55

Lowe, George A., 223; founding member Alta Club, 302n4

Lowe, James (grand chaplain), and cornerstone laying, 241

Loyal League, 189n51, 189n52, 192; Park City mining interests, 189

Lund, Gerald N., author of faith-promoting literature, 350n22

Lund, R. C., as orator, 225

Luttrell Bill, 127n7, 163, 167, 177, 343n6; stalled in Congress, 167

Lyman, Amasa Mason, 12, 15; friction with Brigham Young, 82; life and safety at risk, 82

Mackintosh, R. (founding member Alta Club), 302n4

Madsen, Brigham D., 12n2

Mahoney, James, cited for Coalville murders, 86n6

Manifesto: against practice of polygamy, 220, 221n33; an "official declaration," 220; non-Mormons suspicious of, 221n33, 318; not published in *Doctrine and Covenants* until 1908, 221; proclaimed, printed in *Deseret News*, 220

Marioneaux, Thomas (lawyer), 297

Marquardt, H. Michael, 58n25m

Marshall, John A., 228n10

Marshall, Thomas: buys Salt Lake Gas Co., 206n21; Liberal Party member, 191, 206n21

Marshall, Thomas (Southern Pacific RR official), 262

Masonic ritual, 241, 242; blessing with wine and oil, 241–42; kernels of corn, 241–42; level and plumb, 241–42; square, 241–42

Mauss, Armand, 349

Maxwell, George R., 11, 15, 29, 84, 207, 216, 259, 336, 341, 343; as U.S. marshal serves 260 subpoenas for Lee trial, 129; challenges George Q. Cannon's seat, 153; Force Act riot, 158–59; in conviction of George Reynolds, 63–64; issues contested in Cannon seating,

157; Master Mason, 59n27; on compliance to law, 315; on "Federal Enemies list," 313, 313n52; reports miners will contribute to hiring legal talent for Lee trial, 128; run for congress, 28; to Washington to lobby for Luttrell Bill, 164; worked with Baskin, 108

McAllister, John David Thompson: demolition of Flint's bordello, 123; release of men charged with Coalville murders, 86, 86n6

McAuslan, Peter, 13; leaves Mormonism and Utah because of murders, 82; on murders of apostates, 88

McBride, Dave, teamster named in murder, 90n26

McBride, Judge John R.: declares theocracy in Utah, 169; works with Baskin to oppose Utah statehood, 194

McBride, William Craig (nephew): attends Baskin funeral, 335; son of Martha J. Baskin, 335, 335n42

McClellan, Gen. George B., 47

McClernand, John A.: aligns with Mormons and Carlton of oath, 192; Utah commissioner, 192; votes against anti-polygamy legislation, 192n68

McCornick, William S.: first president of Salt Lake Chamber of Commerce, 302; founder of Alta Club, 302; worked with Baskin on City Council, 302

McCurdy, Justice Solomon P., Robinson inquest, 94

McFarlane, John (counsel defending Lee), 127, 127n11

McGroarty, William, 28, 84, 207, 343; run for congress, 28

McGuffie, James, on power of Mormon leaders, 82

McKean, Judge James Bedell, 216, 259, 289n27, 341; arrives in Utah, 113, 113n32; burial site, 119, 335; first on "Federal Enemies list," 313, 313n52; Relief Corps, protests Faulkner and Teller Bills, 229n13; relieved of appointment, 118

McKee Bill, 177, 343n6

McKinley, Pres. William, 289

McLeod, Rev. Norman: advised not to return to Utah, 93; friend of Dr. Robinson, 92, 92n35, 255n24; testifies on violence, 93

McMillan, Henry G., 171–72, 171n12

McMurdy, Samuel, 137n61

McNece, Rev. Robert G., 228; and Olive Baskin's death, 215; efforts to close saloons on Sunday, 233

McNeil, Franklin, murder of, 88

McRae, Alexander (territorial marshal), 74; brother of Kenneth, killing of, 98–99

McRae, Kenneth (brother of Alexander), killing of, 98–99

Meacham, Morris, charged with murder of Horace Bucklin, 114

Merritt, Judge Samuel Augustus, 216; dissolves injunction against Smith army of unemployed, 270; founding member Alta Club, 302; life threatened during invasion of unemployed, 269; support of Poland Act, 122; validates Baskin departure from Liberal Party, 258

Merritt Bill, 177, 343n6

Miles, Caroline Owens: description of temple ceremonies, 58; supports Edmunds-Tucker Act, 183

Miller, George L., of *Omaha Herald*, 184n28; urges Pres. Cleveland to treat Mormons kindly, 184n28

Miller, Miles, Aiken party murders, 96n55

Miller, Rose (city brothel owner), 234

Miller, Samuel Henry, 174

Miller Hill (mining area), 309

Miller Hill Mining Co., sold by Baskin, 311

Miner, Judge James A.: favors Teller Bill, 224n47; staggered term as supreme court judge, 284; supreme court judge, 283n7

Mineral Flat (American Fork mining claim), 311

Monheim, Henry: architect for City and County Building, 237; short history of, 237n62

Monroe, James, murder of, 85

Mont Moriah Lodge No. 2, Baskin admitted to, 56–57

Moran, P. J., 228n10; joins Tuscarora Society, 229; Liberal ticket candidate, elected to legislature, 223; opponent of Independent-Citizen party, 254

Morgan, Dale, on Utah as a police state, 80

Moritz, Jacob, 228n10

Mormon, civil disobedience, 107, 107n1

Mormon Battalion, 69

Mormon history, revised, 81

Mormonism: narrow path between assimilation and dissolution, 348–49; mainstream acceptance against uniqueness, 348–49

Mormon militia (Utah), 25, 26, 26n7, 45, 46, 50, 61, 77, 96, 105, 125, 126, 131–32, 143, 167n72, 175, 263, 342

Mormons: move west, 24; on belief in freedom of religion denied, 339–40; organized by priesthood, life monitored, 75–76

Mormon scriptures, to be only textbooks in schools, 203

Mormon society, emergence to power, defiance of government, 67

Mormon ward houses, used for schools, 203

Mormon women: as doctors, 33n10; in Mormon societal structure, 33

Morrill, Laban, witness in second Lee trial, 137n61

Morrill, Sen. Justin Smith, 48

Morrill Act, 185; and anti-bigamy, 47, 109; features of, 48

Morrill Bill, and land grants for home-state colleges, 48

Morris, Joseph, killed during apostate rebellion, 143

Morris, Joseph R., charged with bribery, 277

Morris, Richard P. (Salt Lake City mayor), 323

Morrisite rebellion, 162

Morrow, Col. Henry Andrew: commander Camp Douglas, 117; general, 336

Morse, Gilbert, second Lee trial, 136n58

Mortality rates in Salt Lake City, 230

Mountain Dell mine, 309, 310, 311

Mountain law, trumps English common law, 85

Mountain Meadows massacre, 25, 46, 100, 107, 336, 341; calls for military action against Mormons for killings, 46–47; description of events, 46, 46n10; full history remains unfinished, 140; investigations of Cradlebaugh, 55, 126

Mount Olivet Cemetery, 65n55, 109n8, 119, 127n9, 204n10, 215, 232, 335, 355; sexton records for Baskin family, 215n12

Moyle, James H., 204; as potential candidate for Utah governorship, 325; critical of supreme court judges, 282; nominated by Democrats for governor, 298

Murdock, John, and Aiken party murders, 96n55

Murphy v. Ramsey, 191

Murray, Gov. Eli Houston, 214; appointment called victory for "forces of evil," 321n37; awards election certificate to Campbell, 169; called "Gov. Whiskerando," 180; founding member Alta Club, 302; highly regarded in Washington, 181n9; on the Mormons, 317; refusal to sign Utah Territorial bills, 180; resignation called for, 180

Nauvoo, Ill., 24

Nauvoo Brass Band, in Shaver procession, 175

Nauvoo Legion, 111n17, 129, 131, 286

Nauvoo police force, 67

Negley, James Scott, support of Poland Act, 122

Nelson, Alfred H., counsel for brother's widow in personal injury suit, 295–96

Nelson, Charles A., killed in employ of railroad, 295

Nelson, William, 177; author of Associated Press dispatches, 211n37; contributions to public education, 211; kept pistol on desktop, 211n37; Liberal Party member, 211; rumors of evidence tampering, 143; succeeds Maxwell in second Lee trial, 136; *Tribune* editor, 211; U.S. marshal at second Lee trial, 211

Nelson Congressional Bill, 177, 343n6

New Edmunds Bill. *See* Edmund-Tucker Act

Newell, E. P., dedication of City and County Building, 275

New Jerusalem, 24

Noble, John (secretary of interior), 221n33

Non-Mormons, labelled agents of Satan, 320–21

North Star mine, 23

Nye, James, role in Cullom failure, 112

Oaks, Dallin, claims of persecution, 319

Oath of Vengeance, changes in scope, 58n25

Oats, Marvin, killed by Orrin Porter Rockwell, 98

Obedience to law, 315–21; attempts to enforce called persecution, 318

Ogden: city council donates provisions for Kelly's army, 265–66; parade supporting unemployed army, 265

Ogden Mormons, urge breakup of People's Party, 221

O'Meara, W. P., plans vetoed by Baskin, 277

Ophir mining district, 307

Oregon Short Line, 263, 292

Orr, Joseph Milton (Grand Master Utah Lodge), orders no Mormons in Masonic lodges, 57

Paden, Rev. W. M. (Presbyterian pastor), objections to Smoot seating, 292

Page, J. E., 297

Pallbearers at Baskin funeral, 334n40

Palmyra, N.Y., 24

Park, Samuel C. (jeweller), defeats Baskin in mayoral election, 294

Parrish, William R., murder of, 87–88

Patrick, Mathewson T. (U.S. marshal), serves Young warrant for cohabitation, 114

Patriotism, and public schools, 201

Patterson, A. S. (notary public), 172

Paul, Joshua H.: brief history, 325n7; university professor, 325; urges that Baskin be considered for Utah governor position, 325

Paul, Samuel (Worshipful Brother), and cornerstone laying, 239

Peery, Luacine Hoge, death of, 324

People's party, 78, 192–93, 207, 227, 228, 254, 259, 343; break up considered devious, 249; disbands, 221–24; divides into Democrats and Republicans, 227; initially held no political meetings, 169; non-Mormons suspicious about disbanding, 222

Perpetual Emigrating Fund, 77, 158; confiscated by Edmunds-Tucker, 190, 205, 344

Persecution, of Mormons, 317–18; in arresting men for cohabitation, 319

Peters, George S. (U.S. attorney), 205

Peters, John D., 225; legislative committee on education, 225; role in public education, 210–11; work with Baskin for public education legislation, 225

Petition for statehood, 116

Pettibone, Augustus H., 176n33

Peyton, Frank: at death of Olive Baskin, 214; employee of Denver and Rio Grande Railroad, 188; marriage to Kitty Baskin, 188

Peyton, Katherine C. "Kitty" Baskin: cause of death, 214n7; remains moved to Mount Olivet Cemetery, 335

Pierce, Franklin, 228n10

Pierrepont, Edwards (U.S. attorney general), 163n41

Platt, Sen. Orville, 220

Pleasant Valley Junction, Utah, 188

Poland, Luke, 122

Poland Act, 54, 54n8, 126; changes court jurisdiction, 62, 119–20; Maxwell and William Carey lobby for, 120; on judicial process, 122; permits warrants for murders at Mountain Meadows, 122;

provisions of, 120; Utah Bar supports, 119

Polygamy, and challenges to theocracy, 320, 320n33

Potter, Gardner G. "Duff," murder of, 87–88

Potter, Isaac, murder of, 86

Potter, Joseph, attempt to defraud lawyers, 297

Powers, Orlando, 207, 216n15, 336; at disbanding of Liberal Party, 257–58; attends Democratic Convention as Tuscaroran, 229; awarded $10,000, 216, 216n15; claims Independent-Citizen votes procured by LDS Church actions, 254; criticizes Baskin, 252; distrusts People's Party division, 228; feted for successful campaign, 215–16; interview with President Cleveland, 229; Liberal Party campaign manager, nominated by Democrats for congress, 298; organizes Tuscarora Society, 229; photograph, 255; represents Potter in injury case, 297; resigned from Tuscarora Society, from Democratic Committee, 273; testifies against Faulkner and Teller Bills, 229

Pratt, Arthur (son of Orson), 374n48; buys Salt Lake Gas Co., 206n21; deputy marshal, in conviction of George Reynolds, 63; forms special police unit for invasion of unemployed, 263; Liberal, 167n72, 206n21; makes survey of unemployed men, 264; on Independent-Citizen ticket, 254; wins city marshal seat, 255

Pratt, Orson, 167n72; in trial of George Reynolds, 63, 64n48; preaches death for prostitution, 71; speaks at Shaver funeral, 175

Pratt, Sarah Marinda Bates (wife

of Orson Pratt), 167n72; fear of Mormon spies, 71n22

Price, Capt. George F., warns of violence in Utah, 91

Protestant missionaries, and private schools, 201

Proudfoot, Willis T. (architect for City and County Building), 237

Public education: enrollment figures, 210; features of, 210; legislation for free schools passed 1890, 213; opposed by Brigham Young, 202; opposed by Mormons for forty years, 211; primary objectives, 201–202; progress of, 209–10; students labeled Mormon or non-Mormon, 210n35

Queen Victoria, 171, 172n14

Quinn, Michael: culture of violence, 104, 104n141; sexual sin punished by castration, beheading, 104n141

Racehorses, Baskin's interests in, 306–307

Ranney, Ambrose A., on Cannon citizenship, 176n33

Rawlins, Joseph L., 204n10, 231, 274; allegations of secret support by LDS Church, 229; defeats Thatcher for Senate nomination, elected to congress, 229; lobbies for statehood, 227; mentioned by *Broad Ax* for Senate seat, 281n1; potential candidate for Utah governorship, 325; represents Baskin, 278; with Baskin on Shamrock and Katherine mine, 310

Rawlins Bill, enabling act for Utah Statehood, 258

Raybould, A. W., joins Baskin in Imperial Mining and Smelter, 309

Reformation, 26–27, 167; a reign of terror, 71, 72

Reid, Judge Lazarus H., 175

Religious Freedom Restoration Act,
319

Reminiscences of Early Utah, 12, 58, 95,
115, 121, 129, 129n20, 139, 204, 245,
293, 328, 329, 332, 341, 342, 347, 355;
published in Salt Lake City, 326

*Reply to Certain Statements by O. F.
Whitney in His History of Utah*, 12,
347; published, 328

Republican government, defined,
69n9

Republican Party, divides Liberal
vote, 222

Reynolds v. United States (98 U.S. 145
[1879]), 64, 65, 162n42, 320n29

Richards, Charles C., 326n11;
legislator, 207

Richards, Franklin S., 328; against
Edmunds-Tucker Bill, 182; cites
Utah low illiteracy rate, 195; claims
no paupers in Utah, 195; court
injunction confining Kelly's army,
264; defends Lorenzo Snow before
U.S. supreme court, 182; lobbies for
statehood, 227; opposes Cullom-
Struble, 219; works for statehood,
194

Ringwood, Charles: at Force Act riot,
159; city policeman at Robinson
murder, 95n49

Rio Grande Western, 263; on
transport of Carter army, 267

Roberts, Brigham Henry, 289, 291;
brief history, 283; candidate for
congress, 281–82; denied seat
in congress because of multiple
wives, 284; elected to congress, 283;
polygamist, 283, 283n10

Robertson, Reuben Howard, 109,
109n8, 313; assisted with Cullom,
109; founds Wasatch Lodge, 57

Robertson, R. S. (Utah
commissioner), 219

Robie, Frederick (gov. of Maine), 188

Robinson, Dr. John King, 109, 117,
306, 341; alleged his murderers
paraded in support of Baskin, 254–
55; assassins known, 255n24; assured
by Baskin that court challenge
without danger, 92; feared being
killed, 92; inquest of murder,
94–95; marriage, 91; murder makes
non-Mormons fearful, 93–94;
murder of, 91; seeks land for
hospital, property destroyed, 92

Rockwell, Merritt (brother to Orrin
Porter), 98

Rockwell, Orrin Porter: Baskin
named as one of the killers of
Aiken party, 97; charged with
murder of Horace Bucklin, 115;
in John Tobin attack, and Henry
Jones attack, 97; posts bail for
Brigham Young, 109n10; shooting
of Lilburn Boggs, 97; suspected in
Robinson murder, 97

Rocky Mountain Lodge, No. 205
(first lodge in Utah), 56

Rogers, Lindsay R., disbarment case
heard by Baskin, 295–96

Rolapp, Henry H., 328; brief history,
282n4; defeated by Baskin, 282

Romney, Willard Mitt (Mormon
candidate for U.S. presidency),
350n20

Roosevelt, Pres. Theodore, 299;
allegations regarding a Mormon
apostle in congress, 290

Rosborough, John B.: indignant at
lenient sentence for Cannon, 198;
Liberal Party affiliate, 193; of Utah
Democratic Party, 193

Roylance, William, as potential
candidate for Utah governorship,
325

Ruffner, Clara H. (wife of William
Craig McBride), 335, 335n42

Russell, Majors, and Waddell, 111n17

Salem Academy, 32, 32n4

Saloons, open on Sunday, 232–33

Salt Lake City: sewer completed, 278; sewer, cost of, 278; streets paved, sidewalks formed, 231

Salt Lake City LDS temple: cost of, 238n66; drive to finish, dedicated, 237–38; history of, 236n57; tour for non-Mormons, 238

Salt Lake Stock and Mining Exchange, 307

Sandford, Elliot F.: lenient sentence for George Q. Cannon, 197–98; replaces Zane, 206, 206n19; sentencing of George Q. Cannon, 203n19

Sandwich Islands, 156, 156n13, 159, 172

San Joaquin Lode, 307

Saunders, Alvin W., 219

Schaeffer, Chief Justice Michael: decrees Ann Eliza marriage not valid, 167n72; removal asked, 166

Scott, Gen. Winfield, dispatched troops to Utah, 44

Scott, George M.: dedication of City and County Building, 275; Eagle Foundry, 279; elected first non-Mormon mayor of Salt Lake City, 214; mayor improves city infrastructure, 230; mayoral portrait, full-length, 245n86

Scott, John S.: mine owner, 184n27; supports Edmunds-Tucker and benefits of mining for Utah, 184n27

Seaman, John, candidate for presidential elector, 329

Second 1856 handcart company, 13

Sessions, Carlos, 312n45

Sessions, Perrigrine, 312n45

Sexual sins, punishment by death, 104n141. *See also* beheading; castration

Shaffer, John Wilson, supports Cullom, 111

Shaughnessy, Michael (deputy marshal), founding member Alta Club, 302

Shaver, Judge Leonidas, 162, 171n10; brain abscess alleged, 174; cause of death uncertain, rumors of poisoning, 175–76, 175n26; death under suspicious circumstances, 174; decisions adverse to Mormons, 175; funeral and burial incongruous, 175–76; funeral procession, 175; inquest on death, 174–75; poisoning charged by non-Mormons, 176

Shearman, William (Godbeite), 82

Sheets, George (policeman removed by Baskin), 235

Sherman Law, 262

Shilling, Newton Watson (Grand Master), and cornerstone laying, 241

Silences: about Baskin, 348; on benefits that control of theocracy brought, 348

Silver King mine, 262

Sirrine, Samuel D., on death of Gheen, 98–99

Smith, Dr. F. Deming, called "Lt. Col.," leading third group of unemployed, 269

Smith, George A.: avoids cross examination, 130; death of, 130; defends Howard Egan, 85; deposition not accepted in court record, 130; deposition taken in Salt Lake City, 130; drafts resolution honoring Judge Shaver, 175; speaks at Shaver funeral, 175

Smith, Grant H., on Independent-Citizen ticket, 254

Smith, Hyrum (Master Mason), 55

Smith, John Henry (LDS apostle), 199

Smith, John P., killing of, 99

Smith, Joseph, Jr., 24; authored Articles of Faith, 315; Master Mason, 55; violent nature, 67

Smith, Joseph Fielding: hiding in Hawaii, 193n76, labeled Baskin as bitter against the Saints, 322; LDS Church president, 279; testimony before congress, 293

Smith, Judge Elias: child custody, 151n46; collusion in citizenship fraud, 177; Cullom Bill devised by the wicked, 320–21; dismisses death of John P. Smith, 99; dismisses death of Moroni Clawson, 99; dismisses deaths of Brewer and Johnson, 98; dismisses deaths of McRae brothers, 99; dismisses murders as inconsequential, 87–88; false testimony on Cannon citizenship, 172; grants Olive Stafford a divorce, 60, 60n34; labels Governor Murray as agent of Satan, 320–21; lax territorial law and creation of divorce mills, 150–52; puzzled by apostates leaving, 72; ran lucrative divorce mill, 60n34; tribute to Brigham Young, 144–45

Smith, Marcus Aurelius, works for Utah statehood, 194

Smith, Mary Ettie V.: report of Judge Shaver poisoned, 176; report of murder of Wallace Alonzo Clarke Bowman, 99

Smith, William Henry, 211n37

Smoot, Abraham O. (mayor), visit to threaten DeWolfe, 125

Smoot, Reed, 290, 290n29, 291, 328, 344; Baskin supports, 292; hearings, probe secret marriages, loyalty of Mormons to United States, 290–93

Snell, John William, purchases warm springs property from Baskin, 305

Snow, Bishop Warren, castration of Thomas Lewis, 90

Snow, Lorenzo, 278; attends Young's birthday celebration, 286; instructed to end divorce mills, 152;

ordination, 281; polygamy case in U.S. Supreme Court, 182, 182n19

Snow, Zerubbabel, 85; claims office of attorney general, 117; drafts resolution honoring Judge Shaver, 175

Snyder, George, teamster named in murder, 90n26

Sons of Saint George, 55

Sorenson, John Peter, 57

Southern Pacific RR, 268; refuses free transport of unemployed, 264

Spicer, Wells: blames Ark. emigrants for their attack, 130; counsel defending Lee, 127; defense of John D. Lee, 127; second Lee trial, 136

Sprague, E. T. (court clerk), testimony of Cannon citizenship, 171

Springer, William M., 195

Spry, William, defeats Jesse William Knight for Utah governorship, 326

Stafford, Lila (daughter), 151

Stafford, Olive Lavinia Gardner (wife): award from Wells Fargo, 60; concerns of divorce granted by Judge Elias Smith, 151; divorce, 60, 60n34; injured in Wells Fargo crash, 59–60; maiden name restored, 60; sues Wells Fargo, 60

Staines, W. C., and inquest on Judge Shaver's death, 175

Standing, Joseph, missionary murdered in Georgia, 318

Stanley, John, cited for Coalville murders, 86n6

Stanton, Charles E. (city fire chief), as Amorine, 251

Stayner, Arthur, curses DeWolfe, 126

Stealing, punished by death, 71, 86–87, 89

Stegner, Wallace, on Utah as police state, 80

Stenhouse, Thomas B. H., 100,

140; on Gheen's death as blood atonement, 97; on the Reformation, 73; report of Clawson and Smith executions, 99

Steptoe, Lt. Col. Edward J., leaves Utah with women in protection, 861

Stewart, John W., hearing Edmunds-Tucker Bill, 183

Stewart, William Cameron, charged in murders at Mountain Meadows, 129n21

Stewart, William M., 109n9

Stewart Bill, 109n9, 177, 343n6

Stiles, Judge George P., 44, 71; papers burned, 44

Stillson, Jerome B.: investigated for reporting murder attempts, 100; report on Brigham Young, 142–43; represented by Baskin, 100; requests 1857 letter of James Haslam, 143; two attempts at murder of, 100; investigative journalism, 100; Stout, Hosea, at Robinson inquest, 94

St. Mary's congregation, Salt Lake City, 250

St. Omar, Elsie (brothel owner), 234

Stout, Hosea: at murder of Yates, 96; charged with murder of Richard Yates, 114

St. Patrick's congregation, Salt Lake City, 250

Straup, Daniel N., 323

Street, James, 77–78

Strickland, Obed Franklin (founder of Wasatch Lodge), 57

Struble, Isaac, 344; sponsors companion to Cullom Bill, 218. *See also* Cullom-Struble

Struck It Lode, Baskin's estate, 313

Sullivan, P. J. (fire captain), 276

Surprise Mining Company, 310

Suspicions at Mormon divisions to major party affiliations, 227

Sutherland, Jabez Gridley: contends Indians forced whites into Mountain Meadows killings, 129–30; counsel defending Lee, 127; defense of John D. Lee, 127; represents Cannon in citizenship hearing, 159

Sutter's army (unemployed men), 270

Taft, Alphonso (U.S. attorney general), 163n41

Talmage, Dr. James Edward, tribute at Young birthday celebration by, 286

Taylor, John: admits extent of Mormon Church financial holdings, 185n33; death of, 193n76; hand of God in Edmunds-Tucker Bill, 189; president of LDS Church, 169; proponent of theocracy, 340

Telephone service in Salt Lake City, 214n6

Teller Bill, 227, 228, 229; provided for immediate, unqualified statehood for Utah, 224

Thatcher, Moses, mentioned by *Broad Ax* for Senate seat, 281n1

Theocracy: as incompatible with republican government, 339; continuance of to a degree in Utah, 344–45

Theocratic oligarchy, 70

Theodemocracy, defined, 68

Thomas, Gov. Arthur Lloyd, 216, 219, 221n33; acting governor of Utah Terr., overrides Governor Murray, 170; aids passage of Cullom-Struble, 218; as Utah commissioner, says no republican government in Utah, 196; carries education bill to Sen. Edmunds, 208; cornerstone ceremony, 241; favors Teller Bill, 224n47; suspicious of Manifesto, 221n33; vacillated on statehood bills, 227

Thompson, Dr. (John D.), treats John C. Young, 167

Thompson, Eliza Jane Trimble, (wife): march on saloons, temperance movement, 34–35

Thompson, Ezra, elected to third term as mayor, 294

Thompson, James H., 35; Baskin mentor, 32–33; forms Hillsboro Female College, 33; husband to "Mother" Thompson of temperance movement, 35; Republican in political views, 34; served in cavalry in Civil War, 34, 34n15

Thompson, Julia F., report of 1857 visit of George A. Smith to southern settlements, 127

Thompson, William, Jr. (deputy marshal), and death of Edward M. Dalton, 202n7

Thurman, Samuel R., 326n11; charged with cohabitation, 208n26; runs for congress, 207; Sagebrush Democrat, 207

Tithing extracted from contracts, 80n72

Titus, John (chief justice), at Robinson inquest, 94

Tobin, John, near assassination, 87, 87n10

Totalitarian state: features of, 342–43; ingredients for, 74; ingredients in place in Utah, 80–81; in Mormon society, 68–69

Townsend, George Alfred, 108n4, 313n52; as "Bobster," and "Gath," 115; critical description of Baskin, McKean, 115

Townsend Hotel, 99

Trevelyan, George Macauley, 12, 12n3, 15

Trimble, Allen: Ohio governor, 35; secures bail for Baskin, 38n28

Trimble, Eliza Jane (daughter of Gov. Trimble, wife of James H. Thompson), 35

Trumbo, Isaac: asks Baskin for endorsement, 278; lobbies for enabling act, 273–74

Trumbull, Lyman, 108, 108n5

Tucker, Beverly: accused of being paid representative of Mormons, 188; brother of John Randolph, 188

Tucker, John Randolph, 207; admits ignorance of Mormon issues, 183; hearing Edmunds-Tucker Bill, 183; holds of Edmunds-Tucker in committee, 188

Tuscarora Society, 347; disbands, 230; makeup of, 229; number of members, 229

Tuttle, Luther T., 326n11

Twenty-fourth Ohio Infantry, 36; members aware of people's ambivalence, 36

Twinning, H. H., joins Baskin in Imperial Mining and Smelter, 309

Tying, George, 311; joins with Baskin on Miller Company mine, 309

Typhoid, general term, 230

Unemployed men: in Utah, 261; throughout western cities, 268

Union Pacific RR, 265; provides transport of Kelly's army, 265–66; refuses free transport of unemployed, 264

Union Vedette, 93, 113n32

University Club, 305, 305n12, 336

U.S. mail, violated, 74, 75

Utah Commission: set up by Edmunds-Tucker, 190; on Mormons' obedience to law, 317

Utah constitutional amendment 3: aimed at same-gender marriage, 340; defining marriage, 340; limit on marriage Mormons fought for 160 years, 340

Utah Enabling Act, 346

Utah Expedition, 25, 107

Utah legislature, 1878 bill limits 1878 non-Mormon voting, 163

Utah militia. *See* Nauvoo Legion

Utah Northern Rail, 263

Utah Ring, 25, 26, 27, 28; as enemies of the Saints, 108

Utah State Constitution, adopted, 278

Utah statehood: achieved, 278–79; celebrated, 278–79; sixth appeal for, 193

Utah Supreme Court assignments, drawing lots for, 284

Utah Territory: excluded common law, 53; excluded legal population in 1865, 53, 53n1; jury packing with Mormons, 54; polygamy known in Highland County, 45; precedents, 53; probate courts, court jurisdiction, 54, 54n7; subject to federal law, 316

Utah War, 26, 26n7, 45, 46n10, 56, 74, 96, 98, 99, 111n17, 115, 133n42, 171n8; extensive coverage of by *New York Times*, 45, 45n8; nationwide press coverage, 45n9

Vallandigham, Clement Laird: agitation, 36; anti-war stance, 35–36; arrest, 36; flight to Canada, 36, 36n20

Valley Tan (non-Mormon newspaper), 55n11

Van Cott, Waldemar, 328

Van Zile, Philip T. (U.S. district attorney), 172–73

Varian, Judge Charles Stetson, 208n26, 216, 328; critical of supreme court judges, 282; efforts to close saloons on Sunday, 233; nominated for supreme court, 298–99; on compliance to law, 315; validates Baskin departure from Liberal Party, 258

Varnell's Station, missionary Joseph Standing murdered, 318

Vaughn, Dr. John M., murder of, 85

Vocational preparation, and public schools, 202

Voorhees Bill, 177, 343n6; Baskin and McKean lobby, 119; cash needed "to fee" its defeat, 119

Wade, Benjamin F., 109

Wade Bill, 109, 177, 343n6

Walker, Charles Lowell, reports on Baskin and Edmunds-Tucker Bill, 183

Walker, David Fred, with Baskin investment in railroad co., 312

Walker, James R. (founding member Alta Club), 302

Walker, John, murder of, 86

Walker, Joseph R., with Baskin investment in railroad co., 312

Wall, Col. Enos, 218n22; indignation at lenient sentence for Cannon, 198

Ward, Hamilton, 110

Wardell, Martin Douglas: names six Mormon men for murder, 90n26; observes murder, 90

War of the Rebellion, Mormon perception of, 26. *See also* Civil War

Washington Square, as site for City and County Building, 237

Waters, William: observations of Mormons, 73; on power of Brigham Young, 96

Watt, George D.: on Brigham Young, 82; refused fair pay, 13, 15

Watt, Ronald G., 13

Watts, Edwin, absolved by Brigham Young for murder of Levi York, 89

Weller, John B.: at Robinson inquest, 94; former governor of Calif., 94; opinion of cause of murder, 94–95

Wells, Daniel H., 26n7; charged with murder of Richard Yates, 114; early city improvements, 230n19; election riot, 159; had authority to convene court martial, 131; imprisoned after Reynolds trial, 64; in trial of George Reynolds, 63; tells teamster to kill thieves on trail, 89–90; testifies in second Lee trial, 136

Wells, Emmeline B., 323; appears against Edmunds-Tucker Act, 183; wife of Daniel H. Wells, 183

Wells, Heber Manning (son of Daniel H. Wells), 228; at joint legislative meeting to support Smoot, 291; candidate for governor, 277; governor, 323; speaks at Young's birthday celebration, 286

Wells Fargo, coach crash injures Olive Stafford, 59

West, Allen P. (brother), 41

West, Andrew, 337; death alluded to, 253; death of, 37; family of, 41; Masonic tribute to, 38–39; picks fight with Baskin, 37; witness testimony, 38

West, Caleb Walton, 265; activates Utah National Guard, 263; Carter's unemployed army, 267; claims LDS Church influenced Republican victory, 278; congratulates National Guard troops, 266; criticized for handling of unemployed army, 265; governor to Utah, 184; invasion of unemployed from Calif., 262; life threatened during invasion of unemployed, 269; opposes statehood, 195; speaker at City and County Building dedication, 275; speaks for Cullom-Struble, 219; validates Baskin departure from Liberal Party, 258; veto of Mormon education bill, 204–205; visits President Cleveland, 184

West, John (father of Andrew), 41

West, Joseph (brother), 41

West, Joseph A., against Edmunds-Tucker Bill, 182

Weston, Isaac Mellen: beaten, warned to leave Salt Lake City, 93, 93n39; editor of *Union Vedette*, 93

Whedon, D. P., member panel prosecuting Lee, 127n10

Whim, device for raising ore from mine shaft, 309

White, Joel, 87; witness at first Lee trial, 129; witness in second Lee trial, 137n61

Whitney, George E., and Judge McKean dismissal, 118n54

Whitney, Orson Ferguson, 278; opinion of Baskin, 27

Widows, of Civil War would marry Mormons, 26

Wilkinson, Ernest, and following religious leaders in political matters, 344–45

Willden, Ellott, charged in murders at Mountain Meadows, 129n21

William, W. W., teamster named in murder, 90n26

Williams, A. B. (Utah commissioner), says no republican government in Utah, 196

Williams, George Henry (U.S. attorney general), 163n41, 191

Williams, Parley Lycurgus, 204, 205, 207, 209, 210; advocate of public schools, 202; Alta Club President, 303n8; brief history of, 334n39; buys Salt Lake Gas Co., 206n21; critical of supreme court judges, 282; death of Edward M. Dalton, 202n7; defends George Reynolds, 64n50; Liberal, 206n21; on disbarment charges against David Evans, Lindsay R. Rogers, 295; photograph of, *203*; prominent Mason, 59n27;

raises objections to Smoot seating, 292; speaker at Baskin funeral, member Mount Mariah Lodge, 334; sponsors education bill, 207; street altercation with Evans, 296n54; superintendent of schools, 59n27; validates Baskin departure from Liberal Party, 258

Willis, John, Santa Clara ambush, 87

Wilson, Charles, murder of, 86

Wilson, Hattie (brothel owner), 234

Wilson, Jeremiah: opposes Cullom-Struble, 219; works for statehood, 194

Winder, John R., of Central Territorial Committee, 193

Wiseman, Joshua, named by Baskin for Coalville murders, 86n6

Wolff (also Wolf), Sarah Ann: mother of Mary Edna Brown, 331n27; sister of Absolom Wolff, 331n27; wife of Homer Brown, 331n27

Wolff (Wolf), Absolom, perpetrator in Aiken party murders, 96n55, 331n27

Women's Christian Temperance Movement, and Mother Thompson, 35

Woodburn, William: brief history of, 180n6; called "Buttermilk Woodburn," 187n45

Woodburn Bill, 177, 180, 184, 343n6

Woodruff, Pres. Wilford: accepts Republican voting material, 274; death, 281; Edmunds-Tucker calls for destruction of U.S. government, 190; lays capstone of Salt Lake temple, 237; Manifesto, 259, 344; offers prayer at City and County Building dedication, 275; rejects Democratic voting material, 274; support of polygamy, 219

Woods, George L.: denied Cannon election certificate, 160; on voting practices in Utah, 78

Woolley, Bishop Edwin D., advocates violence, 73

Wooten, John H., and Surprise Mining Co., 310, 310n33

Wooten, Joseph A., and Surprise Mining Co., 310, 310n33

Wootton, Francis W. (acting governor), 55

Yates, Richard, murder ordered and stolen property, 96

York, Levi, murder of, 89

Young, Ann Eliza Webb Dee: divorce action, 143; response to Lee mistrial, 132–33

Young, Brigham, Sr.: affidavit, admitted in second Lee trial, 138; arrest for cohabitation, murder, 113; arrest for violation of Morrill Act, 109n10; avoids cross examination, 130; carried in sedan chair at St. George temple ceremony, 141; charged with murder of Richard Yates, 114; conflicting reports of good health, 143–44; death penalty for stealing, 71; declares martial law, 25; deposition taken in Salt Lake City, 130; deposition not accepted in court record, 130; ends Mormon participation in Nauvoo Masonic lodges, 56; extensive reports and opinions of legacy by nation's newspapers, 145–50, 149n35; feigns illness, 130, 130n28; final months of life, 141; funeral, 144; his word is God's word, 79; his death did not end violence, 83; instructs Mormons to vote only for Mormon candidate, 78; newspaper evaluations after execution of John D. Lee, 141–42, 143n11; many responsibilities, 76–77; offers prayer at Judge Leonidas

Young, Brigham, Sr. (*continued*),
Shaver's funeral, 175; one-hundred-
year birthday celebration, 286–87;
cartoon of, 287; orders books
destroyed, 81; photograph of Kraig
Varner sculpture, *288*; proponent
of theocracy, 340; released by
Englebrecht ruling, 116n42; rules in
all things, 76–77; speculation on
cause of death, 144n14; terminal
illness and death, 144; threatens
death to Gov. Alfred Cumming,
70; threatens death to U.S. troops,
47; under house arrest, 116n42;
wears Masonic pin, 56
Young, John C. (son), *Tribune*
reporter attacked, 167
Young, John W. (son), 189; as teamster
of William Dame Company named
in a murder, 90n26; telegraphs
Utah for money for use in congress,
194n77; work must be secret, 189
Young, Joseph A. (son), charged with
murder of Richard Yates, 114
Young, LeGrande, 223n44; speaker
at City and County Building
dedication, 275
Young, Oscar (son), reports father's
health, 141
Young, Willard (son), 143

Zane, John Maxcy (son), 207, 285;
distrustful of Teller statehood,
227; joins Baskin as counsel for
Mammoth Mining Co., 310;
protects money for schools, 206;
provides guards for his father, 83;
son of Charles S. Zane, 206
Zane, Judge Charles Shuster, 215, 216,
218, 331, 336; accuses Dyer of fraud,
205; Baskin response to death
of, cause of death, 327; Baskin
informed of Zane's death, 327; body
guards provided by his son, 83;
body removed for burial in Illinois
near tomb of Abraham Lincoln,
328; candidate for supreme court,
277; death of, 327; dismissed by
Pres. Cleveland, 206; favors Teller
Bill, 224n47, 227; former partner of
Shelby M. Cullom, 205n16; friend
of Lincoln, 205n16; indignation
at lenient sentence for Cannon,
199; invited to tour Salt Lake LDS
temple, 238; joins Baskin as counsel
for Mammoth Mining Co., 310;
Mormons work to remove, 187;
of Abraham Lincoln, 205n16; on
compliance to law, 315; on Mormon
apostates, 74; opposes Baskin for
supreme court, 282–83; protects
public school funds, 206–207;
staggered term in supreme court,
284; validates Baskin departure
from Liberal Party, 258
Zion's Camp, 67
Zion's Cooperative Mercantile
Institution (ZCMI), 80, 185n33, 303

8-16

ML